Contemporary Arguments in Natural Theology

Also available from Bloomsbury

Debating Christian Religious Epistemology, edited by
John M. DePoe and Tyler Dalton McNabb
Four Views on the Axiology of Theism, edited by Kirk Lougheed
Free Will and Epistemology, by Robert Lockie
The Philosophy of Being in the Analytic, Continental, and Thomistic Traditions, by
Joseph P. Li Vecchi, Frank Scalambrino, and David K. Kovacs

Contemporary Arguments in Natural Theology: God and Rational Belief

Edited by Colin Ruloff and Peter Horban

BLOOMSBURY ACADEMIC
LONDON • NEW YORK • OXFORD • NEW DELHI • SYDNEY

BLOOMSBURY ACADEMIC
Bloomsbury Publishing Plc
50 Bedford Square, London, WC1B 3DP, UK
1385 Broadway, New York, NY 10018, USA
29 Earlsfort Terrace, Dublin 2, Ireland

BLOOMSBURY, BLOOMSBURY ACADEMIC and the Diana logo are trademarks of
Bloomsbury Publishing Plc

First published in Great Britain 2021
This paperback edition published 2023

Copyright © Colin Ruloff, Peter Horban and Contributors, 2021

Colin Ruloff and Peter Horban have asserted their right under the Copyright, Designs and Patents Act, 1988, to be identified as Editors of this work.

For legal purposes the Acknowledgments on p. ix constitute an extension of this copyright page.

Cover image: Sean Gladwell © Getty images.

All rights reserved. No part of this publication may be reproduced or transmitted in any form or by any means, electronic or mechanical, including photocopying, recording, or any information storage or retrieval system, without prior permission in writing from the publishers.

Bloomsbury Publishing Plc does not have any control over, or responsibility for, any third-party websites referred to or in this book. All internet addresses given in this book were correct at the time of going to press. The author and publisher regret any inconvenience caused if addresses have changed or sites have ceased to exist, but can accept no responsibility for any such changes.

A catalogue record for this book is available from the British Library.

Library of Congress Cataloging-in-Publication Data

Names: Ruloff, C. P., 1967- editor. | Horban, Peter, editor.
Title: Contemporary arguments in natural theology: God and rational belief / edited by Colin Ruloff and Peter Horban.
Description: London; New York: Bloomsbury Academic, 2021. | Includes bibliographical references and index. |
Identifiers: LCCN 2021000353 (print) | LCCN 2021000354 (ebook) | ISBN 9781350093850 (hardback) | ISBN 9781350093867 (ebook) | ISBN 9781350093874 (epub)
Subjects: LCSH: Natural theology.
Classification: LCC BL175.C66 2021 (print) | LCC BL175 (ebook) | DDC 210–dc23
LC record available at https://lccn.loc.gov/2021000353
LC ebook record available at https://lccn.loc.gov/2021000354

ISBN: HB: 978-1-3500-9385-0
PB: 978-1-3502-4457-3
ePDF: 978-1-3500-9386-7
eBook: 978-1-3500-9387-4

Typeset by RefineCatch Limited, Bungay, Suffolk

To find out more about our authors and books visit www.bloomsbury.com and sign up for our newsletters.

Contents

List of Figures	vi
List of Contributors	vii
Acknowledgments	ix
Introduction *Colin P. Ruloff and Peter Horban*	1

Part 1 Revisiting the Classical Arguments for the Existence of God

1	The Argument from Contingency *Joshua Rasmussen*	17
2	The Kalam Cosmological Argument *Andrew Ter Ern Loke*	35
3	The Ontological Argument *Jason Megill*	51
4	The Fine-Tuning Argument *Michael Rota*	69
5	The Argument from Biological Complexity *Michael J. Behe*	89
6	The Argument from Biological Information *Stephen Meyer*	109
7	The Moral Argument *C. S. Evans and Trinity O'Neill*	129

Part 2 Further Directions in Natural Theology

8	The Argument from Phenomenal Consciousness *J. P. Moreland*	149
9	The Argument from Beauty *Brian Ribeiro*	167
10	The Argument from Certainty *Katherin Rogers*	179
11	The Argument from the Applicability of Mathematics *William Lane Craig*	195
12	The Conceptualist Argument *Greg Welty*	217
13	The Argument from Desire *William A. Lauinger*	235
14	The Argument from Religious Experience *Kai-man Kwan*	251
15	The Wager Argument *Joshua Golding*	271
16	The Argument from the Meaning of Life *Stewart Goetz*	281
17	The Argument from Common Consent *Jonathan Matheson*	293
18	The Argument from Ramified Natural Theology *Sandra Menssen and Thomas D. Sullivan*	311
Index	327

Figures

4.1	Fine-tuning of the cosmological constant	73
4.2	The probability space for a sample problem	76
4.3	Illustration of the probability space for the fine-tuning argument	78
5.1	A mechanical mousetrap with multiple parts.	98
5.2	The bacterial flagellum.	100
6.1	The bonding relationship between the chemical constituents of the DNA molecule.	114

Contributors

Michael J. Behe
Professor of Biology, Department of Biological Sciences
Lehigh University

William Lane Craig
Research Professor of Philosophy
Talbot School of Theology
Biola University

C. S. Evans
Professor of Philosophy
Baylor University

Stewart Goetz
Professor of Philosophy, Department of Philosophy and Religious Studies
Ursinus College

Joshua Golding
Professor of Philosophy
Department of Philosophy
Bellarmine University

Peter Horban
Senior Lecturer, Department of Philosophy
Simon Fraser University

Kai-man Kwan
Professor of Philosophy
Hong Kong Baptist University

William Lauinger
Associate Professor of Philosophy, Religious Studies and Philosophy
Chestnut Hill College

Andrew Ter Ern Loke
Assistant Professor of Philosophy
Hong Kong University

Jon Matheson
Assistant Professor of Philosophy
University of North Florida

Jason Megill
Assistant Professor of Philosophy
Bentley University

Sandra Menssen
Professor of Philosophy
Department of Philosophy
University of St. Thomas

Stephen Meyer
Director
Institute of Science and Culture, Discovery Institute

J. P. Moreland
Distinguished Professor of Philosophy
Talbot School of Theology
Biola University

Trinity O'Neill
PhD candidate, Department of Philosophy
Baylor University

Joshua Rasmussen
Assistant Professor of Philosophy
Azusa Pacific University

Brian Ribeiro
Professor of Philosophy
University of Tennessee

Katherin Rogers
Professor of Philosophy
University of Delaware

Michael Rota
Associate Professor of Philosophy
University of St. Thomas

Colin Ruloff
Instructor of Philosophy
Kwantlen Polytechnic University

Thomas Sullivan
Professor of Philosophy Emeritus
Department of Philosophy
University of St. Thomas

Greg Welty
Associate Professor of Philosophy
Southeastern Baptist University

Acknowledgments

We would like to thank the following publishers and copyright holders for permission to reprint parts of or full previously published articles and chapters:

IVP for material from *Taking Pascal's Wager* by Michael Rota. Copyright © 2016 by Michael Rota. Used by permission of InterVarsity Press, P.O. Box 1400, Downers Grove, IL 60515, USA. ivpress.com.

Oxford University Press for material from Chapter 5 ("Moral Arguments and Natural Signs for God" by C. S. Evans) in C. Stephen Evans, *Natural Signs and Knowledge of God* (Oxford, Oxford University Press, 2010), 107–148.

Taylor & Francis Informa UK Ltd for material from Chapter 10 ("The Argument from Consciousness" by J. P. Moreland) in Paul Copan and Paul K. Moser (eds.), *The Rationality of Theism* (Routledge, 2003), 204–220.

The European Journal for the Philosophy of Religion for material from Brian Ribeiro, "The Theistic Argument from Beauty: A Philonian Critique", *European Journal for the Philosophy of Religion* 5 (2013): 149–158. © EJPR.

The Society of Christian Philosophers for Katherin Rogers, "Evidence for God from Certainty", *Faith and Philosophy* 25 (2008): 31–46.

The Copyright Clearance Center (222 Rosewood Drive Danvers, MA 01923 www.copyright.com) for material from Kai-man Kwan, "Can Religious Experience Provide Justification for Belief in God?", *Philosophy Compass*, 1 (2006): 640–661.

Taylor & Francis Informa UK Ltd for Chapter 41 ("The Wager Argument" by Joshua Golding) in Chad Meister and Paul Copan (eds.), *The Routledge Companion to Philosophy of Religion* (Routledge, 2012), 445–453.

Sincere appreciation and warmest thanks go out to Emily Beattie and Paul Fader for their invaluable help with formatting and organizing the manuscript. Their patience, support, and attention to detail is greatly appreciated.

We would also like to extend our gratitude to Becky Holland for agreeing to take on this project, and for her professionalism, guidance, and support throughout its various stages. Additionally, we would like to thank Merv Honeywood for his excellent work on copyediting the manuscript and compiling the index. Finally, our greatest debt of gratitude is to the two who know us best. This book is for you, Gabrielle and Helene.

Introduction

The book you are holding is a book on natural theology. Natural theology is the practice of attempting to arrive at truths regarding the nature and existence of God independent of divine revelation by relying solely on one's natural cognitive faculties. These faculties may include sense perception, memory, introspection, deductive inference, inductive inference, analogical reasoning, and abductive reasoning or inference to the best explanation. Natural theology stands in contrast to *revealed* theology or *revelation-based* theology, which is the attempt to arrive at truths regarding the nature and existence of God based solely on statements that have been revealed to us by God through various sacred texts such as the Bible, Talmud, or Koran. As its starting point, revealed theology may, for instance, take as authoritative certain New Testament claims about Jesus Christ and then go on to construct a philosophical or theological account of how Christ may simultaneously possess two distinct natures—one human and one divine. Natural theology, by contrast, typically takes as its starting point certain facts about the observable universe—the fact that the cosmos exists, the fact that the universe is fine-tuned, and so on—and then goes on to construct an argument for the existence of God based on these facts. Generally speaking, we might say that natural theology, unlike revealed theology, avoids any appeal to any supernatural sources of information or data, follows the same standards of rational investigation as other philosophical enterprises, and is subject to the same methods of critical evaluation.[1]

One striking feature about the project of natural theology is its sheer longevity. Philosophers across almost every era and tradition have been engaged in the project of natural theology.[2] As far back as the fourth century BC, we find in Book X of Plato's *Laws*, a version of what philosophers now call the "cosmological argument" for the existence of God. Ever since, philosophers have devoted an enormous amount of time and energy articulating, defending, and refining various attempts to show that God exists and that belief in God is rational. Indeed, as noted by William Lane Craig and J. P. Moreland,[3] there has been a bold revival in the field of natural theology over the past two decades. Today's practitioners of natural theology have not only revived and recast all of the traditional arguments in the field, but, by drawing upon recent discoveries in contemporary cosmology, chemistry, and biology, have also developed a range of fascinating new ones. Scores of books and hundreds of academic articles in natural theology (many of which are dauntingly technical and presuppose advanced training in logic and philosophy) continue to be churned out annually by professionally-trained philosophers and theologians. It would not be inaccurate to say that debate about the existence of God is an all-consuming passion of twentieth-century practitioners of natural theology. The practice of natural theology, however, isn't confined to the halls of academia; rather, as Chignell and Pereboom[4] note, the current renaissance in natural theology has spilled over into the popular sphere as well. There are now popular institutes promoting intelligent design, popular apologetics courses, campus debates between theists and atheists, a "New Atheist" movement, Youtube debates between pastors and atheist apologists, and TED talks by famous atheists on attempts to demonstrate the existence of God.

Given this recent explosion in natural theology, it is surprising to find that contemporary formulations of this panoply of arguments have yet to be represented in a single user-friendly volume. The current volume aims to fill this lacuna. Intended primarily for the advanced undergraduate and early graduate student, *Contemporary Arguments in Natural Theology* is a comprehensive, philosophically rigorous, and yet accessible "field guide" to the practice of natural theology. It aims to cover not only the most prominent arguments in natural theology that have been advanced over the past twenty years, but a number of intriguing lesser-known arguments as well, including the conceptualist argument, the argument from information, the argument from mathematics, the argument from common consent, the argument from certainty, and the argument from beauty. As such, the volume should appeal not only to the undergraduate and graduate student in philosophy, but also to the professional researcher in religious studies, theology, biblical studies, and philosophy. We believe that this volume vividly illustrates the creative depth and philosophical breadth of the work being done by some of the very best practitioners of natural theology today.

* * * *

In order to give the reader a broad overview of the book and its structure, we have provided introductory summaries for each of the eighteen chapters.

In Chapter 1 ("The Argument from Contingency"), Joshua Rasmussen advances a two-stage argument for the existence of a maximally great being. Rasmussen begins his argument by describing a puzzle about existence. The puzzle centers on an observation about the *totality* of reality: Suppose, says Rasmussen, we call reality as a whole "the blob of everything." The blob of everything is strange in a way, for, says Rasmussen, nothing beyond the blob explains or causes the blob. But how can any blob exist without any outside cause or explanation? In order to answer this question, Rasmussen suggests that a blob can exist without a cause or explanation so long as that blob includes some *foundational* or *non-dependent* layer. This foundational layer is the bedrock layer of existence. Nothing causes the foundation to exist. Rasmussen calls the theory that the blob of everything includes such a foundational layer "The Foundation Theory." Rasmussen motivates the Foundation Theory by offering two closely-related reasons for thinking that there must be a foundational layer of reality. The first reason comes to us by way of a contemporary formulation of a classic argument for a necessary foundation of contingent things—the so-called "Argument from Contingency." And the second argument comes to us by way of an argument that Rasmussen calls "The Argument from Possible Explanations." After defending each of these arguments and addressing a number of objections to them, Rasmussen goes on to suggest that any necessarily existing foundation will also possess a broad range of theistic attributes, including eternality, supreme existence, and unsurpassable power. The conclusion that Rasmussen arrives at is that a proper explanation of reality will necessarily involve affirming the existence of a supreme God-like being.

In Chapter 2 ("The Kalam Cosmological Argument"), Andrew Loke aims to defend the following argument from a range of objections:

(1) Everything that begins to exist has a cause.
(2) The universe began to exist.
(3) Therefore, the universe has a cause.

Specifically, with respect to premise (2), Loke surveys the relevant literature and argues that, at present, there is no good evidence for thinking that any of the cosmological models that propose that the universe has an infinite past is plausible. On the contrary, says Loke, our best scientific evidence strongly indicates that the universe is past-time finite and had an absolute beginning in time. Loke bolsters his argument for (2) by advancing four arguments, each of which shows that an infinite regress of causes and events is impossible:

(i) the argument from the impossibility of concrete actual infinities
(ii) the argument from the impossibility of traversing an actual infinite
(iii) the argument from the viciousness of dependence regress, and
(iv) the argument from paradoxes.

Loke then turns to a defense of (1). Specifically, Loke responds to worries regarding the causal principle expressed by (1) based on considerations of quantum theory. In this connection Loke also develops an argument for premise (1) which shows that if something (e.g. the universe) begins to exist uncaused, then many other kinds of things/events which can begin to exist would *also* begin to exist uncaused. Loke concludes by examining the nature of the cause of the universe and suggests that it must be uncaused, beginningless, changeless, free, and personal. Hence, concludes Loke, it's rational to believe that a personal creator of the universe exists.

The ontological argument is an argument for the existence of God that begins with premises that do not derive from an observation of the world, but from pure reason alone. In Chapter 3 ("The Ontological Argument"), Jason Megill points out that, although the ontological argument has historically been much maligned, the recent spate of modal versions of this argument are able to overcome many (if not all) of the traditional objections that have been leveled against it. Towards this end, Megill begins his paper by providing a historical overview of some of the major traditional versions of the ontological argument from the early medieval period through to the early modern period. In particular, Megill explicates Anselm's, Descartes', and Leibniz's versions of the ontological argument, along with some of the most common objections to these arguments, including the parody objection, the objection which asserts that existence is not a perfection, and Kant's objection according to which existence is not a predicate. After making a few preliminary comments regarding the notions of possibility (i.e., of what could happen), and necessity (i.e., of what must happen) and defining the notion of a "possible world," Megill then goes on to discuss a pair of important contemporary modal versions of the ontological argument, focusing in particular on Alvin Plantinga's modal ontological argument and Robert Maydole's modal perfection argument. After situating each of these arguments within its appropriate system of modal logic, Megill then examines the most prominent objections to each of these arguments. Megill concludes by describing the current situation with respect to the ontological argument and suggests some avenues of future research.

In Chapter 4 ("The Fine-Tuning Argument"), Michael Rota presents and defends the fine-tuning argument for the existence of God. According to most physicists, the universe is *fine-tuned* for complex biological life, i.e., constructed in such a way that if any of the basic parameters of physics had been ever-so-slightly different, a life-sustaining universe would never have arisen. But, asks Rota, what best explains this fine-tuning? According to Rota, the best explanation for the fine-tuning of the universe is that it was the product of intentional intelligent design. In order to establish this conclusion, Rota begins by presenting the following "core" version of the fine-tuning argument: If the cause of our universe is an intelligent being capable of deliberately designing and producing a universe, then the fact that our universe is fine-tuned is not at all surprising. If, on the other hand, our universe is the result of blind physical processes, then it is enormously improbable and therefore highly surprising that our universe is fine-tuned. Since a fine-tuned universe is not at all surprising on the former hypothesis, but highly surprising on the latter hypothesis, the fact that our universe is fine-tuned constitutes strong evidence for the claim that it was in fact intelligently designed. After responding to two objections to the core version of the argument—viz., Sean Carroll's Star Trek Objection and Elliot Sober's Anthropic Objection—Rota then formulates a more rigorous version of the fine-tuning argument based on Bayes' Theorem. Rota concludes his paper by responding to five common objections to the fine-tuning argument: the objection from uniform probabilities, the objection from divine inscrutability, the necessity objection, the stringent vs. lax laws objection, and the multiverse objection. The conclusion that Rota arrives at is that, all things considered, the existence of fine-tuning provides the theist with significant evidence for thinking that the universe was the product of intelligent design.

In Chapter 5 ("The Argument from Biological Complexity"), Michael Behe argues that advances in our understanding of the molecular level of life in the past fifty years strongly support the conclusion that life is the intentional product of intelligent design. In order to arrive at this conclusion, Behe structures his paper as follows: After an extended discussion regarding the various logical, empirical, and historical features underlying the design argument, Behe goes on to defend the main claim of his paper, viz., the claim that the blind Darwinian processes of natural selection and random genetic variation are unable to account for the gradual evolution of complex, functional systems at the molecular, foundational level of life. In particular, Behe claims that natural selection and random genetic variation are unable to account for the gradual evolution of *irreducibly complex systems*, where an "irreducibly complex system" is a system which is comprised of several well-matched, interacting parts such that the removal of any one of those parts causes that system to cease functioning. The reason why natural selection and random genetic variation are unable to account for such systems, says Behe, is this: natural selection requires some function to exist before it can be selected. But for irreducibly complex systems, the function appears only when the system is *complete*. Thus, the gradual evolutionary construction of irreducibly complex systems cannot be achieved by natural selection and random genetic variation. As an example of an irreducibly complex system, Behe points to the bacterial flagellum, whose construction Behe describes in detail. After responding to various naturalistic attempts to explain the evolution of the flagellum and sketching a further anti-Darwinian argument based on the concept of devolution, Behe arrives at the following conclusion: the best explanation for the existence of complex, functional systems at the molecular level is that such systems are the intentional product of intelligent design.

In Chapter 6 ("The Argument from Biological Information"), Stephen Meyer defends what he calls the "biological argument from information." Since 2006, a series of bestselling books—led by Richard Dawkins' *The God Delusion*—have claimed that science decisively shows that belief in God is fundamentally irrational. Specifically, according to Dawkins along with the so-called "New Atheists," belief in God is irrational because there is no *evidence* for intelligent design in nature. Since, says Dawkins, the wholly undirected processes of natural selection and random genetic mutation can mimic the powers of a designing intelligence without itself being guided or directed by an intelligent agent of any kind, belief in God must be considered a failed hypothesis—tantamount to a delusion. According to Meyer, however, there is powerful evidence of intelligent design in nature that has been ignored by Dawkins and the New Atheists, viz., the digital information contained within the DNA molecule. Confronted with the information-rich DNA molecule, Meyer asks: what best explains this digital information? After surveying and rejecting a wide range of prominent naturalistic explanations for information—including the chemical evolution theory, chance-based scenarios, self-organization scenarios, pre-biotic natural selection, and the RNA world hypothesis—Meyer claims that the digital information contained within the DNA molecule is best explained in terms of the action of a designing intelligence or mind. Meyer then goes on to argue that, contrary to those who oppose the idea of intelligent design, the argument for design from DNA is not based upon ignorance or a desire to "give up on science," but rather upon our growing scientific knowledge of the inner workings of the cell and our experience-based knowledge of the cause and effect structure of the world. Indeed, says Meyer, the argument for design from DNA is based on the same method of scientific reasoning that Darwin himself used and thus there is no good reason to exclude the design hypothesis from consideration as a *bona fide* scientific theory.

In Chapter 7 ("The Moral Argument"), Stephen Evans and Trinity O'Neill defend the moral argument for the existence of God. Specifically, Evans and O'Neill develop an argument for God's existence that is rooted in *moral obligations* or *moral duties*. The guiding idea is this: Most people believe that not everything is permitted; some acts are morally wrong, and some acts are morally obligatory. But if some acts are morally obligatory—that is, if there really are objectively-binding moral obligations—then there must be a God that serves as the ultimate source or ground for such obligations. Hence, God exists. Stated formally, the argument goes as follows:

(1) If there are objectively-binding moral obligations, God exists
(2) There are objectively-binding moral obligations
(3) Therefore, God exists.

After a critical evaluation of Friedrich Nietzsche and J. L. Mackie's reasons for rejecting premise (2), Evans and O'Neill turn their attention to premise (1), i.e., to the claim that objectively-binding moral obligations require God as their source or foundation. As Evans and O'Neill point out, the critic who wishes to cast doubt on (1) but maintain (2) has two main options; (i) the critic may claim that moral obligations require no foundation and are simply brute facts, *or* (ii) the critic may concede that moral obligations require some sort of ground to explain them but claim that something other than God can supply this ground. After rejecting the idea that moral obligations are brute facts, Evans and O'Neill turn their attention to (ii) and evaluate three prominent naturalistic strategies to explain moral obligations. One strategy, the "naturalistic reductive" strategy, attempts to ground moral obligations in facts derived from evolutionary biology and psychology. A second strategy, the "social contract" strategy, attempts to show how a social contract between humans can ground moral obligations. The third strategy, the "self-legislation" strategy, construes moral obligations as a kind of demand that humans, as rational beings, impose on themselves. After highlighting the deep conceptual problems with each of these views, Evans and O'Neill conclude with the following suggestion: the existence of objectively-binding moral obligations is best explained by God who functions as the ultimate source or ground for these obligations.

In Chapter 8 ("The Argument from Phenomenal Consciousness"), J. P. Moreland defends the idea that consciousness—the raw qualitative feel of a mental state—is best explained by theism. Simplified somewhat, Moreland's argument goes as follows: consciousness exists and requires an explanation. The explanation for consciousness is either naturalistic or personal. Since there is no naturalistic explanation of consciousness, the explanation for consciousness must be personal. And if it is personal, then it must be theistic. The existence of consciousness, thus, constitutes good evidence for theism. After explaining the general motivation for each of the steps of his argument, Moreland then provides an extended defense of the main premise of his argument, viz., the premise which asserts that there is no naturalistic explanation for consciousness. Here Moreland provides four reasons for thinking that this premise is true: Firstly, Moreland argues that that there is no good reason for thinking that spatially-arranged matter or physical/chemical reactions in the brain could by themselves conspire to produce consciousness. Secondly, Moreland argues that the regular law-like correlation between types of mental states and physical states is inexplicable on naturalism. Thirdly, Moreland argues that naturalism, when conjoined with the causal closure principle (a principle to which naturalists are committed, according to Moreland), entails a mistaken account of mentality, viz., epiphenomenalism. Fourthly and lastly, Moreland argues that naturalism, when conjoined with evolutionary theory, cannot account for the emergence of consciousness. In the final section of his paper, Moreland examines four prominent rival explanations for consciousness, and concludes with the claim that, all things considered, the existence of consciousness is best explained by theism.

In Chapter 9 ("The Argument from Beauty"), Brian Ribeiro examines a fascinating but understudied form of the design argument which focuses on the *beauty* of the natural world and which asserts that, on that basis, the world requires a divine artist in order to explain its beauty. After motiving the main steps of this argument and discussing how the argument from beauty relates to the more familiar argument from design, Ribeiro then examines four important objections to this argument. According to the first objection, the reason why humans have an aesthetic appreciation of natural beauty (such as the freshly fallen snow or the jagged mountain tops) is that humans have a genetic predisposition, acquired through the pressures of evolutionary selection, to prefer certain natural environments. The second objection that Ribeiro considers is one that challenges an underlying assumption of the argument, viz., the assumption that beauty is an *objective* feature of reality. Since (the objection goes) beauty is merely an expression of subjective preference and nothing more, beauty doesn't require an explanation, contrary to the proponent of the argument. According to the third objection, what we might call the "ugliness objection," the existence of "disteleological" or ugly features of the world counts as strong evidence for thinking that the world is not in fact designed. After presenting a range of potential theistic rejoinders to each of these objections, Ribeiro then defends what he considers the strongest objection to the argument from beauty, what Ribeiro calls the "explanatory regress problem." According to this objection, the argument from beauty should be rejected as it generates a vicious explanatory regress. After carefully examining and rejecting a contemporary response to this objection (due to Mark Wynn), Ribeiro concludes with the following thought: although the theist may have the conceptual resources to respond to the first three objections, the theist is without an adequate response to the fourth objection. Since this is so, Ribeiro is ultimately led to reject the argument from beauty as an unsuccessful piece of natural theology.

In Chapter 10 ("The Argument from Certainty"), Katherin Rogers claims that the fact that human beings have indubitable beliefs about necessary truths such as $2 + 2 = 4$ serves as good evidence for the existence of God or a God-like being. Rogers takes it as a datum to be explained that humans sometimes have "strongly certain" beliefs. As Rogers defines it, a strongly certain belief is characterized by two main features. Firstly, such a belief will be *veridical*. That is, it will be held with a certainty such that the having of the belief will entail the truth of the proposition believed. Secondly, a strongly certain belief will possess a pair of properties which bestow upon it a distinct phenomenology. Specifically, a strongly certain belief will be *luminous*. That is, if I am strongly certain that p, then I know *that* I know that p. Additionally, a strongly certain belief will be *immediate*. That is, if I am strongly certain that p, then I will directly recognize, see, or grasp the content of p. Rogers claims that many human beings have strongly certain beliefs regarding necessary truths such as $2 + 2 = 4$. Not only, says Rogers, is the simple mathematical belief that $2 + 2 = 4$ held by many human beings with certainty, but the belief that $2 + 2 = 4$ is accompanied by a distinct phenomenology, one that is both luminous and immediate.

Armed with the definition of a strongly certain belief, Rogers then asks the following question: what best explains the fact that human beings have strongly certain beliefs regarding necessary truths such as $2 + 2 = 4$? On the plausible assumption that mathematical entities are causally inert abstract entities, Rogers argues that naturalist theories cannot provide an adequate causal explanation for the existence of strongly certain beliefs. This is because, says Rogers, such theories are unable to show how the propositional content of causally inert abstract entities is able to enter into in a chain of physical causes and thereby produce in us strongly certain beliefs. But now, if naturalist theories are unable to provide a causal explanation for the existence of strongly certain beliefs, what then best explains them? According to Rogers, only theism can provide a causally sufficient explanation for the existence of strongly certain beliefs regarding necessary truths. Since God (as an omniscient being) *knows* of such truths, and since God (as an omnipotent being) has the *power* to produce such truths in us, it follows, says Rogers, that the existence of strongly certain beliefs provides the theist with good evidence for the existence of God.

In Chapter 11 ("The Argument from the Applicability of Mathematics"), William Lane Craig presents the argument from mathematics. Philosophers of mathematics are sharply divided as to whether mathematical entities like numbers, sets, functions, and so on, really exist or not. *Realists* hold that such objects exist as mind-independent, causally impotent, abstract entities. *Anti-realists* are united in denying that such objects actually exist. Now one of the central questions facing realists and anti-realists alike is what the physicist Eugene Wigner famously called "the unreasonable effectiveness of mathematics." How is it, for example, that a mathematical theorist like Peter Higgs can sit down at his desk and, by pouring over mathematical equations, predict the existence of a fundamental particle which, thirty years later, scientists are finally able to detect? How is this to be explained? How, that is, do we explain the *applicability* of mathematics? Craig argues that, irrespective of whether one is a realist or an anti-realist about mathematical entities, theism offers a superior explanation for the applicability of mathematics than does naturalism. Consider first, says Craig, realism's take on the applicability of mathematics to the real world. For the *non-theistic* realist, the fact that physical reality behaves in accordance with the dictates of causally-impotent mathematical entities existing beyond space and time is a happy coincidence. By contrast, the *theistic* realist can argue that God has fashioned the world on the structure of the mathematical objects. Now consider anti-realism of a *non-theistic* sort. On mathematical anti-realism, relations which are said to obtain among mathematical objects just mirror the relations obtaining among things in the real world; there is, then, no happy coincidence. Fine; but, asks Craig, what remains wanting on naturalistic anti-realism is an explanation why the physical world exhibits so complex and stunning a mathematical structure *in the first place*. By contrast, the *theistic* anti-realist has a ready explanation of the applicability of mathematics to the physical world: the world exhibits the mathematical structure that it does because God has chosen to create it according to the abstract model he had in mind. Thus, concludes Craig, theism should be considered the superior explanatory account with respect to the applicability of mathematics.

In Chapter 12 ("The Conceptualist Argument"), Greg Welty claims that there are at least five intuitions and four distinct arguments that give us good reason for believing in the existence of propositions. But, says Welty, even though these arguments support a robust propositional-realism, these arguments do not by themselves indicate what *kind* of thing propositions are, metaphysically speaking. As Welty quips, "Are they bits of ink on paper, acoustic waves in the air, or magnetized regions on hard drives? Are they thoughts in one's head, or in all our heads put together? Are they built out of abstract 'stuff' which is neither material nor mental?" On these points, the arguments for propositional-realism are silent. According to Welty, however, whatever propositions turn out to be, propositions must, *at the very least*, satisfy the following six conditions: propositions must (i) be mind-independent, (ii) exist necessarily, (iii) be the bearers of truth-values, (iv) be the kinds of things that can be believed or disbelieved, (v) exist in an infinite number, and lastly, (vi) be the kinds of entities that belong fundamentally to one ontological category. The main realist accounts of propositions that can satisfy these six conditions are, says Welty, conceptualism, nominalism, and Platonism. Conceptualist accounts identify propositions with mental particulars (such as thoughts, whether human or divine). Nominalist accounts identify propositions with material particulars and subdivide into linguistic nominalism (where propositions are written or spoken sentences) and set-theoretic nominalism (where propositions are sets of familiar objects). Platonist accounts identify propositions with abstract entities that are neither mental nor material. But since, argues Welty, only *divine* conceptualism—the version of conceptualism which identifies propositions with the thoughts of a divine transcendent mind—is able to satisfy all six of these conditions, we therefore have good reason to be divine conceptualists about propositions, and therefore good reason to be theists.

In Chapter 13 ("The Argument from Desire"), William Lauinger claims that it's an empirical fact that humans (generally) have a restless innate desire for a kind of fulfillment that is attainable only in an afterlife outside the natural world and only with the help of God. According to the proponent of the argument from desire, the fact that we have this innate desire provides us with good evidence for believing that an afterlife and God both exist. After defending the idea that humans have an innate desire for an afterlife and articulating a key assumption underlying the argument—viz., the assumption that, for any inborn desire that humans have, it is far more reasonable to think that it can be fulfilled than that it cannot be fulfilled—Lauinger then offers the following (somewhat simplified) *inference-to-the-best explanation* formulation of the argument from desire:

(1) Humans generally have an innate desire for a kind of fulfillment that is attainable only in an afterlife outside the natural world and only with the help of God or something like God.
(2) The best explanation for the desire mentioned in (1) is a theistic one, according to which God instilled this desire in humans.
(3) Therefore, we have good reason for thinking that God exists and instilled this desire within humans.

Since, as Lauinger notes, he has already defended premise (1), Lauinger focuses his attention on premise (2). Specifically, Lauinger takes up a prominent objection advanced by Erik Wielenberg. According to Wielenberg, since a plausible naturalistic, evolutionary explanation for the existence of the desire mentioned in premise (1) is readily available, we have good reasons for rejecting premise (2). Lauinger responds to this objection by claiming that Wielenberg has fundamentally misunderstood the nature of desire; although Wielenberg has provided us with a plausible naturalistic evolutionary explanation for the existence of a natural desire for *earthly goods* that are available in infinite abundance, Wielenberg has failed to provide an explanation for the specific kind of desire that is at issue in the argument, viz., the natural desire for a state of fulfillment that *transcends* the natural world. Lauinger concludes by claiming that, although the argument from desire does not compel one to accept its conclusion, the theist who is already inclined to hold that the presence of a transcendent desire points to God is justified in accepting the argument's conclusion.

In Chapter 14 ("The Argument from Religious Experience"), Kai-man Kwan claims that a religious experience (that is, the kind of experience that a subject *takes* to be caused by God or brought about by some supernatural being) can, in certain circumstances, serve as good evidence for the belief that God exists. After laying out the general contours of the argument from religious experience and providing a general survey of some of the various contemporary expressions of this argument, Kwan then responds to a range of stock objections to the argument. From here, Kwan goes on to explain and motivate Richard Swinburne's highly-influential version of this argument, which can be stated as follows:

(1) Many subjects have had experiences such that *it seems* to those subjects as if God were present.
(2) In the absence of any counter-evidence, these subjects are epistemically justified in believing that things are as they seem to be.
(3) Therefore, in the absence of any counter-evidence, subjects who have had the kind of experience mentioned in (1) are justified in believing that God is the cause of their experience and that God exists.

After unpacking a key epistemic principle underlying this argument—what Swinburne dubs the "principle of credulity"—Kwan discusses three important objections to Swinburne's argument. According to the first objection, what Kwan dubs the "no criteria/uncheckability objection," since there is no objective criterion by which one can distinguish veridical religious experiences from non-veridical ones, it's not rational to believe that any particular religious experience is in fact veridical. But if it's not rational to believe that any particular religious experience is veridical, then the proponent of the argument can't use religious experience as evidence *for* the existence of God. According to the second objection, the "naturalistic explanation objection," religious beliefs formed by way of religious experiences should be discredited since they can be given purely naturalistic explanations, i.e., explanations in terms of unconscious psychological processes, various sociological pressures, or neurophysiological processes. Lastly, according to the "conflicting claims objection," since beliefs formed by way of religious experiences differ so wildly from each other and are often mutually contradictory, we should regard all such beliefs with suspicion. After defending the argument against these objections, Kwan concludes his paper by suggesting that, although there are important theoretical issues regarding the epistemic principles upon which the argument from religious experience depends (issues that need to be investigated and further clarified), some version of this argument may well be defensible, especially for those subjects who have had vivid religious experiences themselves.

As Joshua Golding points out at the outset in Chapter 15 ("The Wager Argument"), traditional arguments in natural theology seek to demonstrate that God exists or to show that God's existence is probable on the basis of the evidence of the senses. These may be referred to as *cognitive* arguments. In contrast, the argument known as Pascal's Wager aims to show that it is rational to believe in God, not on the basis of the evidence of the senses, but rather on the potential *value* of having the belief in God. Hence, the Wager may be referred to as a *pragmatic* argument for the existence of God. Golding summarizes Pascal's Wager as follows: We are faced with a decision about whether or not to believe that God exists. In order to decide what to believe, we should base our decision on consideration of what possible effect belief (or disbelief) in God will have on our welfare or happiness. At first glance, it appears that we have everything to gain and nothing to lose if we choose to believe that God exists. For, if we believe that God exists and God *does* exist, we shall attain great happiness in the afterlife. If we believe that God exists and God does *not* exist, we haven't lost much. On the other hand, if we disbelieve that God exists, we shall not attain great happiness under any circumstance. The rational decision according to Pascal, then, is this: we should choose to believe that God exists. Using modern terminology, the option of belief in God "dominates" over the alternative of disbelief, since belief in God has a better result if God exists, and no worse result if God does not exist. After a careful formulation of Pascal's Wager, Goldman then examines a range of standard criticisms of the wager argument. The criticisms concern (i) Pascal's claim that reason is unable to assess whether God exists; (ii) technical worries regarding the notion of infinite value; (iii) Pascal's assumptions linking a belief in God with the attainment of infinite value; and finally, (iv) moral and intellectual worries regarding the pragmatic justification of belief. Goldman concludes by suggesting a few ways in which the proponent of the wager argument may revise the argument so as to evade some of these standard criticisms.

In Chapter 16 ("The Argument from the Meaning of Life"), Stewart Goetz discusses the argument from the meaning of life. Since late in the last century, analytic philosophers have been exploring the meaning of life as a legitimate philosophical topic. The vast majority that have written about the issue have been naturalists. Although theists have been somewhat late to the debate, a number of theists are now beginning to think seriously about the matter. In his contribution Stewart Goetz explains how Christian theism—unlike naturalism—has the better conceptual resources to make possible an ultimately meaningful life. Towards this end, Goetz begins his paper by noting that the question "What is the meaning of life?" admits at least three interpretations: (1) "What, if anything, is the purpose of life?", (2) "What, if anything, makes life worth living?", and (3) "What is the way in which life ultimately makes sense?" Goetz then advances what he considers plausible theistic answers to each of these questions. As an answer to (1), Goetz suggests that theists through the ages have claimed that God creates each one of us for the purpose of experiencing perfect happiness. As an answer to (2), Goetz suggests that, since happiness is intrinsically good, experiencing perfect happiness is what makes life worth living. Finally, as an answer to (3), Goetz claims that life ultimately makes sense only if there is an afterlife in which the experience of perfect happiness can be realized. After developing his answers to (1)–(3), Goetz then turns his attention to the idea of ultimately making sense of things. What he claims to show is that naturalists themselves are committed to the idea of making sense of things, but in order to do this they must ultimately commit themselves to implausible positions regarding issues related to teleology and purpose. Indeed, says Goetz, these positions are so implausible that one must conclude that life is ultimately absurd on a naturalist view of things. In the end, it is clear, says Goetz, that Christian theism ultimately provides a superior explanatory account of the meaning of life than does naturalism.

In Chapter 17 ("The Argument from Common Consent"), Jonathan Matheson presents the common consent argument for theism. According to this argument it is rational for us to believe that God exists because we are aware of so many other people who believe that God exists. Formally, the argument has the following logical structure:

(1) The belief that God exists is prevalent.
(2) God existing is a good explanation for the prevalence of the belief that God exists.
(3) God existing better explains the prevalence of the belief that God exists than any available rival explanation.
(4) Therefore, God exists.

Although not deductively valid, Matheson points out that the proponent of the argument claims that its premises nevertheless provide good *abductive support* for its conclusion—enough to make it rational to believe the conclusion. After motivating the argument and explaining the rationale for each of its premises, Matheson then examines a wide range of objections to the argument. The main objections that Matheson considers are the following: According to the first objection, the argument from common consent essentially commits the appeal to popularity fallacy and, as such, ought to be rejected. According to the second objection, premise (1) is false since theistic belief is not in fact prevalent or not prevalent in the relevant way. According to the third objection, it's important for a particular belief's evidential value to be *independently formed*, i.e., formed in such a way that a person arrives at his or her belief without influence from other group members. But religious beliefs are rarely formed in isolation, and so, fail to have much evidential value. According to the fourth objection, if God exists we should expect much more—if not universal—theistic belief. So even if theistic belief is more prevalent than non-belief, God's existence can't be a good explanation for the prevalence of theistic belief given that there is still *far too much* non-belief. According to the fifth objection, since there are good naturalistic explanations for the prevalence of religious belief, the existence of such explanations strongly undermine premise (3). The overall conclusion that Matheson arrives at is this: a number of complex philosophical issues play an important role regarding whether or not the argument from common consent succeeds as a piece of natural theology. As such, more work needs to be done in these areas to properly assess the strength of this argument.

In Chapter 18 ("The Argument from Ramified Natural Theology"), Sandra Menssen and Thomas D. Sullivan present an argument from ramified natural theology. Traditionally conceived, natural theology aims to demonstrate that God exists without relying on the authority of divine revelation—relying only on evidence that we access through our ordinary cognitive faculties. Ramified natural theology, by contrast, uses that same sort of evidence to argue for a specific claim regarding *a particular religious tradition*. As Menssen and Sullivan point out, an argument in ramified natural theology might begin with the kind of evidence that we access through our ordinary cognitive faculties and conclude with, say, the claim that Jesus Christ was resurrected or the claim that Mohammad was a prophet of God. Other paradigmatic examples of ramified natural theology include Anselm's arguments for the incarnation, Pascal's use of biblical prophecy to defend the deity of Christ, and probabilistic arguments supporting miracle-claims, such as the contention that Jesus rose from the dead. Ramified natural theology, thus, can be understood as natural theology employed *not* in the service of theism in general, but rather in the service of some particular religious tradition.

Menssen and Sullivan attempt to develop an extended example of ramified natural theology which they call "the argument from revelatory content." They begin by introducing an argument-schema or, what they call an "argument-frame." After explaining and justifying each of the steps of the argument-frame and responding to a number of objections to it, they argue that the argument-frame is able to generate a wide variety of specific arguments from revelatory content. From here, they go on to show how the argument-frame might be used to support the revelatory claims of Christianity. Specifically, by drawing extensively upon the insights of St. Thomas Aquinas, they attempt to show how the argument-frame can be used to deploy an argument involving the "fittingness" of the incarnation, and therefore show that that Christian revelatory claim is likely to be true.

Notes

1 Andrew Chignell and Derk Pereboom, "Natural Theology," *Stanford Encyclopedia of Philosophy*, ed. Edward N. Zalta, 2019, https://plato.stanford.edu/entries/natural-theology/
2 Ibid.
3 William Lane Craig and J. P. Moreland, *The Blackwell Companion to Natural Theology* (Wiley-Blackwell, 2012), ix.
4 Chignell and Pereboom.

Part One

Revisiting the Classical Arguments for the Existence of God

1

The Argument from Contingency

Joshua Rasmussen

1. The question of existence

Why does *anything* exist? There are atoms. There are planets. There is you. Why are there any of these things? Why not instead just nothing at all? The purpose of this chapter is to help you investigate a possible answer.[1]

Given the topic of this book, you might expect me to argue that *God* is the answer—i.e., God explains why anything exists. However, this answer has a puzzling consequence. God cannot explain existence unless God already *exists*. This explanation appears circular.

If we want to know why something exists, curiosity typically draws our attention to a broader context. For example, if we wish to understand why a particular fire exists, we might search for a cause of the fire. The cause of the fire is not the fire itself; the cause is something *else*, like a match or lightning strike. In the absence of a broader context that could help us see why something exists, the original mystery seems to remain.

I will seek to shed light on the mystery of existence in two stages. In the first stage, I will show how certain principles of explanation suggest that there is a *foundational* layer of reality, which exists without any outside explanation. In the second stage, I will investigate the nature of this foundation; in particular, I will consider how a foundation could be *relevantly different* from everything else that has an outside explanation, and how we may thereby avoid the problem of circularity. In the end, we will arrive at what may be the ultimate explanation of everything.

2. Why ask why?

Asking *why* is one of the most powerful tools for investigating any topic. I will show how we can use the question—*why?*—to investigate an explanation of everything.

I begin with a simple "why" principle: *explain as much as you can*. This principle will guide our entire inquiry.

Let us unpack the "why" principle. I offer what I call "the Principle of Explanation" (PE), which is one modest translation of the "why" principle: For any fact *F*, if an explanation of *F* is possible, then an explanation of *F* is expectable, other things being equal. This principle is relatively modest as far as principles of explanation go. PE is more modest than the classic Principle of Sufficient Reason (PSR). PSR says that everything whatsoever has a sufficient reason (explanation or cause).[2] By contrast, PE doesn't require that much. Instead, PE expresses a *presumption* to expect an explanation; in other words, explain as much as you can.

Five clarifications are in order. First, when I say some explanation is expectable, I don't mean that someone probably *knows* the explanation. Some explanations may be entirely unknown. For example, it could be that there is ash on the ground because there was a fire, even while no one knows that there was a fire. So I'm thinking of explanations as part of the world—perhaps awaiting discovery.

Second clarification: I am thinking of explanations as expressible in terms of *propositions*. So, for example, the proposition *that there was a fire* may explain the fact (true proposition) *that there is ash on the ground*. If we say the fire itself explains the ash, I understand this talk to be shorthand. I'll say an explanation is *real* (actually obtains) if the proposition that expresses it is true.[3]

Third, an explanation, as I am thinking of it, provides *some* illumination of why or how something is the case without circularity. When I say the explanation is not circular, I mean that at least part of the explanation is *external* to (not wholly included in) the fact to be explained. (I leave to the side the prospect of other notions of "explanation" that allow for circularity.) Example: a theory of common ancestry helps illuminate—and so explains (to some extent)—why genetic similarities exist.

For our purposes, we may say that where F is a fact of the form *the xs exist*, an external explanation of F is in terms of at least one thing that is not among those same xs. For example, an external explanation of the fact that the turtles exist is not entirely in terms of those same turtles.

Fourth, by "expectable," I mean a positive *degree of expectation* (what philosophers sometimes call "epistemic" probability). For example, if someone tosses a six-sided die, and if all sides look equal in size, then you can expect a 1/6 probability (expectation) that the die lands on a given side. In the same way, the expectation in PE is an expectation of a further explanation in light of the record of actual explanations one knows about.

Fifth and finally, the principle allows for exceptions. It says that an explanation is expectable *other things being equal*. In this way, PE can expose a *reason* in support of some explanation, while leaving open whether one may have counterbalancing reasons. The discovery of reasons to think something is true is itself an important part of the discovery of truth.

Now that we have some preliminaries out of the way, I will share a few reasons I think PE can help us extend sight. First, PE successfully predicts many observations. In this respect, PE is like the law of gravity. The law of gravity successfully predicts the many cases of gravitational attraction. Similarly, PE successfully predicts the many cases of explanation. Successful prediction provides evidential support for the theory.

Note that evidential support is *open to defeat*. For example, suppose we found a special massive object that defies gravity. Then we may have reason to restrict the law of gravity. Similarly, if one has reason to think that PE fails to apply to a particular item, then that reason may motivate an exception. Still, even if we found some weird object, that wouldn't undermine the presumptive application to most other objects.

Consider, moreover, that science succeeds by seeking deeper explanations of observations. Without something like PE, it is unclear how scientific practice could have a solid footing, for scientific investigation relies on at least the presumption that there is a further, outside explanation for a given phenomenon (while we might not yet know what it is). Suppose, instead, there is no presumption of any explanation. Then for any given observations, there is no presumption of an explanation of those observations. In that case, every scientific explanation would be suspect.

The ramifications go beyond science. Without PE, it's not even clear how you could infer that anything exists outside your head. For suppose there is no presumption to expect an explanation. Then why expect any external explanation of your existence or inner experiences? You might just as likely be randomly hallucinating.

Now to be clear, I am not suggesting that you must first *explicitly* believe PE to believe that particular things have an explanation. Rather, I think you can begin by directly witnessing clear cases of explanations, such as that your current thoughts have an explanation in terms of previous thoughts. These clear cases then provide a basis for inferring a more general principle, which is implicit in ordinary and scientific reasoning.

Here is a final, reason-based consideration that may also support PE. One may have a direct, intuitive sense that truths, in general, have an explanation. To trigger that sense, take any arbitrary proposition p out of a hat. Suppose p is *true*. We can wonder: why is p true? Why not false? One's very curiosity reflects the sense that there is likely *some* explanation, whatever it might be.

At this point, it may help to sketch the sorts of explanations that might be available in general. So take any true proposition p. Proposition p is either *contingent* (i.e., not necessarily true or necessarily false) or *necessary*. Suppose, first, p is contingent. Then an explanation of p could be in terms of prior causes or tendencies. For example, the fact that there are sheep is explicable in terms of a causal history leading to the first sheep. Next, suppose p is necessary (not contingent). In that case, here are three options: (i) the fact that p is necessary is a reason to think p cannot have an explanation; (ii) p has an explanation in terms of more fundamental necessary truths; or (iii) p is self-explanatory or explained by the fact that it is necessary (if we put aside the *external* explanation requirement).

In light of these options, one could theoretically hold that *every* fact has some explanation, either in terms of prior causes or conditions (if it is contingent) or in terms of itself (if it is necessary).[4] For our purposes, we may leave these (and other[5]) options open.

To review, PE invites us to explain things as far as we can. *Why*? To illuminate our world. The twin lights of reason and experience testify to the illuminating power of explanations. Explanations empower scientific inquiry. Explanations help you see that there is an external world. And, as we will consider next, explanations may help us uncover the nature of ultimate reality.

3. The foundation theory

The next step is to use the "why" tool to investigate reality as a whole. Suppose we call reality as a whole (all things included), "the blob of everything." The blob of everything is strange in a way, for nothing beyond the blob explains or causes the blob (since there is nothing beyond the blob). But how can any blob—of any size or shape—exist without any outside cause or outside explanation?

I offer for your consideration the beginning of an answer. I propose that a blob can exist without any outside cause or explanation if that blob includes some *foundational* (non-dependent) layer. This foundation is the bedrock layer of existence. Nothing causes the foundation to exist. The foundation exists on its own—independently of any outside cause or outside explanation. I call the theory that the blob of everything includes a foundation, "The Foundation Theory."

I will motivate this proposal by offering two related reasons to think that there is a basic, necessary portion of reality capable of being a foundation for *contingent* (i.e., non-necessary) things. The first reason uses the Principle of Explanation (PE) in support of the first stage of a classic *Argument from Contingency*. The second reason is a contemporary argument from possible explanations.

Start with the Argument from Contingency (stage 1):

(1) Something exists.
(2) If everything is contingent, then there is no external explanation of the contingent things (of why there are the contingent things *there are*).
(3) There is an external explanation of the contingent things.
(4) Therefore, not everything is contingent. (from 2 and 3)
(5) Therefore, something is non-contingent. (from 1 and 4)
(6) Therefore, something has necessary existence.

Let us examine each premise. Start with (1): something exists. By "exists," I do not mean anything fancy. I mean that *there are things*, whatever they might be. Even if everything is an illusion, then illusions *exist*.

Why believe anything exists? Here's why: you can see that something exists via your direct awareness of existing things. For example, you are aware of your thoughts. Your awareness of your thoughts is your clearest way of knowing that your thoughts exist. (I do not assume anything about the *nature* of the things that exist. If everything is an illusion, then at least the illusions exist.)

If we suppose instead that nothing exists, then *no one* exists. If no one exists, then there is no one for me to convince. There are no words here. There are no thoughts. There is no you. But there are words, there are thoughts, and there is you. Therefore, something exists.

Next, consider premise (2): if everything has contingent existence, then there is no external explanation of the contingent things. A contingent thing is something that doesn't have necessary existence. So the premise says that if nothing has necessary existence, then there is no external explanation of the fact that there are the contingent (*non-necessary*) things that there are.

Principle (2) follows from the intended meaning of "explanation," which goes beyond what is to be explained. In this case, what is to be explained is the fact *that there are the contingent things that there are*. If we want to know why there are *these* contingent things, an external explanation will not be entirely in terms of those very same things.

Any explanation in terms of contingent things presupposes the very thing we are trying to explain: these very contingent things. Therefore, an external explanation of the contingent things (of the fact that they all exist) will ultimately be in terms of something that is *not* contingent. (This inference doesn't depend upon the *length* of the chain of contingent things: I'll say more about the prospect of an infinite chain in section 5.[6])

Note the term "the contingent things" refers to all the contingent things using plural reference.[7] That is to say, the term "the contingent things" refers to the plural of *all* contingent things (at all times and all places).[8] In referring to the contingent things, I do not assume that they compose a single Big Contingent Thing, over and above the individuals. In the same way, by referring to ten children, I'm not saying those ten children compose a big child.

Turn to premise (3): there is an external explanation of the contingent things. Our explanation-seeking tool (PE) exposes a reason in support of (3). According to PE, for any given fact f, if an explanation of f is possible, some explanation is expectable (other things being equal), where the notion of "explanation" in view is external. In this case, f = the fact that there are the contingent things that there are. According to PE, then, we can expect an external explanation of this fact. (I am assuming it is a fact that there are contingent things. If instead there are *no* contingent things, then everything is a necessary thing. In that case, the *conclusion* of the first stage of the Argument from Contingency is true, and we may then skip ahead to section 6.)

Before moving on, I want to emphasize again that PE is quite modest. The principle merely invites us to seek an explanation as far as we can. If there is an exception (a fact with no external explanation), then perhaps that fact is special. We can identify special exceptions if we have sufficient reason. In any case, PE is at least a *reason* in support of (3), which one may weigh in the balance.

Moreover, in the absence of a counterbalancing reason to think that a given fact admits of no further explanation, one has no reason to treat the given fact as different from every other fact that has a further explanation. In other words, you may explain facts as far as you can.

Let us recap the argument. The key idea is that contingent things have some explanation. To avoid circularity, an explanation of all the contingent things will not be solely in terms of contingent things (on the relevant notion of "explanation"). If that is right, then some non-contingent thing is part of the total explanation of contingent things. Since a non-continent thing is (by definition) a necessary thing, it follows that there is a necessary thing; maybe there are many necessary things, but there is at least one.

This result has far-reaching ramifications, as we shall see in section 6. It will be useful, therefore, to reexamine our steps before we continue. In the next section, I will offer another argument for the same result. Then, in section 5, we will examine some objections.

4. An argument from possible explanations

A more recent type of argument from contingency seeks to display a link between *possible* causes (or possible explanations) and a necessary thing capable of causing or grounding contingent things.

Here is one such argument, what I will call "The Argument from Possible Explanations" (APE):[9]

(1) Every contingent state could *possibly* have some (external) explanation.[10]
(2) If no necessary thing is possible, then some contingent state couldn't possibly have an (external) explanation.
(3) Therefore, some necessary thing is possible.
(4) A necessary thing is either impossible or necessary.
(5) Therefore, some necessary thing is necessary.
(6) Therefore, there is a necessary thing (at least one).[11]

I will suggest a potential justification for each premise. First a clarification: I use the term "could possibly" to convey *consistent with* the truths of reason—i.e., the truths one can see to be true via rational reflection (*a priori*). Truths of reason include, for example, truths of mathematics and logic, like $1 + 1 = 2$.

Next, when I say a proposition is *consistent* with reason, I mean the proposition doesn't *contradict* any truth of reason.

This notion of "possibility" is very broad. It is broader than *physical* possibility—i.e., consistency with what physical things actually exist. There might be physically impossible things that are still logically possible; e.g., it may be *physically* impossible for you to travel faster than the speed of light, but there's nothing *logically* impossible about that. (A priori possibility may also be broader than what is called "*metaphysical* possibility"—i.e., consistency with whatever is ontologically necessary.[12])

The broadness of the notion I have in mind contributes to the modesty of (1). This premise says merely that no principle of reason *rules out* a scenario in which every contingent state could—consistent with reason—have an external explanation. In view of the modesty of (1), I suspect you might find (1) quite plausible in its own right—perhaps self-evident.

In any case, one might also motivate principle (1) via examples. Principle (1) successfully predicts many cases of possible explanations (without appealing to anything ad-hoc or weird). In particular, (1) predicts that it is possible for there to be an explanation of your current thoughts. An explanation of your thoughts is surely possible. Therefore, (1)'s prediction here is successful. As far as I am aware, there are no counterexamples to (1) and no simpler, competing principle with as much predictive success. I leave it to the reader to consider possible exceptions.

As with any principle, (1) is open to defeat, at least in principle. Thus, for example, if you have some reason to think that some contingent state *couldn't* have any explanation, then that reason may defeat (1), at least with respect to that case. In the interest of modesty, we may treat (1) as a rule of thumb (at least): so for any given contingent state, one may expect that state to at least possibly have an external explanation, absent a sufficient reason to think otherwise.

Next, consider premise (2): there is some contingent state that couldn't possibly have an (external) explanation unless some necessary thing is possible. Here's a reason for (2). Let C = the *state of there being the contingent things there are and no others*. C is contingent (since C would fail to obtain if any contingent cause failed to exist). So suppose C could possibly have an explanation. To avoid circularity, the explanation will not be solely in terms of those same contingent things; instead, the explanation will be in terms of something *non-contingent* that could produce or cause contingent things. In other words, if C could possibly have an (external) explanation, then there could possibly be a necessary thing capable of producing or causing contingent things.

If that much is correct, we may then complete the argument as follows. A necessary thing is the sort of thing that is either *necessary* or *impossible*—premise (4). A necessary thing is not impossible—given (3). It follows that a necessary thing is necessary, and therefore actual.

Let us look again at premise (4): a necessary thing is either necessary or impossible. This premise is a consequence of a standard logic of possibility. For our purposes, we may treat this logic as orienting us to a relevant *definition* of "necessary thing." I relegate the technical details to a note at the end of the chapter.[13]

We've covered a lot of ground. I invite you to review the steps carefully. Test them. See what you can see. (To examine additional pathways to a necessary thing that could be a cause of contingent things, see necessarybeing.com or Alexander Pruss and Joshua Rasmussen, *Necessary Existence* (Oxford: Oxford University Press, 2018)).

5. Objections

I will address six common and instructive objections to the Foundation Theory. This list is only a sample. You may have additional objections. The discussion below is an introduction to some of the wider issues at stake.

Objection 1: infinite regress

Suppose every contingent thing depends on another *contingent* thing in an infinite regress of causes. Then no foundation is required, or even possible. If every contingent thing already has a complete contingent cause, there is no place in the chain of causes for a necessary thing to participate.

Reply

Note first that this objection does not target any premise in either of my two arguments for a necessary foundation. Both arguments leave open the prospect of an infinite chain of causes. No premise says that contingent reality is finite.[14]

Second, and more fundamentally, the hypothesis that there is an infinite chain leaves unanswered *why* that chain exists (whether we conceive of the chain as a single thing or as an assemblage of many things). The mere infinity of the chain still leaves something unexplained. To illustrate, suppose you find a hammer in your friend's garage, and you ask, "Where did this hammer come from?" Your friend replies, "Oh, that hammer has always been there." His answer doesn't really address your question, since the age of the hammer—even if infinite—doesn't by itself ultimately explain the existence of the hammer.[15]

Note that even if a chain of causes is *internally* explained (in some sense) by its members, that still doesn't give us an external explanation. PE invites us to look for external explanations as far as we can (to empower science, etc.). We can externally explain a chain of contingent things in terms of a non-contingent foundation (just as we can externally explain any chain of turtles in terms of more fundamental causes), whether or not the chain is infinite.[16] (I say more about external explanations of infinite chains in the next objection.)

Objection 2: the fallacy of composition

It is fallacious to suppose that the totality of contingent things is itself contingent. After all, a totality can have different properties from its parts: for example, the totality of chickens is not a chicken. Similarly, maybe each contingent thing has a cause, while the totality of contingent things is uncaused.

Reply

The version of the Argument from Contingency in this chapter does not depend upon any inference from parts to wholes. In particular, the Principle of explanation (PE) equally applies to totalities (of any size).

To draw out this point, consider the following story. You wake up in an alternative world. In this world, you encounter a forest on a flat planet that extends out infinitely. You then overhear some people talking about the origin of the forest. Their conversation proceeds like so:

Philo   Where did this forest come from?

Nihilo   Don't you know? Every tree in the forest came from another tree. This forest is infinite.

Philo   I've heard that, Nihilo. But I'm still perplexed. Why have any trees ever come from any other trees? Why are there any trees here at all? And why *these* trees?

Nihilo   Explaining each tree suffices to explain all the trees. What is there left to explain?

Philo   There's *something* left unexplained. I see this giant forest. It's huge and impressive. But why is it here? Why not instead an infinite series of *vines*, or *turtles*, or just *nothing at all*? If you explain a bunch of things by citing the activities of those *same* things, then the explanation is circular. A circular explanation is as good as no explanation.

Nihilo   Well, the reason no vines are here is that these trees here take up too much space.[17]

Suddenly, out of nowhere, a new *infinite* forest appears in the sky.[18] Philo and Nihilo run and hide. The End.

This story illustrates a difference between explaining *individuals* (e.g., individual trees) and explaining *groups* (the forest). Even if each individual tree is somehow explained in terms of another tree, all these individual explanations leave something unexplained. We can still wonder why there is the infinite forest at all, or why it exists where it does.

PE invites us to search for an explanation that goes beyond the very fact to be explained. So, if there is a forest, PE invites an explanation that goes beyond the elements of that same forest. In general, an external explanation of x (whether one or many) is in terms of something beyond x itself.

Note also that the Argument from Possible Explanations depends merely on the *possibility* of an external explanation. So even if some infinite forest in the sky *could* somehow grow up without any external explanation, it wouldn't thereby follow that contingent things *couldn't* have an external explanation.

Objection 3: virtual particles

Physicists tell us that "virtual" particles can randomly appear without any explanation. If virtual particles appear uncaused, perhaps the entire cosmos came into existence uncaused, without any explanation.

Reply

The first thing to note is that virtual particles don't literally come from *nothing*. Virtual particles come from prior states of energy. Next, states of energy can provide a *non-deterministic* (non-necessitating) explanation. For example, if state alpha spontaneously transitions to state beta, and if state alpha had a 15% chance of doing so, then this 15% chance provides some (even if slight) explanation of the transition. For the purposes of our arguments, even a slight explanation counts as *some* explanation. (Note: the explanation need not be contrastive, e.g., an explanation of state alpha *rather than* state beta.)

Objection 4: bootstrapping

How does a necessary thing produce contingent things? It seems the very production of contingent things would itself be contingent (because the effects are contingent) yet uncaused (because it is the first production). If something can be contingent and uncaused, why couldn't the universe simply be contingent and uncaused?

Reply

This objection helps us separate different versions of the Argument from Contingency. Some versions rely on the stronger principle that whatever is contingent (whether a thing or an act) must have a prior cause. The arguments in this chapter, by contrast, don't rely on anything that strong. Instead, I say *explain as much as you can*. We can explain carrots and castles, for example, in terms of prior activities; thus, we can expect an explanation of carrots and castles. Same for contingent things: we can explain them in terms of prior activities. Moreover, the activities themselves could also have an explanation in terms of a necessary *tendency* within the necessary thing to non-deterministically produce something. Here is the main point: if we explain things as far as we can, that's enough to expose a reason to think contingent things have an explanation in terms of a necessary thing.

Objection 5: the possibility of nothing

The philosopher David Hume (1779, 58–59) observes that any existing thing is *conceivably* non-existent. For example, I can conceive of a world with no chairs, no trees, and no universe. Therefore, each thing has the real possibility of not existing. A necessary foundation, however, is supposed to have *no* possibility of not existing (cf. Swinburne 2012).[19]

Reply

Hume's thought does not actually touch our particular arguments. To see why, suppose Hume is right that whatever can be conceived of as existing can be conceived of as not existing. And suppose that a necessary concrete thing N can be *conceived of* in the relevant sense. Then either conceivability implies (or gives evidence for) possibility, or it does not. If conceivability does not provide evidence for possibility, then Hume's objection fails at the start: for then we cannot use conceivability to infer that N's non-existence is possible. So, suppose instead that conceivability provides evidence for possibility. Then conceivability provides evidence for *both* the possibility of N and the possibility of no N (since both are conceivable if either is). Yet, these can't both be possible, for we saw that N is either possible or impossible. So, the evidence from conceivability washes out. Either way, then, the objection fails.[20]

Objection 6: brute fact

Everyone is committed to brute, unexplained facts. Whether you locate bruteness in God or in the universe, *something* must be ultimate. So why couldn't the universe be the brute, ultimate reality?

Reply

This objection invites us to consider the next stage of the Argument from Contingency. The Argument from Contingency has two stages. We have only seen the first stage, which is an argument for the *existence* of a necessary foundation. The second stage seeks to identify the *nature* of the foundation. We will turn to the second stage next.

6. Can we say more?

What else might we say about a necessary foundation? I will seek to show that if there is a necessarily existent portion of reality that could be a foundation for contingent things, this necessary portion has the following attributes: (i) independent existence, (ii) eternal existence, (iii) non-limited nature, (iv) unsurpassable power, and (iv) a supreme nature.

To begin, let *n* refer to the totality of whatever exists necessarily (including any mathematical objects and other *abstracta*, if there are any). I shall now give a series of arguments to shed light on some attributes of *n*. I will construct all my arguments using conceptual analysis and the Principle of Explanation (PE).

6.1. Independent existence

By "independent existence", I mean that *n*'s existence doesn't depend on any *prior* reality (whether prior in time or in existence).

Here is an argument for *n*'s independent existence:

(1) *n* is the totality of whatever is necessary (by definition).
(2) No necessary reality is prior to the totality of *all* necessary reality.
(3) No contingent reality is prior to the totality of all necessary reality.
(4) Everything is either necessary or contingent.
(5) Therefore, no reality is prior to *n*.
(6) Therefore, *n*'s existence doesn't depend upon any prior reality.

6.2. Eternal

n is eternal in at least this sense: *n* never comes to exist or ceases to exist. Here is my argument for eternal existence:

(1) Whatever comes to exist or ceases to exist can fail to exist.
(2) *n* cannot fail to exist (since *n* has *necessary existence*).
(3) Therefore, *n* cannot come to exist or cease to exist.
(4) Whatever cannot come to exist or cease to exist is eternal.
(5) Therefore, *n* is eternal.

For the sake of neutrality, I leave open the nature of time; *n* is eternal on any of the major theories of time. Take *eternalism*, which is the position that whatever exists at any time also exists *simpliciter*. If eternalism is true, then *n* is eternal in at least this sense: there is no time at which *n* began or ceased to exist *simpliciter*.[21] Another option is presentism: whatever exists, exists presently. On this option, *n* necessarily exists at whatever time is present (now), since *n* necessarily exists. In any case, *n* cannot come to be or cease to be.

6.3. Non-limited

I begin with a modest proposal: *n* is not a turtle. Perhaps this much is already too obvious. However, seeing *why* it is not a turtle will help us see other things about *n*.

Here is why *n* is not a turtle:

(1) Every turtle is dependent.
(2) *n* is independent.
(3) Therefore, *n* is not a turtle.

Premise (1)—that every turtle is dependent—is justified by a principle of irrelevant differences. The principle is that differences between turtles (size, shape, eating capacity, etc.) are *irrelevant* to account for a difference with respect to being dependent on prior conditions. Therefore, if any turtle depends on a prior condition, every turtle alike is dependent.

Someone might reply that perhaps there is simply no relevant difference between the explained and the unexplained. Perhaps something could be *inexplicably* unexplained.

However, PE is itself a reason to expect an explanation. PE invites us to explain things as far as we can. If we do, then we will explain all turtles, if we can; or we will explain why some turtle is relevantly different from all others.

Next, we have premise (2): *n* is independent. We already saw justification for (2). To review, the independence of *n* follows from the meaning of terms: *n* refers to the totality of necessary reality. There is nothing prior to all necessary reality. Therefore, there is nothing prior to *n* upon which *n* may depend. In that sense, *n* is the ultimate anchor for dependent things.

The reasoning above has additional applications. For example, it applies to *cubes*. In the absence of a reason to think there is a special, uncaused, necessary cube, the presumption is to treat all cubes alike: contingent and dependent. Hence, we have reason to expect that *n* is not a cube.

In general, for any type *t*, in the absence of a reason to think there is a special, uncaused, necessary instance of *t*, the presumption is to treat all instances of *t* alike: contingent and dependent. PE amplifies this reasoning. By the light of PE, we should explain things as far as we can. So, if we can explain an instance of *t*, we have good reason to do so.

We can use this general reasoning to form an argument against positing arbitrary *limits*, such as in size, shape, powers, or in any other attribute that comes in various degrees. Let us say a thing is *limited* (to some extent) if it has some basic attribute (i.e., an attribute not grounded in other attributes) to some non-maximal degree, like a flower with a finite size. Then we have the following argument *against n* being limited in its basic nature:

(1) Whatever is limited (like turtles, giraffes, cubes, etc.) can have an external explanation.
(2) *n* cannot have an external explanation.
(3) Therefore, *n* is not limited (in its basic nature).

The most common response to this argument I have received is a question about whether *n*'s basic limits might be *necessary*. The thought here is that if *n*'s limits hold necessarily, then perhaps they couldn't have any further explanation.

This proposal, however, requires motivation. To my mind, positing unexplained limits is like supposing some event is an exception to the natural order (a miracle). Theoretically, one could have some reason to posit such an exception. Still, anyone who lacks such a reason is in position to expect a further explanation.

Recall the "why" principle: explain as much as you can. We can explain limited things. For example, the hypothesis that an unlimited foundation created limited, contingent things would explain the existence of limited things. I leave it to readers to consider whether there may be sufficient reason to make a special exception in this case. Here, my main point is to draw out the implication of explaining things as far as you can—by the light of PE; if you explain things as far as you can, then you will explain limits as far as you can.

6.4. Unsurpassable power

We may build on the previous results to expose another attribute: n has unsurpassable power, where a *power*, let's say, is a potential to produce an effect. Here's my argument:

(1) n has some power (at least to be a possible cause of contingent things).
(2) If n's power were surpassable, then n would be limited (e.g., would have a basic limit in power).
(3) n is not limited (see 6.3).
(4) Therefore, n's power is unsurpassable (from 2 and 3).

I leave it to the reader to consider the potential implications of unsurpassable power (e.g., whether unsurpassable power would include cognitive powers, powers of moral reflection, etc.).

6.5. Supreme

Finally, here is a reason to think n is *supreme*.

(1) Whatever is not supreme is limited (in some basic respect).
(2) Whatever is limited could conceivably have some external explanation.
(3) n cannot conceivably have an external explanation.
(4) Therefore, n is supreme.

By "supreme", I mean the quality of being maximal with respect to positive properties. A positive property is a property that contributes to the *intrinsic value* of a thing. Examples of positive properties include *knowledge, power,* and *goodness*. A supreme foundation, then, is something that, in total, has no limit with respect to whatever positive properties it has.

There are various questions to consider at this point. Is the concept of "positive" purely subjective, or could there be an objective notion of positive property? Are there counterbalancing reasons to think that the foundation cannot be supreme? What positive properties could the foundation have? I deal with these questions in some detail in Rasmussen 2019.[22] Here I set them aside for further inquiry.

Instead, I will close this chapter by showing how the hypothesis that the foundation is supreme enables a maximally *deep* (or complete) explanation of things. The Foundation Theory provides the beginning of an explanation of at least contingent things. We can still wonder about the nature of the foundation. If the foundation has necessary existence, what sort of thing could have necessary existence? Not a turtle. Not a snake. Then *what*? The deepest answer is going to be in terms of something that we can *see* is relevantly different from dependent, contingent things.

So what is relevantly different from dependent, contingent things? The answer, I propose, is something with a (maximally) supreme nature. A supreme nature is relevantly different from every other nature that can conceivably have a further explanation. Every non-supreme, limited thing could conceivably have an external explanation; for example, a turtle could have an explanation in terms of causal activities or essential tendencies of *n*. Something with a supreme nature, by contrast, *cannot conceivably* have any further explanation. Supremacy itself entails ultimacy. In other words, *if n* is supreme, we can see *why n* must be ultimate, foundational, and independent. We can also see *why n* would have supremely robust existence (necessary existence).[23]

Note that this proposal also gives us a simple, non-arbitrary account of *n*'s basic nature. If the foundation is not supreme, by contrast, then we multiply complexity: a theory of a non-supreme nature will include additional complexity about the details of its particular limits.

I conclude this section with an argument that succinctly summarizes both stages of the argument from contingency:

(1) Without a supreme foundation, the chain of explanations stops inexplicably short.
(2) The chain of explanations doesn't stop inexplicably short (PE).
(3) Therefore, there is a supreme foundation.

7. Results

I note three significant results of our inquiry. First, we saw that reality, in total, has no external explanation (since nothing is outside everything). Second, we saw how a *foundation* of reality (within reality) could provide an ultimate explanation of everything else. Third, we saw how a foundation could provide the *most ultimate* explanation if it has a supreme nature, since anything less than supreme could conceivably have a further explanation.

These results add up to a single, significant result. If you explain things as far as you can, you will arrive at the most supreme explanation possible.[24]

Notes

1. There are different ways to interpret the question; see Andrew Brenner, "What Do We Mean When We Ask, 'Why is There Something Rather Than Nothing?'" *Erkenntnis* 81, no. 6 (2016): 1305–1322. For a survey of contemporary articulations and analyses, see Tyron Goldschmidt (ed.), *The Puzzle of Existence* (New York: Routledge, 2013). Cf. my review in Joshua Rasmussen, "Tyron Goldschmidt: the Puzzle of Existence," *European Journal for Philosophy of Religion* 9 (2) (2017): 235–240.
2. Pruss defends a version of this stronger principle in Alexander Pruss, *The Principle of Sufficient Reason* (New York: Cambridge University Press, 2006).
3. For more on the relationship between true propositions, facts, and the word, see McGrath and Frank, "Propositions," *Stanford Encyclopedia of Philosophy*, (2018): https://plato.stanford.edu/entries/propositions/.
4. For a defense of the general principle that every (contingent) fact has an explanation, see Pruss, *The Principle of Sufficient Reason*, or Michael Della Rocca, "PSR," *Philosophers' Imprint* 10 (2010): 1–13.
5. Joe Schmid suggested to me the possibility that certain necessary truth may be explicable in terms of a necessary truth *in combination with contingent truths*.
6. We may set aside van Inwagen's proposal in Peter van Inwagen, "Why Is There Anything at All?," *Proceedings of the Aristotelian Society* 70 (1996): 95–110, that things exist because an empty world is improbable, for probability doesn't externally explain *the* actual contingent things there are. Cf. Stephen Maitzen, "Questioning the Question," in *The Puzzle of Existence: Why Is There Something Rather Than Nothing?* ed. Tyron Goldschmidt (New York: Routledge, 2013): 252–271.
7. For a discussion of the motivation for plural reference, see George Boolos, "To Be Is To Be a Value of a Variable (or to Be Some Values of Some Variables)," *Journal of Philosophy* 81, (1984): 430–449.
8. Those who think past times do not exist (e.g., *presentists*) may translate what I say in terms of truths about what *did* exist. Compare: an external explanation of all humans, including the humans that *did* exist, is not entirely in terms of humans.
9. For other examples of arguments from possibility, see Joshua Rasmussen, "'From States of Affairs to a Necessary Being," *Philosophical Studies* 148, (2010): 183–200; Joshua Rasmussen, "A New Argument for a Necessary Being," *Australasian Journal of Philosophy* 89, (2011): 351–356; Alexander Pruss and Joshua Rasmussen, *Necessary Existence* (Oxford: Oxford University Press, 2018); Joshua Rasmussen and Christopher Weaver, "Why Is There Anything at All?," in *Two Dozen (or so) Arguments for God*, ed. Jerry Walls and Trent Dougherty (New York: Oxford University Press, 2019).
10. We could try running a related argument using the premise that *possibly* (1) is true. Such an argument would show that in any possible world, there is a contingent state that is only explicable in terms of a necessary thing (its activity or inactivity)—and so (3) is true. The remainder of the argument would be the same. I leave it as an exercise for readers to see how such an argument might work.
11. This argument may remind you of the *ontological* argument, which attempts to deduce the existence of a maximally great being from the premise that such a being is at least possible. However, my argument is importantly different. In particular, I do not assume that the conclusion is even possible. Rather, I *argue* for the possibility of a necessary thing based on an independently supported principle of explanation. Note also that my argument leaves open the reverse possibility that the contingent things have no explanation; the result so far is just that there is a necessary thing that *could* cause

contingent things. We will see what more we might say about a necessary foundation in section 6.

12. In Joshua Rasmussen, *How Reason Can Lead to God* (Downers Grove, IL: InterVarsity Press, 2019), I argue that truths of reason are an essential part of the foundation of existence, and that therefore, this foundation spans both metaphysical possibilities and logical possibilities.

13. Define "x is necessary" = "x exists no matter what *symmetric* possibility is actual," where w is *symmetric* means that if w had been actual, our actual world would still have been possible. We then narrow our scope to symmetric possibilities, with the understanding that a "necessary" thing is something that spans all the symmetric possibilities. Then (4) is true by definition. I give a formal deduction of the actual existence of a necessary thing from its possible existence at joshualrasmussen.com/s5.

14. For arguments that infinite causal chains are metaphysically impossible, see Alexander Pruss, *Infinity, Causation, and Paradox* (Oxford: Oxford University Press, 2018); Robert Koons, "A New Kalam Argument: Revenge of the Grim Reaper," *Noûs* 48, no. 2 (2014): 256–267.

15. Thanks to Paulo Jaurez for suggesting this example to me.

16. If someone thinks an infinite chain of contingent causes *precludes* an explanation of contingent reality, then PE gives them a reason to think the chain is finite. But see Kenneth Pearce, "'Foundational Grounding and the Argument from Contingency," in *Oxford Studies in Philosophy of Religion* 8, ed. Jonathan L. Kvanvig (Oxford: Oxford University Press, 2017) for an account of how an infinite chain of contingent causes could be explained in terms of a more fundamental, necessary ground.

17. I owe this suggested ending to Tyron Goldschmidt.

18. We could stipulate that each tree in the sky forest springs out of another tree (in supertask speed). Then every tree in the sky has an explanation, even while the total forest emerges from nowhere.

19. My discussion of this objection is from Felipe Leon and Joshua Rasmussen, *Is God the Best Explanation of Things?* (Cham: Palgrave Manmillan, 2019).

20. I address contemporary versions of the conceivability objection in Joshua Rasmussen, "Could God Fail to Exist?", *European Journal of Philosophy* 8 (2016): 159–177.

21. Technically, on eternalism, everything counts as "eternal" in this minimal sense. I leave it to the reader to consider what more might be said about n's relationship to time. In particular, one could argue that whatever exists only *sometimes* is arbitrarily limited in temporal duration, whereas by the argument in 6.3, n is not arbitrarily limited in any of its basic features.

22. With respect to the last question, I argue (in Joshua Rasmussen, *How Reason Can Lead to God*, 136–151) that a supreme nature would include the positive properties of knowledge, power, and goodness, since any nature that lacks these properties would include an arbitrary, unexplained *limit* in intrinsic value.

23. For more on how n's great nature could explain n's necessary existence, see T. Ryan Byerly, "From a Necessary Being to a Perfect Being," *Analysis* 9 (2018): 10–17.

24. Special thanks to Zach Blaesi, Cameron Bertuzzi, Bryan Crothers, Amedeo Da Pra Galanti, Hugh Jidiette, Tyron Goldschmidt, Omar Fakhrl, Paulo Jaurez, Alex Malpass, Joe Schmid, Joel Turnbull, Shane Wagoner, and Joe Weinstein for comments on an earlier draft.

Bibliography

Brenner, Andrew, "What Do We Mean When We Ask 'Why is There Something Rather Than Nothing?'," *Erkenntnis* 81, no. 6 (2016): 1305–1322.

Boolos, George, "To Be Is To Be a Value of a Variable (or to Be Some Values of Some Variables)," *Journal of Philosophy* 81 (1984): 430–449.

Byerly, T. Ryan. "From a Necessary Being to a Perfect Being," *Analysis* 9 (2018): 10–17.

Della Rocca, Michael, "PSR," *Philosophers' Imprint* 10 (2010): 1–13.

Goldschmidt, Tyron (ed.), *The Puzzle of Existence,* New York: Routledge, 2013.

Hume, David, *Dialogues Concerning Natural Religion,* Cambridge: Cambridge University Press, 1779.

Koons, Robert, "A New Kalam Argument: Revenge of the Grim Reaper," *Noûs* 48, no. 2 (2014): 256–267.

Leon, Felipe, and Joshua Rasmussen, *Is God the Best Explanation of Things?* Cham: Palgrave Macmillan, 2019.

McGrath, Matthew, and Devin Frank, "Propositions," *Stanford Encyclopedia of Philosophy* (2018): https://plato.stanford.edu/entries/propositions/.

Maitzen, Stephen, "Questioning the Question," in *The Puzzle of Existence: Why Is There Something Rather Than Nothing?* edited by Tyron Goldschmidt, 252–271. New York: Routledge, 2013

Pearce, Kenneth, "Foundational Grounding and the Argument from Contingency," in *Oxford Studies in Philosophy of Religion* 8, edited by Jonathan L. Kvanvig, Oxford: Oxford University Press, 2017.

Pruss, Alexander, *The Principle of Sufficient Reason,* New York: Cambridge University Press, 2006.

Pruss, Alexander, *Infinity, Causation, and Paradox,* Oxford: Oxford University Press, 2018.

Pruss, Alexander, and Joshua Rasmussen, *Necessary Existence,* Oxford: Oxford University Press, 2018.

Rasmussen, Joshua, "From States of Affairs to a Necessary Being," *Philosophical Studies* 148, (2010): 183–200.

Rasmussen, Joshua, "A New Argument for a Necessary Being," *Australasian Journal of Philosophy* 89 (2011): 351–356.

Rasmussen, Joshua, "Could God Fail to Exist?" *European Journal of Philosophy* 8 (2016): 159–177.

Rasmussen, Joshua, "Tyron Goldschmidt: The Puzzle of Existence," *European Journal for Philosophy of Religion* 9, no. 2 (2017): 235–240.

Rasmussen, Joshua, *How Reason Can Lead to God.* Downers Grove, IL: InterVarsity Press, 2019.

Rasmussen, Joshua, and Christopher Weaver, "Why Is There Anything at All?" In *Two Dozen (or so) Arguments for God,* edited by Jerry Walls and Trent Dougherty, New York: Oxford University Press, 2019.

Swinburne, Richard, "What Kind of Necessary Being Could God Be?" *European Journal of Philosophy of Religion* 4 (2012): 1–18.

van Inwagen, Peter, "Why Is There Anything at All?" *Proceedings of the Aristotelian Society* 70, (1996): 95–110.

2

The Kalam Cosmological Argument

Andrew Ter Ern Loke

1. Introduction

The Kalam Cosmological Argument (KCA) is an *a posteriori* argument which starts from the observation of the cosmos and deduces that it has a Creator. In distinction from the Thomist and Leibnizian versions of the Cosmological Argument, the KCA argues for the *beginning of existence*[1] of the cosmos which involves considerations of both contemporary scientific cosmology and philosophical arguments.[2] The KCA as formulated by its noteworthy recent proponent William Lane Craig is as follows:

(1) Everything that begins to exist has a cause.
(2) The universe began to exist.
(3) Therefore, the universe has a cause.

Craig argues that further analyses of the Cause of the Universe show that this Cause possesses various theistic properties, such as being the uncaused First Cause, beginningless, initially timeless, enormously powerful and possessing libertarian freedom.[3] To make the deduction of the properties of the First Cause explicit, I shall reformulate the KCA as follows:

(1) There exists a series of causes-and-effects and changes (= events), and the number of earlier entities is either actually infinite or finite.
(2) If the number of earlier entities is finite, then either earlier and later entities are joined together like a loop such that there is no first member in the series, or the series has a first member i.e. a First Cause and a first change (= first event).
(3) It is not the case that the number of earlier entities is actually infinite.
(4) It is not the case that earlier and later entities are joined together like a loop.
(5) Therefore, there exists a First Cause and a first change (= first event).
(6) Since the First Cause is the first, it must be uncaused.
(7) Since everything that begins to exist has a cause (Causal Principle), the First Cause must be beginningless.

(8) Since the first change (= first event) did not begin to exist uncaused (because of the Causal Principle), the first change (= first event) must have been caused by a First Cause which was initially changeless.
(9) In order to cause the first event from an initial changeless state, the First Cause must have:
  (9.1) The capacity to be the originator of the first event in a way that is undetermined by any prior event, since the First Cause is the first, and:
  (9.2) The capacity to prevent itself from changing, for otherwise the First Cause would not have been initially changeless.
  (9.1). and (9.2.) imply that the First Cause has libertarian freedom.
(10) In order to bring about the entire universe, the First Cause must be enormously powerful.
(11) A First Cause that is uncaused, beginningless, initially changeless, has libertarian freedom, and enormously powerful is a Creator of the Universe.
(12) Therefore, a Creator of the universe exists.

The crucial steps involve ruling out an actual infinite regress (premise 3) and ruling out a loop (premise 4), and establishing the Causal Principle (premise 7) and the libertarian freedom of the First Cause (premise 9). Due to limitation of space, I can only briefly explain the supporting arguments for these steps in what follows; readers are encouraged to check out the sources I cite for further details.

2. Ruling out an actual infinite

2.1. Introduction

It is evident that there exists a series of causes-and-effects and events (such as the event of my beginning of existence in 1975 and the event of the beginning of our universe at the Big Bang 13.8 billion years ago). For example, I came from my parents, my parents came from my grandparents, my grandparents came from my great-grandparents, etc. The question is whether such a series has an actual infinite regress.

In support of the conclusion that the universe has a beginning, Craig utilizes the so-called Standard Big Bang Model, according to which time itself and all physical entities came into existence with the beginning of our universe at the Big Bang 13.8 billion years ago. It has been objected that our universe is not necessarily the totality of all physical things, but a "space-time manifold" that possess some well-defined geometrical properties, and that over the years a number of cosmological scenarios have been proposed in which time and physical entities exist prior to the Big Bang.[4] Nevertheless, there is no adequate evidence for thinking that any of the cosmological models which postulates an infinite number of earlier events is the correct model. On the contrary, such models face various technical difficulties related to the Second Law of Thermodynamics, acausal fine-tuning, or having an unstable or a metastable state with a finite lifetime.[5]

Moreover, there are at least four arguments which demonstrate that an actual infinite regress of causes and events is not the case:

1. The argument from the impossibility of concrete actual infinities.
2. The argument from the impossibility of traversing an actual infinite.
3. The argument from the viciousness of dependence regress.
4. The argument from paradoxes.

Any one of these arguments would be sufficient. Therefore, it is not enough for the objector of finite regress to rebut one of these arguments (e.g. it is not enough to rebut the argument against concrete actual infinities); rather, the objector would need to rebut all four of them (and perhaps others). I shall now briefly explain these arguments.

2.2. Concrete actual infinities cannot exist

The explanation of the first two arguments require a brief explication of the key term "infinite," in particular the distinction between an "actual infinite" and a "potential infinite" (both of which are different from "divine infinite").[6]

An actual infinite is larger than any finite number. Craig utilizes the understanding of an actual infinite set as any set that has a proper subset that is equivalent to it. A proper subset is a subset where "at least one member of the original set is not also a member of the subset." Two sets are said to be equivalent if the members of one set can be related to the members of the other set in a one-to-one correspondence, that is, so related that a single member of the one set corresponds to a single member of the other set and vice versa. Equivalent sets are regarded as having the same number of members. For example, an original abstract actual infinite set of integers (1, 2, 3, 4, 5, 6 ...) has a proper subset of even numbers (2, 4, 6 ...) which has an equivalent number of members as the original actual infinite set.[7] The number of all whole numbers (... −2, −1, 0, 1, 2 ...) is a countable infinite known as aleph-zero.

An actual infinite is conceived as a determinate whole with an infinite number of members, in contrast with a potential infinite which never attains infinity, although it increases perpetually towards infinity as a limit. At any point in time, a potential infinite is finite.[8] Such a collection would be one in which the membership is not definite in number but may be increased without limit.[9] In contrast with aleph-zero, which is a number, ∞ is used for infinity understood as a limit.

When we ask for the causes of the stars we observe, as well as the causes of the causes of their existence, we are asking for causes which actually existed; we are not asking for causes which potentially existed. Likewise, the events that led to the formation of our sun, for example, have already happened, that is, they have already been actualised, and their number is no longer increasing perpetually but a determinate whole. Hence, when we ask whether there is an infinite regress of causes, events, changes or intervals of time, we are asking whether there is an actual infinite regress, and not whether there is a potential infinite regress. For given that the number of causes, events, changes, or intervals of time prior to any event is a determinate whole, it cannot be a potential infinite.

The number of events later than any event, however, can be a potential infinite if the dynamic (A-) theory of time is true. According to this theory, the members of a series of events come to be one after another, and the number of events which have happened would be increasing perpetually if the future is unending (although the number of events which have happened prior to any actual event(s), say the formation of our sun, would not be increasing perpetually but is a determinate whole, as noted above). By contrast, according to a static (B-) theory of time, the members of a series of events do not come to be one after another; rather the series of events is a tenselessly existing manifold all of whose members are equally real. On a static theory of time, the number of later events cannot be a potential infinite; it would be either finite or actually infinite.

In short, the number of events later than any event can be a potential infinite depending on what theory of time is true and whether the future is unending, but the number of events earlier than any event cannot be a potential infinite.[10] The key issue to be addressed is whether the number of earlier events is an actual infinite or finite.

According to the great mathematician David Hilbert, "The infinite is nowhere to be found in reality. It neither exists in nature nor provides a legitimate basis for rational thought . . . The role that remains for the infinite to play is solely that of an idea"[11] (note that by "infinite" Hilbert is referring to an "actual infinite"). Craig has developed and defended Hilbert's arguments, such as the famous Hilbert Hotel thought experiment. Craig explains:

> Let us imagine a hotel with an infinite number of rooms and suppose once more that all the rooms are occupied. There is not a single vacant room throughout the entire infinite hotel. Now suppose a new guest shows up, asking for a room. "But of course!" says the proprietor, and he immediately shifts the person in room #1 into room #2, the person in room #2 into room #3, the person in room #3 into room #4, and so on out to infinity. As a result of these room changes, room #1 now becomes vacant, and the new guest gratefully checks in. But remember, before he arrived, all the rooms were occupied![12]

Craig argues that the absurdities which result from paradoxes such as Hilbert's Hotel indicate that concrete actual infinities cannot exist, and since an infinite temporal regress of events is a concrete actual infinity, it follows that an infinite temporal regress of events cannot exist.[13] While critics have objected that actual infinities are mathematically possible,[14] it should be noted that what is mathematically possible is not always metaphysically possible in the concrete world. For example, the quadratic equation $x^2 - 4 = 0$ can have two mathematically consistent results for "x": 2 or −2, but if the question is "How many people carried the computer home?", the answer cannot be "−2", for in the concrete world it is metaphysically impossible that "−2 people" carried a computer home. Thus the conclusion of "2 people" rather than "−2 people" is not derived from mathematical equations alone, but also from metaphysical considerations: "−2 people" have no causal powers to carry a computer home. One can then proceed to argue that concrete actual infinities such as an actual infinite temporal regress of events violate metaphysically necessary truths concerning causal powers, and explain that none of the purported counter-examples taken from the fields of philosophy, physics, geometry and mathematics is a concrete actual infinite (e.g. they may be abstract actual infinities or potential infinities).[15] Proponents of the Hilbert-Hotel argument can clarify that their argument is directed only against concrete actual infinities and not abstract actual infinities. Concrete entities have causal powers and can be part of a chain of causes and effects, while abstract entities do not have causal powers and therefore cannot account for the origin of things such as our universe.

2.3. It is impossible to traverse an actual infinite

Think about a series of events (whether microscopic or macroscopic). Suppose $event_1$ begins at time t_1, $event_1$ causes $event_2$ at t_2, $event_2$ causes $event_3$ at t_3, and so on. The number of events can increase with time, but there can never be an actual infinite number of events at any time, for no matter how many events there are at any time, there can still be more: If there are 1000 events at t_{1000}, there can still be more (say, 1001 events at t_{1001}); If there are 100,000 events at $t_{100,000}$, there can still be more (100,001 events at $t_{100,001}$), etc. This illustrates that an actual infinite has greater number than the number which can be traversed one-after-another in time.

Since it is impossible to traverse an actual infinite number of events *from* $event_1$, it is likewise impossible to traverse an actual infinite number of earlier events *to* $event_1$, given that the number of events required to be traversed in both cases is the same. Thus the number of events earlier than $event_1$ (and likewise, the number of earlier causes and durations) cannot be an actual infinite. Therefore there must be a first event and a First Cause.

Some objectors have claimed that Zeno's paradoxes of motion indicate that actual infinite sequences are "traversed" all the time. For example, it has been claimed that whenever an object moves from one location to another (e.g. Achilles running across the stadium) it must pass through an infinite number of halfway points.

Craig replies by noting that the argument for the impossibility of traversing an actual infinite has two crucial disanalogies with Zeno's paradoxes of motion. First, in the case of the argument, the events would have to sum up to an actual infinite magnitude in order to avoid a beginning. By contrast, in the case of Zeno's paradoxes, the points that Achilles passes through sum to a distance that is of merely finite magnitude—it has a beginning and an end. Therefore such a scenario does not avoid a beginning. Second, in the case of the argument, the events in a temporal series are actual. By contrast, in the case of Zeno's paradoxes, the interval traversed can be regarded as being potentially infinitely divisible and not actually infinitely divided. In other words, one can keep on dividing the interval by half without ever ending up with an actual infinite number of divisions. The claim that Achilles must pass through an infinite number of halfway points in order to cross the stadium begs the question by assuming that the whole interval is a composition of an infinite number of points.[16]

Sorabji objects that the potentially infinite divisibility of a line entails that there is an actually infinite number of positions at which the line could be divided.[17] Craig and Sinclair reply that Sorabji's argument is guilty of a modal operator shift, inferring from the true claim:

(1) Possibly, there is some point at which x is divided;

to the disputed claim:

(2) There is some point at which x is possibly divided.[18]

Craig and Sinclair observe that it is coherent to maintain that a physical distance is potentially infinitely divisible without holding that there is an actual infinite number of positions where it could be divided.[19] While one might argue that it is possible to have an abstract point in between any two points, it is logically invalid to infer from this to the conclusion that it is possible that an actual infinite number of points can exist together concretely and be traversed. It would be like arguing "because a leaf could be any colour, therefore it can be every colour at the same time." A leaf obviously cannot be of every colour at the same time because of metaphysical constraints. Likewise, the argument from the impossibility of traversing an actual infinite (and also the argument from the impossibility of concrete actual infinities as well as the Grim Reaper paradox, see below) indicates that there are metaphysical constraints which make it impossible for all the points to exist together concretely, even if each point can exist concretely.

Bertrand Russell objects to the argument against an infinite regress by appealing to a negative number series as a counterexample, claiming that there could be an actual infinite series of negative integers ending with minus one and having no first term.[20]

In reply, a negative number series is disanalogous to an actual infinite temporal/causal regress in a crucial way. A negative number series is a case an of abstract actual infinite which exists timelessly rather than as a one-after-another temporal process. Thus, it does not provide a counterexample to the claim that an actual infinite cannot be arrived at via a one-after-another temporal process in the concrete world. While each member of the abstract negative number series . . ., $-n$, . . ., $-3, -2, -1$ is obtained from the preceding member by the addition of a unit, this obtaining is in the form of timeless mathematical relation. It is not the case that the abstract number -2 (say) is brought into existence in time by the addition of a unit to -3. Rather the abstract numbers -2 and -3 have always existed timelessly, and this is unlike a causal series of concrete entities existing in time. One can have an abstract actual infinite number of negative numbers each of which is timelessly separated from zero by a finite number of negative numbers. The existence of each of the numbers in the series is not causally dependent on any previous number, nor is it dependent on the actual infinite number which exists outside of the series. However, to arrive by a one-after-another causal process is a different matter. In contrast with timeless numbers, a temporal series of causes-and-effects are arrived at in time, and each effect in time is causally dependent on a prior cause. The process proceeds one after another, arriving at a finite number at any time. In order to arrive at an actual infinite number of generations one needs to first proceed one generation after another, and the problem is that the result of that process is always finite at any time. One does not arrive at an actual infinite at any time, not at t_{1000}, t_{100000}, etc. Time $t_{infinite}$ cannot be in the series. Actual infinite stands outside the series, timelessly and abstractly. But here we are talking about what happens in a temporal series of events in the concrete world, not timelessly and abstractly. In the concrete world there is never an actual infinite number of generations at any time.

Morriston objects that:

From the fact that we cannot—beginning now—complete the task of enumerating all the events in a beginningless series, it does not follow that the present event cannot arrive or that a beginningless series of events that have already arrived is impossible. To suppose otherwise would be to confuse the items to be enumerated with the enumerating of them—it would be like arguing that there must be finitely many natural numbers because we can't finish counting them.[21]

In reply, arriving at the present from a beginningless past would require the number of events completed to be actual infinite, but an actual infinite is too large to be completed. The problem is not due to our ability to enumerate; rather, it is due to the nature of an actual infinite which is too large to be completed via a one-after-another process. While there can be an infinite number of natural numbers in the abstract, to complete an actual infinite in the concrete is a separate issue and the real issue here. Morriston's objection is thus irrelevant, for it does not reply to the real issue.

Some have objected that the argument begs the question by assuming a beginning. They think that the principle "an actual infinite has greater number than the number which can be traversed one-after-another in time" is only valid for a series with a beginning. However, if the series is beginningless, then it would be the case that one arrives at an actual infinite number of generations of causes-and-effects by the present moment.

In reply, without begging the question by presupposing whether the number of earlier events is infinite or not, think of a series of events in the midst of being constituted. There is one event produced at t_p, there are two events produced at t_p and t_q, there are three events produced at t_p, t_q, and t_r, etc. The number of events is constituted by each event. The whole series is constituted by the parts, in particular by a finite number ("one") following another finite number ("another"), and together they constitute a finite number. This conclusion is based on the nature of the sequential process (Finite + Finite = Finite), and how any concrete series (e.g. of durations) is constituted. The argument is not based on presupposing "a particular time as a starting point" or that the past is not an actual infinite, thus it does not beg the question.

Moreover, the objector is claiming that there is a distinction between arriving at later durations from a particular time (a beginning) and arriving at that particular time from earlier durations, and while it is impossible to arrive at an actual infinite in the former case, it is possible in the latter case. However, whether an actual infinite has greater number than the number of durations and generations of causes-and-effects which can be arrived at via a one-after-another process should be independent of whether it is from a particular time to later durations, or from earlier durations to a particular time. The reason is because the number of elements required to be arrived at via a one-after-another process in both cases is the same. Thus, the objection fails.[22]

2.4. The argument from the viciousness of dependence regress

A dependence regress (i.e., a regress in which each item depends on the prior one) is a vicious regress, and causation is a kind of dependence. Hence infinite causal regresses are vicious.[23] While arguments based on dependence have often been used to demonstrate the impossibility of an infinite regress in the case of an essentially ordered series in the

Thomistic Cosmological Argument, they can be used to demonstrate the impossibility of an infinite regress for an accidentally ordered temporal series of events as well.[24] Think about a series of train wagons in which each train wagon requires a preceding one to pull it if it is to begin to move. Before the last train wagon begins to move, the one before it has to begin to move, and before that train wagon begins to move, the one before it has to begin to move, etc. No matter how many such train wagons there are, none of them would begin to move, because no prior wagon escapes from the problem of having 0 capacity to begin movement. What is required is an engine, a First Puller which does not depend on another train car to pull it, and which has the independent capacity to bring about the beginning of movement. Likewise, suppose that the Causal Principle is true (see Section 4 below), and suppose x has a beginning of existence and x causes the beginning of existence of y. Then x can causally explain the beginning of y only after x begins to exist, but the problem is that x cannot explain why x itself begins to exist. Thus x cannot explain why there are entities (x, y) which begin to exist. If there is something w which begins to exist prior to x, then w can explain why (x, y) begin to exist, but the problem is that w also cannot explain why itself begins to exist. Thus w cannot explain why there are entities (w, x, y) which begin to exist, and relies on there being a prior entity v which also cannot explain why there are entities which begin to exist if v itself begins to exist. Indeed, if every prior entity has a beginning, then no prior entity escapes from the problem of having 0 capacity to explain why there are entities which begin to exist. What is required is a beginningless First Cause, which does not depend on another entity to bring it into existence because it is without a beginning, and which has the independent capacity to bring about the beginning of the first event.[25]

2.5. The argument from paradoxes

Various types of argument from paradoxes have been formulated in the literature.[26] An example is the Grim Reaper Paradox.[27] Suppose you are alive at midnight and there are infinitely many instants from 12:00 a.m. to 1:00 a.m. Grim Reaper #1 will strike you dead at 1:00 a.m. if you are still alive at that time, Grim Reaper #2 will strike you dead at 12:30 a.m. if you are still alive then, Grim Reaper #3 will strike you dead at 12:15 a.m. if you are still alive then, and so on. This leads to a contradiction: you cannot survive past midnight, and yet you cannot be killed by any Grim Reaper at any time.

The Paradox rules out the claim that it is possible to specify an actual infinity of divisions within a finite region of space or time.[28] Moreover, Pruss and Koons argue that the Paradox can be reformulated to demonstrate the impossibility of an actual infinite number of earlier durations by spreading out the Grim Reapers over infinite time rather than over a single hour, for example, by having each Grim Reaper swing his scythe on January 1 of each past year if you have managed to live that long.

3. Can a First Cause be avoided by a causal loop?

Such a causal loop is contrary to the Second Law of Thermodynamics and faces the following problems.

For a causal loop in dynamic (A-) time, the members of a series of events come to be one after another cycles after cycles. Given that an actual infinite regress is impossible, the number of cycles in the past could not have been actually infinite, and thus there must still be a first event and a First Cause.

A static causal loop—in which A requires B to bring it into existence, B requires C to bring it into existence, and C requires A to bring it into existence—is viciously circular. It would be similar to a scenario in which railway wagon A requires wagon B to bring it into motion (i.e. by pulling it), wagon B requires wagon C to bring it into motion, and wagon C requires wagon A to bring it into motion. It is evident that such a viciously circular setup—in which the state of each of the entities in a causal loop is supposed to be dependent on another entity within the loop—would not work. Likewise, in a loop that is supposed to avoid a first cause, the beginning of our universe is required to provide causally necessary conditions for the beginning of existence of other entities within a closed loop, while the beginning of our universe itself requires the existence of these other entities. Such a vicious circular setup would not work as well.[29]

4. Defending the Causal Principle

The Causal Principle has been rejected in recent years by some philosophers due to considerations from quantum-mechanical indeterminacy.[30] However, others have responded that quantum particles emerge from the quantum vacuum which is not non-being, but something with quantum fields (quantum particles are manifestations of fields) which can be acted on by the relevant laws of nature.[31] The Heisenberg uncertainty principle does not imply that it is possible that energy comes from absolutely nothing; it just means that the pre-existing energy (i.e., the vacuum energy which is already present) can (unpredictably) have a very high value in a very short period of time. Additionally, many different interpretations of quantum physics exist, and some of them, such as Everett's Many World's interpretation and Bohm's pilot-wave model, are perfectly deterministic. A number of scientists have argued that Bohm's theory is superior to Bohr's indeterministic theory.[32]

Likewise, while some scientists have claimed that the universe could have begun to exist from nothing,[33] what they mean by "nothing" is not the absence of anything; rather it is something that can behave according to the equations of quantum physics. Cosmologist George Ellis observes that the efforts by these scientists cannot truly "solve" the issue of creation, "for they rely on some structures or other (e.g. the elaborate framework of quantum field theory and much of the standard model of particle physics) pre-existing the origin of the universe, and hence themselves requiring explanation."[34] Even if it is the case that the negative gravitational energy of our universe exactly cancels the positive energy represented by matter so that the total energy of the universe is zero, as portrayed in some cosmological scenarios,[35] this does not imply that the positive and negative energy arose uncaused from zero energy (to conclude otherwise is to commit the fallacy of thinking that "net zero imply no cause").³⁶ One can still ask what is the efficient cause which made the positive and negative energy to be the way they are.

In summary, no compelling scientific evidence has been offered against the Causal Principle. On the other hand, the following Modus Tollens argument can be offered for the Causal Principle. (Note that this is a deductive argument which is immune to the fallacy of generalization or the fallacy of composition which may (or may not)³⁷ beset an inductive argument for the Causal Principle.)

(1) If something x begins to exist uncaused, then y which begins to exist would also begin to exist uncaused.
(2) It is not the case that y begins to exist uncaused.
(3) Therefore it is not the case that something begins to exist uncaused.

Very briefly, the justification for premise 1 is that, if x begins to exist uncaused, then (1.1) there would not be any causally antecedent condition which would make it the case that only x rather than y begins to exist uncaused, and (1.2) the properties of x and the properties of y which differentiate between them would be had by them only when they had already begun to exist, and (1.3) the circumstance is compatible with the beginning of existence of y.

(1.1), (1.2) and (1.3) jointly imply that there would be no essential difference between x and y where beginning to exist uncaused is concerned. To deny the consequent in premise 1, I only have to show that one event around me does not begin to exist uncaused. For example, I do not experience an event such as y = "a rapid increasing in strength of electric fields around me" beginning to exist without causally antecedent conditions such as (say) having to switch on the electric field generator. Since the consequent in premise (1) is false, the antecedent is false, i.e. it is not the case that something begins to exist uncaused.

One might object by claiming that my argument only shows that, if (say) the universe began to exist uncaused, other entities *could* also begin to exist uncaused, not that they *would*.

In reply, "could" concerns possibility, but I am not referring to possible events here. Rather, I am referring to actual events, and arguing that there would be no difference between them where beginning to exist uncaused is concerned if one of them begins uncaused. For example, consider the scenario in which something (say) the universe began to exist and there was also a rapid increasing in strength of electric fields around me. In this scenario these are not just possible events (i.e. it is not merely the case that the universe *could* begin to exist and electric field *could* increase in strength), but actual events, i.e. the universe did begin to exist and electric field did increase in strength. Since (as explained above) there would be no difference between these events where beginning to exist uncaused is concerned if the universe did begin to exist *uncaused*, the increasing in strength of the electric field around me would also began to exist uncaused (e.g. without being preceded by the switching on of an electric field generator). Which is not the case.³⁸

5. The nature of the First Cause

It has been shown that an actual infinite regress of events (= changes) is impossible, and that a causal loop that attempts to avoid a First Cause is metaphysically impossible as well. Thus, there must be a first change requiring a beginningless First Cause which must therefore have been either in (1) an initially changeless-in-timeless state causally antecedent to the first change; or (2) an initially changeless state with an actual infinite past extension on a substantival view of time,[39] causally and temporally antecedent to the first change (this view is proposed by Alan Padgett;[40] according to this view, God exists before creation in an undifferentiated, non-metric time). In either case, the First Cause would be initially changeless. Someone might suggest an alternative possibility that the first change began to exist without causal antecedent, but this is contradicted by the arguments offered for the Causal Principle above.

In the antithesis of his First Antinomy, Kant argues against the idea that time has a beginning by claiming that, if time has a beginning, there will be an empty time before the first moment of time, and no coming to be of a thing is possible in an empty time.[41] Craig has replied that this problem can be resolved by postulating the existence of an initially timeless First Cause with libertarian freedom, and that such an entity freely brought the first event—and with it, the first moment of time—into existence (and as it does so it also enters into time).[42]

To elaborate, for the First Cause that is initially changeless to change, it must have:

1. The capacity to initiate change, for the change cannot be caused by another entity since the First Cause is the First.
2. The capacity to prevent itself from changing initially (i.e., the capacity to prevent the capacity to initiate change from initiating it initially), for otherwise the First Cause would not have been initially changeless.

Now quantum systems are not changeless entities, rather quantum systems are physical systems that are in constant change. Therefore, quantum systems cannot be the First Cause that is initially changeless.[43]

What is required is an entity that is initially changeless, and which—unlike a quantum state—possesses a certain property that enables the entity to initiate the first change, yet also having the capacity to prevent itself from changing initially. The required property fits the description of libertarian freedom, which postulates a personal agent having the power to initiate change as a first mover (without being causally necessitated by prior events), and also having the ability to refrain from exercising this power.[44]

The possession of libertarian agency therefore explains how an entity that is initially changeless could change and cause entities that exist in time. Craig explains that "Such an account of the origin of the universe will work only for agent causation,[45] for only a libertarian agent could interrupt the static reign of being of the First Cause sans the universe." "Only a personal, free agency can account for why the first effect is not coeternal with the first cause."[46]

6. Who created the Creator?

This popular question can be easily answered as follows: things which begin to exist require a cause. On the other hand, if something is without beginning, then it has always existed and therefore was not brought into existence. Such a thing does not require a cause, because it didn't come from nothing; it has always been there. Such a thing can be uncaused, i.e., nothing created it.

Now it has been explained previously that there cannot be an actual infinite regress of causes. Therefore there must be a First Cause which (as explained above) is uncaused, beginningless, has libertarian freedom and is enormously powerful, i.e. an uncaused Creator of the Universe.

7. Conclusion

The question of ultimate origins is one of the biggest questions humans can ever ask.

Our journey in search of an answer has arrived at a First Cause which is uncaused, beginningless, has libertarian freedom, and is enormously powerful. Such a First Cause has all the essential properties of being a Creator of the universe. One might also add that, in order to freely bring about events which follow the amazing laws of nature, the First Cause must be highly intelligent,[47] thus providing further considerations for thinking that the First Cause is a Creator.

It might be asked whether the conclusion that the Creator exists is based on ignorance. For example, when ancient people did not understand certain natural phenomena (such as thunder), they thought that these were caused by the gods (e.g. Thor). As scientific understanding progresses, such explanations are replaced by scientific ones.

In reply, the conclusion of the KCA is not based on ignorance. Rather, it is based on reasons. The argument is not "because we still do not know how to explain the origin of the universe, therefore there must be a Creator." Rather, the argument is because there are reasons (discussed above) for thinking that an actual infinite causal regress is metaphysically impossible and that the regress could not be terminated by a causal loop, therefore there must be a First Cause. It is because there are reasons for thinking that everything that begins to exist has a cause, therefore this First Cause must be beginningless. The rest of the properties of this First Cause are likewise derived on the basis of reasons rather than ignorance, as shown above. While the progress of science would generate newer understandings of the laws of nature as explanations for the phenomena we observe, it would not replace a First Cause (Creator) as an explanation for the existence of all things, including the laws of nature themselves which must have come from this First Cause. Thus the conclusion of the argument cannot in principle be overturned by future scientific discoveries. Rather future discoveries would only enhance our understanding of the wisdom of the Creator through understanding the laws which He had created.[48] [49]

Notes

1. For the theological significance of this, see Andrew Loke, "Creatio Ex Nihilo," in *T&T Clark Companion to Analytic Theology*, ed. J. T. Turner and James Arcadi (London: T&T Clark, 2020); Andrew Loke, "Theological Critiques of Natural Theology: A Reply to Andrew Moore," *Neue Zeitschrift für Systematische Theologie und Religionsphilosophie* 61 (2019): 207–222.
2. In Andrew Loke, *God and Ultimate Origins: A Novel Cosmological Argument* (Cham, Switzerland: Springer Nature, 2017), Chapter 1, I summarize various arguments against scientistic and radical postmodernist views concerning this issue, demonstrate that philosophical arguments are capable of yielding knowledge about reality that are more epistemically certain than scientific discoveries, and explain that science and philosophy can complement each other in the quest for the answer.
3. William Lane Craig and James Sinclair, "The Kalam Cosmological Argument," in *The Blackwell Companion to Natural Theology*, ed. William Lane Craig and J. P. Moreland (Chichester: Wiley-Blackwell, 2012).
4. Stephen Barr, "Modern Cosmology and Christian Theology," in *The Blackwell Companion to Science and Christianity*, ed. Alan G Padgett and J. B. Stump (Chichester: Wiley-Blackwell, 2012), 179–183.
5. William Lane Craig and James Sinclair, "The Kalam Cosmological Argument," in *The Blackwell Companion to Natural Theology*, ed. William Lane Craig and J. P. Moreland (Chichester: Wiley-Blackwell, 2009), 179–182; Peter Bussey, "God as First Cause—a Review of the Kalam Argument," *Science & Christian Belief* 25 (2013), 17–35; Paul Copan and William Lane Craig (eds.), *The Kalam Cosmological Argument*, vol. 2 (New York: Bloomsbury Academic, 2017).
6. Craig explains that God's infinity can be taken to mean that God is metaphysically necessary, morally perfect, omnipotent, omniscient, eternal, etc., and that none of these need involve an actual infinite number of things (e.g. "omnipotence is not defined in terms of quanta of power possessed by God or number of actions God can perform but in terms of His ability to actualize states of affairs." William Lane Craig, "Q&A #106: Is God Actually Infinite?" 2009, available online: http://www.reasonablefaith.org/is-god-actually-infinite.
7. Craig and Sinclair, *The Kalam Cosmological Argument*, 103–105.
8. Ibid.
9. Ibid.
10. Andrew Loke, "On Beginningless Past, Endless Future, God, and Singing Angels: An Assessment of the Morriston–Craig Dialogue," *Neue Zeitschrift für Systematische Theologie und Religionsphilosophie* 58 (2016): 57–66.
11. David Hilbert, "On the Infinite," in *Philosophy of Mathematics*, ed. P. Benacerraf and H. Putnam (Englewood Cliffs, NJ: Prentice-Hall, 1964), 151.
12. Craig and Sinclair, *The Kalam Cosmological Argument*, 109–110.
13. Ibid.
14. James East, "Infinity Minus Infinity," *Faith and Philosophy* 30 (2013): 429–433.
15. Loke, *God and Ultimate Origins*, chapter 2; Andrew Loke, "Is an Infinite Temporal Regress of Events Possible?" *Think* 11 (2012): 105–122.
16. Craig and Sinclair, *The Kalam Cosmological Argument*, 119.
17. R. Sorabji, *Time, Creation and the Continuum* (Ithaca, NY: Cornell University Press, 1983), 210–213, 322–324.
18. Craig and Sinclair, *The Kalam Cosmological Argument*, 114.

19 Ibid.
20 Bertrand Russell, *History of Western Philosophy* (London: Allen and Unwin, 1969), 453.
21 Wes Morriston, "Doubts about the Kalam Argument," in *Debating Christian Theism*, ed. J. P. Moreland, Chad V. Meister, and Khaldoun A. Sweis (Oxford: Oxford University Press, 2013), 26–27.
22 For replies to other objections see Loke, *God and Ultimate Origins*, 62–75.
23 Alexander Pruss, *Infinity, Causation, and Paradox* (Oxford: Oxford University Press, 2018), 27.
24 Loke, *God and Ultimate Origins*, 99–100.
25 Ibid., 85–108.
26 E.g. Pruss, *Infinity, Causation, and Paradox*; Robert Koons, "A New Kalam Argument: Revenge of the Grim Reaper," *Noûs* 48 (2014): 256–267; Ben Waters, "Methuselah's Diary and the Finitude of the Past," *Philosophia Christi* 15 (2013): 463–469.
27 Pruss, *Infinity, Causation, and Paradox*; Koons, "A New Kalam Argument."
28 Stephen Puryear, "Finitism and the Beginning of the Universe," *Australasian Journal of Philosophy* 92 (2014): 619–629.
29 Loke, *God and Ultimate Origins*, chapter 4.
30 Adolf Grünbaum, "Why is There a Universe AT ALL, Rather Than Just Nothing?" *Ontology Studies* 9 (2009): 15.
31 Bussey, "God as First Cause," 33.
32 Jean Bricmont, *Making Sense of Quantum Mechanics* (Cham: Springer Nature, 2016).
33 Lawrence Krauss, *A Universe from Nothing: Why There is Something Rather than Nothing*, (New York: Free Press, 2012).
34 George Ellis, "Issues in the Philosophy of Cosmology," in *Philosophy of Physics*, ed. J. Butterfield and J. Earman (Amsterdam: Elsevier, 2007), Section 2.7.
35 Victor Stenger, *God: The Failed Hypothesis* (Amherst, NY: Prometheus Books, 2007), 116–117.
36 Consider this analogy: the fact that my company's total expenses cancel the total revenue, such that the net profit is zero, does not imply that the expenses and revenue occurred without an efficient cause. We still need to ask what made the expenses and revenue to be the way they are.
37 Loke, *God and Ultimate Origins*, 134–136.
38 For replies to other objections e.g. Graham Oppy, "Uncaused Beginnings Revisited," *Faith and Philosophy* 32 (2015): 205–210; see Loke, *God and Ultimate*, chapter 5; see also Andrew Loke, "Reply to reviews of God and Ultimate Origins," April 4, 2020 at https://www.academia.edu/36933170/Reply_to_reviews_of_God_and_Ultimate_Origins.
39 "Substantival theories are theories that imply time is substance-like in that it exists independently of the space-time relations exhibited by physical processes. On the other hand, relational theories imply time's existence requires there to be some physical process in the universe—such as a movement or a change in a field. In short, no change implies no time." Bradley Dowden, "Time," *Internet Encyclopaedia of Philosophy* (2013): http://www.iep.utm.edu/time/.
40 Alan Padgett, *God, Eternity, and the Nature of Time* (New York: St. Martin's, 1992).
41 Immanuel Kant, *Critique of Pure Reason*, trans. Norman Kemp-Smith (London: Macmillan, 1965), A466/B494.
42 William Lane Craig, "Kant's First Antinomy and the Beginning of the Universe," *Zeitschrift für Philosophische Forschung* 33 (1979): 553–567; Loke, *God and Ultimate*, chapter 6.

43 For other replies to Stephen Hawking and Leonard Mlodinow, *The Grand Design* (New York: Bantam Books 2010); see Loke, *God and Ultimate Origins*, chapter 6.
44 J. P. Moreland, "The Explanatory Relevance of Libertarian Agency," in *Mere Creation*, ed. William Dembski (Downers Grove, IL: InterVarsity Press, 1998), 266–267.
45 William Lane Craig, "Must the Beginning of the Universe Have a Personal Cause?" *Faith and Philosophy* 19 (2002): 94–105.
46 Craig and Sinclair, *The Kalam Cosmological Argument*, 192–194; for replies to other objections, see Loke, *God and Ultimate Origins*, chapter 6.
47 See chapter 4 in this book.
48 For the argument that this Creator has revealed himself in history, see Andrew Loke, *The Origins of Divine Christology* (Cambridge: Cambridge University Press, 2017); Andrew Loke, *Investigating the Resurrection of Jesus* (London: Routledge, 2020).
49 The writing of this article is funded by the Hong Kong Research Grants Council (project number 22603119).

Bibliography

Barr, Stephan, "Modern Cosmology and Christian Theology," in *The Blackwell Companion to Science and Christianity*, edited by Alan G Padgett and J. B. Stump, 179–183, Chichester: Wiley-Blackwell, 2012.

Bricmont, Jean, *Making Sense of Quantum Mechanics,* Cham: Springer Nature, 2016.

Bussey, Peter, "God as First Cause—a Review of the Kalam Argument," *Science & Christian Belief* 25 (2013): 17–35.

Copan, Paul and William Lane Craig (eds.), *The Kalam Cosmological Argument*, vol. 2. New York: Bloomsbury Academic, 2017.

Craig, William Lane. "Kant's First Antinomy and the Beginning of the Universe," *Zeitschrift für Philosophische Forschung* 33 (1979): 553–567.

Craig, William Lane. "Must the Beginning of the Universe Have a Personal Cause?" *Faith and Philosophy* 19 (2002): 94–105.

Craig, William Lane, and James Sinclair, "The Kalam Cosmological Argument," in *The Blackwell Companion to Natural Theology*, edited by William Lane Craig and J. P. Moreland. Chichester: Wiley-Blackwell, 2012.

Craig, William Lane, "Q&A #106: Is God Actually Infinite?" 2009, http://www.reasonablefaith.org/is-god-actually-infinite.

East, James, "Infinity Minus Infinity," *Faith and Philosophy* 30 (2013): 429–433.

Ellis, George, "Issues in the Philosophy of Cosmology," in *Philosophy of Physics*, edited by J. Butterfield and J Earman, Amsterdam: Elsevier, 2007.

Grünbaum, Adolf, "Why is There a Universe AT ALL, Rather Than Just Nothing?" *Ontology Studies* 9 (2009): 15.

Hawking, Stephen, and Leonard Mlodinow, *The Grand Design*, New York: Bantam Books, 2010.

Hilbert, David, "On the Infinite," in *Philosophy of Mathematics: selected readings* edited by P. Benacerraf and H. Putnam, Englewood Cliffs, NJ: Prentice-Hall, 1964.

Kant, Immanuel, *Critique of Pure Reason*, translated by Norman Kemp Smith, London: Macmillan, 1965.

Koons, Robert, "A New Kalam Argument: Revenge of the Grim Reaper," *Noûs* 48 (2014): 256–267.

Krauss, Lawrence, *A Universe from Nothing: Why There is Something Rather than Nothing*, New York: Free Press, 2012.

Loke, Andrew, "Creatio ex nihilo," in *T&T Clark Companion to Analytic Theology*, edited by J. T. Turner and James Arcadi. London: T&T Clark, 2020.

Loke, Andrew, *God and Ultimate Origins: A Novel Cosmological Argument*, Cham, Switzerland: Springer Nature, 2017.

Loke, Andrew, *Investigating the Resurrection of Jesus*, London: Routledge, 2020.

Loke, Andrew, *The Teleological and Kalam Cosmological Arguments Revisited*. Cham, Switzerland: Springer Nature, forthcoming.

Loke, Andrew, "Is an infinite temporal regress of events possible?" *Think* 11 (2012): 105–122.

Loke, Andrew, "On Beginningless Past, Endless Future, God, and Singing Angels: An Assessment of the Morriston-Craig Dialogue," *Neue Zeitschrift für Systematische Theologie und Religionsphilosophie* 58 (2016): 57–66.

Loke, Andrew, "Theological Critiques of Natural Theology: A reply to Andrew Moore," *Neue Zeitschrift für Systematische Theologie und Religionsphilosophie* 61 (2019): 207–222.

Loke, Andrew, *The Origins of Divine Christology*, Cambridge: Cambridge University Press, 2017.

Moreland, J. P., "The Explanatory Relevance of Libertarian Agency," in *Mere Creation*, edited by William Dembski. Downers Grove, IL: InterVarsity Press, 1998.

Morriston, Wes, "Doubts about the Kalam Argument, in *Debating Christian Theism*, edited by J. P. Moreland, Chad V. Meister, and Khaldoun A. Sweis, Oxford: Oxford University Press, 2013.

Oppy, Graham, "Uncaused Beginnings Revisited," *Faith and Philosophy* 32 (2015): 205–210.

Padgett, Alan, *God, Eternity, and the Nature of Time*, New York: St. Martin's, 1992.

Pruss, Alexander, *Infinity, Causation, and Paradox*. Oxford: Oxford University Press, 2018.

Puryear, Stephen, "Finitism and the Beginning of the Universe," *Australasian Journal of Philosophy* 92 (2014): 619–629.

Russell, Bertrand, *History of Western Philosophy*, London: Allen and Unwin, 1969.

Sorabji, R., *Time, Creation and the Continuum*, Ithaca, NY: Cornell University Press, 1983.

Stenger, Victor, *God: The Failed Hypothesis*, Amherst, NY: Prometheus Books, 2007.

Waters, Ben, "Methuselah's Diary and the Finitude of the Past," *Philosophia Christi* 15 (2013): 463–469.

3

The Ontological Argument

Jason Megill

Ontological arguments for God's existence have inspired a vast literature over the last millennium and the debate over these arguments is ongoing. Indeed, the last fifty years in particular have been a golden age for the argument as interesting work on older versions of the argument has been produced and newer modal versions of the argument have been formulated.

In 1078, St. Anselm formulated the first ontological argument.[1] The argument has generated a massive amount of discussion over the ensuing ten centuries, a discussion that continues today. This article provides a broad overview of this discussion. In section 1, I discuss Anselm's original argument and some early objections to it from Gaunilo. In section 2, I discuss work on the argument in the early modern period, focusing upon Descartes' and Leibniz's versions of the argument, as well as noteworthy objections to the argument from Hume and Kant, among others.[2] In section 3, I discuss attempts to rehabilitate the argument in the 20th Century using modal logic, with a special emphasis on Alvin Plantinga's version of the ontological argument[3] In section 4, I conclude by discussing contemporary work on the argument.

1. Anselm's version

The origin of the ontological argument is St. Anselm's *Proslogion*.[4] However, there are various fundamental controversies surrounding the argument. As Oppy points out, some deny that Anselm was even trying to prove God's existence.[5] Most agree that Anselm was attempting to prove God's existence, but others disagree about exactly where in the text the proof is.[6] There is also disagreement about the number of distinct ontological arguments Anselm offers.[7] Still others argue about what the proof even is. Indeed, Oppy has discussed five distinct attempts to clearly state Anselm's argument.[8]

Nevertheless, there is a "standard account" of Anselm's argument of the sort that one might hear, e.g., in an Introduction to Philosophy course; I will focus on this "standard account." It is widely believed that this is a crucial passage in Anselm's formulation of the argument:

> Thus even the fool is convinced that something than which nothing greater can be conceived is in the understanding, since when he hears this, he understands it; and whatever is understood is in the understanding. And certainly that than which a greater cannot be conceived cannot be in the understanding alone. For if it is even in the understanding alone, it can be conceived to exist in reality also, which is greater. Thus if that than which a greater cannot be conceived is in the understanding alone, then that than which a greater cannot be conceived is itself that than which a greater can be conceived. But surely this cannot be. Thus without doubt something than which a greater cannot be conceived exists, both in the understanding and in reality.[9]

The argument is generally taken to be something like the following:

(1) God is, by definition, the "greatest conceivable being." We cannot conceive of a being that is greater than God.
(2) Theists and atheists (or "fools") alike can agree that we at least have the idea of God. They disagree about whether this idea corresponds to something in reality, but nevertheless, we have the idea of this greatest conceivable being.
(3) Suppose, for *reductio*, that we have this idea of the greatest conceivable being but this being does not in fact exist. Just as we have the idea of a unicorn but there are no unicorns, we have the idea of God but there is no God.
(4) But this is a contradiction. Surely it is greater to exist in reality than it is to merely exist as an idea in our heads. A being that exists as only an idea is not as great as one that exists as an idea *and actually* exists in reality. After all, would you prefer to have a 100 dollars in the bank or merely the idea of a hundred dollars in the bank? So, it cannot be the case that the greatest conceivable being only exists as an idea in our heads; this being, which again is by definition the greatest conceivable, must also exist in reality.
(5) So, our assumption in (3) is false; it is not possible for this greatest conceivable being to exist as an idea in our heads yet fail to exist in reality. That is, God exists.

Anselm has attempted to prove the existence of God from the simple claim that we have the idea of God. On the standard account of the ontological argument, one difference between it and many other attempts to prove God's existence is that it is *a priori*; that is, the argument makes no appeal to claims that can only be learned through experience. Many arguments for God's existence rely on at least one premise that can only be known through experience; e.g., the argument from design relies on the empirical claim that living creatures display structure and organization, which suggests that they were designed by an intelligent designer. But the ontological argument doesn't appeal to any claims that involve observing the nature of the world. Moreover, the argument is often said to be "*analytic*," which roughly means that one only needs to appeal to the meanings of the words involved to reach the conclusion; Anselm attempted to prove that God exists from the mere meaning of the phrase "greatest conceivable being." We can infer that someone is an unmarried male if they are a bachelor, and likewise, we can (allegedly) infer that something exists if it is the greatest conceivable being.

One strategy for defeating the argument is to deny premise (2), and indeed, some have denied that we have the idea of God. There are different forms this denial might take. Perhaps the concept of God is perfectly coherent or consistent, but human minds, perhaps because of various limitations or simply because of the incomprehensibility of God, lack the ability to grasp this concept. Perhaps surprisingly, Aquinas, who is known for trying to prove the existence God, rejected the ontological argument; and he did so at least partially because of such of worries. For Aquinas:

> while we can rehearse the words "a being than which none greater can be imagined" in our minds, we have no idea of what this sequence of words really means. On this view, God is unlike any other reality known to us; while we can easily understand concepts of finite things, the concept of an infinitely great being dwarfs finite human understanding. We can, of course, try to associate the phrase "a being than which none greater can be imagined" with more familiar finite concepts, but these finite concepts are so far from being an adequate description of God, that it is fair to say they don't help us to get a detailed idea of God.[10]

Another strategy is to deny that the concept of God is coherent; if the idea of God is incoherent, then obviously we cannot have a coherent idea of God. And it has been argued that the idea of God is incoherent in various ways. One commonplace example is the paradox of the stone: can God create a stone that is so heavy that God cannot lift it? If God can create a stone that God cannot lift, there is something God cannot do, and if God cannot create such a stone, there is something God cannot do; either way, there is at least one thing that God cannot do; but given God's omnipotence, God is supposed to be able to do anything. The paradox of the stone suggests that the idea of God is incoherent or contradictory. But if so, then we really don't have a coherent idea of God after all, and Anselm's argument fails.[11]

One famous, very early objection to the ontological argument was formulated by Gaunilo.[12] Gaunilo produced a "parody" of Anselm's argument, i.e., he devised a slight variation of Anselm's argument that can prove the existence of an absurd entity, which calls Anselm's argument into question. Consider the "greatest conceivable island." This is the most perfect island imaginable; the beaches have just the right number of grains of sand, the coconuts are ideal in every way, and so on. Suppose that we have the idea of this greatest conceivable island. But following Anselm's reasoning, it would be better for this island to exist in reality as opposed to merely existing as idea (for actually existing would make it even greater), and therefore the island exists. But this is absurd; clearly no such island exists. If the basic form of Anselm's argument can be used to prove such absurdities, there must be something wrong with Anselm's argument. Gaunilo's objection continues to generate discussion to this day; see, e.g., Danielyan and Ward for two recent attempts to undermine the objection.[13]

Gaunilo's objection provided a blueprint for later opponents of ontological arguments; even today, a common strategy for defeating ontological arguments is to parody them. Oppy writes:

> Positive ontological arguments—i.e., arguments FOR the existence of god(s)—invariably admit of various kinds of parodies, i.e., parallel arguments which seem at least equally acceptable to non-theists, but which establish absurd or contradictory conclusions. For many positive ontological arguments, there are parodies which purport to establish the non-existence of god(s); and for many positive ontological arguments there are lots (usually a large infinity!) of similar arguments which purport to establish the existence of lots (usually a large infinity) of distinct god-like beings.[14]

Oppy uses the word "invariably," which implies that every extant and even all possible ontological arguments can be parodied in one way or another. One might (and some have) disputed that, but the main point of Oppy's passage stands: the ability to be parodied is a serious issue with many extant versions of the ontological argument and when connoisseurs are confronted with a novel ontological argument, many of them immediately start searching for a parody.

There are additional issues with Anselm's argument; some of these will be discussed as we discuss other, newer ontological arguments.

2. The early modern period

A pivotal period in the history of ontological arguments was the early modern period. The early modern period saw the development of some of the best known versions of—and objections to—the ontological argument.

In the *Meditations*, Descartes formulated an ontological argument that is generally taken to be the following:

(1) God has all perfections. That is, if there is a property that something can have and this property is a perfection, God has that property.
(2) Existence is a perfection.
(3) Therefore, God exists.[15]

This argument has the virtue of simplicity, but it faces objections. One immediate concern is that it isn't clear that existence is a perfection. Even assuming there is some subset of all properties that can be called "perfections," and even assuming we can know which properties are in this set and which are not, it isn't clear that existence is in this set. It might seem odd to claim that existence is a perfection; aren't there some things that are such that it would be better for them not exist? How, for instance, does pancreatic cancer having the property of existence make it more perfect in any way; wouldn't it be better for pancreatic cancer to not exist? Descartes' ontological argument has generated a large literature; see Nolan for a detailed introduction to Descartes's ontological argument,[16] and see, e.g., Alston, Abbruzzese, and Forgie for additional discussion.[17]

Leibniz also did important work on the ontological argument. Recall one concern with the ontological argument discussed above: if the concept of God is somehow inconsistent (and concerns over, e.g., the paradox of the stone suggest that it might be), then we do not in fact have the idea of God, and so trivially cannot show that God's existence follows directly from that idea. Leibniz was acutely aware of this concern and it was the impetus behind much of his work on the argument. Leibniz states the ontological argument only succeeds if

> it is granted that a most perfect being or a necessary being is possible and implies no contradiction, or, what amounts to the same, that an essence is possible from which existence follows. But as long as this possibility is not demonstrated, the existence of God can by no means be considered perfectly demonstrated by such an argument.[18]

Leibniz "often remarks that the ontological argument itself demonstrates only that if it is possible that God exists then God exists."[19] In effect, the argument cannot be considered complete until it is shown that God, or a necessary being, or a being that is such that its very existence follows from essence, is possible. And Leibniz attempted to demonstrate the possibility of God.

> He defines a "perfection" as a "simple quality which is positive and absolute, or, which expresses without any limits whatever it does express" (A VI iii 578/SR 101). And with this definition in hand, Leibniz is then able to claim that there can be no inconsistency among perfections, since a perfection, in being simple and positive, is unanalyzable and incapable of being enclosed by limits.[20]

One way to interpret Leibniz's argument is the following: consider any two perfections, A and B. A and B do not break further down into parts, they are "simple," so taken individually they cannot be broken down into further components that might contradict one another. A, taken in isolation, cannot produce a contradiction, and neither can B, nor any other perfection for that matter. Furthermore, given that A and B are simple, one cannot derive a contradiction between them by breaking A and B up into parts and finding a part of one that contradicts a part of the other. Moreover A, or B, or any perfection, cannot be "limited by" or "interfered with" or contradicted by another perfection because perfections, by definition, cannot be limited. So any perfection can be combined with any other perfection without fear of contradiction; so all perfections can be consistently combined into the same being; so a being that contains all perfections is logically possible.

However, Leibniz still didn't consider the ontological argument complete. He had an additional concern (also discussed above): why think that "existence is a perfection"? Look states:

> Leibniz must also show that existence is itself a perfection, so that a being having all perfections, an *ens perfectissimum*, may be said to exist. More exactly, Leibniz needs to show that *necessary existence* belongs to the essence of God. And this he does in another short piece from this period, writing "Again, a necessary being is the same as a being from whose essence existence follows. For a necessary being is

one which necessarily exists, such that for it not to exist would imply a contradiction, and so would conflict with the concept or essence of this being." ... In other words, if it is the case that a necessary being is the *same* thing as a being whose existence follows from its essence, then existence must in fact be one of its essential properties.[21]

In short, by definition, a necessary being is one that must exist; it would be a contradiction for a necessary being to not exist. So, the existence of a necessary being is logically entailed by the concept of a necessary being.

While Descartes and Leibniz were proponents of the ontological argument, not all early modern philosophers were. Both Hobbes and Hume worried, as Aquinas had before them, that we lack a sufficient grasp of the concept of God for ontological arguments to succeed. Hobbes states:

> Whatever we imagine is *finite*. Therefore there is no idea or conception of anything we call *infinite*. No man can have in his mind an image of infinite magnitude, nor conceive infinite swiftness, infinite time, or infinite force, or infinite power ... And therefore the name of *God* is used, not to make us conceive him (for he is *incomprehensible*, and his greatness and power are inconceivable), but that we may honour him. Also because whatsoever ... we conceive has been perceived first by sense, either all at once or by parts, a man can have no thought representing anything not subject to sense.[22]

While Hume claims that God is

> a Being, *so remote and incomprehensible*, who bears much less analogy to any other being in the universe than the sun to a waxen taper, and who discovers himself only by some faint traces or outlines, beyond which we have no authority to ascribe to him any attribute or perfection.[23]

And Hume raised additional worries for the ontological argument. For example, the ontological argument attempts to establish the existence of a necessary being *a priori*. But Hume was skeptical that there could be a being that necessarily exists, and even if there were, he didn't think we could demonstrate its existence with an *a priori* argument:

> there is an evident absurdity in pretending to demonstrate a matter of fact, or to prove it by arguments a priori. Nothing is demonstrable, unless the contrary is a contradiction. Nothing, that is directly conceivable, implies a contradiction. Whatever we conceive as existent, we can also conceive as non-existent. There is no being, therefore, whose non-existence implies a contradiction. Consequently there is no Being whose contradiction is demonstrable. (D, 9.5/189; cp, EU,12.28–34/ 164–5)[24]

We can imagine that a unicorn exists, but we can just as easily imagine that no unicorns exist. Likewise, we can conceive that a necessary being exists; but we can just as easily conceive that it does not exist. And why think that we can demonstrate the existence of something *a priori*; arguably the truth-value of existence claims can only be known by observing the world. I cannot, for example, reason my way to the claim that there are 24 chairs in the room; I have to look at the world to check.

One notable objection to ontological arguments associated with the early modern period is the claim that "existence is not a predicate"; this objection is still commonly given today. Descartes's version of the argument (and arguably Anselm's version, and at least some other versions as well, etc.) appears to presuppose that existence is a property that things can have, just as being blue, or being large, or being all-powerful is; but is existence like this? Is existence a property at all? This objection was "in the air" following Descartes's *Meditations*; the first person to make it was likely Gassendi. Nolan writes:

> The seventeenth-century empiricist Pierre Gassendi confronted Descartes with this criticism in the Fifth Set of Objections (and deserves credit for being the first to enunciate it) "existence is not a perfection either in God or in anything else; it is that without which no perfections can be present" (AT 7:323; CSM 2:224). As with most of his replies to Gassendi (whom he regarded as a loathsome materialist and quibbler), Descartes responded somewhat curtly.[25]

Hume had a similar worry. But this objection is generally associated with Kant, and when someone objects to ontological arguments by denying that existence is a predicate, they probably have Kant's version of this objection in mind.[26] Consider the idea of a hundred-dollar bill. This idea will have various properties associated with it, the properties of greenness, rectangularity etc. Now consider adding the putative property of existence to that idea. Adding that "property" to the idea does not change the nature of the idea in any way; in a sense, the *idea* of a hundred-dollar bill is the same whether the hundred-dollar bill exists or not. This suggested to Kant that existence is not a property like greenness or rectangularity; indeed, existence is not a property at all. Given that Descartes's argument presupposes that existence is a property, and given that existence is not a property, Descartes' argument cannot succeed. One interesting question is whether more modern versions of the ontological argument, which we discuss shortly, fall prey to Kant's objection. Finally, note that some deny that this objection even applies to all older versions of the argument; Lochhead,[27] for example, denies that Anselm's version of the argument is open to this objection.

3. Twentieth-century modal versions

In the twentieth century, logicians developed systems of formal logic capable of dealing with the notions of possibility, i.e., what could happen, and necessity, i.e., what must happen. Logical systems capable of dealing with possibility and necessity are called "modal logics." Systems of modal logic are generally obtained by adding one or more axioms concerning possibility or necessity to standard first-order logic. These axioms are generally thought to be unproblematic, e.g., no one disputes the so-called axiom T (if necessarily P, then P), though some have occasionally taken issue with the stronger systems of modal logic such as S5 (described in the next paragraph). In contemporary modal logic, an important concept is that of a "possible world." A possible world is one way that a universe can be. The actual world is a possible world; the universe we live in is obviously one way that a universe can be. But it appears that things could have been different than they are in various ways; it seems, for example, that Trump might have lost the 2016 presidential election. So there is presumably a possible world where, e.g., Trump is not president. If something is true in at least one possible world, then it is possibly true; it can be true. If something is true in all possible worlds, it is necessarily true; it must be true. If something is not possible, then it is true in no possible worlds.[28] In what is probably the most important development to the ontological argument since the early modern period, some philosophers have used modal logics to develop new and quite sophisticated versions of the argument called "modal ontological arguments".

There were several important modal ontological arguments formulated in the twentieth century; Gödel's and Malcolm's versions are two examples.[29] But in what follows I'll focus on Plantinga's 1974 version.[30] Plantinga's initial formulation of his argument is complex; he develops and critiques various arguments in the effort to find a workable version. But Plantinga's final argument relies on two definitions. He states that a being is "maximally *excellent*" if it has all the properties God is thought to have in the Western theological tradition, e.g., omnipotence, omniscience, and so on in a given possible world. A being is "maximally *great*" if it is necessarily maximally excellent, i.e., the being is maximally excellent in *all* possible worlds, which would also involve existing in all possible worlds. So, e.g., suppose there is some possible world *w* that contains God and God has all the traditional great-making properties, but in some other world, this being lacks one of the divine attributes (perhaps it is not omniscient). This being is maximally excellent in *w* but not maximally great (because it lacks some greatness in at least one world). However, if this being is maximally excellent in all possible worlds, then it is maximally great. Now, suppose that it is possible that there is a being that is maximally great; that is, there is a possible world that contains a being that is maximally great. But since this being is maximally great, and since maximal greatness entails maximal excellence and existence in all possible worlds, we can infer that this being is "possibly necessary." The being is possible because it exists in *at least one world*, but the being is necessary because by definition it would exist in *all* possible worlds, so it is possibly necessary. "S5" is an axiom in modal logic which states that if something is possibly necessary, it is necessary. So given S5, if a necessary being exists in one possible world, it exists in all possible worlds. (S5 might sound odd, but arguably it follows from the mere meanings of "possibility" and "necessity" in modal logic.) So, given S5, and given the claim that a maximally great being is possibly necessary, it follows that a maximally great being is necessary, and so exists in all possible worlds, including our own. God exists.

Here is the argument presented more systematically:

(1) By definition, a being is "maximally great" if it is "maximally excellent" and existent in all possible worlds.
(2) It is possible that there is a being that is maximally great; a possible world contains a maximally great being. Being maximally great, this being would necessarily exist (by definition). So, a maximally great being is possibly necessary.

(3) If a maximally great being is possibly necessary, a maximally great being is necessary. This is an instance of the modal axiom S5.
(4) Therefore, a maximally great being is necessary. This follows from (2) and (3) with modus ponens. That is, God exists in all worlds, including our own.

Plantinga takes a modest stance with respect to his argument; he doesn't claim that the argument is irrefutable proof that God exists, but he does claim that it at least makes theism rational. He states:

> Our verdict on these reformulated versions of St. Anselm's argument must be as follows. They cannot, perhaps, be said to *prove* or *establish* their conclusion. But since it is rational to accept their central premise [i.e., that such a being is at least possible] they do show that it is rational to accept that conclusion.[31]

However, some deny that Plantinga has succeeded in establishing even his modest goal; Plantinga's argument has spawned a lively debate. Oppy doubts that the argument will, or even should, convince any non-theists. He writes:

> anyone with even minimal rationality who understands the premise and the conclusion of the argument, and who has doubts about the claim that it is rationally permissible to believe that there is an entity which possesses maximal greatness, will have exactly the same doubts about the claim that it is rationally permissible to believe that there is a possible world in which there is an entity which possesses maximal greatness.[32]

One might think that the claim that God is possible is a plausible and fairly weak claim; after all, theists and atheists alike can perhaps agree that God could have existed (even though the atheist denies that God does in fact exist); then with modal logic we move to the claim that God does exist. This is how Plantinga's argument is supposed to work. But Oppy takes issue with this; he is claiming that the atheist has no good reason for even granting that God is possible.

One might also wonder if Plantinga's argument faces Gaunilo-style parodies. It appears we can use Plantinga's argument to prove the existence of various absurd entities. Tooley writes:

> Let P be any property, and define the property of being maximally P as that property possessed by something if and only if it exists, and has P in every possible world. If it is then granted that the property of being maximally P is possibly exemplified, it follows that it is exemplified. This will lead to an overpopulated world. It will also lead to contradictions.[33]

Consider the property of being a "solvent"; suppose that it is possible for something to be a maximal solvent. But then, since it is maximal, it would exist in all possible worlds. Moreover, why can't something possibly have the maximal property of being resistant to solvents? It would then exist as well. So, we can infer the existence of two perhaps absurd entities, and furthermore, the existence of the entities contradicts one another (for one of them dissolves anything, while the other cannot be dissolved).

4. More recent work

There has been continued interest in traditional ontological arguments and modal ontological arguments over the last few decades. For instance, a number of recent review articles on ontological arguments have appeared. As Oppy notes,[34] much of the recent work on ontological arguments appears in compendiums, companions, encyclopedias, and the like. So, for example, there are review discussions of ontological arguments in Leftow,[35] Matthews,[36] Lowe,[37] Oppy,[38] and Maydole.[39] Indeed, there have been entire books devoted to ontological arguments; one example is Szatkowski.[40] I conclude by giving a broad overview of some of the recent literature.

One important development is that a number of new modal ontological arguments have been formulated. One interesting recent example is Maydole's "Modal Perfection Argument."[41] Maydole attempts to prove the existence of a "Supreme Being," i.e., a being that is necessarily the greatest being possible. Like many of the newer arguments, Maydole's argument is quite technical; it is formulated in 2QS5, a system of modal logic. But despite its technicality, one can explain the premises of his argument in prose. The argument depends upon three premises. First, the negation of any "perfection" is not itself a perfection; e.g., assuming that omnipotence is a perfection, the negation of omnipotence is not a perfection. Second, perfections only entail other perfections; so, e.g., if omnibenevolence is a perfection, and other properties (such as "being kind" or whatever) are entailed by omnibenevolence, then these entailments are perfections too. Third, being "supreme," or being necessarily the greatest possible being, is a perfection. There is much to like about Maydole's argument; e.g., he straightforwardly defines the term "perfection" (if it is better to have a given property than not have it, the property is a "perfection"). The argument is also clearly valid; if the premises are true (and *if* we accept the system 2QS5), one can logically derive the claim that a Supreme being exists. Maydole uses his premises to show that a unique Supreme Being is possible; he infers from his premises, for example, that there can be a being such that it is impossible for any being to be greater than it. Then, once Maydole has established that such a being is possible, he is able to infer in 2QS5 that the being is necessary and so exists in all possible worlds.

But like all ontological arguments, the argument faces objections. One worry is that Maydole makes use of the Barcan[42] formula in his proof; Maydole sees this reliance on the formula as the biggest weakness of his argument. The Barcan formula entails some modal claims that some find implausible; e.g., given the Barcan formula, then anything that possibly exists in the actual world does exist in the actual world, but surely there are some things that could have existed in our world but do not (and never will)? One might think it is obvious, for example, that while there could have been dragons, none will ever actually exist in our world; but given the Barcan formula, if dragons possibly exist in our world, they must exist somewhere at some point. Oppy, while noting that the Barcan formula is controversial and should probably be rejected, mounts a different attack; he rejects the second premise of the argument, i.e., that perfections entail only perfections. Oppy states:

> Consider the property of being either supreme or else a mass murderer. That there is such a property is guaranteed by the unrestricted principle of abstraction that belongs to 2QS5. Moreover, it is quite clear that anything that has the property of supremity has this further property. But it is quite unintuitive to suppose that the property of being either supreme or else a mass murderer is a perfection. This is particularly clear when we consider the intuitive gloss that Maydole puts upon perfections: it is plainly not so that the property of being either supreme or else a mass murderer is a property that it is better to have than not. It would have been far better than not had Stalin and Hitler lacked this property. End of story.[43]

Maydole has responded to Oppy, and Oppy has responded in turn.[44] See also Metcalf[45] for an additional criticism of Maydole's argument. Others have recently formulated novel versions of the modal ontological argument. Bernstein[46] e.g., tries to derive God's existence from only two claims, God possibly exists and necessary existence is a perfection; Bernstein also defends his argument from some of the traditional objections.[47]

But not all recent work on ontological arguments are attempts to find new versions of the argument, modal or otherwise; a number of issues are being discussed in the contemporary literature. For instance, some have devised new defenses of Anselm's argument(s). For example, Matthews and Baker[48] argue that some things have unmediated causal powers while other things, like Pegasus, have mediated causal powers, i.e., they can cause things "through the thoughts, depictions, and the literature in which [Pegasus] figures."[49] Armed with this distinction, they formulate a version of Anselm's argument which purportedly does not depend upon existence being a predicate. Mann[50] objects to their argument, however, claiming, for example, that they fail to show that a greatest conceivable being is even logically possible (as we've seen, this is a persistent objection to ontological arguments). While some search for new ways to defend Anselm's proof, others have uncovered novel, previously unnoticed issues with Anselm's argument. One notable example is Millican[51] who argues that Anselm's argument suffers from a rather simple logical error, a scope ambiguity that completely undermines the argument and can be generalized to other versions of the argument. And others are still trying to defend or refute previous ontological arguments aside from Anselm's. For example, Pruss[52] attempts to improve upon Gödel's ontological argument by establishing the possibility of God with more plausible principles than Gödel used.[53]

There has also been some recent debate about the nature and coherence of the divine attributes; this debate is directly relevant to the ontological argument and Anselmian theism in general. For example, Whitcomb[54] drawing on recent debates concerning the concept of "grounding," argues that omniscience is impossible; if so, there cannot be a perfect Anselmian God. Peels[55] offers an interesting rebuttal to Whitcomb, arguing, among other things, that if Whitcomb is correct, then nothing is true and most people believe only false things, which seems implausible.[56]

Perhaps, at some point, the intense current interest in ontological arguments will fade. But given that the argument is a millennium old and still generates heated discussion to this day, it is unlikely that argument will ever be completely ignored.

Notes

1. See St. Anselm's "Proslogion," in *St. Anselm's Proslogion*, edited by M. Charlesworth (Oxford: Oxford University Press, 1965).
2. See René Descartes, *Discourse on Method and The Meditations*, translated with an introduction by F. Sutcliffe (Harmondsworth: Penguin, 1968); G. Leibniz, *New Essay Concerning Human Understanding*, translated by A. Langley (New York: Macmillan, 1886); David Hume, *Dialogues concerning Natural Religion and Other Writings*, ed. D. Coleman (Cambridge: Cambridge University Press, 2007); Immanuel Kant, 1787. *Critique of Pure Reason*, translated by N. Kemp Smith (London: Macmillan, 1933).
3. See Alvin Plantinga, *The Nature of Necessity* (Oxford: Oxford University Press, 1974); M. Gettings, "Gödel's Ontological Argument: A Reply to Oppy," *Analysis* 59, no. 264 (1999): 309–313.
4. St. Anselm, "Proslogion," 1965.
5. Graham Oppy, "Ontological Arguments," *The Stanford Encyclopedia of Philosophy*, ed. Edward N. Zalta, 2019, https://plato.stanford.edu/archives/spr2019/entries/ontological-arguments/, section 8.
6. Ibid.
7. As Oppy (section 9) states:

    Some commentators claim that the main proof is in *Proslogion II*, and that the rest of the work draws out corollaries of that proof (see, e.g., Charlesworth 1965). Other commentators claim that the main proof is in *Prologion III*, and that the proof in *Proslogion II* is merely an inferior first attempt (see, e.g., Malcolm 1960). Yet other commentators claim that there is a single proof which spans at least *Proslogion II-III*—see, e.g., Campbell 1976 and, perhaps, the entire work—see, e.g., La Croix 1972.

8. Ibid., section 8.
9. Ibid.
10. K. E. Himma, "Anselm: Ontological Arguments for God's Existence," *The Internet Encyclopedia of Philosophy*, ed. James Fieser, 2015, https://www.iep.utm.edu/ont-arg/, Section 2.
11. This is not to suggest that the paradox of the stone conclusively refuted Western theism. Theists have offered numerous responses to the paradox over the centuries and plausibly the coherence of omnipotence (and the other divine attributes sometimes attributed to God in Western theism) is an open question. See Kenneth Pearce, "Omnipotence," *The Internet Encyclopedia of Philosophy* edited by James Fieser and Bradly Dowden, 2011, http://www.iep.utm.edu/omnipote/ for an introduction to omnipotence including a brief discussion of the paradox of the stone. See Kenneth Pearce and Alexander Pruss, "Understanding Omnipotence," *Religious Studies* 48 (2012): 403–414 for an example of recent work on the concept of omnipotence.

12 Gaunilo, "On Behalf of the Fool," in *St. Anselm's Proslogion*, ed. M. Charlesworth (Oxford: OUP, 1965).
13 E. Danielyan, "On the Inherent Incoherence of Gaunilo's Island," *Heythrop Journal*, forthcoming; Thomas M. Ward, "Losing the Lost Island," *International Journal for Philosophy of Religion* 83, no. 1 (2018): 127–134.
14 Oppy, "Ontological Arguments," 2019, section 6.
15 Rene Descartes, *Discourse on Method and The Meditations*, 1968.
16 Lawrence Nolan, "Descartes' Ontological Argument," *The Stanford Encyclopedia of Philosophy*, ed. Edward N. Zalta, 2015, https://plato.stanford.edu/archives/fall2015/entries/descartes-ontological/.
17 William Alston, "The Ontological Argument Revisited," in *Descartes: A Collection of Critical Essays*, ed. Doney (New York: Doubleday, 1967): 278–303; John Abbruzzese, "The Structure of Descartes' Ontological Proof," *British Journal for the History of Philosophy* 15 (2007): 253–282; William Forgie, "Is the Cartesian Ontological Argument Defensible?" *New Scholasticism* 50 (1976): 108–121.
18 Quotation from Barry Loewer, "Leibniz and the Ontological Argument," *Philosophical Studies* 34, no. 1 (1978): 105.
19 Ibid.
20 Brandon Look, "Gottfried Wilhelm Leibniz," *The Stanford Encyclopedia of Philosophy*, ed. Edward N. Zalta, 2013, https://plato.stanford.edu/entries/leibniz/, Section 7.
21 Ibid.
22 Thomas Hobbes, 1651, *Leviathan, with selected variants from the Latin edition of 1668*, ed. E. Curley (Indianapolis: Hackett, 1994), 3.12.
23 David Hume, "An Enquiry concerning the Principles of Morals," in *Enquiries concerning Human Understanding and concerning the Principles of Morals*, ed. L. A. Selby-Bigge, rev. P. H. Nidditch (Oxford: Clarendon Press, 1975), 147–148.
24 Hume, "Enquiry" (D, 9.5/189; cp, EU,12.28–34/ 164–5). See also Paul Russell and Anders Kraal, "Hume on Religion," *The Stanford Encyclopedia of Philosophy*, ed. Edward N. Zalta, 2017, https://plato.stanford.edu/archives/sum2017/entries/hume-religion/.
25 Nolan, "Descartes' Ontological Argument," Section 3.
26 Kant, 1787, *Critique of Pure Reason*, 1933.
27 David Lochhead, "Is Existence a Predicate in Anselm's Argument?" *Religious Studies* 2, no. 1 (1966): 121–127.
28 For an introduction to modal logic, see James Garson, *Modal Logic for Philosophers* (Cambridge: Cambridge University Press, 2006). A classic text in modal logic is G. Hughes and M. Cresswell, *A Companion to Modal Logic*. London: Methuen, 1984.
29 See C. Anthony Anderson, "Some Emendations of Gödel's Ontological Proof," *Faith and Philosophy* 7, no. 3 (1990): 291–303 for a clear formulation of Gödel's argument.
30 See Plantinga, *The Nature of Necessity*, 1974.
31 Ibid., 221.
32 Oppy, "Ontological Arguments," section 8.
33 Michael Tooley, "Critical Notice of the Nature of Necessity," *Australasian Journal of Philosophy* 55, no.1 (1977): 102.
34 Oppy, "Ontological Arguments," section 10.
35 B. Leftow, "The Ontological Argument," in *The Oxford Handbook of Philosophy of Religion*, ed. W. Wainwright (Oxford: Oxford University Press, 2005): 80–115.
36 G. Matthews, "The Ontological Argument," in *The Blackwell Guide to the Philosophy of Religion*, ed. W. Mann (Oxford: Blackwell, 2005): 81–102.

37 E. Lowe, "The Ontological Argument," *The Routledge Companion to Philosophy of Religion*, ed. P. Copan and C. Meister (London: Routledge, 2007).
38 Graham Oppy, "The Ontological Argument," in *Philosophy of Religion: Classic and Contemporary Issues*, ed. P. Copan and C. Meister (Oxford: Blackwell, 2007).
39 Robert Maydole, "The Modal Perfection Argument for the Existence of a Supreme Being," *Philo* 6, no. 2 (2003): 299–313.
40 M. Szatkowski, *Ontological Proofs Today* (Frankfurt: Ontos Verlag, 2012).
41 Maydole, "The Modal Perfection Argument for a Supreme Being," 299–313; Maydole, "The Ontological Argument," in *Blackwell Companion to Natural Theology*, ed. William Lane Craig and J. P. Moreland (2009): 553–592.
42 R. Barcan, "A Functional Calculus of First Order Based on Strict Implication," *Journal of Symbolic Logic* 11 (1946): 1–16.
43 Graham Oppy, "Maydole's Modal Perfection Argument," *Philo* 10, no. 1 (2005): 2–3.
44 See Robert Maydole, "On Oppy's Objections to the Modal Perfection Argument," *Philo* 8, no. 2 (2005): 123–130; Graham Oppy, "Maydole's Modal Perfection Argument (Again)", *Philo* 10, no.1 (2007): 72–84.
45 Thomas Metcalf, "Entailment and Ontological Arguments: Reply to Maydole," *Philo* 8, no. 2 (2005): 131–133.
46 C'Zar Bernstein, "Giving the Ontological Argument Its Due," *Philosophia* 42, no. 3 (2014): 665–679.
47 See also Jason Megill and J. M. Mitchell, "A Modest Modal Ontological Argument," *Ratio* 22, no. 3 (2009): 338–359; Jason Megill, "Two Ontological Arguments for the Existence of an Omniscient Being," in M. Szatkowski, *Ontological Proofs Today* (2012): 77–88; and Jason Megill and Amy Reagor, "A Modal Theistic Argument," in M. Szatkowski, *Ontological Proofs Today*, (2012): 55–89 for a few different versions of modal ontological arguments.
48 Gareth Matthews and Lynne Rudder Baker, "The ontological argument simplified," *Analysis* 70, no. 2 (2010): 210–212.
49 Matthews and Baker, "The Ontological argument Simplified," 210.
50 W. Mann, "Locating the Lost Island," *Review of Metaphysics* 66, no. 2 (2012): 295.
51 P. Millican, "The One Fatal Flaw in Anselm's Argument," *Mind* 113 (2004): 437–476.
52 Alexander R. Pruss, "A Gödelian Ontological argument Improved," *Religious Studies* 45, no. 3 (2009): 347–353; Alexander R. Pruss, "A Godelian Ontological Argument Improved Even More," in Szatkowski, *Ontological Proofs Today*, 203–211. See also Johan E. Gustafsson, 'A Patch to the Possibility Part of Gödel's Ontological Proof', *Analysis* 80, issue 2 (2020): 229–240.
53 See also recent work by Ted Parent, "The Modal Ontological Argument Meets Modal Fictionalism," *Analytic Philosophy* 57, no. 4 (2016): 338–352, who objects to modal ontological arguments in a novel way.
54 Dennis Whitecomb, "Grounding and Omniscience," in *Oxford Studies in Philosophy of Religion 4*, ed. Jon Kvanvig (Oxford University Press, 2011).
55 Rik Peels, "Is Omniscience Impossible?" *Religious Studies* 49, no. 4 (2013): 481–490.
56 For other work on the coherence of Anselmian theism, see Yujin Nagasawa, "A New Defence of Anselmian Theism," *Philosophical Quarterly* 58, no. 233 (2008): 577–596; Yujin Nagasawa, *Maximal God: A New Defence of Perfect Being Theism* (Oxford: Oxford University Press, 2017).

Bibliography

Alston, William P., "The Ontological Argument Revisited," in *Descartes: A Collection of Critical Essays*, edited by Doney, New York: Doubleday, 1967: 278–303.

Abbruzzese, John Edward, "The Structure of Descartes' Ontological Proof," *British Journal for the History of Philosophy* 15 (2007): 253–282.

Anderson, C., "Some Emendations on Gödel's Ontological Proof," *Faith and Philosophy* 7, (1990): 291–303.

Anselm, St., "Proslogion," in *St. Anselm's Proslogion*, edited by M. Charlesworth. Oxford: Oxford University Press, 1965.

Aquinas, St. Thomas, "Whether the Existence of God is Self-Evident," in *Summa Theologica* (1a Q2). Thomas More Publishing, 1981.

Barcan, R., "A Functional Calculus of First Order Based on Strict Implication," *Journal of Symbolic Logic* 11, (1946): 1–16.

Benzmüller, C., and B. Woltzenlogel-Paleo, "Automating Gödel's Ontological Proof of God's Existence with Higher-Order Automated Theorem Provers," *Frontiers in Artificial Intelligence and Applications* 263 (2014): 93–98.

Benzmüller, C., and B. Woltzenlogel-Paleo, "The Inconsistency in Gödel's Ontological Argument—A Success Story for AI in Metaphysics," in *Proceedings of the 25th International Joint Conference of Artificial Intelligence*, edited by Subbarao Kambhampati. AAAI Press (2016): 936–942.

Bernstein, C'Zar, "Giving the Ontological Argument Its Due," *Philosophia* 42, no. 3 (2014): 665–679.

Campbell, R., *From Belief to Understanding*, Canberra: ANU Press, 1976.

Charlesworth, M., *St. Anselm's Proslogion*, Oxford: Oxford University Press, 1965.

Descartes, R. *Discourse on Method and The Meditations*, translated with an introduction by F. Sutcliffe, Harmondsworth: Penguin, 1968.

Danielyan, E. "On the Inherent Incoherence of Gaunilo's Island," *Heythrop Journal*, forthcoming.

Forgie, J. William, "Is the Cartesian Ontological Argument Defensible?" *New Scholasticism* 50 (1976): 108–121.

Garson, James, *Modal Logic for Philosophers,* Cambridge: Cambridge University Press, 2006.

Gaunilo. "On Behalf of the Fool," in *St. Anselm's Proslogion*, edited by M. Charlesworth, Oxford: Oxford University Press, 1965.

Gettings, M., "Gödel's Ontological Argument: A Reply to Oppy," *Analysis* 59, no. 264 (1999): 309–313.

Gustafsson, Johan E., "A Patch to the Possibility Part of Gödel's Ontological Proof," *Analysis* 80, issue 2 (2020): 229–240.

Hartshorne, C., *Anselm's Discovery: A Re-Examination of the Ontological Proof for God's Existence*, La Salle, IL: Open Court, 1965.

Himma, K. E., "Ontological Arguments for God's Existence," *The Internet Encyclopedia of Philosophy*.

Hobbes, Thomas, *Leviathan, with selected variants from the Latin edition of 1668*, ed. E. Curley, Indianapolis: Hackett, 1994.

Huges, G., and M. Cresswell, *A Companion to Modal Logic,* London: Methuen, 1984.

Hume, David, "An Enquiry concerning the Principles of Morals," in *Enquiries concerning Human Understanding and concerning the Principles of Morals* edited by L. A. Selby-Bigge, 3rd edition, revised by P. H. Nidditch. Oxford: Clarendon Press, 1975.

Hume, David, *Dialogues concerning Natural Religion and Other Writings*, edited by D. Coleman, Cambridge: Cambridge University Press, 2007.

Kant, Immanuel, *Critique of Pure Reason*, translated by N. Kemp Smith, London: Macmillan, 1933.

Lacewing, M., "Malcolm's Ontological Argument," *Philosophy for AS*, London: Routledge, 2014.

La Croix, R., *Proslogion II and III: A Third Interpretation of Anselm's Argument*, Leiden: Brill, 1972.

Leftow, B., "Anselm's neglected argument," *Philosophy* 77, no. 3 (2002): 331–347.

Leftow, B., "The Ontological Argument," in *The Oxford Handbook of Philosophy of Religion*, edited by W. Wainwright, Oxford: Oxford University Press (2005): 80–115.

Leibniz, G., *New Essay Concerning Human Understanding*, translated by A. Langley, New York: Macmillan, 1886.

Lochhead, David M., "Is Existence a Predicate in Anselm's Argument?" *Religious Studies* 2, no. 1 (1966): 121–127.

Lowe, E., "The Ontological Argument." *The Routledge Companion to Philosophy of Religion*, P. Copan and C. Meister edition. London: Routledge, 2007.

Malcolm, N., "Anselm's Ontological Arguments," *Philosophical Review* 69 (1960): 41–62.

Mann, W., "The Ontological Presuppositions of the Ontological Argument," *Review of Metaphysics* 26 (1972): 260–277.

Mann, W., "Locating the Lost Island," *Review of Metaphysics* 66, no. 2 (2012): 295–316.

Matthews, G., "The Ontological Argument," in *The Blackwell Guide to the Philosophy of Religion*, edited by W. Mann. Oxford: Blackwell (2005): 81–102.

Matthews, Gareth B., and Lynne Rudder Baker, "The Ontological Argument Simplified," *Analysis* 70, no. 2 (2010): 210–212.

Maydole, R., "The Modal Perfection Argument for the Existence of a Supreme Being," *Philo* 6, no. 2 (2003): 299–313.

Maydole, R., "On Oppy's Objections to the Modal Perfection Argument," *Philo* 8, no. 2 (2005): 123–130.

Maydole, R., "The Ontological Argument," in *The Blackwell Companion to Natural Theology*, edited by William Lane Craig and J. P. Moreland, Oxford: Wiley-Blackwell (2009): 553–592.

McDonough, R., "Malcolm, Norman," *Internet Encyclopedia of Philosophy*, 2017.

Megill, Jason, "Two Ontological Arguments for the Existence of an Omniscient Being," in *Ontological Proofs Today*, edited by Miroslaw Szatkowski. Ontos Verlag (2012): 77–89.

Megill, Jason, and J. Mitchell, "A Modest Modal Ontological Argument," *Ratio* 22, no. 3 (2009): 338–349.

Megill, Jason, and Amy Reagor, "A Modal Theistic Argument," in *Ontological Proofs Today*, edited by Miroslaw Szatkowski. Ontos Verlag (2012): 50–77.

Metcalf, Thomas, "Entailment and Ontological Arguments: Reply to Maydole," *Philo* 8, no. 2 (2005): 131–133.

Millican, P., "The One Fatal Flaw in Anselm's Argument," *Mind* 113 (2004): 437–476.

Nagasawa, Yujin, "A New Defence of Anselmian Theism," *Philosophical Quarterly* 58, no. 233 (2008): 577–596.

Nagasawa, Yujin, *Maximal God: A New Defence of Perfect Being Theism*, Oxford: Oxford University Press, 2017.

Nolan, Lawrence, "Descartes' Ontological Argument," *The Stanford Encyclopedia of Philosophy*, edited by Edward N. Zalta, 2015. https://plato.stanford.edu/archives/fall2015/entries/descartes-ontological/.

Oppy, G., "Gödelian Ontological Arguments," *Analysis* 56 (1996): 226–230.
Oppy, G., "Response to Gettings," *Analysis* 60 (2000): 363–367.
Oppy, G., "Maydole's Modal Perfection Argument," *Philo* 10, no. 1 (2005): 72–84.
Oppy, G., "The Ontological Argument," in *Philosophy of Religion: Classic and Contemporary Issues*, edited by P. Copan and C. Meister. Oxford: Blackwell, 2007.
Oppy, G., "'Ontological Arguments," *The Stanford Encyclopedia of Philosophy*, edited by Edward N. Zalta. 2019, https://plato.stanford.edu/archives/spr2019/entries/ontological-arguments/.
Parent, Ted, "The Modal Ontological Argument Meets Modal Fictionalism," *Analytic Philosophy* 57, no. 4 (2016): 338–352.
Pearce, Kenneth L., "Omnipotence," *The Internet Encyclopedia of Philosophy*, 2011, https://www.iep.utm.edu/omnipote/.
Pearce, Kenneth L., and Alexander R. Pruss, "Understanding Omnipotence," *Religious Studies* 48, no. 3 (2012): 403–414.
Peels, Rik, "Is omniscience impossible?" *Religious Studies* 49, no. 4 (2013): 481–490.
Plantinga, A., *God and Other Minds*, Ithaca: Cornell University Press, 1967.
Plantinga, A., *The Nature of Necessity*, Oxford: Oxford University Press, 1974.
Pruss, Alexander R., "A Gödelian Ontological Argument Improved," *Religious Studies* 45, no. 3 (2009): 347–353.
Pruss, Alexander R., "A Godelian Ontological Argument Improved Even More," in *Ontological Proofs Today*, edited by Miroslaw Szatkowski. Ontos Verlag (2012): 50–203.
Russell, Paul, and Anders Kraal, "Hume on Religion," *The Stanford Encyclopedia of Philosophy*, edited by Edward N. Zalta, 2017, https://plato.stanford.edu/archives/sum2017/entries/hume-religion/.
Sobel, J., "Gödel's Ontological Proof," in *On Being and Saying: Essays for Richard Cartwright*, edited by J. Thomson, Cambridge, MA: MIT Press (1987): 241–61.
Szatkowski, M., *Ontological Proofs Today*. Frankfurt: Ontos Verlag, 2012.
Todd, Patrick, "'The Greatest Possible Being Needn't Be Anything Impossible," *Religious Studies* 51, no. 4 (2015): 531–542.
Ward, Thomas M., "'Losing the Lost Island," *International Journal for Philosophy of Religion* 83, no. 1 (2018): 127–134.
Whitcomb, Dennis, "Grounding and Omniscience," in *Oxford Studies in Philosophy of Religion 4*, edited by Jon Kvanvig, Oxford: Oxford University Press, 2011.

4

The Fine-Tuning Argument

Michael Rota

Imagine you have just bought a ticket in an unusual lottery. A large set of cards have been printed, each with a different number printed on it. Only one card has the winning number. Your ticket entitles you to select a single card from the large set of cards, and if you select the winning card, you win a billion dollars. Part of what makes this lottery so unusual is the number of cards, which are each the size of a standard business card: 3.5 inches wide, 2 inches tall, and .016 inches thick. The lottery organizers have placed the cards in boxes that are 1 × 1 × 1 foot cubes. (Each box contains 15,174 cards.) They have then placed the boxes in standard steel shipping containers (40 ft × 8 ft × 8.5 ft on the outside), each holding 2400 such boxes. They have then covered the entire surface area of Texas with 23,088,168,276 such shipping containers, allowing them to accommodate all 840,815,677,008,100,000 cards printed. (That's about 840,816 trillion tickets.) Ever hopeful, you climb into a helicopter, consult a map of Texas, and direct the pilot to fly to what used to be San Antonio. After flying over a nearly-endless sea of shipping containers, you arrive in the San Antonio area and select at random one particular container from among the thousands within close reach. You then disembark and spend a few hours unloading box after box so that you can pick a particular box from near the back of the shipping container. You open that box, hold your breath, and remove one of the cards contained, leaving the other 15,173 behind. The number on your card reads: 74,592,324,578,811,234. The smiling lottery employee accompanying you announces that you have lost.

Then things get interesting. Bob, the next participant in the lottery, has been with you in the helicopter. Now he gets his turn. He directs the pilot to fly to what used to be Corpus Christi, picks a shipping container, picks a box, picks a card, and ... wins the lottery. You later learn that Bob is the nephew of a computer programmer who is an employee at the lottery. Would you be suspicious? If so, you just might like the fine-tuning argument.

The fine-tuning argument (henceforth FTA) takes as its point of departure a relatively recent discovery in physics: our universe would not contain living organisms if a number of its fundamental features had not been just exactly right, or *fine-tuned*, for life. On the assumption that our universe was produced by a supernatural agent, it is not particularly surprising or unexpected that our universe would be life-permitting. But on the assumption that there is no supernatural designer of the universe, it was an incredible coincidence that our universe should have been hospitable to life. Since such a coincidence is so unlikely, the fine-tuning of the universe for life provides strong evidence that our universe is the product of a supernatural designer.

In what follows, this line of thought will be motivated, developed, and confronted with a number of objections.[1] The place to begin is with a close look at the single most striking case of fine-tuning.

1. The cosmological constant[2]

The 2011 Nobel Prize in Physics went to Saul Perlmutter, Brian Schmidt and Adam Riess for an observational discovery relating to the expansion of the universe. This was not the first recognition of their work; in 1998, when their results were originally published, *Science* magazine called the findings the top scientific breakthrough of the year. Physicist Brian Greene of Columbia University relates that many researchers found this discovery to be "the single most surprising observational result to have emerged in their lifetimes."[3] What was the discovery, and why exactly was it so surprising?

To find an answer, we need to start with an earlier discovery about space: it is possible for space to expand or contract. For space to expand isn't just a matter of things in space (like stars) moving farther apart from each other *through* space. Rather, the idea is that space itself can expand. Imagine that you drew two dots on the surface of a balloon and then inflated the balloon so it got bigger. As the surface of the balloon stretched, those two dots would get farther and farther away from each other, even though the dots wouldn't be moving *across* the surface in the way that an ant might crawl across the balloon.

Not only *can* space expand, it *is* expanding, as scientists have known since the early twentieth century. It had been thought that, ever since a time very soon after the Big Bang, space was expanding at a slower and slower rate as time went on; that is, it was thought that the expansion of space was decelerating. Perlmutter, heading one research team, and Schmidt, heading another, independently set out to measure how much the expansion of space was slowing down. To their surprise they discovered that it was not slowing down at all—it was speeding up. And this in turn implied something surprising about what we would ordinarily think of as empty space. "Empty" space, it turns out, experiences a repulsive force (a sort of opposite to gravity). Or perhaps the way to describe it is that a number of fields that permeate space generate that repulsive force. However we describe it, something is causing an acceleration in the expansion of space. The rate of this acceleration is related to a parameter (a number) that scientists refer to as the effective cosmological constant. If the effective cosmological constant is a positive number, space tends to expand at an accelerating rate, and the larger the positive number the more rapid the acceleration. If the effective cosmological constant were a negative number, the expansion of space would decelerate, and then space would begin to contract; the larger the negative number the sooner the contraction would begin. Crucially, the observations of Perlmutter, Schmidt and their research teams allowed for a precise calculation of the value of the effective cosmological constant. Measured in Planck units, it turns out to be an extremely small positive number, almost but not quite zero.[4] Taking account of recent data, it's this: .000000000 0000000000000000000000000000000000000000000000000000000000000000 000000000000000000000000000000000000000000135. That's 1.35×10^{-123} of the relevant units.[5]

Mildly interesting, perhaps, but what's the big deal? Well, the value of the effective cosmological constant isn't a mere piece of trivia. As Nobel Prize-winning physicist Steven Weinberg convincingly argued in the late 1980s, the precise value of the cosmological constant is fundamentally important as far as life is concerned. If the effective cosmological constant were about one thousand times bigger than it is (bigger than about 1 over 10^{120} Planck units), the universe would have expanded too rapidly in its earlier stages, and stars would never have formed. This would have made it very unlikely that life could have evolved anywhere in the universe, since all the chemical elements except the three simplest (hydrogen, helium and lithium) are only produced within stars, and it's very unlikely that there could be living beings made only out of these elements and/or subatomic particles. And if the effective cosmological constant had been negative but a bit less than about negative 1 over 10^{120} Planck units, the universe would have collapsed far too soon, before any life could have evolved.

And now we get to the punch line: given what we know from physics, it was unbelievably unlikely that the value of the effective cosmological constant would have fallen inside the narrow life-permitting range, between about negative 1 over 10^{120} and about positive 1 over 10^{120} of the relevant units.[6] It appears that the cosmological constant could have been anywhere in a *very* large range ("large" relative to the size of the narrow life-permitting band), and if it hadn't been just right, we would not exist.

Let's delve a little deeper. The underlying physical reasons why the value of the effective cosmological constant is what it is are not fully known. That is, it's not fully understood why "empty" space experiences the repulsive force to the degree that it does. Still, at least part of the reason has to do with the energy of various fields that permeate space (the fields that are associated with the fundamental particles, such as the electron or the various quarks). Some fields contribute a positive quantity to the effective cosmological constant, some contribute a negative quantity. But when physicists make their best attempt at estimating the energy that the several known fields should contribute all together, they get a result that is much, much bigger than the observed value. Indeed, that's putting it mildly—what's expected is a value about 10 to the 123rd bigger than the observed value![7] What's going on here? A natural conclusion to draw is that, in addition to the known contributors to the effective cosmological constant, there are also one or more other contributors, as yet unknown. And whatever these other contributors are, they *almost* exactly cancel out the contributions from the fields mentioned above, so that the effective cosmological constant is almost zero.

What is amazing to physicists is that, even though each of the individual contributions to the cosmological constant could have taken any of a huge range of values, it somehow turned out that all of the various individual contributions conspire to almost cancel each other out, *almost but not quite*. A cancellation to exactly zero would suggest the presence of some relatively simple underlying mechanism by which various pairs necessarily cancel each other. But when Perlmutter, Schmidt and Riess discovered that the effective cosmological constant is not exactly zero, this simple explanation was ruled out—and this is why the discovery was so surprising to other physicists. With the prospects exceedingly dim for a simple, elegant solution showing why the cosmological constant has to be zero, we're left with what appears to be an enormous coincidence.

How enormous? One that would make participating in our hypothetical lottery look like a fantastically prudent investment. The chance of winning that lottery (fairly) would be approximately 1 in 10^{18}. The chance of the cosmological constant falling in the life-permitting range (without a universe-designer involved) would be approximately 1 in 10^{120}. Philosophers John Hawthorne and Yoaav Isaacs put this figure in perspective:

> Your odds of guessing a person randomly selected from Rhode Island are around 1 in 1,000,000. Your odds of guessing a person randomly selected from India are around 1 in 1,000,000,000. But your odds of guessing an atom randomly selected from the known universe are a mere 1 in 10^{80}—which is not even close to 1 in 10^{120}.[8]

2. The basic fine-tuning argument

The FTA has been formulated in a number of different versions, and in section 6 a precise formulation will be given. But perhaps it is best to begin with the rough idea. The life-permitting character of the universe is evidence for a universe-designer for the same reason that Bob's winning the lottery is evidence that he cheated. In the case of the lottery, Bob's winning is much, much more to be expected given the hypothesis that he was cheating than it is given the hypothesis that he was not cheating, so his winning is evidence that he cheated. Similarly, a life-permitting universe is much, much more to be expected given a universe-designer than without one, so the life-permitting universe is evidence for a universe-designer.[9]

3. The Star Trek objection

An initial objection to the FTA targets its key empirical premise, namely:

(1) Our universe would not contain life if a number of its fundamental features had not been just right, or fine-tuned, for life.

This claim is well-supported and widely-endorsed by experts.[10] But there are some who challenge it; physicist Sean Carroll of Caltech, for example, has suggested that we don't know enough about different possible forms of life to be confident of (1).[11] Perhaps even if stars hadn't formed, life (of a different sort) would have emerged nonetheless.

This is a sensible objection, but upon inspection it doesn't derail the FTA. The probability that the cosmological constant would have fallen in what is standardly considered the life-permitting range by chance is 1 in 10^{120}. This means that if the entire range of possible values for the cosmological constant were represented by a long line, and the range of life-permitting values were represented by a very short segment of that line, then the long line would be 10^{120} times the length of the short segment. This is reflected in Figure 1 (NOT to scale), in which the entire line segment represents the values of the cosmological constant entertained as possible, and the region between −1 and 1 represents the narrow life-permitting region discussed in standard treatments.[12] In those standard treatments, our key claim, (1), is supported with the observation that if the cosmological constant were to the right of 1, there would be no star formation in the resulting universe, and if the cosmological constant were to the left of −1, the universe would end in a Big Crunch far too soon, plausibly, for life to arise. So begins the original FTA. But suppose, in a concession to Carroll's objection about different forms of life, we allow that life might be a real possibility outside that [−1,1] band. Indeed suppose we allow that the life-permitting band might be a trillion times wider than typically thought, conceding for the sake of argument that some form of life might be able to exist if the cosmological constant had been between −10^{12} and 10^{12} in Figure 4.1.

Even so, the strength of the FTA is barely touched. The range of possible values for the cosmological constant is now $10^{120}/10^{12} = 10^{108}$ times wider than the life-permitting range. So instead of a coincidence of 1 in 10^{120}, the fine-tuning of the cosmological constant by chance would be a coincidence of 1 in 10^{108}, still an unimaginably tiny probability. So even once we address Carroll's concerns by allowing for life in very extreme universes, it's still the case that the universe has to be "just right" to allow for life, because there are 10^{108} undeniably life-excluding universes outside our new life-permitting region for every 1 universe inside of it.

I say "undeniably life-excluding universes" because if the cosmological constant took a value at the left-hand limit in our wider life-permitting band, corresponding to the point marked −10^{12}, the universe would have collapsed 15,000 years after the Big Bang, while if it took a value at our new right-hand limit, corresponding to the point marked 10^{12},

> The universe would contain a thin soup of hydrogen and helium. At most, these particles might occasionally bounce off each other, and head back out into space for another trillion years of lonely isolation.[13]

It is not reasonable to think living organisms could form, survive and reproduce in conditions like those. "At this point," Lewis and Barnes continue:

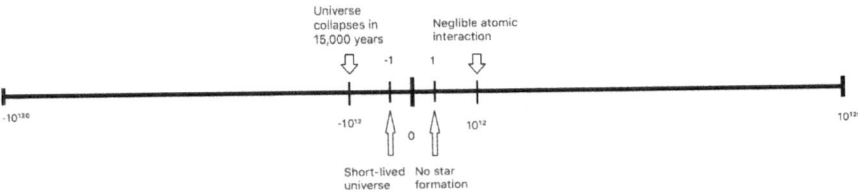

Figure 4.1 Fine-tuning of the cosmological constant.

people often play the science fiction card, and retort that such a simple universe could contain life not as we know it, life so extraordinary and bizarre that our puny human minds could not even conceive of its existence. But the important word here is *fiction*. Any universe in which life can arise must provide the conditions for the storage and processing of information; a thin soup of only hydrogen and helium simply does not provide this.[14]

4. The anthropic objection

The anthropic objection contends that the fine-tuning of the universe for life is sufficiently explained by one simple observation: since we (as living beings within the universe) can only exist in a life-permitting universe, of course we observe a life-permitting universe! *We* couldn't very well expect to observe a universe without life. So while initially it might have appeared improbable that our universe would permit life on the hypothesis that it is the result of some blind physical process, we must remember that because we are living beings produced within our universe we cannot observe our universe to be non-life-permitting. From this it follows, according to the anthropic objection, that our observation of a life-permitting universe was not improbable at all, even on the hypothesis that our universe was the result of a blind physical process.[15]

The first clue that something has gone wrong in this reasoning is that parallel reasoning would have us reject some obviously correct arguments. Suppose you sit before a firing squad, about to be fired on.[16] You aren't hopeless, though, because you have some reason to believe that your cousin, who is on the firing squad, may have convinced the others to intentionally miss you. The signal is given, shots ring out, and you find that all the bullets have missed. Intuitively, it's clear that you've just gained evidence for the hypothesis that the shooters were intending to miss. It is very improbable that they would all miss given the hypothesis that they were trying to hit you, while it is probable that they would all miss on the hypothesis that they were trying to miss. In other words, your evidence (your survival) is much more to be expected if they were trying to miss than if they were trying to hit. Notice, however, that the anthropic objection would have us wrongly conclude that the trying-to-miss hypothesis is given no support at all by your observation that you survived. "You must not forget," it will be urged, "that because you must be alive in order to observe anything at all, you cannot observe a situation in which you didn't survive, and so your observation of a firing-squad survival is not improbable at all, even on the hypothesis that the firing squad was trying to hit you." This can't be right. To press this point, imagine that the firing squad keeps firing, volley after volley for hours, and they miss you every time. Surely you would eventually have evidence that they are not a normal firing squad.[17]

Still, it's one thing to cast doubt on an objection by showing that it proves too much; it's another thing to understand exactly where it goes wrong. The short version (of where it goes wrong) is that the anthropic objection asks us to focus on an irrelevant probability: the probability that the universe is life-permitting given that the universe is the result of a blind physical process *and* we're here to observe it. Okay, *if* we're here to observe it, it must be life-permitting. But we might very well have never been here to observe it! Without a Fine-Tuner in the picture, what is likely is that we would never have been here at all. Since we are here, we have evidence for a universe-designer.

5. The theory of probability

In order to construct a rigorous version of the FTA we will need a few tools, provided courtesy of the theory of probability. First, the *epistemic probability*, for you, of a proposition A is a measure of the level of confidence it is rational for you to assign to A, given all your relevant background information. For example, let A stand for the proposition that a certain coin will land heads when next flipped. If your relevant background information includes only the information that the coin is fair, then the epistemic probability of A will be ½, since you should assign a level of confidence of 50% to the proposition that the coin will land heads. In symbols, $P(A) = .5$.

Second, the *conditional epistemic probability* of a proposition B given another proposition C, written $P(B|C)$, is a measure of the level of confidence it is rational for you to assign to B, given all your relevant background information, plus the assumption (which may or may not be true) that C is known.[18] For example, suppose you are about to draw a card from a standard, shuffled deck of 52 cards, let B be the proposition that the card will be the Queen of Hearts, and let C be the proposition that the card will be red. $P(B)$ is 1/52, but $P(B|C)$ is 1/26. This is because there are 26 red cards in the deck, only one of which is the Queen of Hearts, and so *if* you were to take it as given that the card will be red, then you should judge that there is a 1/26th probability that it will be the Queen of Hearts.

Third, an equation called Bayes' theorem can help us understand how much support some piece of evidence E provides for a hypothesis H, when we know how much E is to be expected if H is true, i.e. when we know $P(E|H)$. To illustrate: suppose we are sitting with a table between us, and on the table there are two decks of cards, a normal deck and a trick deck. Like a normal deck, the trick deck has 52 cards, but unlike a normal deck, the trick deck contains only Aces – 13 Aces of each suit. You however don't know which deck is which. I invite you to point to one of the two decks (without looking at the cards), and then randomly select a card from the deck at which you have pointed. You do so, and find that:

E1 You selected an Ace of Diamonds.

I then ask:

Q1 What is the probability that the deck you selected from was the trick deck?

Before you looked at the card, your answer would have been ½. But now that you've acquired evidence E1, the answer should be more than ½. E1 is evidence that you selected from the trick deck, because there are more Aces of Diamonds in the trick deck than in the normal deck. But how strong is the evidence, exactly? And what is the answer to Q1? Figure 2 can help us here:

Normal Deck				Trick Deck			
2 Clubs	2 Diamonds	2 Hearts	2 Spades				
3 Clubs	3 Diamonds	3 Hearts	3 Spades				
4 Clubs	4 Diamonds	4 Hearts	4 Spades				
5 Clubs	5 Diamonds	5 Hearts	5 Spades				
6 Clubs	6 Diamonds	6 Hearts	6 Spades	Ace of Clubs	Ace of Diamonds	Ace of Hearts	Ace of Spades
7 Clubs	7 Diamonds	7 Hearts	7 Spades				
8 Clubs	8 Diamonds	8 Hearts	8 Spades				
9 Clubs	9 Diamonds	9 Hearts	9 Spades				
10 Clubs	10 Diamonds	10 Hearts	10 Spades				
J Clubs	J Diamonds	J Hearts	J Spades				
Q Clubs	Q Diamonds	Q Hearts	Q Spades				
K Clubs	K Diamonds	K Hearts	K Spades				
A Clubs	A Diamonds	A Hearts	A Spades				

Figure 4.2 The probability space for a sample problem.

Each rectangular region in Figure 4.2 represents a possible outcome after you draw one card from the set of two decks before you. If in fact you pointed to the normal deck, there were 52 different cards you might draw, all equally probable. If in fact you were drawing from the trick deck, there were 52 possible cards to draw: 13 were Aces of Clubs, 13 were Aces of Diamonds, and so on. This makes for a total of 104 equally possible cards. So before you looked at the card you selected, there were 104 possibilities to be kept in mind for what it might be. But once you have looked at the card, most of those possibilities are removed from consideration. Once you see that it is an Ace of Diamonds, you realize that there are only 14 possibilities for what has occurred: you might have drawn the one Ace of Diamonds card in the normal deck, or you might have drawn the first of the 13 Aces of Diamonds in the trick deck, or the second of the 13 Aces of Diamonds in the trick deck, or the third ... etc. You know that the card in your hand is one of those 14 cards, and it could equally well have been any of them. You know, so to speak, that you are somewhere in the shaded area of Figure 4.2. This allows you to answer Q1. Since there are 14 equally probable Ace of Diamonds cards, but only one of them is from the normal deck, there is only a $1/_{14}$ probability that you drew from the normal deck. Likewise, 13 of the 14 Aces of Diamonds you might have drawn are from the trick deck, so there are 13 possible ways to draw an Ace of Diamonds from the trick deck (out of a total of 14 possible ways to draw an Ace of Diamonds). Thus the probability that you have drawn from the trick deck is $13/_{14}$, or about .929. Before acquiring evidence E1, you should think it 50% likely that you pointed at the trick deck, but after acquiring E1, you should think it 92.9% likely!

Bayes' theorem is a rule that allows one to arrive at this same answer, but without drawing a figure.[19] The simplest form of Bayes' theorem relates four quantities:

The probability that some hypothesis is true, if we assume some evidence is known. Here this is P(you selected from the trick deck | E1).

The probability that you should assign to that hypothesis before taking into account the evidence in question. Here, this is P(you selected from the trick deck), which equals ½.

A measure of how much the evidence in question is to be expected if the hypothesis is true. This is the epistemic probability that you would gain that evidence if you take the hypothesis as given. Here it is the probability that you would draw an Ace of Diamonds, supposing that you were drawing from the trick deck, i.e. P(E1|trick), which equals $^{13}/_{52}$ or ¼.

A measure of how much the evidence in question was to be expected. In our example this is P(E1), which equals $^{14}/_{104}$, since out of 104 possible cards, 14 are Aces of Diamonds.

Bayes' theorem enables one to solve for the first of these quantities if the other three are known, and states:

(2) $\qquad P(Hypothesis | Evidence) = \dfrac{P(Hypothesis) \cdot P(Evidence | Hypothesis)}{P(Evidence)}$

In our example, we thus have:

$$P(trick | E1) = \dfrac{P(trick) \cdot P(E1 | trick)}{P(E1)} = \dfrac{(\tfrac{1}{2}) \cdot (\tfrac{1}{4})}{(\tfrac{14}{104})} = \dfrac{13}{14}$$

A final complication: sometimes it is feasible to calculate P(Evidence) only by considering separately how likely the Evidence would be if the Hypothesis were true and how likely it would be if the Hypothesis were false. It turns out that:

P(Evidence) = P(Evidence|Hypothesis) * P(Hypothesis) + P(Evidence|Hypothesis) * P(~Hypothesis)

Together with (2), this implies that:

(3) $\qquad P(H | E) = \dfrac{P(H) \cdot P(E | H)}{P(E | H) \cdot P(H) + P(E | {\sim} H) \cdot P({\sim} H)}$

6. Bayes' theorem and the FTA

Returning now to the FTA, let D be the proposition that *the universe is the causal product of an intelligent agent*.[20] Thus ~D is the proposition that *it is false that the universe is the causal product of an intelligent agent*. Let E be the proposition that *the cosmological constant is in the life-permitting range*. To illustrate the evidential impact of E, imagine that prior to considering the fine-tuning argument, we think the universe

Figure 4.3 Illustration of the probability space for the fine-tuning argument.

is much more likely the product of a blind physical process than of an intelligent agent, and we think that even if the universe were produced by God or some other universe-designer, it can't be guaranteed that the universe-designer would produce a life-permitting universe rather than a lifeless one. In fact suppose that we judge both P(D) and P(E|D) to be about 10%. Attentive to expert opinion regarding the cosmological constant, we recognize that P(E|~D) is tiny.

Figure 4.3 models these judgments, with the narrow column on the right corresponding to D and accounting for 10% of the total area, and the wider column on the left corresponding to ~D and accounting for 90% of the total area. The shaded region in the upper-right includes all the possibilities in which the universe is life-permitting thanks to a universe-designer, and the tiny dot not far from the middle includes the possibilities in which the universe is life-permitting without an intelligent universe-designer. Before taking E into account, we only assigned a 10% level of confidence to the claim that the universe was designed. But to take E into account is to realize that the actual outcome is located in one of the shaded regions—either the tiny dot in a Godless universe, or the larger region in a designed universe. Since the vast majority of the ways of getting a life-permitting universe involve a universe-designer, taking E into account bumps up the epistemic probability of D to something close to 100%. (How close to 100% will depend on the exact ratio between the area of the tiny dot and the area of the shaded region in the upper-right.) Because E is so much more to be expected given D than given ~D, E is powerful evidence for D.

We can use Bayes' theorem and a little algebra to arrive at a more general analysis. From Bayes' theorem, we have:

The Fine-Tuning Argument

$$P(D|E) = \frac{P(D) \cdot P(E|D)}{P(E|D) \cdot P(D) + P(E|\sim D) \cdot P(\sim D)}$$

Now we need some numbers. In concession to the Star Trek Objection, we will assume $P(E|\sim D)$ is $1/10^{108}$ rather than $1/10^{120}$. What shall we estimate for $P(E|D)$? An agent intelligent enough to design a universe would likely understand that the existence of embodied persons like ourselves adds value to a universe, and since a life-permitting cosmological constant is necessary for the existence of embodied persons, such an agent would have a reason to make this universe life-permitting rather than lifeless. Of course such a being might have some countervailing reason to not do so. At the end of the day, how likely is it that an intelligent designer of the universe would produce a life-permitting universe rather than a lifeless one? If I had to guess, I'd say over ½. But let's concede as much as possible to the person who will say that we know very little about what a universe designer might want. Shall we estimate $P(E|D)$ at 1 in 10? 1 in 100? The smaller the number, the weaker the fine-tuning argument will be. In order to rely on a premise that even a skeptic could agree to, let's assume $P(E|D)$ is 1 in a trillion. This gives us:

(4) $$P(D|E) = \frac{P(D) \cdot \frac{1}{10^{12}}}{\frac{1}{10^{12}} \cdot P(D) + \frac{1}{10^{108}} \cdot P(\sim D)}$$

To make the computation simpler, let $\alpha = P(E|\sim D) = \frac{1}{10^{108}}$.

Then $P(E|D) = \frac{1}{10^{12}} = \frac{10^{96}}{10^{108}} = 10^{96} \cdot \alpha$

Thus (4) is equivalent to: $$P(D|E) = \frac{P(D) \cdot 10^{96} \cdot \alpha}{P(D) \cdot 10^{96} \cdot \alpha + P(\sim D) \cdot \alpha}$$

The α terms cancel, and since D and ~D are contradictory propositions, $P(\sim D) = 1 - P(D)$. Substituting, we get:

(5) $$P(D|E) = \frac{10^{96} \cdot P(D)}{10^{96} \cdot P(D) + [1 - P(D)]}$$

Suppose that, prior to considering the evidential impact of fine-tuning, you estimated $P(D)$, the probability that the universe was produced by an intelligent agent, at only 1%. Equation (5) implies that after taking fine-tuning into account, you should be virtually certain the universe was designed, judging the epistemic probability of D to be well over 99.9999999%. If $P(D)$ was 1 in a billion, the same is true. Indeed, even if one put the prior probability of a universe-designer at 1 in 10^{80}, $P(D|E)$ will still be over 99.9999999%.

7. Objections

As with any important philosophical argument, the FTA has been subject to a number of objections. In addition to the anthropic objection and the Star Trek objection, five other issues should be mentioned: uniform probabilities, inscrutability of the divine will, metaphysical necessity, stringent vs. lax laws, and the multiverse. Due to length constraints, I discuss these only briefly, but direct the reader to further resources in the notes.

7.1. Uniform probabilities

Suppose it was possible for the cosmological constant to have been any real number (given a specified unit of measurement). Then how likely is it that the cosmological constant would have been in a given range, e.g. between −1 and 1 of the relevant units? Some philosophers have assumed that in such a case any equally-sized finite range should be assigned equal probability (an assumption of a "uniform probability distribution"), and have accordingly contended that the probability of the cosmological constant's falling within a given finite range must be 0 (for reasons having to do with the infinite number of equally-sized finite ranges within the real number line).[21] If correct, these claims make trouble for the FTA. For a discussion and insightful reply, see Hawthorne and Isaacs (2017).[22]

7.2. Divine inscrutability

The FTA depends on the claim that P(E|D) is much higher than P(E|~D), which in turn depends on the premise that P(E|D) is not astronomically low. Very roughly speaking, the success of the FTA requires that there is at least a decent chance that an intelligent agent designing the universe would select a life-permitting value for the cosmological constant. That's actually putting it too strongly: all the FTA needs is a probability for P(E|D) that is many orders of magnitude higher than the 1 over 10^{108} assigned to P(E|~D). Still, some may say that even this premise is doubtful—perhaps we have no good reason to form a belief about what a universe-designer would or wouldn't likely do. In a recent article Neil Manson presses this sort of objection, discussing the work of several thinkers who take the position that it is inscrutable how likely a life-permitting universe would be given God. (To say the probability of A is inscrutable is to say that A cannot rationally be estimated.)[23]

In response, a distinction should be made between two different epistemic probabilities:

(a) P(the universe is life-permitting | God exists), and
(b) P(the universe is life-permitting | the universe was caused by God).

To evaluate P(X|Y), one takes it as given that Y is true, and then estimates P(X). So to evaluate (a), one would take it as given that God exists, but not take it as given that God has chosen to create anything at all. In contrast, to evaluate (b) one would assume that God has caused the universe to be and then ask how much one could expect the universe to be life-permitting. So if one were discussing (b), questions about how likely God is to create anything at all are irrelevant.[24] The question is whether God (or more generally any universe-designer) would make the universe life-permitting, supposing that the universe-designer was already going to make the universe. In the FTA as presented above, P(E|D) is akin to (b), not (a). In order to evaluate P(E|D), one takes it as given that the universe is the causal product of an intelligent being (and hence one assumes that the universe-designer has already produced the universe). One then asks how much it would be expected that the cosmological constant would be life-permitting. Is P(E|D) inscrutable? Here is an argument that it is not: Assume an intelligent agent A has made something X, but you do not know whether or not X has feature F. It seems to be a general truth that

(6) If A could make X to be F and A could make X to be ~F, and one knows of a good reason for A to make X to be F rather than ~F, and one does not know of any obviously overriding reason for A to make X ~F rather than F, then one should judge that *A's making X to be F* is a real possibility.

Next, for the purpose of evaluating P(E|D), we take it as given that the universe is a causal product of an intelligent agent, and set aside for the time-being our knowledge of the actual features of the universe. We should then reason:

(7) The universe-designer could make the cosmological constant fall within the life-permitting range, and could make it fall outside that range.
(8) We know of a good reason for a universe-designer to make the cosmological constant fall within the life-permitting range, and we do not know of any obviously overriding reason for a universe-designer to make the cosmological constant fall outside that range.

Thus:

(9) We should judge that it is a real possibility that the universe-designer makes the universe to have a life-permitting cosmological constant.

But:

(10) If we should judge that a proposition Y is a real possibility, then Y is not inscrutable.

So:

(11) The proposition that the universe-designer makes the universe to have a life-permitting cosmological constant, given that the universe is the causal product of said universe-designer, is not inscrutable.

A few comments: if it is said that (7) is doubtful, we could modify D to include (7). This would reduce the prior probability P(D) a bit, but not enough to affect the strength of the FTA. In support of (8): because embodied rational life is very valuable, a physical universe with embodied rational beings exhibits more value than a physical universe without such beings. A universe-designer already committed to making a physical universe would therefore have a good reason to create a life-permitting one. In support of (10): judging that Y is a real possibility is equivalent to assigning it at least a non-trivial positive credence. And, it might be added, a positive credence sufficient for the FTA. Could anyone really say that given D, E is a real possibility, but also say that P(E|D) is less than 1 in 10^{80}? That would be like saying "it is a real possibility that I will now successfully guess the identity of an atom randomly selected from the known universe."

7.3. The necessity objection

I have thus far assumed that the cosmological constant could have been otherwise than what it is. But perhaps the features of the universe are metaphysically necessary. If so, then the cosmological constant would have to take the value it does, and a universe-designer would have only one possible "universe blueprint" to work with. Thus, if the features of the universe are metaphysically necessary, the existence of a universe-designer won't raise the probability of a life-permitting universe, so P(E|D) = P(E|~D). An attention to the distinction between metaphysical and epistemic probability and a Bayesian analysis provide a decisive response to this objection.[25]

7.4. Stringent vs. lax laws

Why would a universe-designer create a universe in which the physical laws had to be fine-tuned in order to permit life? Why not just create a universe in which physics made the emergence of life likely for a wide range of parameter values? Reflections on this question can give rise to an objection to the FTA, as work by Jonathan Weisberg has shown. Let O name the proposition that there is life in our universe, and let S be the proposition that the physical laws of our universe are such that only a very narrow range of parameters would allow for life. Roughly, Weisberg's argument is that, whatever evidence O may or may not provide for D, finding out that the universe is fine-tuned adds no additional evidential support for D, because S is no more to be expected given O and D than it is to be expected given O and ~D. Hawthorne and Isaacs give a cogent reply.[26]

7.5. The multiverse objection

The multiverse objection is, in my view, the strongest objection to the FTA. It can be stated as follows:

> Whereas we're accustomed to thinking of the observable universe as the entirety of physical reality, this may be a mistake. Perhaps there is a vast number, possibly an infinite number, of separate universes. These different universes might exhibit a huge array of different physical features, in some the force of gravity being stronger, in others weaker, in some the cosmological constant being larger, in others smaller.

Considered all together, the different universes would make up *the multiverse*, which would be the whole of physical reality. Within the multiverse, the proportion of universes capable of supporting life would indeed be very, very small, but because there would be so many universes in total, there would be many that do support life. If this were the case, we would be wrong to be surprised by the fact that we have found ourselves in a life-permitting universe. Since only the life-permitting universes will contain beings able to observe their own existence, all the observers throughout the vast multiverse will find themselves in life-permitting universes. Each observer will find himself in a universe which appears designed. And since the separate universes are not visible to each other, each observer will be tempted to think, mistakenly, that he is in the only universe. Since the multiverse hypothesis explains our evidential situation, it offers an alternative explanation to design.

So perhaps the correct conclusion from the evidence of fine-tuned life is not the existence of God but the existence of a multiverse. One prominent reply to this objection argues that we have evidence that we are not in a multiverse, because observers in a multiverse should expect not to be stable, long-lived creatures in an orderly sub-region of the universe, but fleeting "Boltzmann brains." For a good discussion, see Lewis and Barnes (2016).[27] A second reply is given by Robin Collins, who points out that not just any multiverse would produce a life-permitting universe. Focusing on the most scientifically well-credentialed multiverse proposal—the inflationary many-universes hypothesis—Collins argues that a number of apparently contingent physical mechanisms and background laws would have to be in place for an inflationary model to yield even a single life-permitting universe. Summarizing a longer discussion, he writes:

> [E]ven if an inflationary/superstring many-universe generator exists, it must have just the right combination of laws and fields for the production of life-permitting universes: if one of the components were missing or different, such as Einstein's equation or the Pauli-exclusion principle, it is unlikely that any life-permitting universes could be produced. In the absence of alternative explanations, the existence of such a system counts as evidence for design since it seems very surprising that such a system would exist with just the right components under the hypothesis that the universe exists as a brute fact without any explanation, but not surprising under the theistic hypothesis. Thus, it does not seem that one can completely escape the evidence of design merely by hypothesizing some sort of many-universe generator.[28]

Still, as Collins acknowledges, on the supposition of an inflationary multiverse the inference to a designer is weakened, since it is not possible to quantify the improbability of the physical mechanisms and background laws needed for an inflationary multiverse to produce a life-permitting universe. According to a third reply, our evidence supports a designer whether or not we're in a multiverse because a theistic multiverse is a possibility, and a theistic multiverse would likely contain a higher proportion of life-permitting universes than would an atheistic multiverse. If we are in a multiverse we should consider both the possibility that we are in an atheistic multiverse and the possibility that we are in a theistic multiverse, i.e. one produced by an intelligent agent. Plausibly, a theistic multiverse will contain a considerably higher proportion of life-permitting universes than would an atheistic multiverse. For any given particular universe in an atheistic multiverse, the chance that it will be life-permitting is extremely low, but for any given particular universe in a theistic multiverse, the chance that it will be life-permitting is not nearly so low, since an intelligent designer would have some reason to make it life-friendly rather than life-excluding. Next, our relevant evidence is not merely that "at least one universe is life-permitting," but that "a given particular universe, the one we're in, is life-permitting." Thus our relevant evidence is much more to be expected on a theistic multiverse hypothesis than on an atheistic multiverse hypothesis.[29]

Notes

1. Approximately 30% of the material in this article is from Michael Rota, *Taking Pascal's Wager: Faith, Evidence and the Abundant Life* (Downers Grove, IL: InterVarsity Press, 2016). Used by permission of InterVarsity Press, P.O. Box 1400, Downers Grove, IL 60515, USA. www.ivpress.com
2. I'm helped in this section by Brian Greene, *The Hidden Reality: Parallel Universes and the Deep Laws of the Cosmos* (New York: Alfred A. Knopf, 2011); Luke Barnes, "The Fine-Tuning of the Universe for Intelligent Life," *Publications of the Astronomical Society of Australia* 29, no. 4 (2012): 529–564; Paul Davies, *Cosmic Jackpot: Why Our Universe Is Just Right for Life* (Boston: Houghton Mifflin, 2007); Leonard Susskind, *The Cosmic Landscape: String Theory and the Illusion of Intelligent Design* (New York: Back Bay Books, 2006); Raphael Bousso, "The Cosmological Constant Problem, Dark Energy, and the Landscape of String Theory," *Pontificiae Academiae Scientiarum scripta varia* 119 (2011): 129–151, arXiv:1203.0307; and Geraint Lewis and Luke Barnes, *A Fortunate Universe: Life in a Finely-Tuned Cosmos* (Cambridge: Cambridge University Press, 2016).
3. Greene, *The Hidden Reality*, 142.
4. A Planck mass is a unit of mass equal to about 0.00002 grams. A Planck length is a unit of distance equal to about 1.6×10^{-33} centimeters. To express the cosmological constant in Planck units, we can express it as a quantity of Planck mass per cubic Planck length.
5. Cf. Bousso, "The Cosmological Constant Problem."
6. Extremely unlikely, that is, assuming that no supernatural agent was involved in the production of the universe.
7. See the discussion in Greene, *The Hidden Reality*, 142–144; Susskind, *The Cosmic Landscape*, 87; and Bousso, "The Cosmological Constant Problem," section 1.2.
8. John Hawthorne and Yoaav Isaacs, "Fine-tuning Fine-tuning," in *Knowledge, Belief, and God: New Insights in Religious Epistemology*, ed. Matthew A. Benton, John Hawthorne, and Dani Rabinowitz (Oxford: Oxford University Press, 2018), 150. Note: I've discussed only the fine-tuning of the cosmological constant, but there

are in fact several other ways in which our universe is "just right" for life, making the apparent coincidence even bigger. For an accessible introduction, see Martin Rees, *Just Six Numbers: The Deep Forces That Shape the Universe* (New York: Basic Books, 2000).

9 It's also relevant here that the hypotheses that Bob cheated, in the one case, and the hypothesis that our universe was produced by an intelligent agent, in the other, are not completely outlandish from the start.
10 See Barnes, "The Fine-Tuning of the Universe for Intelligent Life," 531.
11 Sean Carroll, "Does the Universe Need God?" in *The Blackwell Companion to Science and Christianity*, ed. James B. Stump and Alan G. Padgett (Malden, MA: Wiley-Blackwell, 2012), 190.
12 The scientifically astute will note that 1 unit on this number line corresponds to 1 over 10^{120} Planck units.
13 The quotation is from Lewis and Barnes, *A Fortunate Universe*, 13, and the 15,000 year figure is from Barnes, email communication, February 26, 2015.
14 Lewis and Barnes, *A Fortunate Universe*, 13.
15 This objection has been pressed by Elliott Sober, "The Design Argument," in *Blackwell Guide to the Philosophy of Religion*, ed. W. E. Mann (Oxford: Blackwell, 2004), 117–147. For an extended rebuttal, see Jonathan Weisberg, "Firing Squads and Fine-Tuning: Sober on the Design Argument," *British Journal for the Philosophy of Science* 56, no. 4 (2005): 809–821.
16 Adapted from John Leslie, *Universes* (New York: Routledge, 1989), 13–14.
17 I'm helped here by Luke Barnes.
18 To be more precise, in evaluating $P(B|C)$ we assume we are as yet ignorant about B's truth or falsity.
19 For an advanced introduction to the logic of plausible reasoning and a proof of Bayes' theorem, see E. T. Jaynes, *Probability Theory: The Logic of Science* (Cambridge: Cambridge University Press, 2003), 3–37.
20 To be precise, D is the proposition that the universe is the causal product of one or more intelligent agents, though for the sake of concision I will only say "agent" in the text.
21 See Timothy McGrew, Lydia McGrew, and Eric Vestrup, "Probabilities and the Fine-Tuning Argument: A Sceptical View," *Mind* 110 (2001): 1027–1038; Mark Colyvan, Jay L. Garfield, and Graham Priest, "Problems With the Argument From Fine Tuning," *Synthese* 145, no. 3 (2005): 325–338.
22 John Hawthorne and Yoaav Isaacs, "Misapprehensions about the Fine-Tuning Argument," *Royal Institute of Philosophy Supplement* 81 (2017): 147–154.
23 Neil Manson, "How Not to be Generous to Fine-Tuning Sceptics," *Religious Studies* (2018), 1–15, doi:10.1017/S0034412518000586.
24 Manson focuses on (a), discussing "the probability that there is a life-permitting universe if God exists" and asking "Why would God create anything at all?" ("How Not to be Generous to Fine-Tuning Sceptics," p. 1 and p. 2). But for the formulation of the FTA given here, it is (b) that is relevant.
25 See Rota, *Taking Pascal's Wager*, 121–124, including note 6.
26 See Jonathan Weisberg, "A Note on Design: What's Fine-Tuning Got to Do with It?," *Analysis* 70 (2010): 431–438; Roger White, "What Fine-Tuning's Got to Do with It: Reply to Weisberg," *Analysis* 71 (2011): 676–679; Jonathan Weisberg, "The Argument From Divine Indifference," *Analysis* (2012): 707–714; and Hawthorne and Isaacs, "Fine-Tuning," 150–154.

27 Lewis and Barnes, *A Fortunate Universe*, 313–322.
28 Robin Collins, "The Many-Worlds Hypothesis as an Explanation of Cosmic Fine-Tuning: An Alternative to Design?" *Faith and Philosophy* 22:5 (2005), 654–666, 659.
29 For an elaboration of this approach, see Rota *Taking Pascal's Wager*, 125–134.

Bibliography

Barnes, Luke. "The Fine-Tuning of the Universe for Intelligent Life," *Publications of the Astronomical Society of Australia* 29, no. 4 (2012): 529–564.

Bousso, Raphael, "The Cosmological Constant Problem, Dark Energy, and the Landscape of String Theory," *Pontificiae Academiae Scientiarum scripta varia* 119 (2011): 129–151. arXiv:1203.0307.

Carroll, Sean. "Does the Universe Need God?" in *The Blackwell Companion to Science and Christianity*, edited by James B. Stump and Alan G. Padgett. Malden, MA: Wiley-Blackwell, 2012.

Collins, Robin, "The Many-Worlds Hypothesis as an Explanation of Cosmic Fine-Tuning: An Alternative to Design?" *Faith and Philosophy* 22 (2005): 654–666.

Colyvan, Mark, Jay L. Garfield, and Graham Priest, "Problems With the Argument From Fine Tuning," *Synthese* 145, no. 3 (2005): 325–338.

Davies, Paul, *Cosmic Jackpot: Why Our Universe Is Just Right for Life,* Boston: Houghton Mifflin, 2007.

Greene, Brian, *The Hidden Reality: Parallel Universes and the Deep Laws of the Cosmos,* New York: Alfred A. Knopf, 2011.

Hawthorne, John, and Yoaav Isaacs, "Misapprehensions about the Fine-Tuning Argument," *Royal Institute of Philosophy Supplement* 81 (2017): 147–154.

Hawthorne, John, and Yoaav Isaacs, "'Fine-tuning Fine-tuning," in *Knowledge, Belief, and God: New Insights in Religious Epistemology*, edited by Matthew A. Benton, John Hawthorne, and Dani Rabinowitz, Oxford: Oxford University Press, 2018.

Jaynes, E. T., *Probability Theory: The Logic of Science,* Cambridge: Cambridge University Press, 2003.

Leslie, John, *Universes,* New York: Routledge, 1989.

Lewis, Geraint, and Luke Barnes, *A Fortunate Universe: Life in a Finely-Tuned Cosmos,* Cambridge: Cambridge University Press, 2016.

Manson, Neil, "How Not to be Generous to Fine-Tuning Sceptics," *Religious Studies*, 1–15 (2018), doi:10.1017/S0034412518000586.

McGrew, Timothy, Lydia McGrew, and Eric Vestrup, "Probabilities and the Fine-Tuning Argument: A Sceptical View," *Mind* 110 (2001): 1027–1038.

Rees, Martin, *Just Six Numbers: The Deep Forces That Shape the Universe*. New York: Basic Books, 2000.

Rota, Michael, *Taking Pascal's Wager: Faith, Evidence and the Abundant Life*, Downers Grove, IL: InterVarsity Press, 2016.

Sober, Elliott, "The Design Argument," in *Blackwell Guide to the Philosophy of Religion*, edited by W. E. Mann, Oxford: Blackwell, 2004.

Susskind, Leonard, *The Cosmic Landscape: String Theory and the Illusion of Intelligent Design*, New York: Back Bay Books, 2006.

Weisberg, Jonathan, "A Note on Design: What's Fine-Tuning Got to Do with It?" *Analysis* 70 (2010): 431–438.

Weisberg, Jonathan, "Firing Squads and Fine-Tuning: Sober on the Design Argument," *British Journal for the Philosophy of Science* 56, no. 4 (2005): 809–821.

Weisberg, Jonathan, "The Argument from Divine Indifference," *Analysis* (2012): 707–714.

White, Roger, "What Fine-Tuning's Got to Do with It: Reply to Weisberg," *Analysis* 71 (2011): 676–679.

5

The Argument from Biological Complexity

Michael J. Behe

1. Philosophical aspects of the argument

1.a. General characteristics

This chapter argues that advances in our understanding of the molecular level of life overwhelmingly support the conclusion that, to a very large degree, life is the intended product of a designing mind. Several general characteristics of the design argument will be noted here at the outset.

The first characteristic to note is that the argument for design from biochemistry is in large part an empirical argument. That is, it depends critically on our detailed understanding of the physical structures and processes of life. In turn, that means it depends on the progress of science in elucidating those structures and processes, and that the persuasiveness of the argument can shift with empirical discoveries. Such discoveries have been made since Darwin first put forward his theory.

It has been only since the middle of the twentieth century—a hundred years after Darwin's work, when the double helical structure of DNA and the irregular functional shape of the oxygen-binding protein myoglobin were discovered—that biology has begun to grasp the mechanisms of the molecular foundation of life. Over the past seventy years progress has accelerated enormously with the development of powerful new laboratory tools. An overarching discovery is that the foundational level of life is run by astoundingly complex molecular machinery. That key breakthrough drives much of the argument here. Furthermore, although it is an empirical observation, it is very secure; future work may show life to have greater functional intricacy than we now recognize, but it will not show it to have less.

In addition to empirical data, the argument for design from biochemistry requires logical ties to connect the data to the conclusion. Unlike other writers such as David Hume,[1] who cast the design argument mainly as one from analogy, Steven Meyer,[2] who sees it as an inference to the best explanation, or Elliott Sober,[3] who treats it as a likelihood argument, I consider the design argument to be an inductive one. That is, as we shall see, by considering how we draw conclusions that some inanimate systems were purposely designed, common elements can be extracted to guide us when attempting to decide if some biochemical systems were purposely designed.

The second characteristic of the argument for design from biochemistry to note initially is that, because it is in large part an empirical argument, then much like any good scientific argument it is formally falsifiable[4]—that is, future empirical discoveries may force a revision to, or even overturn, the biochemical design argument. One need not, of course, judge that outcome as probable to acknowledge that all empirical arguments are in principle falsifiable. An important corollary is that the design argument should not be criticized for being what it is—an inductive, empirical argument. Additionally, like any scientific argument, it cannot prove in a logical, deductive sense that all rival explanations are false. Rather, like them, it should be evaluated on how well it fits the empirical evidence.

A related limitation of the biochemical design argument is that it is restricted in scope. It is an argument from *physical evidence* to the conclusion of *design simpliciter*—to the bare conclusion that some physical systems were intentionally arranged. It leaves aside secondary questions for the present, such as: who did the designing? why? how? when? and so on. (In fact, such related questions do not even arise unless we first suspect something to have been designed.) It is not an argument, as is the "Fifth Way" of Thomas Aquinas, from *design* or *teleology* to the conclusion that God exists.[5] The biochemical argument gives reasons to think merely that much of life was purposely arranged. I emphasize that, by itself, it cannot be an argument for the existence of God. Even when successful, it only affirms the existence of an agent with the intelligence and ability to design life. It says nothing about other qualities that philosophical arguments have attributed to God, such as self-existence, incorporeality, eternality, benevolence, omniscience, and omnipotence.[6] Although, for some people, the empirical argument for design from biochemistry may increase the persuasiveness of such traditional philosophical arguments, or decrease the persuasiveness of arguments claiming to disprove the existence of God, taken alone it says nothing definitive about God.

1.b. Recognizing the work of a mind: a purposeful arrangement of parts

To understand the biochemical design argument, we must first understand how we recognize design in general. Philosophers have long grappled with the question of other minds—that is, how can we know that some other beings have minds?[7] After all, we cannot directly perceive the thoughts of other minds with our senses. For all we know, even other people (who physically resemble us), let alone animals, aliens, or more exotic possibilities, may be "zombies"—entities that behave in much the same way that we do, but have no inner mental life.[8] It's a fascinating, difficult, perhaps even unsolvable problem. But there is a more basic, much more accessible question: why do we even *suspect* that some things may have minds? Many things exist to which we are not tempted to attribute a mind: dirt, rocks, sand, and more. So why do we suspect some other things do in fact have minds? Or that things with minds have acted?

The eighteenth-century Scottish philosopher Thomas Reid pointed out that, although it cannot directly be observed, we infer intelligence—the existence of a mind—through its physical, empirical, observable effects:[9]

Now, every judgment of this kind is just one application of *the design principle*, the general principle that intelligence, wisdom, and other mental qualities in the cause can be inferred from their marks or signs in the effect. The things men say and do are effects, of which the speakers and doers are the causes. We perceive the effects through our senses, but the causes are behind the scene. We simply *infer* their existence and their degrees from what we observe in the effects. From wise conduct we infer wisdom in the cause, and so on.

What are those observable marks of intelligence? The relevant definition of *design* is "the purposeful arrangement of parts."[10] Thus the key is this: *because minds can choose to order for a purpose whatever is within their power to manipulate, intelligence is detected by perceiving a purposeful arrangement of parts.* That is *the* way, the *only* way, that we can discern the existence of other minds and their intelligence. Conversely, whenever we see parts that appear to have been arranged intentionally—arranged for a purpose—we conclude with greater or lesser conviction that a mind is behind the arrangement, either proximately or remotely.

For the goal of detecting intelligence, the word *parts* is construed very broadly, as "something determined in relation to something that includes it"[11]—that is, as any facet contributing to the design. In human speech, we purposefully arrange sounds to form words. In writing, we arrange letters. In constructing machinery, we arrange mechanical or electrical parts. In planning a surprise party, we may arrange not only physical objects such as tables and chairs, and written words to write invitations, but also the very timing of events as well, such as when the invitees are to gather in secret and when the guest-of-honor is to be led under pretense to the party's pre-arranged location. Purpose can also be discerned in coordinated motions and gestures. Sign language is a straightforward example. Another is an organism arranging its muscular activity to move itself, such as a runner headed toward a finish line or an eagle swooping toward the surface of a lake. In all of these various illustrations we recognize a mind behind the arrangements.

Design may occur at multiple independent or hierarchical levels, or between undesigned levels. For example, formulating materials to make ink, arranging ink into letters, letters into words, words into sentences, and sentences into paragraphs are all different levels of design;[12] the higher levels (sentences, paragraphs) make use of the lower ones (ink, letters, words), but go beyond each of them. With machinery, many parts (for example, nuts, bolts, gears and so on) may show their own designs in their specific shapes and other properties; the organization of those designed parts is a separate level of design. For any particular example, there may be no reason to suspect purposeful design at a higher or lower level. The chemicals that go into ink may be undesigned, natural inorganic materials. The paragraph into which some ink is arranged may be found on a crumpled piece of paper in a wastebasket, with no indication that it is part of a larger design such as a book or encyclopedia. Similar arguments can be made for machinery, party planning, or any design.

A critical characteristic of the empirical design argument to grasp is that it is *quantitative*—the more parts there are, and the more closely they are arranged to fit the purpose, the much more confident we can be in a conclusion of design. If Scrabble letters were spilled onto a table, we would positively expect to observe some letter or letters to be right-side-up by chance. Right-side-up letters near each other that formed a short word might appear in the mix by accident. But as the spilled letters were seen to form a longer word, sentence, or paragraph, our confidence in design would approach certainty. The same progression happens as mechanical parts form an ever more complex machine, or as the closer and closer timing of events permits a surprise party.

The quantitative aspect of the design argument is a reflection of the fact that, as Thomas Reid noted,[13] we judge the degree of intelligence by the difficulty of arranging parts for a particular purpose. Just as longer words formed by spilled Scrabble letters more strongly indicate design, offering wise counsel to a troubled youth demonstrates more wisdom than giving foolish advice; solving a calculus problem shows more intelligence than adding two integers; building a skyscraper shows more than a beehive; and so on. It is necessary to realize, however, that an agent might be more intelligent than its actions show. For example, a person we see adding two integers might also have the ability to do calculus.

The topic of how one determines what the purpose of an arrangement of parts might be deserves much greater consideration than can be given here. The ultimate, or even proximate, intentions of an intelligent agent may be obscure, and that may interfere with our judgments in marginal cases. Nonetheless, in many other cases at least the proximate purpose is plain from the physical arrangement itself. For example, the arrangement of parts that constitutes a camera strongly attests to its purposeful design, even if the ultimate purpose of the designing agent was to, say, become wealthy. Similarly, the arrangement of the parts of an eye betrays its purposeful design, no matter what the ultimate purpose may be. As a rule of thumb, one should look to the proximate purpose of an arrangement of parts when judging its possible design. Fortunately, the molecular machinery discovered in the cell often exhibits very strong proximate purpose in the arrangement of its parts.

1.c. Cleanthes' implicit induction

I consider the argument for design to be an inductive one, not an argument from analogy or likelihood, or as an inference to the best explanation as others do. In an inductive argument, one can reason from multiple particular instances of a phenomenon to a general conclusion. For example, black clothes, black paint, and black rocks all become warmer in sunlight than otherwise-similar white objects; thus it is probable that the next class of black objects will be found to become warmer in sunlight than otherwise-similar white objects. Notice that the particular instances being compared differ from each other in many ways. Yet the induction holds because the conclusion depends only on one shared property—blackness. Therefore to call such an induction into doubt one would have to show that dissimilarities make a relevant difference to the property under consideration. Furthermore, an induction may be greatly strengthened over time by new knowledge. For example, with progress in understanding the physics and chemistry of light absorption by pigments, the reason that black objects become warmer in the sunshine has been placed on a foundation that is much firmer than that of the simple association with which it began.

Failure to recognize the correct form of a design argument can lead to much confusion. In an analogy, the more attributes that the analogized subjects have in common, the stronger the likelihood they will share an additional characteristic under discussion. In Hume's 1779 classic, *Dialogues Concerning Natural Religion*, which features characters representing different views on natural theology, the skeptical Philo criticizes Cleanthes' argument that the universe is analogous to a human machine and that the analogy demonstrates not only the intelligence but also other attributes of God. Philo objects that the universe strikes him as more like an animal or vegetable than as a machine. In any event, Philo points out, there are many differences between the universe and human artifacts and so the analogy is quite weak. Yet with one example Cleanthes reduces Philo to befuddlement. Cleanthes asks Philo to suppose:[14]

> that an articulate voice were heard in the clouds, much louder and more melodious than any which human art could ever reach; suppose that this voice were extended in the same instant over all nations ... [C]ould you possibly hesitate a moment concerning the cause of this voice, and must instantly ascribe it to some design or purpose?

Philo makes no substantive reply; eventually the dialog drifts on to other topics. What is different about this example?

The difference between Cleanthes' successful voice-in-the-clouds example and his unsuccessful other examples is that the case of the voice is an implicit induction, not an analogy. Whenever we have heard articulate voices we have found them to come from intelligent sources (either proximate or remote). Thus if we heard a voice coming from a cloud we would conclude the same. What's more, we have a deeper reason to conclude the involvement of intelligence. We know that an intelligent agent has the ability to manipulate parts for a purpose. We know of no other cause that has that ability. (Hume has Philo briefly present the design argument also as an inductive argument, but as a particularly careless one—that if we wish to show by induction that our world was designed *in toto*, we must have experience of other worlds that were designed *in toto*.)[15]

In the passage quoted above, Cleanthes tries to push his example further than mere design, so we must be careful to distinguish separate, critical aspects of it. Only the articulate voice—that is, the purposeful arrangement of sounds—is needed to demonstrate an intelligent source. The minimum degree of its intelligence is manifest in whatever message it conveys. Cleanthes adds superfluous attributes—the message's loudness and melodic nature—apparently to steer the conversation toward God himself, but neither of those are needed to demonstrate bare intelligence. One detail—that the voice is heard simultaneously in all nations—is intended, it seems to me, both to push the conclusion toward God and to rule out the possibility that just a single person had an auditory hallucination (by indicating that the knowledge is universally shared). But if, instead of an ephemeral voice, one were discussing a persisting physical object such as a manuscript or a machine—which could be examined by multiple people over time—then hallucination is easily ruled out.

Hume wrote in the eighteenth century. If we moderns heard a voice from a cloud we might think it was a broadcast from an airplane or some other technological trick—no need to think otherwise. Yet whether the voice came from God, aliens in a space ship, a human ventriloquist, a radio, a recording, or some technical trick whose details we did not know, like Cleanthes we would certainly "ascribe it to some design or purpose." We would easily recognize the intelligence in the purposefully arranged sounds of the message.

Whether the agent behind the voice were friendly, hostile, or indifferent to us is much more difficult to conclude than whether it is simply intelligent, as is the question of whether the agent is also an omnipotent being responsible for the whole universe. Like others before and after him, Cleanthes ran into trouble by confounding separate issues and trying to claim too much. Design itself is abundantly clear in the empirical observation of a purposeful arrangement of parts. Drawing conclusions beyond mere design requires other kinds of arguments. However, the possible lack of soundness of downstream arguments—concerning who, what, how, why, and so on—does not negate the original conclusion of purposeful design.

With the preceding discussion as background, the inductive biochemical argument for design can be stated as follows:

(1) We know from experience that intelligent beings can have purposes and that, to achieve a purpose, they can choose to arrange whatever is within their power to manipulate. As a result, the action of an intelligent being can be detected by perceiving a purposeful arrangement of parts.

(2) Whenever we are familiar with a causal chain that produces a sufficiently complex, purposeful arrangement of inanimate parts, we always find one of the causes to be an intelligent agent, acting either proximately or remotely in the causal chain.

(3) The molecular basis of life consists of inanimate molecules (such as proteins, polysaccharides, lipids, and nucleic acids). In living beings, these molecules are often found combined in extraordinarily complex, purposeful arrangements.

(4) Claims of marvelous abilities for Darwinian processes notwithstanding, we know of no unintelligent process that, when examined in sufficient detail, mimics the ability of intelligence to arrange parts for a purpose.

(5) By (1), (2), (3), and (4) we are justified in concluding that a cause of many complex, functional, molecular aspects of life was an intelligent being, acting either proximately or remotely.

A fundamental difference between living and non-living systems is reproduction and the consequent ability of life to undergo variation and selection. As I will argue in the rest of this chapter and as I've shown at much greater length in previous writings,[16] however, although those factors can affect life marginally they are thoroughly unable to account for the machinery of life. Reproduction, variation, and selection have no ability to arrange parts for a purpose. Therefore, the inductive argument for design applies to both animate and inanimate systems.

2. Empirical aspects of the argument

2.a. A very brief history

The first part of this chapter discussed the logical underpinnings of the design argument. I now turn to a discussion of the progress of science on relevant empirical topics.

For virtually all of recorded history most people believed nature in general and life in particular to have been purposely designed. For example, in *On the Usefulness of the Parts of the Body*, the Greek pagan Galen—the most eminent physician of the classical era—concluded that the human body is the result of a "supremely intelligent and powerful divine Craftsman," that is, "the result of intelligent design."[17] Fifteen hundred years after Galen, the English clergyman William Paley made the strongest argument for design to that date, incorporating into it much biology that had been unknown to Galen. The very anatomies of the eye, muscles, blood vessels, and more were strong pointers to design, he argued, for the same reason that deducing a pocket-watch found in a field was designed:[18] "For this reason, and for no other, namely, that when we come to inspect the watch, we perceive that its several parts are framed and put together for a purpose ... [T]he inference we think is inevitable, that the watch must have had a maker." When multiple parts are ordered to each other, and by that arrangement the system acquires the ability to perform a function such as keeping time, then the inference to design is powerfully justified, thought Paley.

Although he admired Paley's work in his youth, as a result of his own discoveries while acting as the ship's naturalist of the HMS *Beagle* Charles Darwin later proposed that a hitherto-unrecognized natural process could mimic a designing intelligence: random variation sifted by natural selection. In brief, Darwin saw that there was variation in each species. Some members of a species might be bigger than others, some faster, some brighter in color. He realized that not all organisms that were born could survive to reproduce, simply because the limited resources of nature would not permit an unlimited expansion of a species' population size. From that Darwin reasoned there would be a struggle for those limited natural resources. A member of a species whose biological variation gave it an edge in the struggle to survive would have an increased chance to leave offspring—that is, natural selection. If the variation could be inherited, then the next generation would be enriched in organisms that carried it, and the next generation even more so, until the variation became the norm. At that point the species as a whole would have changed from what it had been. Many subsequent repetitions of the same process, starting from other random variations, might over long times change a species into something quite different from the ancestral form.

It seemed to be a promising idea. However, Darwin was severely handicapped by the relatively primitive state of biological knowledge of his time. For example, in the mid-nineteenth century physicists and chemists still debated whether molecules were real entities.[19] And the cell, which is now known to be the foundation of life, was then thought to be simple—in the words of Ernst Haeckel, a "simple little lump of albuminous combination of carbon."[20] Thus Darwin and his contemporaries were ignorant of a tacit-yet-key factor of his theory—the nature of heredity.

Scientific progress in the twentieth century revealed that the basis of life occurs at the cellular and molecular levels. Beginning with Watson and Crick's elucidation of the double helical structure of DNA[21] and Kendrew's solving of the structure of myoglobin,[22] research in the second half of the twentieth century showed that the foundation of life is run by large, complex, molecular machines, and that mutations in the machinery were far more likely to damage it than to improve it. Accelerating progress in the twenty-first century in the ability to sequence DNA has allowed scientists to determine the identities of many beneficial mutations. As discussed below, a large majority of those, too, damage, rather than improve, molecular machinery.

2.b. Problems for Darwin's theory

(i) The critical question of randomness

To properly evaluate the intelligent design argument, it is crucial to distinguish the question of the descent of modern organisms from ancient ancestors from the question of what might have driven that process—what might have caused such fantastic changes to occur? As noted by Ernst Mayr,[23] what is often referred to as a single idea—"Darwin's theory"—is actually an amalgam of a handful of separable ideas: 1) species change with time; 2) the common descent of all organisms (branching evolution); 3) the gradualness of evolution (no saltations, no discontinuities; 4) the multiplication of species (the origin of diversity); 5) natural selection (the directional driver of evolution), which in Darwin's time implicitly included the idea of random variation. Mayr points out that, although most biologists in the decades after the publication of *The Origin of Species* readily accepted the proposal of common descent, they were skeptical of Darwin's proposed mechanism of evolution. That remains the case for many biologists today as modifications and revisions to Darwin's theory continue to be proposed.[24] It is specifically the *Darwinian mechanism* that the argument for design from biochemistry challenges. It does not challenge the proposals of common descent, or gradualness, or other parts of Darwin's theory, but only the role of randomness.

(ii) The major conceptual difficulty for Darwin's theory

The preeminent conceptual difficulty for Darwin's mechanism as the chief driver for the development of life is its need to account for the gradual evolution of life's intricate, complex, functional systems without intelligent guidance. The Oxford biologist Richard Dawkins explains the need for gradual evolution:[25]

> A key feature of evolution is its gradualness. This is a matter of principle rather than fact ... Evolution is very possibly not, in actual fact, always gradual. But it must be gradual when it is being used to explain the coming into existence of complicated, apparently designed objects, like eyes. For if it is not gradual in these cases, it ceases to have any explanatory power at all.

Yet many aspects of life certainly do not appear to be amenable to gradual evolutionary construction. Within a decade of the publication of the *Origin of Species* the English biologist St. George Mivart challenged the theory on the grounds of the "incipient stages of useful structures." Many biological systems, Mivart argued, could not plausibly have been useful to an organism as inchoate structures.[26]

> "Natural Selection," simply and by itself, is potent to explain the maintenance or the further extension and development of favourable variations, which are at once sufficiently considerable to be useful from the first to the individual possessing them. But Natural Selection utterly fails to account for the conservation and development of the minute and rudimentary beginnings, the slight and infinitesimal commencements of structures, however useful those structures may afterwards become.

Although he tried to respond to some of Mivart's examples in later editions of the *Origin*, Darwin's attempts were once again severely hamstrung by a lack of understanding of the molecular and cellular foundation of life. Consider Darwin's oft-cited example of possible evolutionary steps leading to the vertebrate eye, beginning with a light-sensitive spot, proceeding through a pinhole eye, then to an eye with a lens.[27] Yet Darwin had no idea of the many complex molecular structures that underlie any of those structures. As he wrote of the light-sensitive spot, "How a nerve comes to be sensitive to light hardly concerns us more than how life itself originated."[28] Whether or not his hypothetical scheme was workable depended on a multitude of factors that resided at a level of life that was unknown to him.

Related to Mivart's argument about the "incipient stages of useful structures" is the argument of "irreducible complexity," which becomes clearest at the molecular, foundational level of life. I defined *irreducible complexity* in 1996 in *Darwin's Black Box* as "a single system which is composed of several well-matched, interacting parts that contribute to the basic function, and where the removal of any one of the parts causes the system to effectively cease functioning." To illustrate the concept for the general reading public, I pointed to the example of a common mechanical mousetrap consisting of multiple pieces. Each of the five larger pieces (platform, spring, hammer, holding bar, and catch) pictured in Figure 5.1 is needed for the mousetrap to work. There are also several small staples holding the larger pieces together. The correct placement of the staples is also needed for the function of the system. Furthermore, several of the pieces have complex shapes and other properties that are needed for system function. A mechanical mousetrap is a relatively simple machine. By extension, more complex machinery is very likely to be irreducibly complex (IC) as well.

If any IC systems occurred at the molecular level of life, the difficulty they would present to Darwin's mechanism is readily apparent. Natural selection requires some function to exist before it can be selected. Yet for IC systems, the function appears only when the system is complete. Thus the straightforward conclusion is that evolutionary construction of IC systems cannot be guided by a Darwinian mechanism.

Since the introduction of this concept twenty-five years ago, two main lines of response have been offered by Darwinian biologists. First, H. Allen Orr pointed to the writings of the early twentieth-century geneticist H. J. Muller, who wrote that a new feature *B* may be added to an already functioning organ *A*, and over time that new

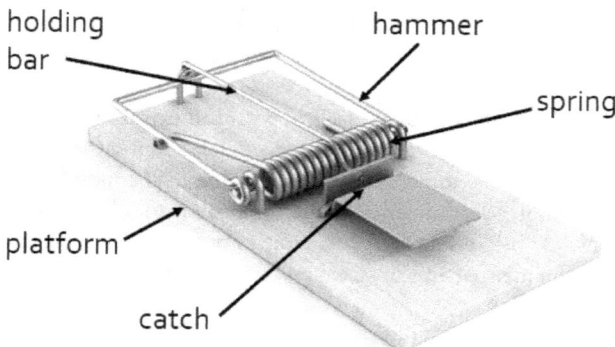

Figure 5.1 A mechanical mousetrap with multiple parts (Ilin Sergey/Shutterstock).

feature is integrated so thoroughly that removing it breaks the functions of both *A* and *B*.[29] Thus—although by hypothesis it developed gradually—the combined organ might appear to need both parts *A* and *B*. Unfortunately, as I criticized it, the argument is fatally vague.[30] What *A* and *B* may represent at the molecular level Muller had no way of knowing and Orr does not say. It is quite difficult to see what parts *A* and *B* would correspond to for a mousetrap. As we'll see below, the same difficulty applies for molecular machinery.

The second main line of response by Darwinian biologists to the problem of irreducible complexity is to speculate about indirect routes to complex systems. Brown University biologist Kenneth Miller has argued that parts of a mousetrap might be useful in other roles, for example as a tie clip, paper weight, and so on.[31] However, as H. Allen Orr agreed, indirect routes to a complex structure that switch functions/roles are very unlikely to be successful. As he wrote:[32]

> Second, we might think that some of the parts of an irreducibly complex system evolved step by step for some other purpose and were then recruited wholesale to a new function. But this is also unlikely. You may as well hope that half your car's transmission will suddenly help out in the airbag department. Such things might happen very, very rarely, but they surely do not offer a general solution to irreducible complexity.

Selection on a simple paperweight would not be expected to produce a tie clip, and selection on a tie clip would not be expected to produce a mousetrap. Like the first main line of response, the second one also remains utterly unsupported by experiment.

(iii) The unexpectedly, extraordinarily intricate physical foundation of life

Beginning in the 1950s with the development of X-ray diffraction techniques for the elucidation of the structures of DNA and proteins, science has steadily uncovered more and more of the molecular workings of life. Even several decades ago Bruce Alberts, then president of the National Academy of Sciences, could write:[33]

> We have always underestimated cells. Undoubtedly we still do today. But at least we are no longer as naive as we were when I was a graduate student in the 1960s... The chemistry that makes life possible is much more elaborate and sophisticated than anything we students had ever considered... Indeed, the entire cell can be viewed as a factory that contains an elaborate network of interlocking assembly lines, each of which is composed of a set of large protein machines. Why do we call the large protein assemblies that underlie cell function protein machines? Precisely because, like the machines invented by humans to deal efficiently with the macroscopic world, these protein assemblies contain highly coordinated moving parts.

Since Alberts wrote those words, the recognized sophistication of the machinery of life has increased enormously. In order to give the lay reader a taste of the functional complexity of the molecular level of life, below I briefly describe one example of such machinery.

(1) *The structure of the bacterial flagellum*

The bacterial flagellum is literally an outboard motor that some bacteria use to swim. Since its very structure so clearly embodies its purpose, the flagellum has rightly been called the "poster child" of intelligent design.[34] As illustrated by the cartoon in Figure 5.2, the structure consists of a number of discrete parts that work together to produce flagellar rotary motion. As labeled in the figure, the long, whip-like, tail filament acts as a propeller, pushing against the watery environment as it is rotated by the motor, propelling the bacterium forward. The propeller is attached to the drive shaft of the structure by means of a "hook" region, which acts as a universal joint. The purpose of a universal joint is to smoothly transmit the rotary motion from the plane of the motor to the propeller, which is oriented in a different plane. The motor itself is constructed to use a flow of acid (protons) from the exterior of the cell to the interior to power its rotation, much as the flow of water over a dam can turn a turbine. The motor is encircled by a stator against which the motor pushes, and which keeps the apparatus stationary within the plane of the bacterial cell's membrane. Other parts of the flagellum act as a bushing to allow the drive shaft to pass through the cell membrane.

The description above, of course, is quite superficial. Each of the parts mentioned itself consists of one or more complex proteins, many of whose specific structural details are necessary for its subfunction. As an example, consider just the flagellar hook. Details of the working of the hook/universal joint have recently been elucidated by the powerful new technique of cryoelectron microscopy. The structure was seen to be composed of multiple copies of the ~400-amino-acid-residue protein FlgE arranged

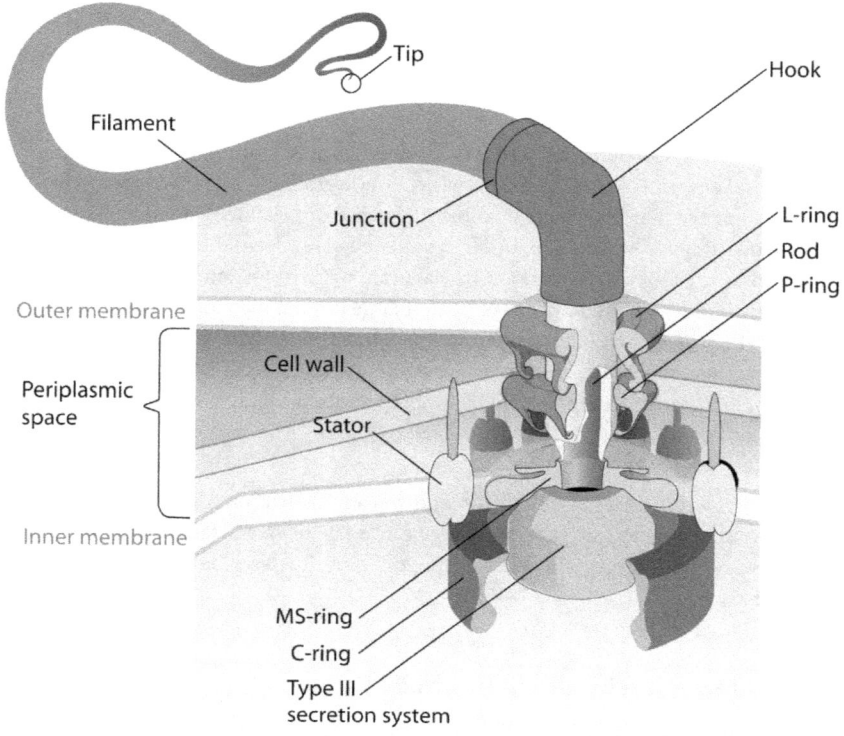

Figure 5.2 The bacterial flagellum (Wikimedia Commons).

into eleven protofilaments that form a hollow microtubular structure. In order for the reader to glimpse its complexity, a short excerpt from the paper is provided below:[35]

> Dynamic changes in intermolecular interactions. The smooth compression and extension of the protofilament [of the hook] are achieved also by dynamic changes in intersubunit interactions. The overall changes of intersubunit interactions can be depicted well by comparing two sets of models, each consisting of an array of four neighboring subunits, in which the middle two subunits are from the shortest and longest protofilaments, respectively. Domains D0 and Dc form one compact domain D0–Dc consisting of the N- and C-terminal α-helices and a long β-hairpin (residues 1–71 and 358–402), and this domain is tilted by about 17° from the tubular axis of the hook. Within each protofilament, the bottom of the N-terminal helix of the upper subunit is located on the top of the C-terminal helix with relatively large gaps of 6.3 and 12.5 Å in the short and long protofilaments, respectively. The bottom of the C-terminal helix of the upper subunit axially overlaps with the top of the C-terminal helix of the lower subunit to allow their mutual sliding for protofilament compression and extension. The relative disposition of the C-terminal helices between the neighboring protofilaments is

well maintained between subunits 0 and 5 but shows a slight axial shift between subunits 0 and 6 and a larger axial shift between subunits 0 and 11. Residues Gly 329–Asp 330 of subunit 0 at the tip of a short β-hairpin of domain D1 interact with residues Ala 39–Asp 40 of subunit 5 in the distal part of the long β-hairpin of domain Dc, and this interaction does not change by protofilament compression and extension, indicating the importance of the long β-hairpin of domain Dc for the structural stability of the hook....

As the above excerpt illustrates, a profound lesson of science's deeper penetration into the molecular foundation of life is that, for molecular machinery to function, an astounding number of details must be attended to.

(2) Regulation of flagellum construction

The structure of molecular machinery such as the flagellum is the end result of a process of carefully coordinated construction. Unlike human-made machines, which can be assembled by factory workers fitting the proper pieces in the proper order, cellular machines have to be put together by a fully automated process. At the least, this requires the protein pieces of the final machinery to have geometrically and chemically complementary surfaces with which to bind specifically to the proper neighboring pieces in the final assembly and to avoid improper interactions with incorrect proteins. Lacking such binding surfaces, the pieces would float apart. Thus, even if analogous proteins that had all other properties of the flagellum components were present in a cell, but lacked the necessary complementary surfaces to bind their correct partners, no functioning machine would be produced.

For particularly complex machinery such as the flagellum much more is required.[36] The protein pieces of the machinery have to be available at the correct time and place. This requires the assistance of other proteins that do not appear in the final structure but are necessary for its construction. Briefly, the multiple genes coding for proteins of the flagellum are grouped together in a bacterial genome.[37] The first gene to be activated is a "master regulator", which codes for a protein that activates a second set of genes. This set contains the components of the flagellum that appear in its base—inside the cell and cell membrane—and that are needed to help build the more distant parts. Among the genes activated by the master regulator is one that codes for a secondary regulator that activates a second set of flagellar genes, ones that code for the middle regions. Among the genes activated by the secondary regulator is one that codes for a tertiary regulator that activates the last set of genes, ones that code for the outside region of the flagellar tail and cap. Among these genes are also ones that code for chaperone proteins—proteins which bind to and escort component parts to the flagellum construction sites but which do not appear in the final structure.

3. Criticism and replies

As part of a discussion of why the irreducibly complex nature of the bacterial flagellum is a severe difficulty for Darwinian evolution and a strong pointer to purposeful design, in 1996 in *Darwin's Black Box* I surveyed the scientific literature and showed there was up to that point no serious scientific work directed at showing how such a complex, functional structure could be produced by random mutation and natural selection. Fully a decade later several Darwinian biologists agreed with that assessment and issued a call to arms for the research to begin. Under the uncertain section-title "An experimental research programme?" the authors candidly admitted that no research had been done on flagellum evolution until that point.[38] "In recent years, flagellar biologists have made astonishing progress in understanding the structure, function and regulation of bacterial flagella ... However, the flagellar research community has scarcely begun to consider how these systems have evolved."

Since its publication in 2006, however, the authors' challenge hasn't been taken up, either by other researchers or by the authors themselves. Twenty-five years after *Darwin's Black Box* highlighted the difficulty, the stunningly complex molecular machine is no closer to receiving a Darwinian account. This includes any possible scenario in which the type III secretory system (TTSS) might have been a stepping stone on a Darwinian pathway to the flagellum. Because it contains proteins similar to some of the proteins of the flagellum, some biologists speculated that such might be the case.[39] However, no experiments or detailed explanations showing how a Darwinian mechanism might have produced the TTSS, flagellum, or a transition between the two have been published. What's more, the current consensus is that the TTSS is likely to have been derived from the flagellum rather than the reverse.[40] Yet a scenario in which an unexplained, more-complex machine loses parts to give rise to a functioning, less-complex machine is not a Darwinian explanation for either.

3.a. Comparative difficulty

In discussing the evolution of such an enormously complex molecular machine as the bacterial flagellum, it can be quite difficult to do justice to the scale of the problem. The previous quotation from a paper on the details of just the hook region was one attempt to do so. Another way to begin to grasp the scale is to consider the challenge to the Darwinian mechanism of explaining even a much simpler interactive structure. Arguably the simplest biochemical structure that requires two components to interact is a disulfide (sometimes spelled "disulphide") bond. A disulfide bond is formed when the side chains of two cysteine amino acid residues react with each other. Thus, to form a disulfide bond, two cysteines are required—one by itself is insufficient. An analogy from ordinary life is a simple hook-and-eye latch, which can be used to hold a door closed. The hook or eye by itself doesn't work for that purpose; the combination is needed.

Yet even the formation of a simple disulfide bond by Darwinian processes is difficult to account for. In 2008 the journal *Biology Direct* published a theoretical, "concept" paper entitled "The Look-ahead Effect of Phenotypic Mutations," which concerned the problem. As the authors wrote,[41] "The evolution of complex molecular traits such as disulphide bridges often requires multiple mutations. The intermediate steps in such evolutionary trajectories are likely to be selectively neutral or deleterious. Therefore, large populations and long times may be required to evolve such traits."

The journal editor Eugene Koonin was excited about the prospect of addressing that fundamental problem within a Darwinian framework. Acting as one of the reviewers of the manuscript himself, he commented:[42]

> The idea of this paper is as brilliant as it is pretty obvious ... in retrospect. A novel solution is offered to the old enigma of the evolution of complex features in proteins that require two or more mutations (emergence of a disulphide bond is a straightforward example) ... From my perspective, this is a genuinely important work.

In the intervening years the proposal has not received much attention, and there are a number of difficulties with it.[43] However, my point here is that the enthusiasm Koonin (a prominent scientist) exhibits in his comment bespeaks the severe difficulty of accounting in Darwinian terms for even the *simplest* example of cooperativity at the molecular level of life. Yet a theory that can't easily account for a simpler example is quite unlikely to account for a much more complex one.

3.b. Devolution

The difficulty of accounting for the evolution of the early stages of complex systems—including irreducible ones—is the chief conceptual problem for the Darwinian mechanism, because a blind, undirected process cannot plan ahead. The difficulty was evident even in the nineteenth century when the molecular basis of life was unknown. As science has advanced, further severe fundamental problems have been uncovered. The most serious of these is the nature of the molecular changes—mutations—underlying helpful, positively selected organismal traits.

As we now know, mutations are changes in molecules—in the protein machinery of the cell and the DNA that codes for it. Thus properly evaluating the scope of Darwin's mechanism requires the ability to identify and track underlying mutations over many generations. That was for all intents and purposes impossible to do in the necessary detail until just the past few decades. It has only been about twenty years since the technology to easily sequence DNA has become available. As the sophistication of the technology increases and its price decreases, more and more pertinent data are accumulating.

As I discussed in *Darwin Devolves* (2019), a surprising result of evolutionary DNA sequencing experiments is that the large majority of beneficial mutations that sweep through a species's population as a consequence of natural selection have been found to actually *degrade* or *destroy* preexisting genes. The phenomenon appears to be universal; it can be seen over short and long time scales, and in organisms ranging from bacteria to mammals. For example, a handful of mutations have been selected in the past ten thousand years in populations of humans who live in malarious regions of the world.[44] The mutations confer a measure of resistance to the deadly disease. Yet most of the mutations break pre-existing genes. Apparently the loss of the gene is less deleterious to the species than is susceptibility to malaria. In the largest laboratory evolution experiment ever reported with microorganisms—lasting more than 50,000 generations and involving trillions of *E. coli* cells—the thirty most beneficial, highly selected mutations all likely degraded or destroyed the genes in which they occurred.[45] Most mutations that are associated with the distinctive traits of dog breeds likewise are degradative,[46] as are most beneficial mutations distinctive for polar bears.[47] Random mutation and natural selection thus explain some adaptations, but not the building up of complex molecular systems.

Natural selection will cause a sufficiently beneficial mutation to sweep to fixation in a population, so that every member of a species then has the mutant gene. Thus beneficial degraded or nonfunctional genes will take over a population, causing a steady depletion of the species' genetic patrimony. This seems likely to be an insuperable problem for an unintelligent, undirected evolutionary mechanism such as Darwin proposed. As I argued in *Darwin Devolves*, there are compelling empirical reasons to think that Darwinian processes can produce new species and genera by degradative evolution, but cannot reach the biological classification level of family.

4. Conclusion

In the nineteenth century Charles Darwin proposed a novel non-design explanation for the complex features of life—natural selection sieving random variations in populations of creatures. However, accelerating progress in science has demonstrated that the foundation of life lies at the molecular level. There the tasks of life are accomplished by machinery of staggering complexity and detail, much of it irreducible. Such interactive systems are profound challenges to any undirected, unintelligent mechanism. Progress in the new millennium shows that most helpful, beneficial mutations work to degrade or destroy genes. Thus, as a candidate to explain major constructive changes in life, Darwin's mechanism has been thrown into severe doubt.

The work of a mind can be recognized in a purposeful arrangement of parts. Purposeful arrangements fill the foundation of life. The special characteristics of life compared to inanimate systems—that is, reproduction, and the potential for variation and selection—possess no ability to purposefully arrange parts. Thus the argument for intelligent design applies to both animate and inanimate systems. From these considerations we can confidently conclude that much of life was purposely designed.

Notes

1 David Hume, *Dialogues Concerning Natural Religion*, 1779, London: Penguin Books, 1990.
2 S. C. Meyer, *Signature in the Cell: DNA and the Evidence for Intelligent Design*, New York: HarperOne, 2009, 155–159.
3 E. Sober, "The Design Argument," in *God and Design: the Teleological Argument and Modern Science*, ed. Neil A. Manson, New York: Routledge, 2003, 27–54.
4 K. R. Popper, *Realism and the Aim of Science: the Postscript to the Logic of Scientific Discovery*, Totowa, NJ: Rowman and Littlefield, 1983.
5 Thomas Aquinas, *Summa Theologiae*, New York: Benziger Bros., 1947.

6   E. Feser, *Five Proofs of the Existence of God,* San Francisco: Ignatius Press, 2017.
7   A. Avramides, "Other Minds," *The Stanford Encyclopedia of Philosophy,* ed. Edward N. Zalta, 2019, https://plato.stanford.edu/archives/sum2019/entries/other-minds/.
8   R. Kirk, "Zombies," *The Stanford Encyclopedia of Philosophy,* ed. Edward N. Zalta, 2019, https://plato.stanford.edu/archives/spr2019/entries/zombies/.
9   T. Reid, *Essays on the Intellectual Powers of Man,* 1785, New York: Garland Pub., 1971, Essay VI, Chapter VI.
10 "design," The Free Dictionary, https://www.thefreedictionary.com/design
11 "part," The Free Dictionary, https://www.thefreedictionary.com/part
12 M. Polanyi, "Life's Irreducible Structure," *Science* 160 (1968): 1308–1312.
13 Reid, *Essays on the Intellectual Powers of Man.*
14 Ibid.
15 Ibid.
16 M. J. Behe, *Darwin's Black Box: the Biochemical Challenge to Evolution,* New York: The Free Press, 1996; M. J. Behe, *The Edge of Evolution: the Search for the Limits of Darwinism,* New York: The Free Press, 2007; M. J. Behe, *Darwin Devolves: the New Science about DNA That Challenges Evolution,* New York: HarperOne, 2019.
17 M. J. Schiefsky, "Galen's Teleology and Functional Explanation," *Oxford Studies in Ancient Philosophy* 33 (2007): 369–400.
18 William Paley, *Natural Theology* (New York: The American Tract Society, 1802), 9–10.
19 J. C. Maxwell, "Molecules," *Nature* 8 (1873): 437–441.
20 J. Farley, *The Spontaneous Generation Controversy from Descartes to Oparin,* Baltimore: The Johns Hopkins University Press, 1979, 73.
21 J. D. Watson and F. H. Crick, "Molecular Structure of Nucleic Acid," *Nature* 171 (1953): 738.
22 J. C. Kendrew et al., "'Structure of Myoglobin: a Three-dimensional Fourier Synthesis at 2 Å. Resolution," *Nature* 185 (1960): 422–427.
23 E. Mayr, *What Evolution Is,* New York: Basic Books, 2001, 86.
24 K. Laland et al., "Does Evolutionary Theory Need a Rethink?," *Nature* 514 (2014): 161–164.
25 R. Dawkins, *River out of Eden: a Darwinian View of Life,* New York: Basic Books, 1995, 83.
26 S. Mivart, *On the Genesis of Species,* London: Macmillan, 1871.
27 Charles Darwin, *Origin of Species,* 1872, 6th edition, New York: New York University Press, 1988.
28 Darwin, *Origin of Species,* 151.
29 H. A. Orr, "Darwin v. Intelligent Design (Again)," *Boston Review,* (1996): 28–31.
30 M. J. Behe, "Reply to My Critics: a Response to Reviews of *Darwin's Black Box: the Biochemical Challenge to Evolution,*" *Biology and Philosophy* 16 (2001): 685–709.
31 K. Miller, "The Mousetrap Analogy or Trapped by Design," http://www.millerandlevine.com/km/evol/DI/Mousetrap.html.
32 Orr, "Darwin v. Intelligent Design (Again)."
33 B. A. Alberts, "The Cell as a Collection of Protein Machines: Preparing the Next Generation of Molecular Biologists," *Cell* 93 (1998): 291–294.
34 K. R. Miller, "The Flagellum Unspun," in *Debating Design: from Darwin to DNA,* eds. William A. Dembski, Michael Ruse, Cambridge: Cambridge University Press, 2004, 81.
35 T. Kato et al., "Structure of the Native Supercoiled Flagellar Hook as a Universal Joint," *Nature Communications* 10 (2019): 5295–5302.

36 T. Minamino and K. Namba, "Self-assembly and Type III Protein Export of the Bacterial Flagellum," *Journal of Molecular Microbiology and Biotechnology* 7 (2001): 5–17.
37 P. Aldridge and K. T. Hughes, "Regulation of Flagellar Assembly," *Current Opinion in Microbiology* 5 (2001): 160–165.
38 M. J. Pallen and N. J. Matzke, "From *The Origin of Species* to the Origin of Bacterial Flagella," *Nature Reviews Microbiology* 4 (2006): 784–790.
39 M. H. Saier, Jr., "Evolution of Bacterial Type III Protein Secretion Systems," *Trends in Microbiology* 12 (2004): 113–115.
40 S. S. Abby and E. P. Rocha, "The Non-flagellar Type III Secretion System Evolved from the Bacterial Flagellum and Diversified into Host-cell Adapted Systems," *PLoS Genetics* 8 (2012): e1002983.
41 D. J. Whitehead et al., "The Look-ahead Effect of Phenotypic Mutations," *Biology Direct* 3 (2008): 18.
42 E. V. Koonin, "Reviewer's Comment on Whitehead et al.," *Biology Direct* 3 (2008): 18.
43 M. J. Behe, "The Old Enigma," *Uncommon Descent*, 2009, http://behe.uncommondescent.com/2009/04/%E2%80%9Cthe-old-enigma%E2%80%9D-part-3-of-3/.
44 R. Carter and K. N. Mendis, "Evolutionary and Historical Aspects of the Burden of Malaria," *Clinical Microbiology Reviews* 15 (2002): 564–594.
45 O. Tenaillon et al., "Tempo and Mode of Genome Evolution in a 50,000-generation Experiment," *Nature* 536 (2016): 165–170; R. Maddamsetti et al., "Core Genes Evolve Rapidly in the Long-term Evolution Experiment with *Escherichia coli*," *Genome Biology and Evolution* 9 (2017): 1072–1083.
46 J. J. Schoenebeck and E. A. Ostrander, "Insights into Morphology and Disease from the Dog Genome Project," *Annual Review of Cell and Developmental Biology* 30 (2014): 535–560.
47 S. Liu et al., "Population Genomics Reveal Recent Speciation and Rapid Evolutionary Adaptation in Polar Bears," *Cell* 157 (2014): 785–794.

Bibliography

Abby, S. S., and E. P. Rocha, "The Non-flagellar Type III Secretion System Evolved from the Bacterial Flagellum and Diversified into Host-cell Adapted Systems," *PLoS Genetics* 8 (2012): e1002983.

Alberts, B. A. "'The Cell as a Collection of Protein Machines: Preparing the Next Generation of Molecular Biologists," *Cell* 93 (1998): 291–294.

Aldridge, P., and K. T. Hughes, "Regulation of Flagellar Assembly," *Current Opinion in Microbiology* 5 (2001): 160–165.

Aquinas, Thomas, *Summa Theologiae*, New York: Benziger Bros., 1947.

Avramides, A., "Other Minds," *The Stanford Encyclopedia of Philosophy*, edited by Edward N. Zalta, 2019, https://plato.stanford.edu/archives/sum2019/entries/other-minds/.

Behe, M. J., *Darwin's Black Box: The Biochemical Challenge to Evolution*, New York: The Free Press, 1996.

Behe, M. J., *Darwin Devolves: The New Science about DNA That Challenges Evolution*, New York: HarperOne, 2019.

Behe, M. J., "Reply to My Critics: a Response to Reviews of *Darwin's Black Box: the Biochemical Challenge to Evolution*," *Biology and Philosophy* 16 (2001): 685–709.

Behe, M. J., *The Edge of Evolution: the Search for the Limits of Darwinism*, New York: The Free Press, 2007.
Behe, M. J., "The Old Enigma," *Uncommon Descent*, 2009, http://behe.uncommondescent.com/2009/04/%E2%80%9Cthe-old-enigma%E2%80%9D-part-3-of-3/
Carter, R., and K. N. Mendis, "'Evolutionary and Historical Aspects of the Burden of Malaria," *Clinical Microbiology Reviews* 15 (2002): 564–594.
Darwin, C., 1872, *Origin of Species*, 6th edition. New York: New York University Press, 1988.
Dawkins, R., *River out of Eden: a Darwinian View of Life*, New York: Basic Books, 1995.
Farley, J., *The Spontaneous Generation Controversy from Descartes to Oparin*, Baltimore: The Johns Hopkins University Press, 1979.
Feser, E., *Five Proofs of the Existence of God*, San Francisco: Ignatius Press, 2017.
Hume, David, *Dialogues Concerning Natural Religion*. London: Penguin Books, 1779.
Kato, T., et al., "Structure of the Native Supercoiled Flagellar Hook as a Universal Joint," *Nature Communications* 10 (2019): 5295–5302.
Kendrew, J. C., et al., "Structure of Myoglobin: A Three-dimensional Fourier Synthesis at 2 Å. Resolution," *Nature* 185 (1960): 422–427.
Kirk, R., "Zombies," *The Stanford Encyclopedia of Philosophy*, edited by Edward N. Zalta, 2019, https://plato.stanford.edu/archives/spr2019/entries/zombies/.
Koonin, E. V., "Reviewer's Comment on Whitehead et al.," *Biology Direct* 3 (2008): 18.
Laland, K., et al., "Does Evolutionary Theory Need a Rethink?" *Nature* 514 (2014): 161–164.
Liu, S., et al., "Population Genomics Reveal Recent Speciation and Rapid Evolutionary Adaptation in Polar Bears," *Cell* 157 (2014): 785–794.
Maddamsetti, R., et al., "Core Genes Evolve Rapidly in the Long-term Evolution Experiment with *Escherichia coli*," *Genome Biology and Evolution* 9 (2017): 1072–1083.
Mayr, E., *What Evolution Is*, New York: BasicBooks, 2001.
Maxwell, J. C., "Molecules," *Nature* 8 (1873): 437–441.
Meyer, S. C., *Signature in the Cell: DNA and the Evidence for Intelligent Design*, New York: HarperOne, 2009.
Miller, K. R., "The Flagellum Unspun," in *Debating Design: from Darwin to DNA*, edited by William A. Dembski, Michael Ruse, Cambridge: Cambridge University Press, 2004.
Miller, K., "The Mousetrap Analogy or Trapped by Design," http://www.millerandlevine.com/km/evol/DI/Mousetrap.html.
Minamino, T., and K. Namba, "Self-assembly and Type III Protein Export of the Bacterial Flagellum," *Journal of Molecular Microbiology and Biotechnology* 7 (2001): 5–17.
Mivart, S., *On the Genesis of Species*, London: Macmillan, 1871.
Orr, H. A., "Darwin v. Intelligent Design (Again)," *Boston Review* (1996): 28–31.
Paley, William, *Natural Theology*, New York: The American Tract Society, 1802.
Pallen, M. J., and N. J. Matzke, "From *The Origin of Species* to the Origin of Bacterial Flagella," *Nature Reviews Microbiology* 4 (2006): 784–790.
Polanyi, M., "Life's Irreducible Structure," *Science* 160 (1968): 1308–1312.
Popper, K. R., *Realism and the Aim of Science: The Postscript to the Logic of Scientific Discovery*, Totowa, NJ: Rowman and Littlefield, 1983.
Reid, T.m 1785. *Essays on the Intellectual Powers of Man*, New York: Garland Pub., 1971.
Saier, M. H., Jr., "Evolution of Bacterial Type III Protein Secretion Systems," *Trends in Microbiology* 12 (2004): 113–115.
Schiefsky, M. J. "Galen's Teleology and Functional Explanation," *Oxford Studies in Ancient Philosophy* 33 (2007): 369–400.

Schoenebeck, J. J., and E. A. Ostrander, "Insights into Morphology and Disease from the Dog Genome Project," *Annual Review of Cell and Developmental Biology* 30 (2014): 535–560.

Sober, E., "The Design Argument," in *God and Design: the Teleological Argument and Modern Science*, edited by Neil A. Manson, 27–54, New York: Routledge, 2003.

Tenaillon, O., et al., "Tempo and Mode of Genome Evolution in a 50,000-generation Experiment," *Nature* 536 (2016): 165–170.

Watson, J. D., and F. H. Crick, "Molecular Structure of Nucleic Acid," *Nature* 171 (1953): 738.

Whitehead, D. J., et al., "The Look-ahead Effect of Phenotypic Mutations," *Biology Direct* 3 (2008): 18.

"design," The Free Dictionary, https://www.thefreedictionary.com/design

"part," The Free Dictionary, https://www.thefreedictionary.com/part

6

The Argument from Biological Information

Stephen Meyer

1. Introduction

Contrary to the clear biblical affirmation that a personal God exists and can be known "from the things that are made" (Romans 1:20), prominent—and self-appointed – spokesmen for science have frequently claimed that modern science has shown that belief in God is no longer credible. For example, starting in 2006 and 2007 a spate of bestselling books, led by Richard Dawkins' bestselling *The God Delusion*, popularized this idea. Dawkins and other "New Atheists" argued that science shows the existence of God to be a delusion or as one book put it "a failed hypothesis."[1] Why? Because, according to Dawkins[2] and others, there is no evidence for intelligent design in nature Instead, in their view, Darwin explained away all evidences of design.

Indeed, the modern version of Darwin's theory, called neo-Darwinism, asserts that the wholly undirected processes of natural selection and random mutations is fully capable of producing the intricate designed-like structures in living systems. As evolutionary biologist Francisco Ayala[3] notes, Darwinism accounts for "design without a designer." Moreover, modern neo-Darwinism affirms that natural selection can mimic the powers of a designing intelligence without itself being guided or directed by an intelligent agent of any kind. Thus, Dawkins has argued that living organisms may look designed, but that appearance is entirely illusory.[4] Since, further, he asserts that before Darwin the design argument was always the strongest argument for God's existence, belief in God is now extremely improbable—tantamount to a delusion.

Yet, Dawkins and other New Atheists have overlooked at least one key piece of evidence: the mysterious digital code present in the DNA molecule within the inner recesses of even the simplest living cells. Indeed, the discovery of the information-bearing properties of DNA and other large biomacromolecules now provides a scientific basis for a compelling reformulating the classical argument from design—the very argument that Dawkins and the New Atheists claim is dead.

2. The DNA enigma

In 1953 when Watson and Crick discovered the structure of DNA, they also discovered that DNA stores information in the form of a four-character alphabetic code. Strings of precisely sequenced chemicals called *nucleotide bases* store and transmit the assembly instructions—the information—for building the crucial protein molecules and protein machines the cell needs to survive.

Crick later developed this idea with his famous "sequence hypothesis," according to which the chemical parts of DNA (the nucleotide bases) function like letters in a written language or symbols in a computer code. Just as letters in an English sentence or digital characters in a computer program may convey information depending on their arrangement, so too do certain sequences of chemical bases along the spine of the DNA molecule convey precise instructions for building proteins.

Moreover, DNA sequences do not just have a mathematically measurable degree of improbability. Thus, they do not just possess "information" in the strictly mathematical sense of the theory of information developed by the famed M.I.T. scientist Claude Shannon in the late 1940s. Instead, DNA contains information in the richer and more ordinary dictionary sense of "alternative sequences or arrangements of characters that produce a specific effect." DNA base sequences convey instructions. They perform functions and produce specific effects. Thus, they do not possess mere "Shannon information," but instead what has been called "specified" or "functional information."[5] Indeed, like the precisely arranged zeros and ones in a computer program, the chemical bases in DNA convey instructions in virtue of their "specificity" of arrangement. Thus, Richard Dawkins[6] notes that "the machine code of the genes is uncannily computer-like" and software developer Bill Gates observes that "DNA is like a computer program."[7] Similarly, biotechnology specialist Leroy Hood describes the information stored in DNA as "digital code."[8]

But if this is true, how did the *functionally specified information* in DNA arise? Is this striking appearance of design the product of actual design or a natural process that can mimic the powers of a designing intelligence? This question is related to a longstanding mystery in biology—the question of the origin of the first life. Indeed, since Watson and Crick's discovery, scientists have increasingly come to understand the centrality of information to even the simplest living systems. DNA stores the assembly instructions for building the many crucial proteins and protein machines that service and maintain even the most primitive one-celled organisms. It follows that building a living cell in the first place requires assembly instructions stored in DNA or some equivalent molecule. As origin-of-life researcher Bernd-Olaf Küppers has explained, "The problem of the origin-of-life is clearly basically equivalent to the problem of the origin of biological information."[9]

Today the question of how life first originated is widely regarded as a profound and unsolved scientific problem, largely because of the mystery surrounding the origin of functionally specified biological information. This essay will examine the various attempts that have been made to solve this mystery—what I call "the DNA enigma" – and it will argue that intelligent design, rather than an undirected mechanism that merely mimics the powers of a designing intelligence, best explains it. It will then suggest that the evidence of intelligent design in living cells can—when coupled with discoveries in in modern physics—underwrite a renewed and robust natural theology.

3. Early theories of the origin of life

Darwin's theory sought to explain the origin of new forms of life from simpler forms. It did not explain how the first life—presumably a simple one-celled organism—might have arisen to begin with. Nevertheless, in the 1860s and 1870s scientists assumed that devising a materialistic explanation for the origin of life would be fairly easy and, therefore, they did not worry that one-celled organisms might betray evidence of design.

Instead, scientists at the time assumed that life was essentially a rather simple substance called protoplasm that could be easily constructed by combining and recombining simple chemicals such as carbon dioxide, oxygen, and nitrogen. German evolutionary biologist Ernst Haeckel likened cell "autogeny," as he called it, to the process of inorganic crystallization. Haeckel's English counterpart, T. H. Huxley, proposed a simple two-step method of chemical recombination to explain the origin of the first cell. Just as salt could be produced spontaneously by adding sodium to chloride, so they thought a living cell could be produced by adding several chemical constituents together and then allowing spontaneous chemical reactions to produce the simple protoplasmic substance that they assumed to be the essence of life.[10]

During the 1920s and 1930s, a more sophisticated version of this "chemical evolutionary theory" was proposed by a Russian biochemist named Alexander I. Oparin. Oparin, like his nineteenth-century predecessors, suggested that life could have first evolved as the result of a series of chemical reactions. Nevertheless, he envisioned that this process of chemical evolution would involve many more chemical transformations and reactions and hundreds of millions of years. Oparin postulated these additional steps and additional time because he had a more accurate understanding of the complexity of cellular metabolism than did Haeckel and Huxley.[11] Nevertheless, neither he nor anyone else in the 1930s fully appreciated the complexity—and information-bearing properties—of the DNA, RNA and proteins that make life possible.

Though Oparin's theory appeared to receive experimental support in 1953 when Stanley Miller simulated the production of the amino acid "building blocks" of proteins under ostensibly prebiotic atmospheric conditions, his textbook version of chemical evolutionary theory is riddled with difficulties. Miller's simulation experiment is now understood by origin-of-life researchers to have little, if any, relevance to explaining how amino acids—let alone their precise sequencing which is necessary to produce proteins—could have arisen in the actual atmosphere of the early earth. Moreover, Oparin proposed no explanation for the origin of the information in DNA (or RNA) that present-day cells use to build proteins. As a result, a search for prebiotic chemical mechanisms to explain the origin of biological information has ensued. Since the 1950s, three broad types of naturalistic explanations have been proposed by scientists in an attempt to explain the origin of the information necessary to produce the first cell.

4. Beyond the reach of chance

One naturalistic view of the origin of life is that it happened exclusively by chance.[12] Since the late 1960s, however, few serious scientists have supported this view.[13] Since molecular biologists began to understand how the digital information in DNA directs the construction of protein synthesis in the cell, many calculations have been made to determine the probability of formulating functional proteins and nucleic acids (DNA or RNA molecules) at random. Even assuming extremely favorable prebiotic conditions (whether realistic or not) and theoretically maximal reaction rates, such calculations have invariably shown that the probability of obtaining functionally sequenced (information-rich) biomacromolecules at random is, in the words of physicist Ilya Prigogine and his colleagues, "vanishingly small ... even on the scale of ... billions of years."[14]

Even so, origin-of-life scientists recognize that the critical problem is not just generating an improbable sequence of chemical constituents—an improbable arrangement of nucleotide bases in DNA, for example. Instead, the problem is relying on a random search or shuffling of molecular building blocks to generate one of the very rare arrangements of bases in DNA (or amino acids in proteins) that also *perform a biological function*. Very improbable things do occur by chance. Any hand of cards or any series of rolled dice represents an improbable occurrence. Observers often justifiably attribute such events to chance alone. What justifies the elimination of chance is not just the occurrence of a highly improbable event but also the occurrence of an improbable event that conforms to a discernible pattern (either what statisticians call a "conditionally independent pattern" or what I call a "functionally significant pattern" (i.e., one that accomplishes a discernable purpose).

If, for example, someone repeatedly rolls two dice and turns up a sequence such as 9, 4, 11, 2, 6, 8, 5, 12, 9, 6, 8, and 4, no one will suspect anything but the interplay of random forces, though this sequence does represent a very improbable event given the number of possible numeric sequences that exist corresponding to a sequence of this length. Yet rolling 12 (or 1200!) consecutive sevens in a game that rewards sevens will justifiably arouse suspicion that something more than chance is in play.

Origin-of-life researchers employ this kind of statistical reasoning to justify the elimination of the chance hypothesis. Christian de Duve, for example, has made this logic explicit in order to explain why chance fails as an explanation for the origin of life:

> A single, freak, highly improbable event can conceivably happen. Many highly improbable events—drawing a winning lottery number or the distribution of playing cards in a hand of bridge—happen all the time. But a string of improbable events—drawing the same lottery number twice, or the same bridge hand twice in a row—does not happen naturally.[15]

In my book, *Signature in the Cell*, I perform updated calculations of the probability of the origin of even a single *functional* protein or corresponding *functional* gene (the section of a DNA molecule that directs the construction of a particular protein) by chance alone. My calculations are based upon recent experiments in molecular biology establishing the extreme rarity of functional proteins in relation to the total number of possible arrangements of amino acids corresponding to a protein of a given length. I show that the probability of producing even a single functional protein (a gene product) of modest length (150 amino acids) by chance alone stands at a "vanishingly small" 1 chance in 10^{164}.

Moreover, in *Signature*, I not only demonstrate that the probability of a single functional protein arising at any given time is absurdly small, but also that the probability is even extremely small *in relation to* all the opportunities that have existed for that event to occur since the beginning of time (what are called the "probabilistic resources" of the universe). I show that even if every event in the entire history of the universe (where an event is defined minimally as an interaction between elementary particles) were devoted to producing combinations of amino acids of a given length (an extravagantly generous assumption), the number of combinations thus produced would still represent a tiny portion—less than 1 out of a trillion trillion—of the total number of possible amino acid combinations corresponding to a functional protein— *any* functional protein—of that given length. In short, it is extremely unlikely that even a single protein would have arisen by chance on the early Earth even taking the probabilistic resources of the entire universe into account. For this and other similar reasons, serious origin-of-life researchers now consider "chance" an inadequate causal explanation for the origin of biological information.[16]

5. Self-organization scenarios

Because of these difficulties, many origin-of-life theorists after the mid–1960s addressed the problem of the origin of biological information in a different way. Rather than invoking chance events or "frozen accidents," many theorists suggested that the laws of nature or law-like forces of chemical attraction might have generated the information in DNA and proteins. Some have suggested that simple chemicals might possess "self-ordering properties" capable of organizing the constituent parts of proteins, DNA and RNA into the specific arrangements they now possess. Just as electrostatic forces draw sodium (Na+) and chloride ions (Cl–) together into a highly-ordered patterns within a crystal of salt (NaCl), so too might amino acids with special affinities for each other arrange themselves to form proteins. Kenyon and Steinman developed this idea in a book entitled *Biochemical Predestination*.[17]

Prigogine and Nicolis proposed another theory of self-organization based on their observation that open systems driven far from equilibrium often display self-ordering tendencies. For example, gravitational energy will produce highly ordered vortices in a draining bathtub; and thermal energy flowing through a heat sink will generate distinctive convection currents or "spiral wave activity."[18]

For many current origin-of-life scientists, self-organizational models now seem to offer the most promising approach to explaining the origin of biological information.

Nevertheless, critics have called into question both the plausibility and the relevance of such models. Ironically, perhaps the most prominent early advocate of self-organization, Dean Kenyon, has now explicitly repudiated his own and similar theories as both incompatible with empirical findings and theoretically incoherent.

The empirical difficulties attendant to self-organizational scenarios can be illustrated by examining the structure of the DNA molecule. The diagram below shows that the structure of DNA depends upon several chemical bonds. There are bonds, for example, between the sugar molecules (designated by the pentagons) and the phosphate molecules (designated by the circled Ps) that form the twisting backbones of the DNA helix. There are bonds fixing individual (nucleotide) bases to the sugar-phosphate backbones on each side of the molecule. Notice, however, that there are no chemical bonds (and thus forces of attraction), between the bases that run along the spine of the helix. Yet it is precisely along this axis of the molecule that the genetic instructions in DNA are encoded.

Further, just as magnetic letters can be combined and recombined in any way to form various sequences on a metal surface, so too can each of the four bases A, T, G, and C attach to any site on the DNA backbone with equal facility, making all sequences equally probable (or improbable). The same type of chemical bond (an N-glycosidic bond) occurs between the bases and the backbone regardless of which base attaches.

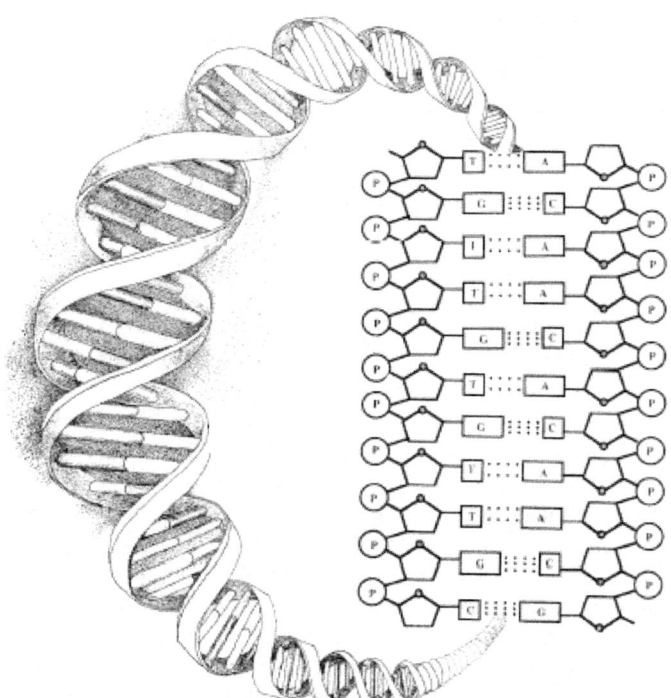

Figure 6.1 The bonding relationship between the chemical constituents of the DNA molecule. Note that no chemical bonds exist between the nucleotide bases along the message-bearing spine of the DNA helix. Courtesy of Fred Heeren.

All four bases are acceptable; none is preferred. Thus, *differences in* bonding affinity do not determine the arrangement of the bases—that is, forces of chemical attraction do not account for the information in DNA.

For those who want to explain the origin of life as the result of self-organizing properties intrinsic to the material constituents of living systems, these rather elementary facts of molecular biology have devastating implications. The most logical place to look for self-organizing properties to explain the origin of genetic information is in the constituent parts of the molecules carrying that information. But biochemistry and molecular biology make clear that the forces of attraction between the constituents in DNA, RNA, and protein do not explain the sequence specificity (the information) present in these large information-bearing molecules.

Significantly, information theorists insist that there is a good reason for this. If chemical affinities between the constituents in the DNA message text determined the arrangement of the text, such affinities would dramatically diminish the capacity of DNA to carry information. Consider what would happen if the individual nucleotide "letters" (A, T, G, C) in a DNA molecule *did* interact by *chemical* necessity with each other. Every time adenine (A) occurred in a growing genetic sequence, it would likely drag guanine (G) along with it. Every time cytosine (C) appeared, thymine (T) would follow. As a result, the DNA message text would be peppered with repeating sequences of A's followed by G's and C's followed by T's.

Rather than having a genetic molecule capable of unlimited novelty, with all the unpredictable and aperiodic sequences that characterize informative texts, we would have a highly repetitive text awash in redundant sequences—much as happens in crystals. Indeed, in a crystal the forces of mutual chemical attraction do completely explain the sequential ordering of the constituent parts, and consequently crystals cannot convey novel information.

Bonding affinities, to the extent they exist, cannot be used to explain the origin of information. Self-organizing chemical affinities create mantras, not messages.

The tendency to confuse the qualitative distinction between "order" and "information" has characterized self-organizational research efforts and calls into question the relevance of such work to the origin of life. Self-organizational theorists explain well what doesn't need explaining. What needs explaining is not the origin of order (whether in the form of the repetitive sequences of chemical constituents in crystals, or the symmetrical patterns evident in swirling tornadoes or the "eyes" of hurricanes), but the origin of *information*— the highly improbable, aperiodic, and yet specified sequences that make both communication and biological function possible.[19]

6. Chance and necessity: prebiotic natural selection

Of course, many theories of chemical evolution have not relied exclusively on either chance or law-like necessity alone, but have instead attempted to combine the two types of explanations. For example, after 1953 Oparin revised his original theory of chemical evolution. In so doing, he attempted to explain the origin of biological information as the product of the law-like process of *natural selection* acting on the chance interactions of simple non-living molecules. Yet Oparin's notion of prebiotic natural selection soon encountered obvious difficulties.

First, the process of natural selection presupposes the differential reproduction of living organisms and thus a pre-existing mechanism of self-replication. Yet, self-replication in all extant cells depends upon functional (and, therefore, to a high degree sequence-specific, information-rich) proteins and nucleic acids. Yet the origin of such information-rich molecules is precisely what Oparin needed to explain. Thus, many rejected his postulation of pre-biotic natural selection as question begging. As the evolutionary biologist Theodosius Dobzhansky insisted, "pre-biological natural selection is a contradiction in terms."[20] Or as Christian de Duve has explained, theories of prebiotic natural selection "need information which implies they have to presuppose what is to be explained in the first place."[21]

7. The RNA world

More recently, some have claimed that another scenario—the RNA World hypothesis, combining chance and prebiotic natural selection—can solve the origin-of-life problem and with it, presumably, the problem of the origin of genetic information. The RNA world was proposed as an explanation for the origin of the interdependence of nucleic acids and proteins in the cell's information-processing system. In extant cells, building proteins requires genetic information from DNA, but information in DNA cannot be processed without many specific proteins and protein complexes. This poses a chicken-or-egg problem. The discovery that RNA (a nucleic acid) possesses some limited catalytic properties similar to those of proteins suggested a way to solve that problem. "RNA-first" advocates proposed an early state in which RNA performed both the enzymatic functions of modern proteins and the information-storage function of modern DNA, thus allegedly making the interdependence of DNA and proteins unnecessary in the earliest living system.

Nevertheless, many fundamental difficulties with the RNA-world scenario have emerged. First, synthesizing (and/or maintaining) many essential building blocks of RNA molecules under realistic conditions has proven either difficult or impossible.[22] Second, naturally occurring RNA possesses very few of the specific enzymatic properties of proteins necessary to extant cells. Indeed, RNA catalysts do not function as true enzyme catalysts. Enzymes are capable of coupling energetically favorable and energetically unfavorable reactions together. RNA catalysts, so-called "ribozymes," are not capable of doing this. Third, RNA-world advocates offer no plausible explanation for how primitive RNA replicators might have evolved into modern cells that do rely almost exclusively on proteins to process and translate genetic information and regulate metabolism.[23] Fourth, attempts to enhance the limited catalytic properties of RNA molecules in so-called ribozyme engineering experiments have inevitably required extensive investigator manipulation, thus simulating, if anything, the need for intelligent design, not the efficacy of an undirected chemical evolutionary process.

Most importantly for our present considerations, the RNA-world hypothesis presupposes, but does not explain, the origin of sequence specificity or information in the original functional RNA molecules. Indeed, the RNA-world scenario was proposed as an explanation for the functional interdependence problem, not the information problem. Even so, some RNA-world advocates seem to envision leapfrogging the sequence-specificity problem. They imagine sections of RNA arising by chance on the pre-biotic earth and then later acquiring an ability to make copies of themselves—that is, to self-replicate. In such a scenario, the capacity to self-replicate would favor the survival of those RNA molecules that could do so and would thus favor the specific sequences that the first self-replicating molecules happened to have.

This suggestion merely shifts the information problem out of view, however. To date scientist have been able to design RNA catalysts that will copy only about 10% of themselves.[24] For strands of RNA to perform even this limited replicase (self-replication) function, however, they must, like proteins, have very specific arrangements of constituent building blocks (nucleotides in the RNA case). Further, the strands must be long enough to fold into complex three-dimensional shapes (to form so-called tertiary structures). Thus, any RNA molecule capable of even limited function must have possessed considerable (specified) information content. Yet explaining how the building blocks of RNA arranged themselves into functionally specified sequences has proven no easier than explaining how the constituent parts of DNA might have done so, especially given the high probability of destructive cross-reactions between desirable and undesirable molecules in any realistic pre-biotic soup. As de Duve has noted in a critique of the RNA-world hypothesis, "hitching the components together in the right manner raises additional problems of such magnitude that no one has yet attempted to do so in a prebiotic context."[25]

8. The return of the design hypothesis

If attempts to solve the information problem only relocate it, and if neither chance nor physical-chemical necessity, nor the two acting in combination, explains the ultimate origin of specified biological information, what does? Do we know of any entity that has the causal powers to create large amounts of specified information? We do. As information scientist Henry Quastler recognized, the "creation of new information is habitually associated with conscious activity."[26]

Experience affirms that functionally specified information routinely arises from the activity of intelligent agents. A computer user who traces the information on a screen back to its source invariably comes to a mind, that of a software engineer or programmer. Similarly, the information in a book or newspaper column ultimately derives from a writer—from a mental, rather than a strictly material, cause.

But could this intuitive connection between information and the prior activity of a designing intelligence justify a rigorous scientific argument for intelligent design? I first began to consider this possibility during my Ph.D. research at Cambridge University in the late 1980s. At that time, I was examining how scientists investigating origins events developed their arguments. Specifically, I examined the method of reasoning that historical scientists use to identify causes responsible for events in the remote past.

I discovered that historical scientists often make inferences with a distinctive logical form (known technically as *abductive inferences*).[27] Paleontologists, evolutionary biologists and other historical scientists reason like detectives and infer *past* conditions or causes from *present* clues. As Stephen Jay Gould noted, historical scientists typically "infer history from its results."[28]

Nevertheless, as many philosophers have noted, there is a problem with this kind of historical reasoning, namely, there is often more than one cause that can explain the same effect. This makes reasoning from present clues (circumstantial evidence) tricky because the evidence can point to more than one causal explanation or hypothesis. To address this problem in geology, the nineteenth-century geologist Thomas Chamberlain[29] delineated a method of reasoning he called "the method of multiple working hypotheses."

Contemporary philosophers of science such as Peter Lipton have called this the method of "inference to the best explanation."[30] That is, when trying to explain the origin of an event or structure from the past, scientists often compare various hypotheses to see which would, if true, best explain it.[31] They then provisionally affirm the hypothesis that best explains the data as the one that is most likely to be true. But that raised an important question: exactly what makes an explanation best?

As it happens, historical scientists have developed criteria for deciding which cause, among a group of competing possible causes, provides the best explanation for some event in the remote past. The most important of these criteria is called "causal adequacy." This criterion requires that historical scientists, as a condition of a successful explanation, identify causes that are known to have the power to produce the kind of effect, feature or event that requires explanation. In making these determinations, historical scientists evaluate hypotheses against their present knowledge of cause and effect. Causes that are known to produce the effect in question are judged to be better candidates than those that are not. For instance, a volcanic eruption provides a better explanation for an ash layer in the earth than an earthquake because eruptions have been observed to produce ash layers, whereas earthquakes have not.

One of the first scientists to develop this principle was the geologist Charles Lyell who also influenced Charles Darwin. Darwin read Lyell's *magnum opus*, *The Principles of Geology*, on the voyage of the *Beagle* and employed its principles of reasoning in *The Origin of Species*. The subtitle of Lyell's *Principles* summarized the geologist's central methodological principle: *Being an Attempt to Explain the Former Changes of the Earth's Surface, by Reference to Causes Now in Operation*.[32] Lyell argued that when scientists seek to explain events in the past, they should not invoke unknown or exotic causes, the effects of which we do not know. Instead they should cite causes that are known from our uniform experience to have the power to produce the effect in question.[33] Historical scientists should cite "*causes now in operation*" or presently acting causes. This was the idea behind his uniformitarian principle and the dictum: "The present is the key to the past." According to Lyell, our *present* experience of cause and effect should guide our reasoning about the causes of *past* events. Darwin himself adopted this methodological principle as he sought to demonstrate that natural selection qualified as a *vera causa*, that is, a true, known or actual cause of significant biological change.[34] He sought to show that natural selection was "causally adequate" to produce the effects he was trying to explain.

Both philosophers of science and leading historical scientists have emphasized causal adequacy as the key criterion by which competing hypotheses are adjudicated. But philosophers of science also have noted that assessments of explanatory power lead to conclusive inferences only when it can be shown that there is *only one known cause* for the effect or evidence in question.[35] When scientists can infer a *uniquely plausible* cause, they can avoid the fallacy of affirming the consequent and the error of ignoring other possible causes with the power to produce the same effect.[36]

9. Intelligent design as the best explanation?

What did all this have to do with the DNA enigma? As a Ph.D. student I wondered if a case for an intelligent cause could be formulated and justified in the same way that historical scientists would justify any other causal claim about an event in the past. My study of historical scientific reasoning and origin-of-life research suggested to me that it was possible to formulate a rigorous scientific case for intelligent design as an inference to the best explanation, specifically, as a best explanation for the origin of biological information. The action of a conscious and intelligent agent clearly represents a known (presently acting) and adequate cause for the origin of information. Uniform and repeated experience affirms that intelligent agents produce information-rich systems, whether software programs, ancient inscriptions, or Shakespearean sonnets. Minds are clearly capable of generating functionally specified information.

Further, the functionally specified information in the cell also points to intelligent design as the *best* explanation for the ultimate origin of biological information. Why? Experience shows that large amounts of such information (especially codes and languages) *invariably* originate from an intelligent source—from a mind or a personal agent. In other words, intelligent activity is *the only known cause of* the origin of functionally specified information (at least, starting from a non-living source, that is, from purely physical or chemical antecedents). Since intelligence is the only known cause of specified information in such a context, the presence of functionally specified information sequences in even the simplest living systems points definitely to the past existence and activity of a designing intelligence.

Ironically, this generalization—that intelligence is the only known cause of specified information (starting from a non-biological source)—has received support from origin-of-life research itself. During the last fifty years, every naturalistic model proposed has failed to explain the origin of the functionally specified genetic information required to build a living cell.[37] Thus, mind or intelligence, or what philosophers call "agent causation," now stands as the only cause known to be capable of generating large amounts of information starting from a non-living state.[38] As a result, the presence of specified information-rich sequences in even the simplest living systems would seem to imply intelligent design.

When I first noticed the subtitle of Lyell's book, referring us to "*causes now in operation*," a light came on for me. I immediately asked myself a question: "What causes 'now in operation' produce digital code or specified information?" Is there a known cause—a *vera causa*—of the origin of such information? What does our uniform experience tell us? As I thought about this further, it occurred to me that by Lyell's and Darwin's own rule of reasoning and test of a sound scientific explanation, intelligent design should qualify as the currently best scientific explanation for the origin of biological information. Why? Because we have independent evidence—"uniform experience"—that intelligent agents are capable of producing specified information and, as origin-of-life research itself has helped to demonstrate, we know of no other cause capable of producing functional specified information starting from a purely physical or chemical state.

Scientists in many fields recognize the connection between intelligence and information and make inferences accordingly. Archaeologists assume that a scribe produced the inscriptions on the Rosetta stone. The search for extraterrestrial intelligence (SETI) presupposes that any specified information imbedded in electromagnetic signals coming from space would indicate an intelligent source.[39] As yet, radio astronomers have not found any such information-bearing signals. But closer to home, molecular biologists have identified information-rich sequences and systems in the cell, suggesting, by the same logic, the past existence of an intelligent cause for those effects.

Indeed, our uniform experience affirms that specified information—whether inscribed in hieroglyphics, written in a book, encoded in a radio signal, or produced in an RNA world ribozyme engineering experiment—*always* arises from an intelligent source, from a mind and not a strictly material process. So the discovery of the functionally specified digital information in the DNA molecule provides strong grounds for inferring that intelligence played a role in the origin of DNA. Indeed, whenever we find specified information and we know the causal story of how that information arose, we always find that it arose from an intelligent source. It follows that the best, most likely explanation for the origin of the specified, digitally encoded information in DNA is that it too had an intelligent source. Intelligent design best explains the DNA enigma.

10. Who is the designer?

The *theory* of intelligent design itself does not identify the designing intelligence responsible for life. Instead, it merely affirms based upon uniform experience that an intelligence of some kind must have played a role. Nevertheless, the theory does not prohibit scientists from engaging in further philosophical reflection about the nature and probable identity of the designing intelligence responsible for life. Thus, the *evidence* of intelligent design may well have larger religious implications.

And there are two basic options. Either the intelligence responsible for life is an intelligent being within the cosmos or beyond the cosmos. Either the designer is an immanent intelligence or a transcendent one—an alien or God.

There are good reasons for thinking that the latter option provides a better explanation.

First, though some atheists and agnostic scientists have postulated an immanent intelligence as an explanation for the origin of the first life on earth, such a postulation does not actually solve the problem of the ultimate origin of biological information. Francis Crick[40] and Fred Hoyle,[41] for example, both proposed so-called panspermia models. They suggested that life was intelligently designed (and/or seeded) by an intelligence within the cosmos—a space alien or extra-terrestrial agent—rather than by a transcendent intelligent God. Richard Dawkins has also proposed this as an explanation for any possible "signature of intelligence" within the cell provided that scientists understand that the alien intelligence itself must have evolved by a purely undirected evolutionary process.[42]

Yet purely undirected chemical processes have not been able to account for the origin of the first life on earth precisely because they have not been able to explain the key signature of intelligence, namely, the information present in DNA. How then does invoking these same kind of undirected processes at work in outer space solve the problem of life's ultimate origin? Clearly, it does not. Instead, explaining the origin of life by reference to other life, albeit intelligent and extraterrestrial, only begs the question of the ultimate origin of life, and the information necessary to produce it.

Second (as Rota has argued in Chapter 4 of this book), modern physics has now revealed evidence of design in the very fabric of the universe. Since the 1960s physicists have recognized that the initial configurations of mass and energy at the beginning of the universe as well as the laws and constants of physics are finely tuned, against all odds, to make life possible. Even slight alterations in the values of many independent factors—such as the expansion rate of the universe, the cosmological constant, the precise strength of gravitational or electromagnetic attraction, or the ratios between the strength of these different forces as well as the precise mass of the electron and proton—would render life impossible. Physicists now refer to these factors as "anthropic coincidences" and to the fortunate convergence of all these coincidences as the "fine-tuning of the universe."

Many have noted that this fine-tuning strongly suggests design by a preexistent intelligence. As physicist Paul Davies has put it, "the impression of design is overwhelming."[43] Or as Fred Hoyle commented, "a commonsense interpretation of the facts suggests that a superintellect has monkeyed with physics, as well as chemistry and biology, and that there are no blind forces worth speaking about in nature."[44] Many physicists now concur.

To circumvent the vast improbabilities associated with the cosmic fine-tuning, some physicists have postulated the existence of a vast number of parallel universes in order to increase the amount of time and number of trials available to produce the fine-tuning. In these "multiverse" scenarios any event, no matter how improbable, must happen somewhere in some other parallel universe. So long as life had some probability of arising, it has to arise in some possible world—or so this thinking goes. Unfortunately, as I show in my forthcoming book *Return of the God Hypothesis*, advocates of these multiverse proposals have overlooked an obvious problem. All speculative cosmologies that posit multiple universes, whether based on string theory, inflationary cosmology or a combination of the two, must posit mechanisms for generating multiple separate universes. And yet, in each case, these mechanisms themselves require extensive prior fine-tuning. In so doing, these multiverse proposals beg the question of the ultimate origin of the fine-tuning needed to make our universe and life possible. These proposals presuppose but do not explain the origin of the fine-tuning.

Yet, in our experience systems that manifest fine-tuning—the presence of an extremely improbable ensemble of parameters, conditions or events that are in turn necessary to produce a significant or functional outcome—invariably arise from the activity of a designing intelligence, a fine-tuner. In *Return of the God Hypothesis*, I show that for this and other reasons theistic design now provides a better explanation of the fine-tuning than any multiverse model or other purely naturalistic cosmology.

Moreover, it is important to remember that the fine-tuning of the laws and constants of physics, and especially the fine-tuning of the initial conditions of the universe, have been present from the very beginning of the universe itself. Thus, the cosmological fine-tuning cannot be explained by any intelligent agent that arose after the beginning of the universe from within the cosmos. Indeed, if intelligent design best explains the fine-tuning, then the designing intelligence responsible for the fine-tuning must have had the capability of setting the fine-tuning parameters and initial conditions from the moment of creation. Yet, clearly, no intelligent being *within* the cosmos that arose after the beginning of the cosmos could be responsible for the fine-tuning of the laws and constants of *physics* that made its existence and evolution possible. Such an intelligent agent "inside" the universe might reconfigure or move matter and energy around in accord with the laws of nature. Nevertheless, no such being subject to those laws could possibly change the constants of physics, simply by changing the material *state* of the universe. Similarly, no intelligent being arising after the beginning of the universe could have retrospectively set the exquisitely fine-tuned initial conditions of the universe upon which its later evolution and existence would depend. It follows that an immanent intelligence (an extraterrestrial alien, for instance) fails to qualify as an adequate causal explanation for the origin of the cosmic fine-tuning.

Thus, even if we concede as a logical possibility that an immanent intelligence might explain the ultimate origin of life somewhere else in the cosmos, the alien intelligence hypothesis does not explain either the ultimate origin of life in the universe or the fine-tuning of the universe—to say nothing of the origin of the universe itself. Instead, if intelligent design best explains the fine-tuning of the universe, then the kind of intelligence necessary to explain the fine-tuning of the universe must in some way pre-exist, or exist independently of, the material universe.

Since theism conceives of God as having an existence independent of the material universe—either in a timeless eternal realm or in another realm of time independent of the time in our universe—it can account for (a) the origin of the universe in time (i.e., at a beginning) and (b) the fine-tuning of the universe from the beginning of time. In other words, since theism posits the prior (either ontological or temporal) existence of a transcendent intelligent agent, the creative and causal act of such an agent in choosing to design the universe with a specific suite of life-friendly parameters would explain the origin of the fine tuning from the beginning of the universe. Thus, theism can provide a causally adequate explanation for the origin of the fine-tuning, whereas an immanent intelligence within the cosmos cannot. (Note positing a deistic creator would also provide an adequate causal explanation for the origin of the fine-tuning. Nevertheless, it would not provide an adequate explanation for the evidence of design in living systems that arises long *after* the beginning of the universe, since a deistic creator by definition limits itself to setting the universe in motion and does not act within the universe after its creation.)

Of course, many will still dismiss the evidence of design in life and the universe precisely because it does have implications supportive of theistic belief. Many have attempted to stigmatize the theory of intelligent design as nothing but "religion masquerading as science."

Yet the distasteful implications of the evidence for intelligent design (from an atheistic or materialistic point of view) are not grounds for dismissing it. To say otherwise confuses the evidence for a theory and its possible implications. Many scientists initially rejected the Big Bang theory because it seemed to challenge the idea of an eternally self-existent universe and pointed to the need for a transcendent cause of matter, energy, space, and time. But scientists eventually accepted the theory despite such apparently unpleasant implications because the evidence strongly supported it. Today a similar metaphysical prejudice confronts the case for intelligent design. Nevertheless, it too must be evaluated on the basis of the evidence not our philosophical preferences or concerns about its possible religious implications. As Antony Flew—the long-time atheistic philosopher who later came to accept the evidence for intelligent design and the scientific case for God—insisted, we must "follow the evidence wherever it leads."

That's good advice for all of us, and perhaps especially good advice for the New Atheists such as Richard Dawkins who have prematurely concluded that science has "buried God." Just the opposite now seems to be the case, just as St. Paul wrote in Romans 1:19–20.[45]

Notes

1   Victor Stenger, *God: The Failed Hypothesis* (New York: Oxford University Press, 2007).
2   Richard Dawkins, *The Blind Watchmaker: Why the Evidence of Evolution Reveals A Universe Without Design* (New York: W.W. Norton and Company, 1986).
3   Francisco Ayala. "Darwin's Greatest Discovery: Design Without Designer," *Proceedings of the National Academy of Sciences* 104 (2007): 8567.
4   Richard Dawkins, *The Blind Watchmaker*, 1.
5   R. M. Hazen, "Functional Information and the Emergence of Biocomplexity," *Proceedings of the National Academy of Sciences* 104 (2007): 8574–8581.
6   Richard Dawkins, *River Out Of Eden: A Darwinian View Of Life*. (New York: Basic, 1995), 17.
7   Bill Gates, *The Road Ahead*. (New York: Viking, 1995), 188.
8   Leroy Hood and David Galas, "The Digital Code of DNA," *Nature* 421 (2003): 444–448.
9   Bernd-Olaf Küppers, *Information and the Origin of Life*. (Cambridge: MIT Press, 1990), 170–172.
10 Stephen Meyer, *Of Clues And Causes: A Methodological Interpretation Of Origin of Life Studies* (Cambridge: Cambridge University Press, 1990), 143–161.
11 Harmke Kamminga, *Studies in the History if Ideas on the Origin of Life*. (London: University of London Press, 1980), 222–245.

12 G. Wald, "The Origin Of Life," *Scientific American* 191 (1954): 44–53.
13 Robert Shapiro, *Origins: A Skeptic's Guide to the Creation of Life on Earth*. (New York: Summit Books, 1986), 121; Harmke Kamminga, *Studies in the History of Ideas on the Origin of Life*, 303–304.
14 Ilya Prigogine, G. Nicolis, and A. Babloyantz, "Thermodynamics of Evolution," *Physics Today* 23 (1972): 23.
15 Christian de Duve, "The Beginnings of Life on Earth," *American Scientist* 83 (1995): 437.
16 Christian de Duve, "The Constraints of Chance," *Scientific American* (1996): 112; Francis Crick, *Life Itself*. (New York: Simon and Shuster, 1981), 89–93.
17 Dean Kenyon and Gary Steinman, *Biochemical Predestination* (New York: McGraw-Hill, 1969).
18 Ilya Prigogine and G. Nicolis, *Self-Organization in Nonequilibrium Systems* (New York: Wiley, 1977), 339–53, 429–447.
19 Hubert P. Yockey, *Information Theory and Molecular Biology* (Cambridge: Cambridge University Press, 1992), 274–281.
20 Theodosius Dobzhansky, "Discussion of G. Schramm's Paper," in Sidney W. Fox, *The Origins of Prebiological Systems and of their Molecular Matrices* (New York: Academic Press, 1965), 310.
21 Christian de Duve, *Blueprint For A Cell: The Nature And Origin Of Life* (Burlington, NC: Neil Patterson Publishers, 1991), 187.
22 Robert Shapiro, "Prebiotic Cytosine Synthesis: A Critical Analysis and Implications For The Origin Of Life," *Proceedings of the National Academy of Sciences* 96 (1999): 4396–4401.
23 I. Wolf Huri and Eugene V. Koonin, "On the Origin of the Translation System and the Genetic Code in the RNA World by Means of Natural Selection, Exaptation, and Subfunctionalization," *Biology Direct* 2 (2007): 14.
24 Wendy K. Johnston, Peter J. Unrau, Michael S Lawrence, Margaret E. Glasner, and David P. Bartl, "RNA-Catalyzed RNA Polymerization: Accurate and General RNA-Templated Primer Extension," *Science* 292 (2001): 1319–1325.
25 Christian de Duve, *Vital Dust: Life as a Cosmic Imperative*. (New York: Basic Books, 1995), 23.
26 Henry Quastler, *The Emergence of Biological Organization* (New Haven: Yale University Press, 1964), 16.
27 Charles S. Peirce, *Collected Papers*, vol. 2, edited by C. Hartshorne and P. Weiss. (Cambridge, MA: Harvard University Press, 1931), 372–388.
28 Stephen J Gould, "Evolution and the Triumph of Homology: Or, Why History Matters," *American Scientist* 74 (1986): 60–69.
29 Thomas C. Chamberlain, "The Method of Multiple Working Hypotheses," *Science* 15 (1890): 92–96, reprinted in *Science* 148 (1965): 754–759.
30 Peter Lipton, *Inference to the Best Explanation* (London and New York: Routledge, 1991), 1.
31 Peter Lipton, *Inference to the Best Explanation*, 1.
32 Charles Lyell, *Principles of Geology: Being an Attempt to Explain the Former Changes of the Earth's Surface, by Reference to Causes Now in Operation* (London: John Murray, 1830–1833).
33 Charles Lyell, *Principles of Geology*, vol. 1, 75–91.
34 V. Kavalovski, *The Cera Causa Principle: A Historico-Philosophical Study of a Meta-Theoretical Concept from Newton through Darwin* (Chicago: University of Chicago Press, 1974), 78–103.

35 Michael Scriven, "Explanation and Prediction in Evolutionary Theory," *Science* 130 (1959): 480.
36 Meyer, Stephen C., *Of Clues and Causes: A Methodological Interpretation of Origin of Life Studies*, 96–108.
37 Charles Thaxton, Walter L. Bradley and Roger Olsen, *The Mystery of Life's Origin*, New York: Philosophical Library, 1984, 42–172; Robert Shapiro, *Origins: A Skeptic's Guide to the Creation of Life on Earth*; Hubert Yockey, *Information Theory And Molecular Biology*, 259–293; Charles Thaxton and Walter Bradley, "Information and the Origin of Life," in *The Creation Hypothesis: Scientific Evidence for an Intelligent Designer*, ed. J. P. Moreland (Downers Grove, IL: InterVarsity Press, 1994), 173–210; Stephen Meyer, *Signature in the Cell* (San Francisco: HarperOne, 2009).
38 Of course, the phrase "large amounts of specified information" begs a quantitative question, namely, "How much specified information would the minimally complex cell have to have before it implied design?" In Stephen C. Meyer, *Signature in the Cell: DNA and the Evidence for Intelligent Design* (San Francisco: HarperOne, 2009), I give and justify a precise quantitative answer to this question. I show that the *de novo* emergence of 500 or more bits of specified information reliably indicates design.
39 T. R. McDonough, *The Search for Extraterrestrial Intelligence: Listening for Life in the Cosmos* (New York: Wiley, 1987).
40 Francis Crick, *Life itself* (New York: Simon & Schuster, 1981), 15–16.
41 Fred Hoyle and Chandra Wickramasinghe, *Evolution from Space* (London: Dent, 1981), 24–27.
42 Ben Stein, *Expelled: No Intelligence Allowed*, DVD, Directed by Nathan Frankowski (Los Angeles: Premise Media, 2008).
43 Paul Davies, *The Cosmic Blueprint: New Discoveries In Nature's Creative Ability to Order the Universe* (New York: Simon and Schuster, 1988), 203.
44 Fred Hoyle, "The Universe: Past and Present Reflections," *Engineering and Science* (November 1981): 8–12.
45 *Postscript*: In Meyer's *Signature in the Cell: DNA and the Evidence for Intelligent Design*, I respond in detail to various objections to the case for intelligent design sketched in this short article. I address objections such as: "intelligent design (a) is religion, (b) is not science, (c) makes no predictions, (d) is based on flawed analogical reasoning, (e) is a fallacious argument from ignorance," and many others. I direct intrigued, but still skeptical, readers to my book for a more thorough consideration of popular objections to my argument. I also provide more extensive documentation there supporting the claims presented in the scientific discussion provided in this paper.

Bibliography

Ayala, Francisco J., "Darwin's Greatest Discovery: Design without Designer," *Proceedings of the National Academy of Sciences* 104 (2007): 8567–8573.
Chamberlain, Thomas C., "The Method of Multiple Working Hypotheses," *Science* (old series) 15 (1890): 92–96. Reprinted in *Science* 148 (1965): 754–759.
Crick, Francis, *Life Itself*. New York: Simon & Schuster, 1981.
Davies, Paul, *The Cosmic Blueprint: New Discoveries in Nature's Creative Ability to Order the Universe*, New York: Simon and Schuster, 1988.
Dawkins, Richard, *The Blind Watchmaker: Why the Evidence of Evolution Reveals a Universe without Design*, New York: W. W. Norton & Company, 1986.

Dawkins, Richard, *River out of Eden: A Darwinian View of Life*, New York: Basic, 1995.
de Duve, Christian, *Blueprint for a Cell: The Nature and Origin of Life*, Burlington, NC: Neil Patterson Publishers, 1991.
de Duve, Christian, "The Beginnings of Life on Earth," *American Scientist* 83 (1995): 249–50, 428–37.
de Duve, Christian, *Vital Dust: Life as a Cosmic Imperative*, New York: Basic, 1995.
de Duve, Christian, "The Constraints of Chance," *Scientific American* (1996): 112.
Dobzhansky, Theodosius, "Discussion of G. Schramm's paper," In *The Origins Of Prebiological Systems and of their Molecular Matrices*, edited by Sidney W. Fox, 309–315, New York: Academic Press, 1965.
Dose, K., "The Origin of Life: More Questions than Answers," *Interdisciplinary Science Review* 13 (1988): 348–356.
Gates, Bill, *The Road Ahead*, New York: Viking, 1995.
Gould, Stephen Jay, "Evolution and the Triumph of Homology: Or, Why History Matters," *American Scientist* 74 (1986): 60–69.
Hazen, R. M., Patrick L. Griffin, James M. Carothers, and Jack W. Szostak, "Functional Information and the Emergence of Biocomplexity," *Proceedings of the National Academy of Sciences* 104, no. 1 (2007): 8574–8581.
Hood, Leroy, and David Galas, "The Digital Code Of DNA," *Nature* 421 (2003): 444–448.
Hoyle, Fred, "The Universe: Past and Present Reflections," *Engineering and Science*, November 1981, 8–12.
Hoyle, Fred, and Chandra Wickramasinghe, *Evolution from Space*, London: Dent, 1981.
Johnston, Wendy K., Pater J. Unrau, Michael S. Lawrence, Margarat E. Glasner, and David P. Bartl, "RNA-catalyzed RNA Polymerization: Accurate and General RNA-Templated Primer Extension," *Science* 292 (2001): 1319–1325.
Kamminga, Harmke, *Studies in the History of Ideas on the Origin of Life*, London: University of London Press, 1980.
Kavalovski, V., *The Cera Causa Principle: A Historico-Philosophical Study of a Meta-Theoretical Concept from Newton through Darwin*, Chicago: University of Chicago Press, 1974.
Kenyon, Dean, and Gary Steinman, *Biochemical Predestination*, New York: McGraw-Hill, 1969.
Küppers, Bernd-Olaf, *Information and the Origin of Life*, Cambridge: MIT Press, 1990.
Lipton, Peter, *Inference to the Best Explanation*. London and New York: Routledge, 1991.
Lyell, Charles, *Principles of Geology: Being an Attempt to Explain the Former Changes of the Earth's Surface, by Reference to Causes now in Operation*. London: John Murray, 1830–1833.
McDonough, T. R., *The Search For Extraterrestrial Intelligence: Listening for Life in the Cosmos*, New York: Wiley, 1987.
Meyer, Stephen C., *Of Clues and Causes: A Methodological Interpretation of Origin of Life Studies*, Cambridge: Cambridge University Press, 1990.
Meyer, Stephen C., *Signature in the Cell: DNA and the Evidence for Intelligent Design*, San Francisco: HarperOne, 2009.
Meyer, Stephen C., *Return of the God Hypothesis: Three Scientific Discoveries that Reveal the Mind Behind the Universe*, San Francisco: HarperOne, 2021.
Peirce, Charles S., *Collected Papers*, vol. 2, edited by C. Hartshorne and P. Weiss, Cambridge, MA: Harvard University Press: 1931.
Prigogine, Ilya, Grégoire Nicolis, and Agnessa Babloyantz, "Thermodynamics of Evolution," *Physics Today*, 23 November 1972, 23–31.

Prigogine, Ilya, and G. Nicolis, *Self-Organization in Nonequilibrium Systems,* New York: Wiley, 1977.

Quastler, Henry, *The Emergence of Biological Organization,* New Haven, CT: Yale University Press, 1964.

Scriven, Michael, "Explanation and Prediction in Evolutionary Theory," *Science* 130 (1958): 477–482.

Shapiro, Robert, *Origins: A Skeptic's Guide to the Creation of Life on Earth.* New York: Summit Books, 1986.

Shapiro, Robert, "Prebiotic Cytosine Synthesis: A Critical Analysis and Implications for the Origin of Life," *Proceedings of the National Academy of Sciences, USA* 96 (1999): 4396–4401.

Stein, Ben, *Expelled: No Intelligence Allowed,* DVD, directed by Nathan Frankowski, Los Angeles: Premise Media, 2008.

Stenger, Victor J., *God: The Failed Hypothesis,* New York: Prometheus Books, 2007.

Thaxton, Charles, and Walter L. Bradley, "Information and the Origin of Life." In *The Creation Hypothesis: Scientific Evidence For An Intelligent Designer*, edited by J. P. Moreland, 173–210, Downers Grove, IL: InterVarsity Press, 1994.

Thaxton, Charles, Walter L. Bradley, and Roger Olsen, *The Mystery of Life's Origin,* New York: Philosophical Library, 1984.

Wald, G., "The Origin of Life," *Scientific American* 191 (1954): 44–53.

Wolf, Huri I., and Eugene V. Koonin, "On the Origin of the Translation System and the Genetic Code in the RNA World by Means of Natural Selection, Exaptation, and Sufunctionalization," *Biology Direct* 2 (2007): 1–25.

Yockey, Hubert P., *Information Theory and Molecular Biology,* Cambridge: Cambridge University Press, 1992.

7

The Moral Argument

C. S. Evans[1] and Trinity O'Neill

1. Introduction

Moral arguments for God's existence were quite prominent in philosophy in the nineteenth and early twentieth centuries, being defended by such thinkers as Cardinal Newman, Hastings Rashdall, W. R. Sorley, and somewhat more recently by A. E. Taylor, Austin Farrer, and H. P. Owen. The most well-known use of the argument is C. S. Lewis's amazingly popular *Mere Christianity*. While the recent philosophical literature on this type of argument is relatively sparse in comparison with that of some other arguments, the influence of Lewis's popular treatment of the argument shows that it remains plausible to lay people, regardless of professional philosophers' views. There are many types of moral argument for God. However, this essay will focus on a theoretical type of argument that holds God is required to explain a type of moral fact.

The essence of the argument is expressed vividly by Ivan Karamazov in Dostoevsky's novel, *The Brothers Karamazov*: "Without God everything is permitted." Most people are convinced that not everything is permitted. Some acts are morally wrong and are forbidden; other acts are obligatory. Ivan holds that if there were no God, then such moral obligations would not exist. If one holds that moral obligations do exist, then there must be a God, understood as the being responsible for such obligations' existence.

To facilitate discussion of the individual premises involved, here is the argument in explicit form:

1. If there are objectively-binding moral obligations, then God exists.
2. There are objectively-binding moral obligations.
3. (Probably) God exists.

Premise (1) is equivalent to the Dostoevskian-type claim that unless God exists, there will be no objectively-binding moral obligations. "Objectively-binding moral obligations" refers to duties that hold independently of an agent's beliefs or desires. While there could be obligations to develop or inhibit various character traits (e.g., a duty to become more compassionate, less cruel, etc.), the focus here will be on obligations to perform or refrain from various actions. Since the argument is logically valid, those who reject it must deny or question one or both of the two premises. This essay will consider each premise in turn.

First, however, consider what counts as a successful argument of this sort. Must a successful argument be a "proof"? If "proof" means a logically valid argument with premises that no reasonable person could deny, it seems highly unlikely that anyone could produce a proof of God's existence. Yet, it also seems highly likely that the same will be true of arguments for any substantive philosophical claim. There are no proofs in that sense for the claim that humans have or lack free will, or that they have or lack a soul. Invariably, arguments for such controversial claims will have premises that some reasonable people will doubt. So, even if an argument for God's existence does not amount to a proof, this does not show the argument is without value. The primary value of philosophical arguments is to clarify the "cost" of rejecting an argument's conclusion. A person who is unwilling to pay this cost will find the argument convincing. Some who already believe the conclusion will find their convictions strengthened by the argument. Those who continue to reject the conclusion will minimally have a clearer understanding of the implications of this rejection.

2. Are There Objectively-Binding Moral Obligations?

If a "proof" is a valid argument with undeniable premises, then our previously outlined moral argument fails as a proof, because one can attack premise (2) by denying that there are any objectively-binding moral obligations. Friedrich Nietzsche holds this view, although he also offers some support for premise (1). In his *Genealogy of Morals*, Nietzsche explains how humans came to believe in moral obligations, even though "*there are no moral facts whatever.*"[2] For Nietzsche, belief in moral obligations arose from the social relation of creditor to debtor. Those who live in community are indebted to the community for the advantages it brings.[3] This indebtedness developed into indebtedness to real or mythical ancestors who are thought to have provided the community's foundations. These ancestors are magnified to astounding proportions, and ultimately, some ancestor "must necessarily be transfigured into a *god*."[4] The debt owed to the community becomes the debt owed to god, and the god's will then becomes the source of obligations. When the god becomes the monotheistic God of Christianity and Judaism, those obligations take on the overriding, serious character that characterizes what we call "morality."

For Nietzsche, then, "morality" (at least in Western cultures) is dependent on belief in the Judeo-Christian God. In one instance of his comments on secular moralists who try to retain moral obligations without religious foundations, Nietzsche observes:

> In England, in response to every little emancipation from theology one has to reassert one's position in a fear-inspiring manner as a moral fanatic. That is the *penance* one pays there.—With us it is different. When one gives up Christian belief one thereby deprives oneself of the *right* to Christian morality. For the latter is absolutely *not* self-evident: one must make this point clear again and again, in spite of English shallowpates.[5]

Nietzsche similarly criticizes Kant's attempt to show that moral obligations could be grounded in autonomous reason. He says, "Kant's success is merely a theologian's success."[6] The Categorical Imperative is the invention of someone "who feel[s] that [he] needs the strongest words and sounds, the most eloquent gestures and postures, in order to be effective *at all.*"[7] Hence, Nietzsche's account of the origin of our belief in moral obligations provides some support for premise (1) of the moral argument presented earlier, for Nietzsche holds that the moral beliefs, not merely of Christians, but even Kantians, utilitarians, and Marxists, depend on belief in God, even if they do not recognize this.[8] Nevertheless, for Nietzsche, the claim that there are objectively moral obligations is just false, the product of "a shameful act of historical falsification."[9]

One might question Nietzsche's particular explanation of how beliefs in moral obligations arose and yet still accept his conviction that these beliefs are in error. This is roughly the view of J. L. Mackie, who defends what he calls an "error theory" of morality.[10] For Mackie, the correct philosophical analysis of our moral beliefs shows that they commit us to moral facts that are both objective and also motivating. Although this view of morality has "a firm basis in ordinary thought and even in the meanings of moral terms," that does not show that moral entities (such as obligations) to which the beliefs commit us really exist.[11] Such entities, per Mackie, would be "queer" kinds of things, like nothing that science discovers, and so he concludes that moral beliefs are simply false. There are no moral facts, and thus no real moral obligations.

The examples of Nietzsche and Mackie show that one can doubt the truth of premise (2) of the moral argument. The critic might boldly affirm that there are no objective moral obligations, as Nietzsche and Mackie do, or be content with the more modest claim that we cannot be sure that there are such things. This stance casts doubt on premise (2), which strongly suggests that this argument fails as a conclusive proof of God's existence. Nevertheless, as already noted, it is doubtful that *any* philosophical arguments measure up to such a high standard. So, although this moral argument does not definitively establish its conclusion, this does not show that it is not a valuable argument with rational support for its conclusion.

The defender of the argument might well point out the high cost of rejecting premise (2). For, as C. S. Lewis astutely observed, the same people who reject objective moral obligations as "illusion" will frequently be found "exhorting us to work for posterity, to educate, revolutionise, liquidate, live and die for the good of the human race."[12] This demonstrates the difficulty of avoiding all moral ideals as objectively binding. Our moral experience often suggests that some acts are really wrong and others are really right. Such experience is far from a proof, but it demonstrates that, even if we can doubt the claim that there are objective obligations, it is a *reasonable* claim. Perhaps this is why many of Nietzsche's and Mackie's atheistic compatriots want to keep premise (2) and instead question premise (1) of the moral argument. Contemporary secular utilitarians and Kantians, for example, think that moral obligations are indeed objectively binding, but they deny that such obligations depend on God.

3. Do Objectively-Binding Moral Obligations Require God as Their Foundation?

So, how might critics of the argument cast doubt on premise (1), while keeping premise (2)? And how might defenders of the argument support premise (1)? Critics can cast doubt on the claim that moral obligations require God as their foundation in two ways: first, by maintaining that moral obligations require no foundation and are simply brute facts; second, by conceding that moral obligations require some ground to explain them but maintaining that something other than God can supply this. Defenders of the argument then face a complex task if they wish to support premise (1). They must defend the claims (a) that moral obligations require some kind of explanation, (b) that God does provide an explanation, and (c) that the proposed non-theistic explanations are inadequate.

The position that moral obligations are brute facts is perhaps the most difficult to attack. Almost no one denies that some facts are ultimate facts and therefore are themselves inexplicable or "brute." Theists, for example, typically hold that the universe itself is not a brute fact; it is explained as God's creation. God's existence, however, is not explained by anything else. Given that there are *some* brute facts, why should not moral facts be among them? If moral facts are brute, it becomes difficult to demonstrate that someone would be wrong to insist that facts about moral obligations are ultimate and inexplicable. Erik Wielenberg has recently made such a claim about morality; it is just a brute fact about the universe that some kinds of actions are morally right and others are morally wrong.[13] Wielenberg's position once again shows that the moral argument is not a conclusive proof.

However, even if we cannot prove that moral obligations require an explanation, there are considerations that suggest that they do. George Mavrodes, for example, has argued that moral facts about obligations would be downright odd or "queer" if we believed that the universe we live in was a "Russellian universe," having the qualities Bertrand Russell believed it had.[14] Russell himself gave a memorable statement of what such a universe would be like, which Mavrodes quotes at length:

> That man is the product of causes what had no prevision of the end they were achieving; that his origin, his growth, his hopes and fears, his loves and his beliefs are but the outcome of accidental collocations of atoms; that no fire, no heroism, no intensity of thought and feeling, can preserve an individual life beyond the grave; that all the labors of the ages, all the devotion, all the inspiration, all the noonday brightness of human genius, are destined to extinction in the vast death of the solar system, and that the whole temple of man's achievements must inevitably be buried beneath the debris of a universe in ruins—all these things, if not quite beyond dispute, are yet so nearly certain that no philosophy which rejects them can hope to stand. Only within the scaffolding of these truths, only on the firm foundation of unyielding despair, can the soul's habitation henceforth be safely built.[15]

Mavrodes subsequently argues that moral obligations in a Russellian universe would be very odd, and would seem to require some kind of explanation. Later on, however,

Mavrodes considers a position similar to Wielenberg's, one that simply considers it to be "an ultimate fact about the universe that kindness is good and cruelty is bad."[16]

Mavrodes admits that this view is not easily refuted: "Since it involves no argument, there is no argument to be refuted. And ... its central contention is not self-contradictory."[17] Nevertheless, Mavrodes points out that a world in which such facts are "brute facts" does not seem very much like a Russellian world. One would think that in a Russellian world, basically a naturalistic world in which everything reduces to the basic particles of physics, moral facts would not be "deep." Rather, a world in which there are ultimate moral facts seems more like Plato's view of the world than Russell's. And a Platonic world, though not necessarily theistic, has usually seemed to be "congenial ... to a religious understanding of the world." In the Platonic view of reality, moral obligations reflect the basic character of reality itself, which suggests that ultimately the universe is not simply "accidental collocations of atoms."[18]

Probably for this reason, many philosophers who are committed to a naturalistic understanding of morality have not been content with the claim that facts of moral obligations are simply ultimate, brute facts, but have rather tried to give such facts an explanation. The need for explanation can be seen in cases where philosophers like Mackie, who are committed to naturalism but do not believe that any such explanation can be supplied, simply stop believing in objective moral obligations altogether, and accept an error theory. Alternatively, such philosophers might follow Gilbert Harman and adopt a "relativistic" account of moral obligations.[19] On Harman's account, "absolute" moral values, including objectively-binding moral obligations, must be rejected because we cannot find a "location" for them in the world as explained by science.[20] Since we cannot explain such moral obligations naturalistically, Harman rejects them altogether, and instead gives an account of moral obligations grounded in the interests and agreements of concrete individuals. The binding force of morality, to the degree it has any, comes from human persons. Since a person can always opt out of such agreements, there are really no objectively-binding obligations. Objective moral obligations, in a naturalistic world, would be surprising, and therefore the kind of thing one would expect to be explained.

4. Naturalistic Explanations of Moral Obligations

There are at least three possible alternatives for a naturalistic explanation of moral obligations. One is to attempt to show how facts about human biology and psychology can explain moral obligations that are binding on humans. We will call these "naturalistic reductive accounts." A second strategy is to attempt to show how a social agreement or contract among humans can explain moral obligations. The third is the Kantian-type strategy of attempting to see moral obligations as a kind of demand that humans, as rational beings, make on themselves. We will now look at each of these options.

(i) Naturalistic reductive accounts

One way that naturalists explain moral obligations is to ground them in the value we ascribe to the states of affairs that are the consequences of our actions. If one can identify some natural quality (pleasure, etc.) as "good" and others as "bad," and if we assume a general "obligation" to maximize good outcomes and minimize bad ones, then one could explain obligations as grounded in natural facts. Classical utilitarianism in its various forms is a good illustration of this strategy.

Contemporary thinkers have developed this strategy in quite sophisticated ways. One way is to ground moral obligations in an account of the good derived from contemporary evolutionary biology. Larry Arnhart attempts this in *Darwinian Natural Right: The Biological Ethics of Human Nature*.[21] Arnhart believes that contemporary biology provides a basis for determining what human desires are "natural" (i.e., part of human nature); such desires are those that are "hard-wired" and cannot be altered without altering our biological nature. Arnhart grants that not everything that we desire is actually desirable, but he argues that natural desires that are rooted in our nature must be regarded as desirable by creatures such as ourselves, and thus good.

There are a host of difficulties that arise with this kind of naturalistic account. First, as G. E. Moore famously argued, the identification of the good with any particular natural property can always be challenged.[22] Just because some human beings desire an outcome, it does not follow that the outcome is actually desirable. Arnhart, for example, says that one of our "natural" desires is a desire to dominate and control others.[23] Biologically, Arnhart may be on solid ground in claiming that this is a pervasive human trait, but it seems highly dubious to infer that domination and control of others is good.

Moreover, even if we concede that we can recognize certain outcomes as good, facts about moral obligations cannot necessarily be derived from facts about what is good. Suppose someone in your city desperately needs a kidney to survive. You have two good kidneys, could donate one without significant risk, and your kidney is a good match for the one who needs it. In this situation, if you donate the kidney, the result seems to be a very good one. No doubt such a decision on your part would also be a morally good thing to do. Few people, however, would argue that you have a moral *obligation* to donate the kidney. To generate a moral obligation to donate the kidney, we need something more than the goodness of the outcome of the act.

Additionally, the problem is not merely that the goodness of an outcome is insufficient to generate a moral obligation. Rather, sometimes the acts that would bring about the best results are positively immoral and we have an obligation not to do them. Suppose, for example, that a law enforcement officer can only prevent a race riot with hundreds of deaths by surrendering one innocent person to a vigilante mob. Even if a better result would be obtained by such an action, we cannot definitively say that the law enforcement officer has an obligation to give up the innocent person. Rather, the officer more plausibly has an obligation *not* to do this. Consequentialists have attempted to respond in various ways to such problems, but the issues remain.

Nonetheless, even if the foregoing could be solved, there is one more serious problem that faces any attempt to base moral obligations on a naturalistic account of good. Even the utilitarian or consequentialist typically agrees that impartiality is an important dimension of moral obligations. Moral obligations are not simply obligations to produce good results. Morally, we must ask not merely whether the results of our actions are good, but also ask for whom they are good. Utilitarians and other consequentialists usually insist that our moral duties are not simply to do what benefits ourselves, or even what benefits our family and friends, but what benefits others too. Indeed, they often insist on strict impartiality, in which one is morally obligated to consider the needs and desires of other persons, and even sentient animals generally, equally with one's own needs and desires.

The question is how to explain this obligation of impartiality. It certainly cannot be argued that such impartiality is "natural" in the sense of being the way most people generally behave. Consequentialists concede that taking such an impartial moral stance is a difficult achievement that few people realize in any substantial way. Most of us care more about ourselves, our friends, and our families than for others. The naturalistic consequentialist may say here that the aforementioned impartial stance is simply the viewpoint of a rational person who is looking at things dispassionately. Such a person is taking "the moral point of view."[24] But what generates our duty to do so?

We can agree that this view of how the good should be sought is how things would look to an impartial "ideal observer." However, humans are not such ideal observers. The questions remain *why* a person ought to take such an impartial "moral point of view" or care how a (fictitious) ideal observer would view our behavior. It might make a difference if the ideal observer were an actual person (God?) whose evaluation mattered to us. Perhaps a person who looks on the world from a moral standpoint will look at things in such an impartial way. However, this is not the only way humans can look at things, and it is difficult to see what answer the naturalist can give to the question why human persons *should* adopt such a moral standpoint. One of the most basic features of moral obligations then seems to be unexplained by the view that our duties are simply to maximize good consequences.

We could of course attempt to explain moral behavior in various ways by looking for the natural causes of such behavior. Various attempts have been made to show that altruistic, impartial behavior is somehow grounded in our nature, as understood by evolutionary biology. For example, some have theorized that altruistic behavior has a genetic basis.[25] Nevertheless, even if these theories succeed in explaining why humans sometimes behave in moral ways, it is mysterious how such facts could explain the existence of genuine moral *obligations*. For whatever an obligation may be, it is not simply a tendency to behave in some particular way, and no biological explanation of why humans might care about other humans seems capable of explaining why they *should* care about them.

(ii) Social contract theories

A different strategy may attract those who think it is difficult or even impossible to explain moral obligations with naturalistic reductive accounts: perhaps we can explain moral obligations as the result of a human contract. Moral obligations, while not reducible to biology or other natural facts, are then constructed by humans, and God is unnecessary to explain them.

If we ask why humans should make such an agreement, the answer seems to be that it is in our self-interest to do so. Human persons who lived in what we might call a moral "state of nature" in which there are no moral obligations would find their situation to be undesirable in many ways. Thomas Hobbes famously described a political state of nature as one in which humans are at "war" with each other, and in which life is "solitary, poor, nasty, brutish and short."[26] Similarly, in a moral state of nature, humans would be free to pursue their own individual desires at the expense of others, but then the goods that cooperative action makes possible would be severely imperiled. While our moral duties often forbid us to do what is to our advantage, the defender of the social agreement view of morality argues that, overall, the "acceptance of duty is truly advantageous."[27]

The social agreement that is the ground of morality on this view is one in which people accept certain behavioral constraints provided others do the same. I will not lie, steal, or break my promises, provided you also do not lie, steal, or break your promises. Note that the agreement is reciprocal and conditional on others' behavior. It would not be rational to give up your rights to privilege personal well-being if other people continue to privilege their own well-being and refuse to take your well-being into account. David Gauthier, who defends this kind of account, says that the person who promises to keep the agreement should not be a "dupe." Instead, a person should respect the agreement only if others do so too. Thus, "she ensures that those not disposed to fair co-operation do not enjoy the benefits of any co-operation, thus making this unfairness costly to themselves, and so irrational."[28]

The social agreement explanation of moral obligations is plausible, for morality often "pays off." Even a dishonest shopkeeper may be deterred from cheating customers by the worry that he could lose business if discovered. However, there are basic problems with the social agreement account of morality. Some concern whether such an account can adequately explain all of the actual obligations we have (more on these later), and some concern the nature of the agreement itself. Regarding the nature of the agreement, we might ask whether the agreement is actual or merely hypothetical—i.e., one that people would accept if they had the opportunity to do so. Either option presents problems.

If the agreement is an actual one, we might ask when the agreement is supposed to have been entered into, and how it was created. Perhaps this problem can be solved by noting that agreements can be tacit and implied; perhaps no explicit agreement is necessary. There are more serious problems. First, has everyone actually made a commitment to such an agreement? What about the person who is a hit man for the Mafia, or the individual who is a racist and believes he can behave as he wishes towards members of some other race? Second, if the moral rules that govern our lives together rest on actual agreements, why should we think that there is only one such agreement? Surely different communities can and will opt for different rules. If the rules are to be such that everyone in the community will accept them, then they most likely will reflect the differences in resources, status, and power that different individuals have. Rich people would likely agree with a rule that no one should steal from others, but reject a rule that rich people should offer assistance to the disadvantaged.[29] If different groups agree on different sets of moral rules, then moral obligations will not really be objective, but relative to specific communities.

Furthermore, it is unclear why the agreement should be viewed as binding in the way moral obligations are supposed to be binding. After all, most agreements are not open-ended, but valid for a particular period of time, and many agreements have provisions that allow individuals to "opt out." It is hard to see why it would not be reasonable for individuals to choose to opt out of any agreement with rules that might seriously disadvantage them. And there are times when doing what is moral does disadvantage a person, at least when judging advantages by the criteria appropriate to a naturalistic worldview, which presumably includes achieving things like wealth, health, and reputation. However, one feature most in need of explanation is the fact that moral obligations are objectively binding; they are always applicable to everyone. Moral rules lack this feature when they hold due to an agreement that we can opt out of.

Another set of problems involves the scope of any actual agreement that might be made. Since the agreement's motivation is self-interest, it is reasonable to make such an agreement only with those who might benefit, or at least not harm oneself, under the agreement. However, there are many persons (e.g., those with mental or physical handicaps, or who live in desperately poor countries) who cannot realistically be expected to benefit or pose any kind of threat to us. Such people, then, are effectively outside the scope of any such agreement. Nevertheless, those who believe in the reality of objective moral obligations usually also believe that we have obligations towards individuals in such categories, and even that our obligations here are especially important ones. It is hard to see how such obligations could result from an actual agreement motivated by self-interest.

The other possibility, then, is where the agreement is seen as hypothetical, rather than actual. For example, one might claim that the rules of morality are the rules that people would accept if they were ignorant of their status in society. If one was going to choose the moral rules for humans to live by but did not yet know what one's situation in life would be (e.g., whether one will be male or female, rich or poor, etc.), then the rules one would accept would more likely be fair and impartial to all than in the case of an actual agreement.[30] To favor rules that disadvantage certain groups is risky if one potentially belongs to such a group.

However, different problems emerge here. Most fundamentally, it is difficult to see how *actual* obligations are grounded in a purely hypothetical agreement between fictitious persons. For example, it might be true that if one attended the local symphony, and afterwards heard an appeal for funds to allow the symphony to continue, one would promise to make a substantial contribution. And if one made such a promise, it seems reasonable that one would be obligated to make the contribution. However, it is hard to see how an assumed hypothetical fact that one would make such a promise in a situation that does not hold obligates one to make a contribution. It might be good to make a contribution, but it is not something one has a duty to do. Nor is a duty created merely by a hypothetical fact about a promise that one would make in a certain situation, when no such agreement has been made, and the actual situation is quite different.

Both actual agreements and hypothetical agreements face other formidable difficulties. First, the agreement is a conditional one, where the individual promises to live by certain rules *if* others do so too. However, we have good empirical reasons to think that others will not always do this. For example, suppose that a community where cheating does not occur is better off than a society where cheating is rampant. Although an individual might be tempted to cheat to secure some good (a better job, admission to a school, etc.), it would be reasonable for a person to agree to refrain from cheating if others do so too, because there will be many undesirable consequences if cheating is widespread. Unfortunately, in the actual world, cheating is widespread. Hence, even if a person promised (or was willing to promise) not to cheat *if* others also agreed, no obligation to refrain from cheating would result. If one knows that others will actually cheat, then the condition for agreement has vanished. If one does not want to be a "dupe," one will see that not cheating gives rise to personal disadvantage in a society of cheaters.

Another difficulty is that of "free-riders" and "parasites." From a self-interested perspective, it might make the most sense to agree to live by the rules of morality, provided others do too, but nevertheless selectively break those rules. One might object that if we break the rules, we will be punished by others. However, there will be cases where violations are undetectable and then no punishment will happen. Hence, the best strategy would be to agree to the rules of morality, and keep them in all cases where violations would likely be detected, but deviate from those rules in cases where violations cannot be detected and some significant advantage can be secured. Then one will have the best of both worlds: a reputation for being morally good and the option of acting immorally in advantageous cases.

(iii) Self-legislation theories

The final option we will consider for explanations of moral obligations is to see them as self-imposed. This is the view developed by Immanuel Kant, who saw moral obligations as laws that humans autonomously legislate. On this view, humans are both authors and subjects of the moral law. Kant is often interpreted by contemporary philosophers as developing an account of morality that makes God unnecessary for morality, and this is the kind of view that we will consider now.

Note that the historical Kant may not have held such a view, since he thought that belief in moral obligation was linked to belief in God in various ways. First, Kant famously argued that a commitment to morality required belief in God as what he called a "postulate of practical reason."[31] More significantly perhaps, Kant did not think that humans create or invent the moral law by their legislation. Rather, they add something like their own reflective endorsement to a principle that is in some sense objective. One way of seeing this is that Kant held that to be a moral being is to be a member of what he called the "kingdom of ends," and he also taught that God was the "head" of this kingdom.[32] As head of the kingdom of ends, God is also the author of the moral law in a profound sense. So, despite holding that the moral law was a principle that reason autonomously endorsed, Kant also held that it was proper to see the moral law as a divine command.[33]

When Kant's notion of self-legislation is interpreted in a secular way that sees no significant role for God in the kingdom of ends, at least two types of difficulties emerge. The first concerns the character of the moral law as self-commanded, and the second concerns the content of the moral law.

The first type of difficulty is memorably described by Kierkegaard:

> Kant was of the opinion that man is his own law (autonomous)—that is, he binds himself under the law which he himself gives himself. Actually, in a profounder sense, this is how lawlessness or experimentation are established. This is not being rigorously earnest any more than Sancho Panza's self-administered blows to his own bottom were vigorous.[34]

Kierkegaard's thought here is clearly that a law, especially a moral law, must be able to bind us if it is to be a genuine law. However, a self-given law lacks this binding force, since if the self has the power to enact the law, it must also have the power to rescind it, and will likely be tempted to do just that when morality goes against what a person wants to do. Kierkegaard's intuition here is shared by Elizabeth Anscombe, who argued that "the concept of legislation requires superior power in the legislature." Anscombe claims that the idea of "legislating for oneself" is like claiming that every decision a person makes is a "vote" that always turns out to be a majority of 1–0.[35]

The second type of problem that afflicts this Kantian-inspired move is determining the content of the moral law. If we interpret the self-legislation model as individuals inventing the moral law, then any content appears arbitrary.[36] Kant did not think the moral law was arbitrary, but that the "categorical imperative" could be derived merely from the rational form of the concept of law, which he saw as universality: "I ought never to act except in such a way *that I can also will that my maxim should become a universal law.*"[37] However, almost from the beginning, Kant's critics have objected that this requirement is so formal and abstract that it fails to specify any determinate content; humans can consistently will almost anything as a universal law without contradicting themselves.

Kant gives several versions of the categorical imperative, which he claims are equivalent to the original version, although many philosophers question this. However, perhaps one of the more promising forms of the principle is the one where Kant urges us to "*act in such a way that you always treat humanity, whether in your own person or in the person of any other, never simply as a means, but always at the same time as an end.*"[38] Kant thought that a rational being necessarily valued himself/herself as an end, and that rational consistency required that a rational being necessarily value other rational beings as well. This principle does have a better chance of delivering moral content than Kant's purely formal version of the categorical imperative.

This is probably why contemporary Kantian Christine Korsgaard relies on a version of this principle when she attempts to develop a contemporary account of how humans themselves can ground the moral law. Though Korsgaard follows Kant in seeing the source of normativity to be the law-like, universal "form" that is constitutive of our "reflective endorsement" of a possible way of acting, she admits that this universal form cannot give fully determinate content to the moral law.[39] She makes a distinction, one Kant himself does not clearly make, between the categorical imperative and the moral law.[40] The categorical imperative rules out some maxims as possible laws, because not every principle can be consistently willed as a universal law. However, for Korsgaard, the particular maxims that have authority for an individual ultimately stem from the identity of that individual, since "a view of what you ought to do is a view of who you are."[41] Since people can and do conceive of their identities very differently, people who conceive of their identities differently will see themselves as having different obligations, and will actually have different obligations on Korsgaard's view.

Korsgaard attempts to limit the relativistic implications here by arguing that whatever practical identity a person takes must include a recognition of their own value as a human being. Essentially, "our identity as moral beings—as people who value themselves as human beings—stands behind our more particular practical identities."[42] If we assume that valuing ourselves in this way implies we should value other humans as well, then we are close to the Kantian formula that persons must be valued as ends in themselves, never only as means.[43]

Such a formula certainly captures something deep about our moral obligations. The question does not concern the truth of the claim that human persons have intrinsic worth and dignity, and therefore should be valued as ends, but the reason why this is true. Korsgaard sees herself as developing a "constructivist" account of morality, where moral truths are the product of human reflection and deliberation, and this constructivism is seen as an alternative to "substantive realism" about morality, which sees moral properties as intrinsic to objective entities and states of affairs.[44] However, recognizing all human beings as creatures who possess intrinsic worth and dignity seems suspiciously like substantive realism.

For Korsgaard, the ground of obligation is our "practical identity," and the moral law is rooted in a legislative affirmation of our identity as human beings, one shared with all other humans. Nevertheless, not everyone conceives of practical identity in this way, seeing all other humans, like oneself, as beings with intrinsic worth who must be valued as ends in themselves. Unfortunately, this raises a dilemma for a view like Korsgaard's. People do have some choice about how they define their identity. If they are making a mistake when they do not construe their practical identity as Korsgaard (and Kant) think they should, moral realism appears right after all, since they fail to recognize an objective truth: that all human persons have intrinsic worth. If they are not making a mistake, then it appears that to opt for an identity that sees human persons as having worth is just a "radical choice," similar to the "existentialist" move that sees morality as grounded in a contingent choice.

Korsgaard might try to avoid this dilemma by arguing that, although any identity that does not affirm the value of humanity is a kind of mistaken identity, the mistake is not one of failing to recognize some substantive moral truth, but failing to solve a practical problem in the "right" way, the way that "reason" requires. However, it is hard to see how other solutions can be "wrong" if it is not the case that humans as such have the value that morality presupposes they have. Surely, the many cultures that have failed to recognize the intrinsic worth of all humans are not fundamentally lacking in rationality. Even Aristotle, the man who virtually invented logic and defined the western conception of rationality, saw women and slaves as naturally inferior beings, who lacked the fundamental rights that a Kantian believes all humans possess. This strongly suggests that the Kantian principle of valuing all human persons is not an inescapable result of practical reasoning per se, but rather seems practically rational only to those who recognize the intrinsic value of human persons.

That one's personal identity is ultimately contingent is something Korsgaard implicitly admits, when she concedes that our identity as a moral agent "does not always swamp other forms of identity," which means that it is not the case that moral obligations always trump other kinds of obligations.[45] Korsgaard might respond that the value we ought to attribute to human persons simply derives from the value we necessarily place on our own reason. If we reflectively attempt to decide how we should live our lives, we cannot help but value reflection itself, and our lives as reflective beings, and reason will require that we value other persons as reflective beings too.

One problem with this response concerns whether our value as humans depends on our actual ability to engage in rational reflection. This is doubtful. Special moral duties apply to humans who lack the actual ability to reflect rationally—infants, the severely mentally ill, etc. They have intrinsic worth and dignity that cannot be grounded in any actual rational ability. Theists may well argue here that there is still something about morality that needs explaining, namely why humans have intrinsic moral value, regardless of any actual rational ability. At this point, a different type of argument from morality to God can be constructed. On the theistic view, God must be seen as supremely real and good, and the source of the reality and goodness of everything other than himself. Theists will maintain that humans' intrinsic value or dignity can be explained if they are understood as creatures made in God's image, which may but need not include any *actual* rational ability. An alternative would be to see humans' intrinsic value or dignity as stemming from the love God has for all of us.

So, to review our progress, if we define a proof of God's existence as a valid argument with undeniable premises, then the moral argument as developed here is not a proof. One can doubt the existence of objective moral obligations, and thus cast doubt on premise (2). There are also ways that critics might doubt premise (1) by looking at alternative explanations of moral obligations that do not posit God. However, we have also examined the liabilities of these attempts to undermine the argument, and each has a cost. Error theories like those of Mackie and Nietzsche carry the cost of denying many deeply-held moral convictions. Reductivist, social contract, and self-legislation theories also have costs, and in many cases seem to inadequately explain important features of morality.

5. Why Should God Be Obeyed?

How does God explain the existence of moral obligations? The theist may hold that God is the rightful sovereign of the universe. As such, God has the authority to establish moral laws for his human subjects, just as human rulers have the authority to establish legal laws. God is the sovereign of the universe because the universe is God's creation, and it is reasonable to hold that a divine person has authority over his handiwork.

Someone who rejects this might still recognize that humans have good reasons to obey God. For example, normally we have good reason to be grateful to someone who has given us a great good, and that such a debt of gratitude means we should try to please our benefactor. However, every good that any person has ultimately comes from God, and thus the debt of gratitude owed to God far exceeds the debt we could owe to anyone else. Some might also argue that it is reasonable to obey God because God, who is completely good and loving, has created humans to become his friends and enjoy eternal life with him. God's laws, as expressed in his commands, represent the path humans must follow to become God's friends.

Note that this theistic view of moral obligations does not require a "voluntaristic" stance where all moral properties arbitrarily depend on God's will. Rather, it holds that there are truths about God and the good that are presupposed by God's laws. God's laws should be obeyed because he is himself good and because we can see that it is good to obey his laws.[46]

6. Conclusion

In sum, for those who accept a certain conception of moral obligations, moral arguments have genuine force, despite failing to reach the standard of proof. By contrast, the cost of denying the reality of moral obligations seems high. Non-theistic explanations of moral obligations seem very implausible to many and are subject to powerful objections. That God—understood as the perfectly good creator of the universe (if such a God exists)—is the ruler of the universe and has the authority to establish laws for that universe is intuitively plausible. Unsurprisingly, many still believe that moral obligations require a religious foundation. This does not mean that non-believers cannot believe in morality and seek to live moral lives. It is not a psychological claim that one must be religious to be motivated to live morally. Many people may be motivated to live morally simply by conscience, which religious believers may see as a God-given faculty. The claim is that belief in moral obligations provides good reasons to believe in God for many people who see moral obligations as requiring an explanation and think that God provides the explanation that is needed.

Notes

1. This chapter is an extensively modified version of material taken from C. Stephen Evans, *Natural Signs and Knowledge of God: A New Look at Theistic Arguments* (Oxford: Oxford University Press, 2010), Chapter 5: "Moral Arguments and Natural Signs for God," 109–131, and is used by permission of Oxford University Press.
2. This quotation is from Friedrich Nietzsche, *Twilight of the Idols*, in *Twilight of the Idols; The Anti-Christ*, trans. R. J. Hollingdale, intro. Michael Tanner (London: Penguin Books, 1990), 66.
3. Friedrich Nietzsche, *On the Genealogy of Morals*, trans. Walter Kaufmann and R. J. Hollingdale (New York: Vintage, 1967), 71.
4. Nietzsche, *On the Genealogy of Morals*, 89 (Nietzsche's emphasis).
5. Nietzsche, *Twilight of the Idols*, 80 (Nietzsche's emphasis).
6. Nietzsche, *The Anti-Christ*, 133.
7. Friedrich Nietzsche, *The Gay Science: With a Prelude in German Rhymes and an Appendix of Songs*, ed. Bernard Williams, trans. Josefine Nauckhoff, poems trans. Adrian Del Caro, Cambridge Texts in the History of Philosophy (Cambridge: Cambridge University Press, 2001), 32–33.
8. Nietzsche, *The Gay Science*, 199.

9   Nietzsche, *The Anti-Christ*, 149.
10 J. L. Mackie, *Ethics: Inventing Right and Wrong* (London: Penguin Books, 1990).
11 Mackie, *Ethics: Inventing Right and Wrong*, 32.
12 C. S. Lewis, *Miracles*, 1947 (San Francisco: HarperOne, 2001), 57.
13 See Erik Wielenberg, "In Defense of Non-Natural, Non-Theistic Moral Realism," *Faith and Philosophy* 26, no. 1 (2009): 23–41.
14 George Mavrodes, "Religion and the Queerness of Morality," in *Rationality, Religious Belief, and Moral Commitment*, ed. Robert Audi and William Wainwright (Ithaca, NY: Cornell University Press, 1986), 213–226.
15 From Bertrand Russell, "A Free Man's Worship," in *Mysticism and Logic* (New York: Barnes and Noble, 1917), 47–48. Quote in Mavrodes, "Religion and the Queerness of Morality," 215.
16 Mavrodes, "Religion and the Queerness of Morality," 224.
17 Ibid.
18 Ibid.
19 See Gilbert Harman, "What is Moral Relativism?," in *Explaining Value and Other Essays in Moral Philosophy* (Oxford: Oxford University Press, 2000). Harman is discussed below in looking at views of morality as grounded in social agreements.
20 Gilbert Harman, "Is There a Single True Morality?," in *Explaining Value and Other Essays in Moral Philosophy*, 83.
21 Larry Arnhart, *Darwinian Natural Right: The Biological Ethics of Human Nature* (New York: State University of New York Press, 1998).
22 See G. E. Moore, *Ethics*, Home University Library of Modern Knowledge 52 (New York: Holt, 1912).
23 Larry Arnhart, *Darwinian Natural Right*, 29–36.
24 Kurt Baier, *The Moral Point of View: A Rational Basis of Ethics* (Ithaca, NY: Cornell University Press, 1958).
25 Frans de Waal, *Good Natured: The Origins of Right and Wrong in Humans and Other Animals* (Cambridge, MA: Harvard University Press, 1996), 135–136.
26 Thomas Hobbes, *Leviathan*, in *Cambridge Texts in the History of Political Thought*, ed. Richard Tuck (Cambridge: Cambridge University Press, 1996), 89.
27 David Gauthier, *Morals by Agreement* (Oxford: Clarendon Press, 1986), 2.
28 Gauthier, *Morals by Agreement*, 179.
29 Gilbert Harman argues that the principles of morality are relative in just this way, and thinks that this is due to the fact that they are grounded in actual agreements humans have made, agreements that reflect the different bargaining positions different people bring to the table, so to speak. See Gilbert Harman and Judith Jarvis Thomson, *Moral Relativism and Moral Objectivity*, Great Debates in Philosophy (Cambridge, MA: Blackwell, 1996), 23.
30 John Rawls, *A Theory of Justice* (Cambridge, MA: Belknap, 2005), 136–142.
31 Immanuel Kant, *Critique of Practical Reason*, trans. Lewis White Beck, The Library of Liberal Arts 52 (New York: Bobbs-Merrill, 1956), 128–136.
32 Kant, *Critique of Practical Reason*, 135–136.
33 Kant, *Critique of Practical Reason*, 134.
34 *Søren Kierkegaard's Journals and Papers*, ed. and trans. Howard V. Hong and Edna H. Hong (Bloomington, IN: Indiana University Press, 1967), Volume 1, entry 188, 76.
35 Elizabeth Anscombe, "Modern Moral Philosophy," *Philosophy* 33 (1958): 1–19.
36 See Alasdair MacIntyre, *After Virtue: A Study in Moral Theory* (London: Duckworth, 1981), 40–45, for a critique of the idea of "radical choice."

37   Immanuel Kant, *Groundwork of the Metaphysic of Morals*, trans. H. J. Paton, Harper Torchbooks, The Academy Library (New York: Harper & Row, 1964), 70.
38   Kant, *Groundwork of the Metaphysic of Morals*, 96.
39   See Christine Korsgaard, *The Sources of Normativity* (Cambridge: Cambridge University Press, 1996), 92–98.
40   Korsgaard, *The Sources of Normativity*, 98–100.
41   Korsgaard, *The Sources of Normativity*, 117.
42   Korsgaard, *The Sources of Normativity*, 121.
43   Ibid.
44   Korsgaard, *The Sources of Normativity*, 112.
45   Korsgaard, *The Sources of Normativity*, 125.
46   For a fuller account of how God has authority over the universe, see C. Stephen Evans, *God and Moral Obligation* (Oxford: Oxford University Press, 2013), chapters 2 and 4.

Bibliography

Anscombe, Elizabeth. "Modern Moral Philosophy." *Philosophy* 33 (1958): 1–19.

Arnhart, Larry. *Darwinian Natural Right: The Biological Ethics of Human Nature*. New York: State University of New York Press, 1998.

Baier, Kurt. *The Moral Point of View: A Rational Basis of Ethics*. Ithaca, NY: Cornell University Press, 1958.

Evans, C. Stephen. *God and Moral Obligation*. Oxford: Oxford University Press, 2013.

Evans, C. Stephen. *Natural Signs and Knowledge of God: A New Look at Theistic Arguments*. Oxford: Oxford University Press, 2010.

Gauthier, David. *Morals by Agreement*. Oxford: Clarendon Press, 1986.

Harman, Gilbert and Judith Jarvis Thomson. *Moral Relativism and Moral Objectivity*. Great Debates in Philosophy. Cambridge, MA: Blackwell, 1996.

Harman, Gilbert. *Explaining Value and Other Essays in Moral Philosophy*. Oxford: Oxford University Press, 2000.

Hobbes, Thomas. *Leviathan*, edited by Richard Tuck. Cambridge: Cambridge University Press, 1996.

Hong, Howard V. and Edna. V. Hong (eds., trans). *Søren Kierkegaard's Journals and Papers*. Bloomington, Indiana: Indiana University Press, 1967.

Kant, Immanuel. *Critique of Practical Reason*, translated by Lewis White Beck. The Library of Liberal Arts 52. New York: Bobbs-Merrill, 1956.

Kant, Immanuel. *Groundwork of the Metaphysic of Morals*, translated by H. J. Paton, Harper Torchbook. The Academy Library. New York: Harper & Row, 1964.

Korsgaard, Christine. *The Sources of Normativity*. Cambridge: Cambridge University Press, 1996.

Lewis, C. S. *Miracles*. 1947. San Francisco: HarperOne, 2001.

Mackie, J. L. *Ethics: Inventing Right and Wrong*. London: Penguin Books, 1990.

MacIntyre, Alasdair. *After Virtue: A Study in Moral Theory*. London: Duckworth, 1981.

Mavrodes, George. "Religion and the Queerness of Morality." In *Rationality, Religious Belief, and Moral Commitment*, edited by Robert Audi and William Wainwright, 213–226. Ithaca, NY: Cornell University Press, 1986.

Moore, G. E. *Ethics*. Home University Library of Modern Knowledge 52. New York: Holt, 1912.

Nietzsche, Friedrich. *On the Genealogy of Morals*, translated by Walter Kaufmann and R. J. Hollingdale. New York: Vintage, 1967.

Nietzsche, Friedrich. *The Gay Science: With a Prelude in German Rhymes and an Appendix of Songs*, edited by Bernard Williams, translated by Josefine Nauckhoff and Adrian Del Caro. Cambridge: Cambridge University Press, 2001.

Nietzsche, Friedrich. "Twilight of the Idols," in *Twilight of the Idols* and *The Anti-Christ*, translated by R. J. Hollingdale. Including an introduction by Michael Tanner. London: Penguin Books, 1990.

Rawls, John. *A Theory of Justice*. Cambridge, MA: Belknap, 2005.

Russell, Bertrand. *Mysticism and Logic*. New York: Barnes and Noble, 1917.

Waal, Frans de. *Good Natured: The Origins of Right and Wrong in Humans and Other Animals*. Cambridge, MA: Harvard University Press, 1996.

Wielenberg, Erik. "In Defense of Non-Natural, Non-Theistic Moral Realism." *Faith and Philosophy* 26, no. 1 (2009): 23–41.

Part Two

Further Directions in Natural Theology

8

The Argument from Phenomenal Consciousness

J. P. Moreland

1. Introduction

Consciousness is among the most mystifying features of the cosmos. Geoffrey Madell opines that "the emergence of consciousness, then, is a mystery, and one to which materialism signally fails to provide an answer."[1] Naturalist Colin McGinn claims that its arrival borders on sheer magic because there seems to be no naturalistic explanation for it: "How can mere matter originate consciousness? How did evolution convert the water of biological tissue into the wine of consciousness? Consciousness seems like a radical novelty in the universe, not prefigured by the after-effects of the Big Bang; so how did it contrive to spring into being from what preceded it?"[2] Finally, naturalist William Lyons argues that "[physicalism] seem[s] to be in tune with the scientific materialism of the twentieth century because it [is] a harmonic of the general theme that all there is in the universe is matter and energy and motion and that humans are a product of the evolution of species just as much as buffaloes and beavers are. Evolution is a seamless garment with no holes wherein souls might be inserted from above."[3]

Lyons' reference to souls being "inserted from above" appears to be a veiled reference to the explanatory power of theism for consciousness. Some argue that, while finite mental entities may be inexplicable on a naturalist worldview, they may be explained by theism, thereby furnishing evidence for God's existence. In this chapter, I shall defend this argument from consciousness (hereafter, AC) by describing two relevant issues in scientific theory acceptance, presenting a summary of AC, characterizing naturalism and showing why mental entities are recalcitrant facts for naturalists and evaluating three explanations of consciousness that serve as rivals for AC.

2. Preliminary points

Two preliminaries are important. First, for two reasons I shall assume that theism and naturalism are the only worldviews relevant to the chapter: These are, indeed, the only live options for many who debate this topic; in any case, other worldviews (e.g., Buddhism) are far from univocal in their commitment to the reality of consciousness or of the cosmos itself. Second, I shall assume a commonsense understanding of mental states such as sensations, thoughts, beliefs, desires, volitions and the selves that have them. So understood, mental states are in no sense physical since they possess *five* features not owned by physical states:

(a) there is a raw qualitative feel or a "what it is like" to have a mental state such as a pain;
(b) at least many mental states have intentionality—*ofness* or *aboutness*—directed towards an object;
(c) mental states are inner, private and immediate to the subject having them;
(d) they require a subjective ontology—namely, mental states are necessarily owned by the first person sentient subjects who have them;
(e) mental states fail to have crucial features (e.g., spatial extension, location) that characterize physical states and, in general, cannot be described using physical language.

Space considerations prevent me from arguing for these claims, but this is not necessary for present purposes, since many (but not all) critics of AC assume with its advocates a dualist construal of consciousness.[4]

3. Two issues in scientific theory acceptance

While theism and naturalism are broad worldviews and not scientific theories, two issues that inform the adjudication between rival scientific theories are relevant to AC. First, there is the issue as to whether some phenomenon should be taken as *basic* for which only a description and not an explanation or as something to be explained in terms of *more basic* phenomena. For example, attempts to explain uniform inertial motion are disallowed in Newtonian mechanics because such motion is basic on this view, but an Aristotelian had to explain how or why a particular body exhibited uniform inertial motion. Thus, what is basic to one theory may be derivative in another.

Issue two is the *naturalness* of a postulated entity in light of the overall theory of which it is a part. The types of entities postulated, along with the sorts of properties they possess and the relations they enter should be at home with other entities in the theory. Some entity (particular thing, process, property, or relation) e is natural for a theory T just in case either e is a central, core entity of T or e bears a relevant similarity to central, core entities in e's category within T. If e is in a category such as substance, force, property, event, relation, or cause, e should bear a relevant similarity to other entities of T in that category.

This is a formal definition and the material content given to it will depend on the theory in question. Moreover, given rivals R and S, the postulation of e in R is *ad hoc* and question-begging against advocates of S if e bears a relevant similarity to the appropriate entities in S, and in this sense is "at home" in S, but fails to bear this relevant similarity to the appropriate entities in R.[5]

The issue of naturalness is relevant to theory assessment between rivals in that it provides a criterion for advocates of a theory to claim that their rivals have begged the question against them or adjusted their theory in an inappropriate, *ad hoc* way. And though this need not be the case, naturalness can be related to basicality in this way: Naturalness can provide a means of deciding the relative merits of accepting theory R, which depicts phenomenon *e* as basic, vs. embracing S, which takes *e* to be explainable in more basic terms. If *e* is natural in S but not in R, it will be difficult for advocates of R to justify the bald assertion that *e* is basic in R and that all proponents of R need to do is describe *e* and correlate it with other phenomena in R as opposed to explaining e. Such a claim by advocates of R will be even more problematic if S provides an explanation for e.[6]

4. The argument from consciousness

AC may be expressed in inductive or deductive form. As an inductive argument, AC may be construed as claiming that given theism and naturalism as the live options fixed by our background beliefs, theism provides a better explanation of consciousness than naturalism and, thus, receives some confirmation from the existence of consciousness.

AC may also be expressed in deductive form. Here is one deductive version of AC:

(1) Genuinely non-physical mental states exist.
(2) There is an explanation for the existence of mental states.
(3) Personal explanation is different from natural scientific explanation.
(4) The explanation for the existence of mental states is either a personal or natural scientific explanation.
(5) The explanation is not a natural scientific one.
(6) Therefore, the explanation is a personal one.
(7) If the explanation is personal, then it is theistic.
(8) Therefore, the explanation is theistic.

Theists such as Robert Adams[7] and Richard Swinburne[8] have advanced a slightly different version of AC which focus on mental/physical correlations and not merely on the existence of mental states. Either way, AC may be construed as a deductive argument.

Premises (2), (4), and (5) are the one most likely to come under attack. We are granting (1) for the sake of argument.[9]

(3) turns on the fact that personal explanation differs from event causal covering law explanations employed in natural science. Associated with *event* causation is a covering law model of explanation according to which some event (the *explanandum*) is explained by giving a correct deductive or inductive argument for that event. Such an argument contains two features in its *explanans*: a (universal or statistical) law of nature *and* initial causal conditions.

By contrast, a *personal* explanation (divine or otherwise) of some basic result R brought about intentionally by person P where this bringing about of R is a basic action A will cite the intention I of P that R occur and the basic power B that P exercised to bring about R. P, I, and B provide a personal explanation of R: agent P brought about R by exercising power B in order to realize intention I as an irreducibly teleological goal.

To illustrate, suppose we are trying to explain why Wesson simply moved his finger (R). We could explain this by saying that Wesson (P) performed an act of endeavoring to move his finger (A) in that he exercised his ability to move (or will to move) his finger (B) intending to move the finger (I). If Wesson's moving his finger was an expression of an intent to move a finger to fire a gun to kill Smith, then we can explain the non-basic results (the firing of the gun and the killing of Smith) by saying that Wesson (P) performed an act of killing Smith (I3) by endeavoring to move his finger (A) intentionally (I1) by exercising his power to do so (B), intending thereby to fire the gun (I2) in order to kill Smith. An explanation of the results of a non-basic action (like going to the store to get bread) will include a description of an action plan. A personal explanation does not consist in offering a mechanism, but rather, in correctly citing the relevant person, his intentions, the basic power exercised, and in some cases, offering a description of the relevant action plan.[10]

Advocates of AC employ the difference between these two modes of explanation to justify premise (2). Briefly, the argument is that given a defense of premise (4) and (5), there is no natural scientific explanation of mental entities. Since both modes of explanation are *ones people use all the time*, there is no reason to take mental entities as brute facts and there is precedent for proffering a personal explanation for them.

Premise (7) seems fairly uncontroversial. To be sure, Humean style arguments about the type and number of deities involved could be raised at this point, but these issues would be intramural theistic problems of small comfort to naturalists.[11] That is, if the explanation for finite conscious minds is supernatural, then naturalism is false. (4) will be examined in conjunction with four alternatives to AC that reject it:

That leaves (5). At least four reasons have been offered for why there is no natural scientific explanation for the existence of mental states (or their regular correlation with physical states):

(a) *The uniformity of nature*. Prior to the emergence of consciousness, the universe contained nothing but aggregates of particles/waves standing in fields of forces relative to each other. The story of the development of the cosmos is told in terms of the rearrangement of micro-parts into increasingly more complex structures according to natural law. On a naturalist depiction of matter, it is brute mechanical, physical stuff. The emergence of consciousness seems to be a case of getting something from nothing. In general, physico-chemical reactions do not generate consciousness, not even one little bit, but they do in the brain, yet brains seem similar to other parts of organisms' bodies (e.g., both are collections of cells totally describable in physical terms). How can like causes produce radically different effects? The appearance of mind is utterly unpredictable and inexplicable. This radical discontinuity seems like an inhomogeneous rupture in the natural world. Similarly, physical states have spatial extension and location but mental states seem to lack spatial features. Space and consciousness sit oddly together. How did spatially-arranged matter conspire to produce non-spatial mental states? From a naturalist point of view, this seems utterly inexplicable.

(b) *Contingency of the mind/body correlation*. The regular correlation between types of mental states and physical states seems radically contingent. Why do pains instead of itches, thoughts or feelings of love get correlated with specific brain states? No amount of knowledge of the brain state will help to answer this question. For the naturalist, the regularity of mind/body correlations must be taken as contingent brute facts. But these facts are inexplicable from a naturalistic standpoint, and they are radically *sui generis* compared to all other entities in the naturalist ontology. Thus, it begs the question simply to announce that mental states and their regular correlations with certain brain states is a natural fact. As naturalist Terence Horgan acknowledges, "in any metaphysical framework that deserves labels like 'materialism,' 'naturalism,' or 'physicalism,' supervenient facts must be explainable rather than being *sui generis*."[12] Since on most depictions, the theistic God possesses libertarian freedom, God is free to act or refrain from acting in various ways. Thus, the fact that the existence of consciousness and its precise correlation with matter is contingent fits well with a theistic personal explanation that takes God's creative action to have been a contingent one. God may be a necessary being, but God's choice to create conscious beings and to correlate certain types of mental states with certain types of physical states were contingent choices, and this fits nicely with the phenomena themselves.

(c) *Epiphenomenalism and causal closure.* Most naturalists believe that their worldview requires that all entities whatever are either physical or depend on the physical for their existence and behavior. One implication of this belief is commitment to the causal closure of the physical. On this principle, when one is tracing the causal antecedents of any physical event, one will never have to leave the level of the physical. Physical effects have only physical causes. Rejection of the causal closure principle would imply a rejection of the possibility of a complete and comprehensive physical theory of all physical phenomena—something that no naturalist should reject. Thus, if mental phenomena are genuinely non-physical, then they must be epiphenomena— effects caused by the physical that do not themselves have causal powers. But epiphenomenalism is false. Mental causation seems undeniable and, thus, for the naturalist the mental can be allowed to have causal powers only if it is in some way or another identified with the physical. The admission of epiphenomenal non-physical mental entities may be taken as a refutation of naturalism. As naturalist D. M. Armstrong admits, "I suppose that if the principles involved [in analyzing the single all-embracing spatio-temporal system which is reality] were completely different from the current principles of physics, in particular if they involved appeal to mental entities, such as purposes, we might then count the analysis as a falsification of Naturalism."[13]

(d) *The inadequacy of evolutionary explanations.* Naturalists are committed to the view that, in principle, evolutionary explanations can be proffered for the appearance of all organisms and their parts. It is not hard to see how an evolutionary account could be given for new and increasingly complex physical structures that constitute different organisms. However, organisms are black boxes as far as evolution is concerned. As long as an organism, when receiving certain inputs, generates the correct behavioral outputs under the demands of fighting, fleeing, reproducing and feeding, the organism will survive. What goes on inside the organism is irrelevant and only becomes significant for the processes of evolution when an output is produced. Strictly speaking, it is the output, not what caused it, that bears on the struggle for reproductive advantage. Moreover, the functions organisms carry out consciously *could just as well have been done unconsciously*. Thus, both the sheer existence of conscious states and the precise mental content that constitutes them is outside the pale of evolutionary explanation. As Howard E. Gruber explains:

> the idea of either a Planful or an Intervening Providence taking part in the day-to-day operations of the universe was, in effect, a competing theory [to Darwin's version of evolution]. If one believed that there was a God who had originally designed the world exactly as it has come to be, the theory of evolution through natural selection could be seen as superfluous. Likewise, if one believed in a God who intervened from time to time to create some of the organisms, organs, or functions found in the living world, Darwin's theory could be seen as superfluous. Any introduction of intelligent planning or decision-making reduces natural selection from the position of a necessary and universal principle to a mere possibility.[14]

We have looked at four reasons why many scholars, including many naturalists hold that naturalism requires the rejection of consciousness construed along dualist lines. Speaking of the conjunction of naturalism and evolution, naturalist Paul Churchland asserts:

> The important point about the standard evolutionary story is that the human species and all of its features are the wholly physical outcome of a purely physical process ... If this is the correct account of our origins, then there seems neither need, nor room, to fit any nonphysical substances or properties into our theoretical account of ourselves. We are creatures of matter. And we should learn to live with that fact.[15]

5. The naturalistic worldview

At this point, it may be wise to look briefly at the nature of naturalism as a worldview to gain further insight into why consciousness is such a problem for naturalists. Naturalism usually includes:

1) different aspects of a naturalist epistemic attitude (for example, a rejection of so-called "first philosophy" along with an acceptance of either weak or strong scientism);[16]
2) a Grand Story which amounts to an etiological account of how all entities whatsoever have come to be told in terms of an event causal story described in natural scientific terms with a central role given to the atomic theory of matter and evolutionary biology;
3) a general ontology in which the only entities allowed are those that bear a relevant similarity to those thought to characterize a completed form of physics.

For most naturalists, the ordering of these three ingredients is important. Frequently, the naturalist epistemic attitude serves as justification for the naturalist etiology, which, in turn, helps to justify the naturalist's ontological commitment. Moreover, naturalism seems to require a coherence among the postulates of these three different areas of the naturalistic turn. For example, there should be a coherence among third-person scientific ways of knowing; a physical, evolutionary account of how our sensory and cognitive processes came to be; and an ontological analysis of those processes themselves. Any entities that are taken to exist should bear a relevant similarity to entities that characterize our best physical theories; their coming-to-be should be intelligible in light of the naturalist causal story; and they should be knowable by scientific means.

For our purposes, it is important to say a bit more about naturalist ontological commitments. A good place to start is with what Frank Jackson calls the location problem.[17] According to Jackson, given that naturalists are committed to a fairly widely-accepted physical story about how things came to be and what they are, the location problem is the task of locating or finding a place for some entity (for example, semantic contents, mind, agency) in that story. As an illustration, Jackson shows how the solidity of macro-objects can be located within a naturalist worldview. If solidity is taken as impenetrability, then given the lattice structure of atoms composing, say, a table and chair, it becomes obvious why they cannot penetrate each other. Given the naturalist micro-story, the macro-world could not have been different: the table could not penetrate the chair. Location is necessitation.

There are three constraints for developing a naturalist ontology and locating entities within it:

(a) Entities should conform to the naturalist epistemology.
(b) Entities should conform to the naturalist Grand Story.
(c) Entities should bear a relevant similarity to those found in chemistry and physics or be shown to depend necessarily on entities in chemistry and physics.

Regarding the naturalist epistemology, all entities should be knowable by third-person scientific means. Regarding the Grand Story, one should be able to show how any entity had to appear in light of the naturalist event causal story according to which the history of the cosmos amounts to a series of events governed by natural law in which micro-parts come together to form various aggregates with increasingly complex physical structures. The four arguments listed above, in one way or other, claim that consciousness cannot be located in the naturalist ontology under the relevant constraints.

Given theism and naturalism as rivals, theists who employ the argument from consciousness seek to capitalize on the naturalistic failure to come to terms with consciousness by offering a rival explanation for its appearance. That failure is why most prominent naturalists (e.g., John Bishop, Daniel Dennett, D. M. Armstrong, Paul Churchland, David Papineau and Jaegwon Kim) reject premise (1) of AC ("Genuinely non-physical mental states exist") and either eliminate or, in one way or another, identify conscious states with physical ones.[18]

Unfortunately for naturalists, consciousness has stubbornly resisted treatment in physical terms. Consciousness has been recalcitrant for naturalists and (1) is hard to dismiss. Aware of this problem, various alternatives to theism and AC have been provided which accept (1). In this section, we shall look at the main options. John Searle's Biological Naturalism, Naturalistic Emergentism, Panpsychism, and Colin McGinn's Agnostic "Naturalism."

6. The chief rivals to AC

6.a. Searle's biological naturalism

John Searle has developed a naturalistic account of consciousness which would, if successful, provide justification for rejecting premise (5) of AC.[19] According to Searle, for fifty years philosophy of mind has been dominated by scientific naturalists who have advanced different versions of strict physicalism because it was seen as a crucial implication of taking the naturalistic turn. For these naturalists, if one abandons strict physicalism, one has rejected a scientific naturalist approach to the mind/body problem and opened oneself up to the intrusion of religious concepts and arguments about the mental.

By contrast, Searle's own solution to the mind/body problem is biological naturalism: While mental states are exactly what dualists describe them to be, nevertheless, they are merely emergent biological states and processes that causally supervene upon a suitably structured, functioning brain. Brain processes cause mental processes, which are not ontologically reducible to the former. Consciousness is just an ordinary (i.e., physical) feature of the brain and, as such, is merely an ordinary feature of the natural world.

Given that he characterizes consciousness as dualists do, why does Searle claim that there are no deep metaphysical implications that follow from biological naturalism? More specifically, why is it that biological naturalism does not represent a rejection of scientific naturalism which, in turn, opens the door for religious concepts and explanations for the mental? Searle's answer to this question is developed in three steps.

In Step One, he cites several examples of emergence (liquidity, solidity, features of digestion) that he takes to be unproblematic for naturalists and claims that emergent consciousness is analogous to the unproblematic cases.

In Step Two, he formulates two reasons why consciousness is not a problem for naturalists: (i) The emergence of consciousness is not a problem if we stop trying to picture or image consciousness. (ii) In standard cases (heat, color), an ontological reduction (e.g., identifying a specific color with a wavelength) is based on a causal reduction (e.g., claiming that a specific color is caused by a wavelength) because of our pragmatic interests are in reality, not appearance.

In these cases we can distinguish the *appearance* of heat and color from the *reality*, place the former in consciousness, leave the latter in the objective world, and go on to define the phenomenon itself in terms of its causes. We can do this because our interests are in the reality and not the appearance. The ontological reduction of heat to its causes leaves the appearance of heat the same. Regarding consciousness, we are interested in the appearances, and thus the irreducibility of consciousness is merely due to pragmatic considerations, not to some deep metaphysical problem.

In Step Three, Searle claims that an adequate scientific explanation of the emergence of consciousness consists in a detailed, law-like set of correlations between mental and physical state tokens. Part of his justification for this is that some explanations in science do not exhibit the type of necessity that explains why certain things must happen (e.g., macro-impenetrability) given that other things have obtained (e.g., micro-structure). Searle cites as an example the inverse square law, which is an explanatory account of gravity that does not show why bodies have to have gravitational attraction.

Several things may be said in response to Searle's position. Regarding Steps One and Two, his cases of emergence (rigidity, fluidity) are not good analogies to consciousness since the former are *easy* to locate in the naturalist epistemology and ontology, but the latter is *not*. Given a widely accepted physicalist description of atoms, molecules, lattice structure, and the like, the rigidity or fluidity of macro-objects follows necessarily. But there is no clear necessary connection between any physical state and any mental state. For example, given a specific brain state normally "associated" with the mental state of being appeared to redly, inverted qualia worlds (worlds with that physical state but radically different mental states "associated" with it), zombie worlds (worlds with that physical state and no mental states at all) and disembodied worlds (worlds with beings possessing mental states with no physical entities at all) are still metaphysically possible. It is easy to locate solidity in a naturalist framework but the same cannot be said for consciousness. This is why there has been turmoil for naturalists in philosophy of mind but not in the philosophy of solidity. Searle's emergent entities follow necessarily given the naturalist Grand Story, but consciousness does not.

Further, the emergence of genuinely new properties in macro-objects that are not part of the micro-world (e.g., heat construed as warmth, color construed commonsensically as a quality) presents problems for naturalists in the same way consciousness does and, historically, that is why they were placed in consciousness. Contrary to Searle, they were not so placed because of the pragmatics of our interests. For example, historically, the problem was that if so-called secondary qualities were kept in the mind-independent world, there was no explanation for why they emerged on the occasion of a mere rearrangement in micro-parts exhaustively characterized in terms of primary qualities.

It is this straightforward ontological problem not the pragmatics of reduction or the attempt to image consciousness that presents difficulties for naturalism: How do you get secondary qualities or consciousness to come-to-be by merely rearranging purely physical entities bereft of the emergent features? Given their existence, why are secondary qualities and conscious states regularly correlated with purely physical states similarly bereft?

In fact, the emergence of mental properties is more like the emergence of normative (e.g., moral) properties than the properties of solidity or digestion. Even the atheist J. L. Mackie admitted that the emergence of moral properties provided evidence for a moral argument for God's existence analogous to AC: "Moral properties constitute so odd a cluster of properties and relations that they are most unlikely to have arisen in the ordinary course of events without an all-powerful god to create them."[20]

Regarding Step Three, "explanations" in science that do not express the sort of necessity we have been discussing are better taken as *descriptions*, not *explanations*. For example, the ideal gas equation is a description of the behavior of gases. An explanation of that behavior is provided by the atomic theory of gas. Curiously, Newton himself took the inverse square law to be a mere description of gravity and not an explanation; so Searle's own example counts against him. Further, given theism and AC, along with our earlier discussion of scientific theory acceptance, it is question-begging and *ad hoc* for Searle to assert that mental entities and mental/physical correlations are basic, since such entities are natural in light of theism but unnatural given philosophical naturalism.

Our current belief that there is no causal necessity to specific mind/brain correlations is not due to our ignorance of how the brain works, but on an understanding of the radical differences between mental and physical entities. As fellow naturalist Jaegwon Kim notes, the correlations are not explanations. They are the very things that need explaining, and, given a proper understanding of the real questions, no naturalistic explanation seems to be forthcoming:

> How could a series of physical events, little particles jostling against one another, electric current rushing to and fro ... blossom into a conscious experience? ... Why shouldn't pain and itch be switched around? ... Why should *any* experience emerge when these neurons fire?[21]

By misconstruing the problem, Searle fails to address the real issue and, weighed against AC, his position is inadequate.

6.b. Naturalistic emergence

For those who accept the existence of genuine, irreducible, non-physical conscious states and, at the same time, desire to avoid AC, the most popular current strategy is to appeal to some sort of natural emergence. In the contemporary literature, this strategy takes two forms: a strictly naturalist account and some sort of panpsychism view. I will discuss the naturalist account in this section, and panpsychism in section 6.c.

According to the strictly naturalist account, matter at the most basic level—the microphysical level—is or will be completely describable within an ideal physics. That description will be able to capture the complete nature of basic matter, and it will entail that basic matter is bereft of any mental entities, including mental potentialities. Nevertheless, when matter reaches a certain, "appropriate" level of complexity, a completely new range of *sui generis* emergent properties, especially conscious properties, appears.

I have already noted that emergent properties do not fit into a naturalist epistemology, Grand Story or ontology, so I shall not repeat my reasoning here. However, I would like to point out that, given the proper depiction of naturalism and theism as a rival theory, it is *ad hoc* and question-begging for the naturalist simply to help herself to emergent properties when they are not natural for naturalism but are at home with and fit into a theistic worldview.

Moreover, keep in mind that in the first half of the twentieth century, emergent properties were defined epistemologically:[22] Property P is an emergent property of some particular x at level l_n just in case P is a property of x at l_n, and no amount of knowledge of (or descriptive statements about) entities at subvenient levels below l_n would justify a prediction of (or logically entails a descriptive statement about) P at l_n. In this sense an emergent property (or a statement about it) is surprising, unexpected, and utterly brute relative to knowledge of (or statements about) lower levels. Thus, the prior probability of emergent properties, given strong naturalism would be zero.

Thus, genuinely emergent (as opposed to structurally supervenient) properties simply does not belong in a naturalist ontology. Besides this, there are other problems with the idea of emergent properties, given naturalism.

For one thing, an appeal to emergent properties has always seemed suspect to me if it is offered as an explanation: "emergence" is not a solution, but a *name for the problem to be solved*. It is a label and that's all. Moreover, as a label, it leaves open other empirically equivalent views, viz., that the new kind of property may reside in a new substance or be due to God's regular intention that the property appear under the same set of circumstances. As Timothy O'Connor has noted, if the law-like link between occurrent subvenient properties and their associated occurrent emergent properties is contingent, as I have argued earlier in this chapter, then the only adequate explanation for the link and the appearance of an emergent property is God's direct activity and stable intention that things be so.[23] Now it seems to many, perhaps most philosophers who do not start with a prior commitment to strong physicalism that the link is indeed contingent as seen in a number of well-known thought experiments.

Further, emergence seems to be a case of getting something from nothing, a case of magic without a Magician. If matter is relevantly similar to what current physics and chemistry tell us, and it is bereft of any sort of mental entities, then matter does not have mental potentialities. Given this, it is hard to see how the mere spatial rearrangement of, say, atomic simples to form a more complicated spatial structure would be an adequate cause for bringing into existence a completely new sort of entity.

Finally, sorites problems are lurking in the neighborhood. Could this emergent property, say being painful, be instantiated with one less atomic part in the subvenient base when that base is the "right" level of complexity? Surely the answer is yes. How about two less atomic parts? And so on. *Sans* ontological vagueness, at some point, the emergentist must say that the subtraction of one small atomic part has a huge, disproportionate metaphysical effect on the disappearance of the emergent property or properties, e.g., all the irreducibly mental properties constituting consciousness.

But how can such a significant metaphysical effect be due to such an insignificant cause? And why was the "right" level of complexity one atomic part greater than the actual level? And the very notion of "the right level of complexity" is completely vacuous. Why? What is the right level? Answer: Whatever the level is when the emergent property appears. When does the emergent property appear? When the right level of complexity is reached. There are no independent criteria for identifying the "right level of complexity" besides the appearance of the so-called emergent property.

6.c. Panpsychism

In light of these problems, especially the difficulty of getting something from nothing, some philosophers such as Thomas Nagel and David Skrbina have turned to a version of panpsychism to explain the origin of consciousness.[24] Roughly, panpsychism is the view that either all objects or all basic entities (those without proper parts) or some relevant range of basic entities have phenomenal consciousness, e.g., there is a what-it-is-like to be an electron (strong panpsychism) or an attenuated, incipient form of consciousness (weak panpsychism). When these relevant entities are brought together in the right way, unified macro-consciousness as we find in humans and sentient animals emerges. It does seem that panpsychism solves the problem of getting something from nothing since, in some way or another, macro-consciousness emerges from and is the actualization of micro-consciousness. Still, there are several problems that, taken together, justify a rejection of panpsychism.

First, as I observed above, the mental-physical link's contingency is a serious problem, one that panpsychism does not solve. Again, panpsychism is merely a label for and not an explanation of the phenomena to be explained. As Geoffrey Madell notes, "the sense that the mental and the physical are just inexplicably and gratuitously slapped together is hardly allayed by adopting . . . a pan-psychist . . . view of the mind, for [it does not] have an explanation to offer as to why or how mental properties cohere with physical."[25]

Second, as I have argued elsewhere, setting aside issues about the origin of macro-consciousness, theism is more rational than panpsychism.[26] If that is right, then since AC fits into a theistic as opposed to a mere panpsychist worldview and theism explains the contingency of the link between conscious and physical states while panpsychism does not, AC is preferable to panpsychism. Moreover, panpsychism faces the sorites problem regarding the precise conditions for macro-consciousness to appear.

Finally, it is hard to see how the holistic, non-atomistic unity of consciousness can be explained by the mere rearrangement of entities with attenuated or fully actualized consciousness. Surely such a process would produce an aggregate of independent conscious base entities such that there would be no unified whole "over and above" these entities that would have its own what-it-is-like, its own first-person point of view. This issue is called the *combination problem*. This may be the most serious difficulty facing panpsychism and, in my view, panpsychists have failed to solve it.[27]

6.d. McGinn's agnostic "naturalism"

Naturalist Colin McGinn has offered a different response to AC.[28] Given the radical difference between mind and matter as it is depicted by current or even an ideal future physics, there is no naturalistic solution that stays within the widely accepted naturalist epistemology and ontology. Darwinian explanations fail as well because they cannot account for why consciousness appeared in the first place. What is needed is a radically different kind of solution to the origin of mind, one that must meet two conditions: (i) It must be a naturalistic solution. (ii) It must depict the emergence of consciousness and its regular correlation with matter as necessary and not contingent facts.

McGinn claims that there must be two kinds of unknowable natural properties that solve the problem. There must be some general properties of matter that enter into the production of consciousness when assembled into a brain. Thus, all matter has the potentiality to underlie consciousness. Further, there must be some natural property of the brain he calls C* that unleashes these general properties.

The temptation to take the origin of consciousness as a mystery, indeed, a mystery that is best explained theistically, is due to our ignorance of these properties. However, given C* and the general properties of matter, the unknowable link between mind and matter is ordinary, commonplace and necessitates the emergence of consciousness. Unfortunately, evolution did not give humans the faculties needed to know these properties and, thus, they are in principle beyond our grasp. We will forever be agnostic about their nature. However, they must be there since there must be some naturalistic explanation of mind as all other solutions have failed.

McGinn offers two further descriptions of these unknowable yet ordinary properties that link matter and mind: (i) They are not sense perceptible. (ii) Since matter is spatial and mind non-spatial, they are either in some sense pre-spatial or are spatial in a way that is itself unknowable to our faculties. In this way, these unknowable properties contain at least the potentiality for both ordinary spatial features of matter and the non-spatial features of consciousness as judged by our usual concept of space.

In sum, the mind/matter link is an unknowable mystery due to our cognitive limitations resulting from our evolution. And since the link is quite ordinary, we should not be puzzled by the origin of mind, and no theistic explanation is required.

Does McGinn's solution succeed? For at least three reasons, it must be judged a failure. First, given McGinn's agnosticism about the properties that link mind and matter, how can McGinn confidently assert some of their features? How does he know they are non-sensory, pre-spatial or spatial in an unknowable way? How does he know some of these properties underlie all matter? Indeed, what possible justification can he give for their reality? The only one he proffers is that we must provide a naturalistic solution and all ordinary naturalistic ones either deny consciousness or fail to solve the problem. But given the presence of AC, McGinn's claims are simply question-begging. Indeed, his agnosticism seems to be a convenient way of hiding behind naturalism and avoiding a theistic explanation. Given that theism enjoys a positive degree of justification prior to the problem of consciousness (see other chapters in this volume), he should avail himself of the explanatory resources of theism.

Second, it is not clear that his solution is a version of naturalism, except in name only. In contrast to other entities in the naturalist ontology, McGinn's linking properties cannot be known by employment of the naturalist epistemology, nor are they relevantly similar to the rest of the naturalist ontology. Thus, it becomes vacuous to call these properties "naturalistic." McGinn's own speculations strike one as *ad hoc* in light of the inadequacies of naturalistic explanations. In fact, McGinn's solution is actually closer to an agnostic form of panpsychism than to naturalism. Given AC, McGinn's solution is an *ad hoc* readjustment of naturalism.

Third, McGinn does not solve the problem of consciousness, he merely relocates it. Rather than having two radically different entities, he offer us unknowable properties with two radically different aspects, e.g., his links contain the potentiality for ordinary spatiality and non-spatiality, for ordinary materiality and mentality. Moreover, these radically different aspects of the linking properties are just as contingently related as they seem to be without a linking intermediary. The contingency comes from the nature of mind and matter as naturalists conceive it. It does not remove the contingency to relocate it as two aspects of an unknowable third intermediary with both.

7. Concluding remarks

In closing, it is not without significance that the existence and *prima facie* contingency of consciousness are problems that have attracted a lot of attention for several decades. Given the importance of locating issues in philosophy of mind in the context of rival worldviews, it becomes apparent that debates about the relative merits of naturalism and theism are part of the background concerns. Since the mid-80s, it has been increasingly apparent that consciousness is genuinely and irreducibly mental and that the mental/physical link is radically contingent. The growing adoption of versions of panpsychism are, among other things, attempts to avoid AC. The incorporation of consciousness into a naturalist worldview is implausible, *ad hoc*, and question-begging. And I, for one, would not bet too much on the future of panpsychism. As I have tried to argue, the existence of consciousness is best explained by theism. Clarifying and defending AC provide insight into why this is the case, or so say I.

Notes

1. Geoffrey Madell, *Mind and Materialism* (Edinburgh: Edinburgh University Press, 1988), 141.
2. Colin McGinn, *The Mysterious Flame* (New York: Basic Books, 1999), 13–14. See G. K. Chesterton's claim that the regular correlation between diverse entities in the world is magic that requires a Magician to explain it in *Orthodoxy* (John Lane Company, 1908; repr., San Francisco: Ignatius Press, 1950), chapter five.
3. William Lyons, "Introduction," in *Modern Philosophy of Mind*, ed. by William Lyons, (London: Everyman, 1995), lv. In context, Lyons remark is specifically about the identity thesis, but he clearly intends it to cover physicalism in general. Similarly, while he explicitly mentions an entity in the category of individual—the soul—the context of his remark makes clear that he includes mental properties and events among the entities out of step with scientific materialism.
4. For defenses of dualism see William Hasker, *The Emergent Self* (Ithaca, NY: Cornell University Press, 1999); J. P. Moreland and Scott Rae, *Body & Soul: Human Nature and the Crisis in Ethics* (Downers Grove, IL: InterVaristy Press, 2000); Richard Swinburne, *The Evolution of the Soul* (Oxford: Clarendon Press, rev. ed., 1997); Charles Taliaferro, *Consciousness and the Mind of God* (Cambridge: Cambridge University Press, 1994).
5. For example, suppose theory S explains phenomena in terms of discrete corpuscles and actions by contact, while R uses continuous waves to explain phenomena. If some phenomenon x was best explained in corpuscularian categories, it would be ad hoc and question-begging for advocates of R simply to adjust their entities to take on particle properties in the case of x. Such properties would not bear a relevant similarity to other entities in R and would be more natural and at home in S.
6. For example, suppose that R is Neo-Darwinism and S is a version of punctuated equilibrium theory. Simply for the same of illustration, suppose further, that R depicts evolutionary transitions from one species to another to involve running through a series of incrementally different transitional forms except for some specific transition *e* which is taken as a basic phenomenon, say, the discrete jump from amphibians to

reptiles. S pictures evolutionary transitions in general, including e, as evolutionary jumps to be explained in certain ways that constitute S. In this case, given the presence of S, it would be hard for advocates of R to claim that their treatment of e is adequate against S. Phenomenon e clearly counts in favor of S over against R.

7   See Robert Adams, "Flavors, Colors, and God," reprinted in *Contemporary Perspectives on Religious Epistemology*, ed. by R. Douglas Geivett and Brendan Sweetman (New York: Oxford University Press, 1992), 225–240.

8   See the following works by Richard Swinburne: *The Evolution of the Soul*, 183–196; *The Existence of God* (Oxford: Clarendon, 1979), chapter nine; *Is there a God?* (Oxford: Oxford University Press, 1996), 69–94; and "The Origin of Consciousness," in *Cosmic Beginnings and Human Ends*, ed. by Clifford N. Matthews, Roy Abraham Varghese (Chicago and La Salle, Illinois: Open Court, 1995), 355–378.

9   I have already listed five features of mental properties and events that justify the claim that they are not physical properties and events. It is beyond the scope of this chapter to defend the irreducible mental nature of mental properties and events against strict physicalist alternatives. Our focus is the more limited one of comparing AC with rivals that accept premise one. For a defense of a dualist construal of consciousness, see the sources in note 4.

10 For a more detailed defense of this premise, see J. P. Moreland, "Searle's Biological Naturalism and the Argument from Consciousness," *Faith and Philosophy* 15 (1998): 68–91.

11 Regarding the *number* of deities, the principle of economy would move us in the direction of one rather than a plurality of deities: why posit multiple entities when one entity will suffice? Regarding the *type* of deity, arguments for God's existence are—or should be—generally modest in what they attempt to show (e.g., the design argument is not intended to show that God is *all*-knowing (or supremely good or the Uncaused Cause). Furthermore, bringing the various arguments together furnishes us with a much less pared down understanding of this God, is sufficient to render us personally accountable to this Being, and does not in any way conflicting with the revealed God of Judeo-Christian theism.

12 Terence Horgan, "Nonreductive Materialism and the Explanatory Autonomy of Psychology," in *Naturalism*, ed. Steven J. Wagner and Richard Warner (Notre Dame: University of Notre Dame Press, 1993), 313–314.

13 D. M. Armstrong, "Naturalism: Materialism and First Philosophy," *Philosophia* 8 (1978): 262.

14 Howard E. Gruber, *Darwin on Man: A Psychological Study of Scientific Creativity* (Chicago: University of Chicago Press, 1974), 211.

15 Paul Churchland, *Matter and Consciousness* (Cambridge, MA: MIT Press, 1984), 21.

16 The *strong* version of scientism maintains that science provides us with the *sole* basis of knowledge; the *weaker* version claims that science furnishes us with the *most certain* basis of knowledge, even if other disciplines provide more weakly justified beliefs or knowledge.

17 Frank Jackson, *From Metaphysics to Ethics* (Oxford: Clarendon Press, 1998), 1–5.

18 John Bishop, *Natural Agency* (Cambridge: Cambridge University Press, 1989); Daniel Dennett, *Elbow Room* (Cambridge, MA: MIT Press, 1984); D. M. Armstrong, *Universals and Scientific Realism Volume I: Nominalism & Realism* (Cambridge: Cambridge University Press, 1978), 126–135; D. M. Armstrong, "Naturalism: Materialism and First Philosophy," *Philosophia* 8 (1978): 261–276; Churchland, *Matter and Consciousness*; David Papineau, *Philosophical Naturalism* (Oxford: Blackwell

Publishers, 1993); Jaegwon Kim, *Mind in a Physical World* (Cambridge, MA: MIT Press, 1998); Jaegwon Kim, *Philosophy of Mind* (Boulder, CO: Westview Press, 1996).
19 See John Searle, *The Rediscovery of the Mind* (Cambridge, MA: MIT Press, 1992).
20 J. L. Mackie, *The Miracle of Theism* (Oxford: Clarendon Press, 1982), 115.
21 Kim, *Philosophy of Mind*, 8.
22 For a classic comparison of the epistemic and ontological characterizations of emergent properties, see Ernest Nagel, *The Structure of Science* (Indianapolis: Hackett, 1979), 366–380.
23 See Timothy O'Connor, *Persons & Causes* (New York: Oxford University Press, 2000), footnote 8, 70–71. I have argued that the causal relation between mental and physical states is, in fact, due to God's direct activity and stable intention that things remain a certain way. See Moreland, *Consciousness and the Existence of God*.
24 See Thomas Nagel, *Mind & Cosmos* (Oxford: Oxford University Press, 2012); David Skrbina, *Panpsychism in the West* (Cambridge, MA: MIT Press, 2005).
25 Geoffrey Madell, *Mind and Materialism* (Edinburgh: Edinburgh University Press, 1988), 3.
26 See Moreland, *Consciousness and the Existence of God*, 117–126.
27 For more on this, see Moreland, *Consciousness and the Existence of God*, 128–131. David Chalmers has offered a different solution to the origin of macro-phenomenal consciousness. See his "Panpsychism and Panprotopsychism," in *Panpsychism: Contemporary Perspectives*, ed. by Godehard Bruntrup and Ludwig Jaskolla (New York: Oxford University Press, 2016), 19–47. Space considerations prevent me from addressing Chalmers' quite nuanced view. It is clear, however, that he distinguishes his position (constitutive Russellian panprotopsychism plus broad physicalism) from any form of emergentism. For those unfamiliar with his theory, the following (inadequate) precis will most likely be unhelpful. But for those who are, here are some critical bullet points: (1) It is highly speculative and does not solve the sorites problem, the contingency problem or the unity-of-consciousness problem since Chalmers' subject of consciousness is a composite object. (For more on this problem, see the source cited in note 5 above.) (2) It is hard to see how the simple spatial re-arrangement of entities with proto-consciousness (aka., conscious precursors, proto-phenomenal properties, preconscious properties) that lack what-it-is-like to be those entities can give rise to full-blown phenomenal consciousness. This difficulty is not due to an epistemic gap between narrow physicalism and phenomenal consciousness as Chalmers would have it. Rather, it arises from broad physicalism along with his characterization of the categorical quiddities in the terms just mentioned. (3) When we conceive of zombies, we do not conceive of structural zombies; rather, we conceive of broad physical zombies. That is, we conceive of zombies with the same physical structural features as we have, along with physical stuff playing the role of quiddities. We strongly conceive that such zombies could be conscious or unconscious *while leaving everything that is physical the same*.
28 McGinn, *The Mysterious Flame*.

Bibliography

Adams, Robert, "Flavors, Colors, and God," reprinted in *Contemporary Perspectives on Religious Epistemology*, edited by R. Douglas Geivett and Brendan Sweetman, New York: Oxford University Press, 1992.

Armstrong, D. M., "Naturalism: Materialism and First Philosophy," *Philosophia* 8 (1978): 262.

Armstrong, D. M., *Universals and Scientific Realism Volume I: Nominalism & Realism*, Cambridge: Cambridge University Press, 1978.

Bishop, John, *Natural Agency*, Cambridge: Cambridge University Press, 1989.

Chalmers, David, "Panpsychism and Panprotopsychism," in *Panpsychism: Contemporary Perspectives*, edited by Godehard Bruntrup and Ludwig Jaskolla, New York: Oxford University Press, 2016.

Chesterton, G. K., *Orthodoxy*, 1908, reprinted with notes and an introduction, San Francisco: Ignatius Press, 1950.

Churchland, Paul, *Matter and Consciousness*, Cambridge, MA: MIT Press, 1984.

Dennett, Daniel, *Elbow Room*, Cambridge, MA: MIT Press, 1984.

Gruber, Howard E., *Darwin on Man: A Psychological Study of Scientific Creativity*, Chicago: University of Chicago Press, 1974.

Hasker, William, *The Emergent Self*, Ithaca, NY: Cornell University Press, 1999.

Horgan, Terence, "Nonreductive Materialism and the Explanatory Autonomy of Psychology," in *Naturalism*, edited by Steven J. Wagner and Richard Warner, Notre Dame: University of Notre Dame Press, 1993: 313–314.

Jackson, Frank, *From Metaphysics to Ethics*, Oxford: Clarendon Press, 1998.

Kim, Jaegwon, *Mind in a Physical World*, Cambridge, MA: MIT Press, 1998.

Kim, Jaegwon, *Philosophy of Mind*. Boulder, CO: Westview Press, 1996.

Lyons, Williams, "Introduction," in *Modern Philosophy of Mind*, edited by William Lyons, London: Everyman, 1995.

Mackie, J. L., *The Miracle of Theism*, Oxford: Clarendon Press, 1982.

Madell, Geoffrey, *Mind and Materialism*, Edinburgh: Edinburgh University Press, 1988.

McGinn, Colin, *The Mysterious Flame*, New York: Basic Books, 1999.

Moreland, J. P., and Scott Rae, *Body & Soul: Human Nature and the Crisis in Ethics*, Downers Grove, IL: InterVarsity Press, 2000.

Moreland, J. P., "Searle's Biological Naturalism and the Argument from Consciousness," *Faith and Philosophy* 15 (1998): 68–91.

Moreland, J. P., *Consciousness and the Existence of God*, Routledge, 2008.

Nagel, Ernest, *The Structure of Science*, Indianapolis: Hackett, 1979.

Nagel, Thomas, *Mind & Cosmos*, Oxford: Oxford University Press, 2012.

O'Connor, Timothy, *Persons & Causes*, New York: Oxford University Press, 2000.

Papineau, David, *Philosophical Naturalism*, Oxford: Blackwell Publishers, 1993.

Searle, John, *The Rediscovery of the Mind*, Cambridge, MA: MIT Press, 1992.

Skrbina, David, *Panpsychism in the West*, Cambridge, MA: MIT Press, 2005.

Swinburne, Richard, *Is there a God?* Oxford: Oxford University Press, 1996.

Swinburne, Richard, *The Evolution of the Soul*, 1986, rev. ed. Oxford: Clarendon Press, 1997.

Swinburne, Richard, *The Existence of God*, Oxford: Clarendon Press, 1979.

Swinburne, Richard, "The Origin of Consciousness," in *Cosmic Beginnings and Human Ends*, ed. by Clifford N. Matthews and Roy Abraham Varghese, 355–378 Chicago and La Salle, IL: Open Court, 1995.

Taliaferro, Charles, *Consciousness and the Mind of God*, Cambridge: Cambridge University Press, 1994.

9

The Argument From Beauty

Brian Ribeiro

1. Introduction

Conceived in a broad and intuitive way, the teleological argument (or, the design argument) holds that, given the ordered beauty of the world, its delicate arrangement of parts, and its suitability as a habitation for humans and other forms of life, we can legitimately infer that our world is the work of some supernatural Designer. Historically speaking, presentations of the design argument have tended to focus our attention on the *orderliness* of the world (i.e., its being subject to natural laws which do not change, and so on). In ancient philosophical theology, this orderliness of the world was construed along the lines of *organic models*: The world is like an animal body, with an organic unity. In modern times, the theist's analogy has generally turned away from the organic model of animal bodies toward the model of *complicated mechanisms*: "Look round the world," Cleanthes says in Hume's *Dialogues*, "Contemplate the whole and every part of it: You will find it to be nothing but one great machine, subdivided into an infinite number of lesser machines, which again admit of subdivisions to a degree beyond what human senses and faculties can trace and explain."[1] Each of these different versions of the design argument looks from the world's *orderliness* to the need for a divine Designer to order it.[2]

But the design argument can also be presented in another, less commonly considered version which focuses its attention on the world's *beauty* and which argues that natural beauty is itself a clear indication of the world's having been the product of conscious intention and design. To a very rough first approximation, if nature itself is beautiful like art, and if art requires an artist to make it beautiful, then perhaps nature itself needs an Artist. Call that *the theistic argument from beauty*. This beauty-based variant of the design argument has been defended by a number of philosophers and philosophical theologians. Suggestions of it can be found in the famous "ascent passage" of Plato's *Symposium*, as well as in the *Confessions* of Saint Augustine, and more recently F. R. Tennant, Peter Forrest, Mark Wynn, and Richard Swinburne have all defended various versions of it.[3] For example, Forrest claims that if he "had to choose one feature of the universe that *most clearly supports theism*, it would have to be the beauty of things rather than the suitability of the universe for life."[4] Explaining and elaborating this thought, Forrest insists that the argument from beauty has four distinct advantages over the usual design arguments:

> The first is that [beauty] is harder to understand in naturalistic terms than is the suitability of the universe for life. The second is that ... beauty is best understood as the result of divine generosity, and like all the best gifts, its enjoyment is an end, not a means. This supports belief in anthropic rather than ananthropic theism. The third is that a sense of the beauty of creation acts as a counterweight to the emotional impact of suffering and malice, which, as I concede, provide prima facie grounds for atheism even after the undermining of all articulate formulations of the argument from evil. Finally, [the fourth is that] the theocentric understanding of beauty results in the emotional responses of both awe and gratitude, which is important because religious faith is widely granted to involve the emotions as well as the intellect.[5]

Thus, we seem to have a prima facie case for thinking that the argument from beauty deserves more careful consideration than it has generally received. If Forrest is correct, the argument from beauty may even be stronger than the standard design argument that focusses on orderliness instead.

In presenting and defending his version of the argument from beauty, F. R. Tennant claims that the world itself is "saturat[ed]" with natural beauty. Such *widespread* natural beauty, Tennant argues, is relatively unlikely to have emerged without being brought about by artistic intentions. After all, in the human case, our works are rarely beautiful unless they are consciously designed with that end in mind.[6] But if such widespread natural beauty really *is* "relatively unlikely to obtain in the absence of artist intent," then that suggests that the world itself is (at least probably) the product of artistic intent.[7] Now, in my view, the argument from beauty is at its strongest when the focus is on the beauty of *non-human nature*, so I believe Tennant's version is well-conceived. Moreover, as Wynn has noted, recent empirical work on human reactions to natural beauty strongly suggests that human attraction to many kinds of natural landscapes is both cross-cultural and stable.[8] And while our appreciation of (i) human artistic products (e.g., the masterworks of Shakespeare, Bach, or Picasso)[9] or of (ii) the beauty of the human form[10] seems possible (and perhaps even relatively easy) to explain in naturalistic terms, our aesthetic appreciation of (iii) the wonders of non-human nature – the freshly fallen snow, or the jagged mountain tops, or the grasses waving in the wind – seems somewhat harder to explain *naturalistically*.[11] Let's focus on cases of type (iii) then. Can cases of type (iii) be explained naturalistically? And, if so, how do the proposed naturalistic explanations of type (iii) cases measure up against proposed theistic explanations of those same cases?[12]

2. First objection: "Beauty can be explained naturalistically"

Perhaps the best known of these naturalistic explanations of our aesthetic appreciation of natural scenes is E. O. Wilson's "biophilia" hypothesis, which proposes that humans may have a partially genetic predisposition, acquired through evolutionary selection, to (aesthetically) prefer certain natural environments.[13] Given that proposed naturalistic explanations do exist, recent defenders of the argument from beauty have spent some time trying to address the objection that, since naturalistic explanations of the world's beauty (to humans) are available, theistic explanations are not needed. Let me briefly summarize the case that defenders like Mark Wynn have put forward in response, while simultaneously laying out the logic of the biophilia hypothesis. Essentially, the theistic response is two-fold, consisting of a concessive reply and a confrontational reply.[14]

The first (concessive) response is that, at most, a naturalistic explanation like Wilson's biophilia hypothesis provides a partial explanation of human beings' aesthetic responses to nature. The biophilic idea is that humans respond positively to environments which, in their evolutionary past, proved conducive to their interests. Thus, environments which provide adequate security, food resources, potable water, and so on would, on the biophilic hypothesis, be environments which humans find beautiful. Take a specific case: if potable water is absolutely essential to human life, it makes sense to imagine that current humans may have a partially genetic predisposition, acquired through evolutionary selection, to be (aesthetically) attracted to sources of potable water. But can the actual degree of humans' aesthetic appreciation of, say, certain waterfalls or mountain streams be *fully accounted for* by this biophilic reasoning? In other words, it might seem that humans like (e.g.) some waterfalls *more* than would be required by (or explained by) the biophilic hypothesis. Perhaps, then, while the biophilia hypothesis provides a partial explanation of humans' aesthetic responses to nature, it does not provide a complete explanation thereof, thus *leaving room* for appeals to theistic explanations as well. This is the concessive response.

The second (confrontational) response is that there seem to be some cases of aesthetic appreciation by humans of natural environments for which a naturalistic explanation like Wilson's biophilia hypothesis does not provide even a partial explanation. If the biophilic hypothesis holds that humans respond positively to environments which, in their evolutionary past, proved conducive to their interests, then why do humans also respond with aesthetic appreciation to environments which seem *hostile* to human interests? For example, consider the arid beauty of desert landscapes, or the beauty of blue-ice glaciers. Or sunset in the vast, untamed Everglades. Or the underwater brilliance along the Great Barrier Reef. Conditions in these environments threaten to freeze us, or fry us, or subject us to death by dehydration, drowning, or dangerous predators, yet humans still find them all to be beautiful. Wynn asks us to "[c]onsider ... the oddity of the expression "How *ugly* the desert (or the snowfield) was!"[15] It seems that to avoid any need of theistic explanations, the naturalist would need a naturalistic explanation for why humans find environments hostile to their own interests and survival attractive. Yet the very ideas that make the biophilia hypothesis seem reasonable would instead predict human aversion to such environments.

3. Second objection: "Beauty is (purely) subjective"

Even if the argument from beauty can be defended against competitor naturalistic explanations of our human appreciation of natural beauty—and that debate is on-going, of course—another obvious objection looms just around the corner. If beauty is merely subjective—merely "in the eye of the beholder" as we say—then perhaps beauty doesn't need much of an explanation after all. So, must the defenders of the argument from beauty first establish that beauty is an objective feature of reality? And if so, how can they do that? They would need to settle the oldest debate in philosophical aesthetics.[16] And any theistic argument which rested upon such a highly-contested aesthetic doctrine would lose much of its force/appeal.

Whether the argument from beauty requires that beauty be an objective feature of reality or not is a disputed issue among the defenders of the argument. Some, like Tennant, see no significant problem for the argument if beauty turns out to be subjective; others, like Swinburne, hold that the argument may need "an objectivist understanding of the aesthetic value of the universe, in order to have significant strength."[17] This disagreement indicates that at least some of the argument's defenders (like Swinburne) think the argument might require "an objectivist understanding of the aesthetic value of the universe." Perhaps they are right. If so, this would tend to diminish the probative power of the argument by linking it to a highly-debatable view. Let me, however, briefly suggest two other lines of response to which the argument's defenders might appeal.

First, the objection that "beauty is (purely) subjective" is at its most alarming when it amounts to a complete individualization of standards of beauty—you have your standards and I have mine: *De gustibus non est disputandum* ("There is no disputing about taste"). While this situation might seem to sometimes describe conflicting human reactions to art, it seems less apt as a way of describing human reactions to natural beauty—or at least natural landscapes—about which, empirical research suggests, there is aesthetic agreement which is both cross-cultural and stable.[18] Of course, even if there really is stable and cross-cultural agreement about which landscapes are beautiful, that would not, *ipso facto*, prove that beauty is objective. Perhaps humans simply have built-in, shared patterns of aesthetic response—the beauty is not in the landscape, but in the human eyes which view it. This would make beauty *intersubjective*, but not yet objective.

Let's suppose that this intersubjective account of natural beauty is all that the argument's defenders have at their disposal. Would, then, their argument be lacking in "significant strength," as Swinburne put it? I'm not sure I see that it would, and this brings us to the second line of response. It seems that God might give humans the gift of experiencing a world saturated with natural beauty in either of two ways: (1) He might make an objectively beautiful world and then equip human creatures with the perceptual and cognitive faculties necessary to experience the (objective) beauty He has created, or (2) He might instead make a world which, while not objectively beautiful—perhaps only God is objectively beautiful—was such that it would be perceived as beautiful and be pleasurably experienced by (the minds of) the human creatures He has chosen to create. Frankly, story (2) accounts for human perceptions of beauty, conceived of a divine gift, and therefore requiring a theistic explanation. Story (1) does all those things as well, but it does no more. So why should the defenders of the argument from beauty need to defend story (1) when story (2) will do?

4. Third objection: "The world also contains ugliness"

The standard versions of the design argument, focusing on the orderliness of the world, find themselves confronting the objection that world appears to also contain very many disteleological features, which one would not expect to find in a (properly) designed system. Thus, the existence of such disteleological features might be regarded as evidence that our system is not in fact a (properly) designed system at all. A wide range of apparently disteleogical features has been suggested under the general heading of the "problem of evil." Some of these spring to mind quite naturally when we consider the earth as a proposed habitation for us or of the operation of our human bodies. If our bodies and our habitation have been designed by a designer than which there is no greater, then why does the earth contain natural disasters, scarcity of resources, or diseases, and why are our bodies subject to physical and mental abnormalities, as well as physical and mental pain and suffering? Of course this question admits of a variety of answers, called theodicies, which attempt to show that such *apparently* disteleological features are not *actually* disteleological at all.

Now, the version of the design argument we are considering, which focuses on the *beauty* of the world, finds itself confronted by a parallel kind of objection. To wit, the world appears to also contain some natural ugliness, something one might not expect to find in a product of divine artistic expression. One might ask, why does the world contain "the harsh call of crows," "the unsightly leaking of sap from a splintered tree limb," "the [human's] insipid and unwieldy elbow," the deep-sea anglerfish or the Amazonian aruana, "sticky and stinky swamps, boring groupings of trees, misplaced shrubbery," not to mention "vomit, puss, bile, phlegm, and faeces"?[19]

I believe the defenders of the argument from beauty have two strategies of response to this "problem of ugliness." First, it seems to me—even as a critic of the argument myself—that the datum here (viz., widespread, naturally-occurring beauty) is not at all easy to discount or dismiss by appeals to contrary features (like natural ugliness). In contrast to apparently *disteleological* features (of which, it seems to me, there are very many), how much naturally-occurring *ugliness* is there? Certainly there is some, and a proponent of the "problem of ugliness" might insist that any expression of divine artistry ought to contain *zero* ugliness.[20] However, this renders the objection somewhat less plausible. Surely an artistic product as vast as a universe makes room for some ugliness, if only to set off or accent the abundant beauty therein—a few dark spots, a few discordant notes, to draw the viewer or the listener in and provide contrast, thereby enhancing the whole.[21] Given this response, the anti-theistic objection becomes, allowing that the world might contain some natural ugliness, is there a degree of ugliness in the world such that a divine artist would not be likely to have included that much? I suppose someone might insist that there is simply *too much* natural ugliness in our world for it to be (likely to be) the work of any divine artist, though I confess that this line of objection seems much less forceful to me than the corresponding objections driven by disteleology. There just seems—to me—to be *far more* (apparent) disteleology in the world than (apparent) ugliness. Still, those who wish to defend and develop the argument from beauty would be well served to explore how to rework standard theodicies for use against this "problem of ugliness."

5. Fourth objection: "This reasoning invites an explanatory regress"

So far we have considered naturalistic explanations of humans' aesthetic experiences of nature, worries about the possible subjectivity of beauty, and worries about the problem posed by the existence of natural ugliness. Each of these poses a significant challenge to the argument from beauty, though I have also suggested various lines of response which the argument's defenders have developed or might seek to develop. The fourth and final objection we will consider is, I believe, the strongest of them all. I will begin by laying out the objection, and then we will take some time to carefully articulate a theistic response. The objection in question is one I will be calling *Philo's explanatory regress objection*, and it is developed by Hume (through the character of Philo) in Part IV of the *Dialogues concerning Natural Religion*.[22]

5.1. Philo's explanatory regress objection

Let's start with the Indian philosopher mentioned by Locke in several passages of his *Essay concerning Human Understanding*.[23] If the world needs to be *supported* by resting on the back on an *elephant*, what supports the elephant? If you say the *elephant* is resting on the back of a *mighty tortoise*, then what supports the tortoise? One makes no real progress in addressing a question ("What supports X?") if the same question can be seen to simply re-emerge at the next level in the proposed explanation. One finds, instead that, to avoid an infinite regress, something must be a "brute" support, not supported by anything else.

Now consider a standard design argument focused on the world's orderliness. That kind of argument holds that since the world is so orderly, its order requires an explanation. If we make that demand into a general principle we get something like this: Things of great intricacy and complexity require an explanation and cannot be accepted as "brute" inexplicable facts.[24] But then what about the orderly divine mind that (allegedly) brings order to our world? Mustn't that divine mind be *at least as complex* as the world? Indeed, one would think it must be *much more complex*. But then, given our principle, the divine mind itself would require an explanation. If, faced with this worry, the theist proposes to treat the order of the divine mind as a "brute" inexplicable fact,[25] why can't the critic simply suggest (with equal justification) that *the world itself* may have that status? After all, the point is that everyone—theists and non-theists alike—must accept *some* "brute" inexplicable fact or else accept an explanatory regress *ad infinitum*. In contrast, the theist had seemed to suggest, in presenting the design argument, that the design argument helps to *remove some mystery* which had puzzled us, but in fact the design argument only pushes the mystery (if there is one) back one step. Moreover, given that everyone must accept some kind of "brute" inexplicable fact, why not keep one's metaphysics more elegant and just stop at the world itself? Moving one step further and stopping at God flies in the face of Occam's Razor and, worse yet, does so without any corresponding explanatory gains.[26] This is just what Philo says to Cleanthes at the conclusion of Part IV of the *Dialogues*:

If I am still to remain in utter ignorance of causes and can absolutely give an explication of nothing, I shall never esteem it any advantage to shove off for a moment a difficulty which you acknowledge must immediately, in its full force, recur upon me. Naturalists, indeed, very justly explain particular effects by more general causes, though these general causes themselves should remain in the end totally inexplicable: but they never surely thought it satisfactory to explain a particular effect by a particular cause which was no more to be accounted for than the effect itself. An ideal system, arranged of itself, without a precedent design, is not a whit more explicable than a material one which attains its order in a like manner; nor is there any more difficulty in the latter supposition than in the former.[27]

Now, just as the *order* of the divine mind is claimed to explain the *order* of the world, in a parallel way the *beauty* of, and in, the divine mind is claimed to explain the *beauty* of the natural world. But, as we have seen, this merely raises a further question: to wit, what explains the beauty of, and in, the divine mind? Supposing beauty to have a divine origin in the beauty of, and in, God's mind, what then explains that *divine beauty*? If beauty truly is such that it rarely emerges in the absence of artistic intent, then must we hypothesize an artistic Super-God to put the beauty into God? And, if so, must we hypothesize a *Super*-Super-God to put the beauty into Super-God, and so on *ad infinitum*? Thus it would seem that the argument from beauty can offer us no explanatory gains, since the divine beauty is *at least* as puzzling as worldly beauty is, if we imagine this divine beauty as a brute fact that is beyond explanation. Indeed, the situation is arguably *worse* when the "brute" inexplicable fact is *divine beauty*, since divine beauty would presumably *greatly exceed* worldly beauty, making it all the more in need of explanation. So, to summarize, moving (inferentially) beyond worldly beauty to divine beauty flies in the face of Occam's Razor, without corresponding explanatory gains, and may in fact give us an even more puzzling *explanandum* (viz., the glorious divine beauty itself). Can the defender of the argument from beauty solve this difficulty?

5.2. Wynn's reply to Philo and a Philonian counter

Among the defenders of the argument from beauty, at least one has explicitly noted the apparent problem for that argument posed by Philo's explanatory regress objection.[28] In section 5.1, I proposed that the argument from beauty seems to offers us no explanatory gains, since the divine beauty is at least as puzzling as worldly beauty is, *if we imagine this divine beauty as a brute fact that is beyond explanation*. However, this is precisely what Wynn proposes to challenge. Wynn argues that Philo's objection can be met if "God's beauty is to be explained by reference to God's own activity, so that it is after all explained, *and not merely posited as a 'brute fact.'*"[29] I now want to attempt to lay out Wynn's response to Philo's objection in some detail, and I want to try to explain why I think that Wynn's responsive is inadequate.

Wynn develops his response to the explanatory regress objection in Chapter 6 of his *God and Goodness*.[30] However, Wynn's response to the explanatory regress objection is not articulated *qua* response to the objection, leaving the reader the task of trying to understand how the material in Chapter 6 responds to the objection. We can start by considering one *unpromising* way of understanding the (purported) divine self-expression found in natural beauty. Suppose that *God's own beauty* is somehow echoed or mirrored in natural beauty. Two problems immediately suggest themselves. First, *how* then does God's own beauty produce natural beauty? The painter of a beautiful painting need not be a beautiful painter: Ugly artists can make strikingly beautiful art. Second, if we imagine some form of "overflowing" of the divine beauty, of which natural beauty is the spillage (as it were), this leaves that same divine beauty as an utterly "brute" fact of the sort Wynn is concerned to avoid. After all, what would then explain the divine beauty?

Thus, what we are seeking (with help from Wynn's Chapter 6) is an understanding of natural beauty that makes it more an active *expression* of (rather than an imitative overflowing of) the Designer. If we can connect natural beauty to *divine activity*, as Wynn seeks to, then perhaps we can make some progress toward understanding how natural beauty can be explained by something (viz., divine activity) that is not itself in need of further explanation, without being problematically "brute."

Toward this end, Wynn claims that the *integrated beauty of the world itself* is a product of the divine mind. Worldly beauty reflects and points to divine beauty: "[T]he many diverse forms of existence which we encounter in the cosmos, when taken together, provide our clearest image of God."[31] For it was the divine mind which designed and brought about the "radiantly attractive synthesis" of things that is evident in creation.[32] So, again, worldly beauty reflects and points toward divine beauty. But this divine beauty, says Wynn, "is to be explained by reference to God's own activity," namely God's synthetic or integrative work in producing a "radiantly attractive" creation.[33]

Focusing the discussion on divine activity, then, seems to be Wynn's approach, and he spends most of Chapter 6 articulating and evaluating several competitor accounts of divine activity.[34] It seems to me, however, that nothing in any of these several accounts—including the account outlined roughly in the previous paragraph—offers us any hope of resolving Philo's explanatory regress objection, so I am prepared to stipulate that Wynn can consider any of those accounts as established (for the sake of argument). Still, I believe Philo's objection remains unanswered. Here's why. If God's *activity* includes (among other things) *designing things*, then this reply collapses back into Philo's original objection to the standard design argument: after all, artists are indeed "designers" in a broad sense. So even if God's beauty isn't just a fact about Him, but rather a fact about His (designing) *activities*—achieving that "radiantly attractive synthesis" of created things—still we can wonder how such complex abilities came to reside in God. If at this point we are told this is simply "brute"—it's the nature of God—then Wynn has failed to meet his argumentative burden: On Wynn's account, God's beauty—which is rooted in His extraordinary design skills—is ultimately as "brute" as the bruteness of those design skills themselves. Wynn's proposal had been to avoid such bruteness, but once the details of his approach are made clear, it is likewise clear that his proposal leads us right back to Philo's original complaint.

Collecting these points together, it therefore seems that we can either think of natural beauty in relation to *God's own beauty* (of which the former is an imitative overflowing), or else we can think of natural beauty as *the fulfillment of a project of divine artistry*, conceived and executed via various divine activities. But the first interpretation—imitative overflowing—invites the explanatory regress (i.e., so who made *God* beautiful?) or else collapses into an assertion of the bruteness of God's beauty (to which we might reply with an equally justified assertion of the bruteness of natural beauty). And the second interpretation—a project of divine artistry—merely highlights the connections between the argument from beauty and the standard design arguments by treating natural beauty (like natural orderliness) as the expression of the activities of the divine mind. But if so then the second interpretation (which is Wynn's view, I believe) actually takes us back to Philo's original worry, to wit: We are trying to explain "a particular effect by a particular cause which was no more to be accounted for than the effect itself. An ideal system, arranged of itself, without a precedent design, is not a whit more explicable than a material one which attains its order in a like manner; nor is there any more difficulty in the latter supposition than in the former."[35] Or, as Wynn himself states the objection early in his book, "the argument lacks any explanatory force because it postulates a further set of facts as much in need of explanation as those which it purports to explain."[36]

To avoid a vicious explanatory regress perhaps all disputants must accept some "brute" facts. Perhaps we must accept certain "brute" facts about beautiful things as well. But choosing to accept the bruteness of the beauty of, and in, the divine mind is no improvement over accepting the bruteness of natural beauty. Thus, the attempt to argue from natural beauty to the likely existence of a divine Artist fails. *Gloria in excelsis Philo.*

6. Concluding remarks

The theist who wishes to defend the argument from beauty is faced with the task of answering (at least) the four objections we have considered. Although I regard myself as a critic of the argument from beauty, I believe a resourceful theist can respond to the first three objections in ways that seem promising. I'm not sure the theist can decisively defeat those three objections, but were I a theist moved by the argument from beauty, I don't think any (or all) of the first three objections would lead me to reject the argument. However, I have argued that the fourth objection is a different case. While at least one sophisticated and well-developed response to the fourth objection exists, I have argued that that response is inadequate. Of course, we might ask whether Wynn's strategy can be further or more successfully developed. Or can my criticisms of Wynn's strategy be answered or shown to be misdirected? These remain questions to be considered.

We began the discussion by considering Forrest's observation that if there is "one feature of the universe that *most clearly supports theism*, it would have to be the beauty of things rather than the suitability of the universe for life."[37] In my view, Forrest's claim is both provocative and intriguing. I myself have conceded that the datum on which this argument rests—viz., the widespread abundance of natural beauty—is very hard to discount or dismiss. Can such natural beauty be shown to be an expression of, and thus a sign or indication of, the activity of a Divine Artist? That is the question with which we began and—as befits the never-ending pursuits of philosophy—that is the question with which we shall end.[38]

Notes

1. David Hume, *Dialogues Concerning Natural Religion*, 2nd edn., ed. Richard H. Popkin (Indianapolis: Hackett Publishing Company, 1998), 15.
2. On this historical shift from organic to mechanistic analogies, see Mark Wynn, *God and Goodness* (London: Routledge, 1999), 11–13, which provides references to several ancient and modern examples.
3. See Plato, *Symposium,* 210a–212c; Augustine, *Confessions,* 11.4; F. R. Tennant, *Philosophical Theology*, 2 vols. (Cambridge: Cambridge University Press, 1928/1930), Vol. 2, 89–93; Peter Forrest, *God Without The Supernatural* (Ithaca: Cornell University Press, 1996), 38–41, 133–135; Wynn, *God and Goodness*, esp. Chapter 1 ("Providence and Beauty"); and Richard Swinburne, *The Existence of God*, 2nd edn. (Oxford: Clarendon Press, 2004), 121–122, 188–191. Wynn's *God and Goodness* is far and away the most developed account of the argument from beauty and, as such, it will receive proportionately more attention in my discussion later in this chapter.
4. Peter Forrest, *God Without The Supernatural*, 39 (my emphasis).
5. Ibid.
6. Tennant, *Philosophical Theology*, Vol. 2, 91–92. Wynn provides a helpful analysis of Tennant's argument (see *God and Goodness*, 16–20).
7. The phrase quoted here is borrowed from Wynn, *God and Goodness*, 21.
8. See, e.g., the extensive survey of available research provided by Roger S. Ulrich, "Biophilia, Biophobia, and Natural Landscapes," in *The Biophilia Hypothesis*, ed. Stephen R. Kellert and Edward O. Wilson (Washington, DC: Island Press, 1993), 73–172. Ulrich (ibid.) is cited and discussed by Wynn (*God and Goodness*, 24 ff).
9. Richard Dawkins addresses (and critiques) the argument from beauty based on great works of art. See Dawkins, *The God Delusion* (Boston: Mariner Books, 2008), 110–112. However, Dawkins does not consider either the beauty of the human form or—more importantly in my view—the beauty of non-human nature in his discussion.
10. See Forrest, *God Without the Supernatural*, 134 n.15, 135.
11. Tennant, *Philosophical Theology*, Vol. 2, 92–93.
12. I should note, before moving on, that some philosophers have tried to connect (i) worldly beauty to (ii) a theistic belief, but without viewing the connection between (i) and (ii) *argumentatively* (i.e., without treating the theistic belief in question as the conclusion of an *inference*). For a famous contemporary example of this non-inferential approach, one specifically drawing our attention to various cases of worldly beauty, see all of the following works by Alvin Plantinga: 'Is Belief in God Properly Basic?' *Noûs* 15, no. 1 (1981): 46–47; "Reason and Belief in God," in *Faith and Rationality*, ed. Alvin Plantinga and Nicholas Wolterstorff (Notre Dame: University of Notre Dame Press, 1983), 18, 80–82; *Warranted Christian Belief* (New York: Oxford University Press, 2000), 170–177. In any case, herein I will be focusing exclusively on the claim that worldly beauty can be put to use in developing an *argument* in the tradition of natural theology.
13. See Edward O. Wilson, *Biophilia* (Cambridge, MA: Harvard University Press, 1984); see also Kellert and Wilson, *The Biophilia Hypothesis* (Washington, DC: Island Press, 1993).

14 For Wynn's discussion, see *God and Goodness*, 26–35.
15 Wynn, *God and Goodness*, 32.
16 Hume's classic essay "Of the Standard of Taste" makes an excellent and engaging entry-point to this debate. See David Hume, "Of the Standard of Taste," in *Of the Standard of Taste and Other Essays*, ed. John W. Lenz (Indianapolis: Bobbs-Merrill, 1965). For further discussion, along with helpful references to the historical and contemporary literature, see Crispin Sartwell's entry on "Beauty" for the *Stanford Encyclopedia of Philosophy*, which is archived in a permalink here: <https://plato.stanford.edu/archives/win2017/entries/beauty/>.
17 Tennant, *Philosophical Theology*, Vol. 2, 89–90; Swinburne, *Existence of God*, 191.
18 For references to the research literature, see Ulrich, "Biophilia, Biophobia, and Natural Landscapes."
19 This is a nearly complete listing of all the *naturally-occurring* examples provided by Scott Aikin and Nicholas Jones, "'An Atheistic Argument from Ugliness," *European Journal for Philosophy of Religion* 7, no. 1 (2015): 211–212. I am setting aside those of their examples which involve "terrible art" by "Ratt or Thomas Kinkade" (ibid., 211) for reasons analogous to those given above when discussing cases of beautiful art. We are interested in *naturally-occurring* beauty and ugliness.
20 This would be analogous to the logical version of the problem of evil, where it is held that *any evil* in the world (no matter how little) is inconsistent with the existence of a supremely perfect being: Either God exists, or evil exists, but they cannot possibly coexist in any conceivable world.
21 Cf. G. W. Leibniz, *Theodicy* (La Salle: Open Court, 1985), 130; cf. also Aikin and Jones, "'Atheistic Argument from Ugliness," 212–214, esp. on the "necessary counterpart" and "perspectival" theodicies.
22 See esp. Hume, *Dialogues*, 30–33. See also ibid., 42–43 and 55–56.
23 See John Locke, *An Essay concerning Human Understanding*, ed. Peter H. Nidditch (Oxford: Clarendon Press, 1975), 2.13.19 and also 2.23.2. Hume alludes to the same story (*Dialogues*, 31). (N.B.: Popkin's edition of Hume's *Dialogues* offers an incorrect reference to Locke's *Essay* 2.13.2—see Popkin's note 13 at *Dialogues*, 31. But that reference should read either 2.13.*19* or 2.*23*.2.)
24 Notice that this principle is actually much weaker (and so more defensible) than a standard version of the principle of sufficient reason.
25 As Cleanthes, Hume's defender of the design argument, does here: "[Y]ou [Philo] ask me what is the cause of this cause? I know not; I care not; that concerns not me. I have found a Deity and here I stop my inquiry. Let those go farther who are wiser or more enterprising" (Hume, *Dialogues*, 32–33).
26 Cf. Hume, *Dialogues*, 36–37.
27 Ibid., 33.
28 See Wynn, *God and Goodness*, 13 and 22–23, where the explanatory regress is clearly stated.
29 Ibid., 23 (my emphasis).
30 I have confirmed this through personal (email) communication with Professor Wynn, who has assured me that his reply to the objection is contained in the material found in Chapter 6 of *God and Goodness*.
31 Wynn, *God and Goodness*, 153.
32 For the quoted phrase, see, e.g., ibid., 155, 156, and 158.
33 For the quoted phrase, see ibid., 23.

34 For further details, see ibid., 141–168, perhaps especially 155–156 (which Wynn specifically emphasized in our correspondence).
35 Hume, *Dialogues*, 33.
36 Wynn, *God and Goodness*, 13.
37 Forrest, *God without the Supernatural*, 39 (my emphasis).
38 For discussion, comments, and suggestions which have improved this paper I would like to thank Colin Ruloff, Crisler Torrence, Mark Wynn, and the participants at the 2012 Central Division meeting of the Society of Christian Philosophers.

Bibliography

Aikin, Scott, and Nicholas Jones, "An Atheistic Argument from Ugliness," *European Journal for Philosophy of Religion* 7, no. 1 (2015): 209–217.
Augustine, *Confessions,* 2nd edition, translated by F. J. Sheed, Indianapolis: Hackett Publishing, 2006.
Dawkins, Richard, *The God Delusion,* Boston: Mariner Books, 2008.
Forrest, Peter, *God without the Supernatural,* Ithaca: Cornell University Press, 1996.
Hume, David, *Of the Standard of Taste and Other Essays,* edited by John W. Lenz, Indianapolis: Bobbs-Merrill, 1965.
Hume, David, *Dialogues Concerning Natural Religion,* 2nd edition, edited by Richard H. Popkin, Indianapolis: Hackett Publishing, 1998.
Kellert, Stephen R., and Edward O. Wilson, eds. *The Biophilia Hypothesis.* Washington, DC: Island Press, 1993.
Leibniz, G. W., *Theodicy,* La Salle: Open Court, 1985.
Locke, John. *An Essay concerning Human Understanding*, edited by Peter H. Nidditch, Oxford: Clarendon Press, 1975.
Plantinga, Alvin, "Is Belief in God Properly Basic?" *Noûs* 15, no. 1 (1981): 41–51.
Plantinga, Alvin, "Reason and Belief in God," in *Faith and Rationality*, edited by Alvin Plantinga and Nicholas Wolterstorff, 16–93. Notre Dame: University of Notre Dame Press, 1983.
Plantinga, Alvin, *Warranted Christian Belief,* New York: Oxford University Press, 2000.
Plantinga, Alvin, and Nicholas Wolterstorff, eds., *Faith and Rationality,* Notre Dame: University of Notre Dame Press, 1983.
Plato, *Plato on Love,* edited by C. D. C. Reeve, Indianapolis: Hackett Publishing, 2006.
Sartwell, Crispin, "Beauty," in *Stanford Encyclopedia of Philosophy*, edited by Edward N. Zalta, https://plato.stanford.edu/archives/win2017/entries/beauty/>.
Swinburne, Richard, *The Existence of God,* 2nd edn, Oxford: Clarendon Press, 2004.
Tennant, F. R., *Philosophical Theology,* 2 vols., Cambridge: Cambridge University Press, 1928/1930.
Ulrich, Roger S., "Biophilia, Biophobia, and Natural Landscapes," in *The Biophilia Hypothesis*, edited by Stephen R. Kellert and Edward O. Wilson, Washington, DC: Island Press, 1993: 73–172.
Wilson, Edward O., *Biophilia,* Cambridge, MA: Harvard University Press, 1984.
Wynn, Mark, *God and Goodness,* London: Routledge, 1999.

10

The Argument from Certainty

Katherin Rogers

The fact that human beings can have indubitable beliefs about necessarily true propositions is evidence for the existence of God because the best causal explanation for the existence of such beliefs involves positing a being with two properties which, in combination, render their possessor at least god-*like*. This being has the sort of causal power that could produce beliefs in human minds, and it somehow possesses (or has immediate access to) necessarily true propositions *necessarily*. Aspects of the physical universe might have the former property, but nothing in the physical universe possesses the latter. I will focus on a specific sort of certainty and on beliefs about mathematical propositions. Some of the claims on which I base my argument are controversial, but they are defensible and worthy of consideration.

I will take it as a datum to be explained that human beings sometimes have "strongly certain" beliefs. I am using "belief" in a rough and general way such that it is legitimate to refer to an instance of knowledge or a rational intuition as a "belief". A more fine-grained analysis might distinguish between "belief" and knowledge or the sort of "seeming" that constitutes rational intuition, but the catch-all term serves my purposes here. A strongly certain belief is characterized by several features. First it is veridical. It is held with a certainty such that having the belief entails the truth of the proposition believed. A variety of different epistemologies might allow room for such a certainty, and I do not need to fill out my conception in accord with one rather than another. My argument can proceed so long as it is granted that there are some beliefs which are held in such a way that what is believed cannot be false.

In addition to being veridical, introspection suggests that, as occurrent, strongly certain beliefs possess a set of properties which bestow upon them a recognizably unique phenomenology. I do not propose a complete description of the experience of having a strongly certain belief, and it is plausible to think that there may be real characteristics which are too subtle to distinguish consciously, but which contribute to the felt *sui generis* nature of the strongly certain belief. There are, however, two key properties which can be isolated and described. First, strongly certain belief will be "luminous". That is, if I am strongly certain that x, then I know that I know that x. And secondly – though I think this quality is intimately related to the first, and perhaps really just another aspect of a single phenomenon – strongly certain belief will be "immediate". It will be characterized by a direct recognition perhaps best described phenomenologically through the standard metaphors of intuition, a "seeing" or "grasping" of the object or content of the belief. This sense of immediacy is only strengthened by careful consideration. With perception one might prima facie have some sense of immediately "seeing" one's monitor screen, but upon being told about one's eyes, photons, etc. one will grant that there is at the very least a many-linked causal story to tell connecting one's seeing and one's monitor. Strong certainty is not like that. There are no intermediaries between the intellectual "seeing" and the content seen, and careful consideration of the experience of "seeing" the content of one's belief only confirms the experience of immediacy.

The claim that some beliefs are held with strong certainty does not entail that every human thinker has strongly certain beliefs. Perhaps some people have none. Nor does it entail that if one person believes a proposition with strong certainty, then anyone who understands that proposition must also hold it with strong certainty. It should be noted that there are many reasonable analyses of what it means to be "certain" of some belief which fall short of strong certainty. On these analyses it is consistent that "I am certain that x" and yet it is not the case that x. In that situation the phenomenology of my belief would differ from that of a strongly certain belief – I would not know that I know x, and I would not "grasp" x immediately. Call instances of less-than-strong certainty, "weak" certainty.

A paradigm instance of a strongly certain belief is, "I exist". If I am strongly certain right now that I exist, then it is true that I exist. And I know that I know I exist. Timothy Williamson mounts an attack on the claim to luminosity in many of the standard examples, but even Williamson has to grant the possibility of a few luminous beliefs including "that one exists".[1] Moreover I "grasp" my own existence, I "see" myself with a sort of pure immediacy. Here it seems to me that my cognitive access to myself fits the sort of experience which William Alston calls intuitive knowledge. He quotes H.H. Price to the effect that "such knowledge 'is simply the situation in which some entity or some fact is directly present to consciousness.'" Alston goes on to explain, "I cannot be in the state of knowledge that p so construed, without its being the case that p; for that state just consists of the presence of that fact to my consciousness; without that fact there could be no such state. Knowledge is not a state that could be just what it is intrinsically without the actual existence of the object; it has no intrinsic character over and above the presence of that object to consciousness."[2]

It seems to me that, in addition to being strongly certain that I exist, I have strongly certain beliefs about some necessary truths, like the basic laws of logic and some of the simpler mathematical propositions.[3] In this paper I will focus on strongly certain mathematical belief. The problem of the causes of knowledge of mathematical truth has already been discussed by philosophers of mathematics, and looking at how they frame the question will be useful. The content of strongly certain belief in simple mathematical propositions is interestingly different from the case of "I exist". In addition to my "grasp" of the bare proposition, like "2+2=4", there is recognition of the necessity of the proposition. It seems to me that this recognition of the necessity is included in the grasping of "2+2=4". A child might understand that "2+2=4" without understanding what it means for some proposition to be necessarily true, but if the child does not see that "2+2=4" in such a way that he automatically applies it in any instance, he does not really grasp it. If he really *gets* "2+2=4", a bit of Socratic questioning would soon elicit the fact that he sees that "2+2=4" must be true always and everywhere. So if I have a strongly certain belief that "2+2=4", and recognition that this is a necessary truth is included in that belief, then 2+2 *does* equal 4 necessarily, I know that I know this, and I have an immediate grasp of it.

It should be admitted first, though, that there are philosophers who deny the possibility of strong certainty. There are those – Quine springs to mind – who insist that even the claims of mathematics do not constitute necessary truth. "The proverbial necessity of mathematical truth resides merely in our exempting the mathematical sentences when choosing which one of a refuted block of sentences to revoke. We exempt them because changing them would reverberate excessively through science."[4] This sort of fallibilism is a difficult thesis to defend, however. Either the fallibilist offers an argument for his position or he does not. If he does not, then we have no reason to accept his counterintuitive conclusion that even apparently necessary truths like 2+2=4 might be false. But if he does give an argument, then it will have premises, and the premises will inevitably be more dubious than the claim that 2+2=4 is a necessary truth. Quine's story about belief acquisition begins, "Our intake of information about the world consists only of the triggering of our nerve endings by light rays and molecules from our environment,..." and goes on to make a series of claims about conditioning, animal expectations, the molding influence of evolution, language acquisition, etc. etc. etc.[5] This story about belief acquisition concludes to, among other things, the point about the in-principle-revokable nature of our mathematical commitments. But any of these claims is far, far more dubious than "'2+2=4' cannot possibly be false." One can read Quine's epistemic story as a version of a fallibilist argument. If this causal story of how we come to any and all of our beliefs is correct, then it follows that any belief, including 2+2=4, is revokable. If this argument is valid – in a sense that is the claim of the present paper – then it seems a reductio showing that this causal story of how we come to our beliefs must be mistaken. Any argument for this skepticism about necessary truth must face the same sort of criticism, mutatis mutandis.

A more moderate fallibilist might say that there are necessary truths, but we have no infallible way to recognize them. We cannot know that we know, and we do not have the sort of "grasping of the content" that strong certainty entails. To such a one I can only respond that I find myself incapable of entertaining the belief that I might be wrong about 2+2 equaling 4. Perhaps the fault lies with my imagination or perhaps the more moderate fallibilist simply holds the belief that 2+2=4 in a somewhat different way than I do.

It seems to me that I have a strongly certain belief that 2+2=4, and I can only ask the reader to introspect regarding his own beliefs. The question I want to address is, how did I come to have such a belief? My belief itself is a contingent phenomenon, and therefore it has a cause. I will argue that such an effect is most plausibly ascribed to God or (a god-like being). It is important here to distinguish between the causal question which I am asking, and the different, epistemic, question of how I can trust my belief that 2+2=4. I am *not* engaged in the sort of project which occupied Descartes in the First Meditation. Descartes holds that one could be brought to doubt even the simple rules of arithmetic if presented with the hypothesis of the evil genius. And then it is only by eliminating that hypothesis through the introduction of God that we can defeat skepticism.

The claim that the evil genius might deceive even with regard to what is most clearly and distinctly perceived generates the famous criticism of Descartes known as the Cartesian circle: How can we possibly mount an argument for knowledge of God, or anything else, if we have cast our most fundamental beliefs and our basic noetic abilities into doubt? Unlike Descartes I am not invoking God to solve some problem of ubiquitous doubt. In positing strongly certain belief in the basic laws of logic and simple mathematical propositions I deny Descartes' skeptical claim about these necessary truths. Mark Heller suggests this move as a solution to the Cartesian circle and argues that it follows that it is not necessary to introduce God to improve our epistemic status with regard to what is clearly and distinctly perceived.[6] That seems to me to be correct. If I have strongly certain belief that 2+2=4, my epistemic status regarding that belief really couldn't get any better. I need no further justification. My simply having it is sufficient to my epistemic needs. Though my discussion has epistemic ramifications, I am not asking about justification or reliability. Rather I am asking a question about adequate explanation: How did I come to have this (inherently justified, completely reliable) strongly certain belief?

My argument, then, is not of the same sort as Plantinga's in Chapter 12 of *Warrant and Proper Function*, where the naturalist hypothesis is seen as a defeater for the reliability of belief. My argument is closer to Augustine's in Book 2 of *On Free Will*: The evident fact of our knowledge of mathematical truth, which knowledge could not have its source in the contingent physical universe, shows that there is an eternal, immutable, and transcendent realm of such truth which must be identified with God.

The distinction between the question of epistemic reliability, which I am *not* addressing, and the question of adequate causal explanations, is so important that perhaps a simple analogy will help to reinforce it. Suppose it is a metaphysical necessity that Snickers Bars have peanuts. Suppose I (occurrently) know that this is the case. Then if I know I have a Snickers Bar in my hand, I know I have a candy bar with peanuts in my hand. Here the peanuts correspond to the veridical nature of the strongly certain belief. If I have a strongly certain belief I cannot even entertain the possibility of its being false. Period.

If I take my Snickers Bar as "given" then I need not look for some additional explanation for the presence of the peanuts. But Snickers Bars are contingent. I might demand a causal explanation for the Snickers Bar itself, and the fact of the peanuts might play an important role in shaping my causal theory. Suppose I hypothesize that the candy bar factory down the street provides an adequate causal explanation for the existence of the Snickers Bar. But suppose I discover that, while the factory does produce various sorts of candy bars, nothing in the factory is capable of inputting peanuts. I will not decide that this Snickers Bar does not have peanuts, since I see that it does and I believe that it must. I am committed to the metaphysical necessity of peanuts in Snickers Bars. But since I know this Snickers Bar has peanuts, and I know that the factory down the street cannot produce candy bars with peanuts, I know that it is not the cause of the Snickers Bar. I must look elsewhere for an explanation – I must find a factory which has the capacity to add peanuts to candy bars.

I do not question the reliability of my strongly certain beliefs, but they are contingent phenomena and so I aim to find a causal explanation for their existence. But an adequate causal explanation will involve causal factors which are capable of producing beliefs that have the inherently veridical nature and the unique phenomenology of strong certainty. I will argue that naturalistic causal theories fail to explain all that needs explaining. By "naturalism" I mean the view that the only things with causal power are things which are part of the spatio-temporal universe. By this definition a "naturalist" might believe in non-causal platonic abstracta. I will focus on mathematical beliefs since contemporary discussion of mathematical platonism has already brought some relevant difficulties with naturalism to light.[7]

For the time being I will assume that mathematical entities are platonic abstracta and that mathematical truths like "2+2=4" are about abstract objects, though at the end of the paper, when the topic is the relationship of God to mathematical truth, some qualifications will be proposed. In any case mathematical truths are about some sort of "things" which are not spatio-temporal and are not aspects of the physical universe. Certainly this is controversial.[8] But the alternative to platonism is to suggest that numbers, for example, *are* aspects of the physical universe. And then it should follow that they might come into or go out of being with the birth and death of the universe as we know it, or that it would not have been the case that 2+2=4 if some radically different physical universe, or none at all, had existed. My strong certainty that 2+2=4 entails that it is not possible that 2+2=4 fail to obtain, and so any attempt to see this mathematical truth as an aspect of the changing and inherently contingent physical universe must be rejected.

If mathematical entities are platonic abstracta then presumably they are causally inert. How then to offer a causal explanation for strongly certain beliefs, given that the human knower is located in time and space?[9] The difficulty lies in the fact that an adequate theory of the causes of knowledge must presumably allow for the content of the knowledge, the thing known, to play *some* role in the causal explanation. This is a common claim. A theory of the causes of perceptual knowledge which held that the objects of perception are entirely outside of the causal chain producing the knowledge would seem a very odd theory. Could it even be considered an explanation of my *seeing a tree*, if no tree at all were involved in the explanation? The point can be put even a bit more strongly if one assumes something like a Kripkean analysis of meaning and reference in which a "chain of communication" reaching back to the thing being referred to is a necessary part of establishing the very *meaning* of a term such that belief would be impossible without the causal connection.[10] Later in this paper I will have occasion to revisit this assumption that an adequate causal theory of knowledge must involve some connection between the knower and the known, even when the known is necessary truth, but let it stand for now.

Could we argue that the theory of evolution offers a causal explanation which can successfully relate the knower to the known in such a way as to explain strongly certain belief? The standard (radically simplified) evolutionary story about the causes of beliefs which have epistemic reliability goes something like this: 1. Eons of evolution have produced human beings with belief-producing mechanisms. 2. These belief-producing mechanisms produce beliefs that are likely to be "useful" (i.e. will help the believer survive and reproduce). 3. Beliefs that are useful are likely to be true. So evolution produces reliably true beliefs.

Even some staunch defenders of natural proofs for the existence of God hold that evolution is adequate to explain how our true beliefs come to be. In *Is There a God?* Richard Swinburne argues that Darwinism is adequate to explain the connection between the believer and the world. How would this come about?

> The answer is evident: animals with beliefs are more likely to survive if their beliefs are largely true. False beliefs – for example, about the location of food or predators – will lead to rapid elimination in the struggle for food or predators [sic]. If you believe that there is no table present, when there is one, you will fall over it, and so on. Those in whom the brain states which give rise to beliefs are connected by causal chains to the outside world, in such a way that the causal chain is normally only activated by a state of affairs which causes the brain state which in turn causes the belief that the state of affairs holds, will normally hold true beliefs about the world and in consequence be more likely to survive.[11]

Recently philosophers from very different camps have raised serious doubts that evolution could really be expected to produce epistemically reliable cognitive faculties.[12] But for the purposes of my argument I can grant that evolution is the source of mechanisms which produce beliefs which are likely to be useful and hence are likely to be true, especially when the issue is food or predators. But what about strongly certain belief that 2+2=4? A very pressing problem is this: Given that this content is causally inert, what could possibly "activate" the causal chain which causes the brain state which causes the belief? I will return to this below in discussing Nagel. First I will focus on a somewhat different issue regarding the special status of strongly certain beliefs – their inherently veridical nature and unique phenomenology which includes luminosity and immediacy.

In the evolutionary story nature produced beliefs which are "likely to be useful and hence true". But that *likely* entails "possibly not useful and, even if useful, possibly not true." For any given belief produced through this mechanism it is possible that it is not really a useful belief. Roger Penrose suggests that mathematical beliefs may have arisen as an accidental, and potentially harmful, side-effect of the useful ability to understand about food and predators. He offers a splendid cartoon in which a brainy pre-historic fellow is having a moment of illumination with respect to Mammoth hunting, while his (even brainier) compadre studies geometry in the dirt, unaware that he is about to be pounced on by a saber-toothed tiger.[13] One could even argue that, unlikely as it seems, whole categories of beliefs, perhaps all beliefs, are mere epiphenomena which play no genuine causal role in the survival and reproduction of the believer.

The connection between "produced by eons of evolution" and "useful" seems likely, but is not necessary. It is possible that any given belief, or even the whole belief-producing mechanism, may fail to be useful. The connection between "useful" and "true" in the evolutionary story is not necessary either. One could tell many a plausible tale in which holding systematically false beliefs, perhaps about one's own talents and importance, proves more useful for the metaphorical "purposes" of evolution than believing the truth would have done. It seems reasonable to suppose that in general the beliefs that *seem* useful, are useful, and that the reason they are useful is that they are true. But the evolutionary causal story, if it is indeed the story of how we come by *all* of our beliefs, seems to entail the possibility that none of our beliefs are useful and the possibility that none of them are true. But given that I am strongly certain that 2+2=4 I know it is not possible that all my beliefs are false. The causal story which appeals to purely naturalistic evolutionary processes proposes that *all* of our beliefs – the true and the false beliefs about contingent phenomena, and the true and the false beliefs about necessary truths (I might easily have a false belief about a complex arithmetical proposition) –are the effects of the same evolutionary processes. But this causal explanation fails for our strongly certain beliefs because there is nothing in the story to account for the inherently veridical nature of these beliefs.

Moreover there is no explanation for the unique phenomenology of the strongly certain beliefs. If all of our beliefs are the effects of the same causes, whence the luminosity and the immediacy of the strongly certain beliefs given that these properties do not, *could* not, characterize other less certain beliefs? A causal story which connects the knower to the known through the usefulness of belief seems ill-suited to explaining the fact that I "know that I know", when it seems obvious that luminosity would not contribute to a belief's enabling the believer to reproduce. Further, the evolutionary story ought to undermine the sense of immediacy which is part of the experience of strong certainty. It proposes that I believe that 2+2=4 because eons of evolution favored the survival of those who held that sort of belief. This suggests a long, involved causal chain, where none of the links consists in any immediate "grasping" 2+2=4. But this story strikes me as doubtful, whereas I do "see" that 2+2=4. Unlike with perceptual knowledge, this causal theory does not incline me to reassess the immediacy of my "seeing" that 2+2=4. Instead I conclude that something is lacking from the causal story. And, finally, remember that the strongly certain belief concerning "2+2=4" recognizes the necessity of the claim. The evolutionary account offers no explanation for our modal knowledge, since it seems clear that recognizing the contingency or necessity of certain propositions does not play a role in our success as reproducers.[14]

Thomas Nagel agrees that the processes of evolution are not sufficient to explain true belief, but goes on to dismiss the "religious proposal" in favor of:

> some systematic aspect of the natural order that would make the appearance of minds in harmony with the universe something to be expected....[There] are specific conditions of the primordial state of our universe that, given its general laws, will lead to the formation of molecules, galaxies, organisms, consciousness, and intelligence. My hypothesis is only that the laws are such as to make not only the first but also the last of these developments intelligible, given the initial conditions that lead to the development of some organisms or other.[15]

But what, in the physical universe, might "activate" a causal chain resulting in strongly certain belief? Nagel grants that the story which hopes to explain the reliability of belief through their evolutionary "use" is not likely to succeed. Still, there must be some causal explanation of belief, and presumably it must point to some connection between the belief and its content. Whatever one might hope for from a "systematic aspect of the natural order" which explains "minds in harmony with the universe," it seems overly optimistic to expect to discover a connection between the minds and platonic abstracta which would allow strong certitude concerning the necessary truth of 2+2=4. The natural order, a contingent phenomenon, simply is not in a position to bridge the gap between itself and the world of necessary abstracta. The evolutionary causal story for strong certainty fails because the attempt to trace the cause of true beliefs through the evolutionary development of useful beliefs cannot explain the special nature of the strongly certain belief. But *any* naturalist story must suffer an even more fundamental failure. If there are platonic abstracta and necessary truths, then they are not aspects of the contingent, physical universe, and therefore if the causal processes which produce the molecules, the galaxies etc. are purely physical, they cannot supply a connection between the contingent knower and the abstract, necessary, known. A platonic abstractum cannot "activate" a spatio-temporal causal chain. That being the case, there will be no naturalist causal explanation for the veridical nature, the luminosity, and the immediacy of the strongly certain belief in a necessary truth like 2+2=4. (George Bealer's analysis of rational intuition may reinforce this point when he argues that intuition, "intellectual seeing", and perceptual seeing, by and large, cannot overlap. He writes, "...most things that can seem intellectually to be so cannot seem sensorily to be so, and conversely."[16]).

But perhaps the naturalist can deny my assumption that the causal explanation of the strongly certain belief must show some sort of causal connection between the knower and the known, between the belief and its content. Seeing that there can be no "natural" causal connection between the knower and the abstracta known, the naturalist might argue that there can be strongly certain beliefs, like the belief that 2+2=4, which are amenable to a causal explanation in which the abstract content simply does not play a role. Perhaps our strongly certain beliefs are just "thrown up" somehow, with no connection to the abstracta, and yet nonetheless, what "grounds" our strong certitude is the fact that the proposition about the platonic abstracta is true. Let us say that our beliefs are caused only by natural processes. Once you have explained the natural processes you have given a complete explanation for the existence of the belief. Some of our beliefs are held with strong certainty and are about platonic abstracta. We have strong certainty because the proposition is true, but there is absolutely no *causal connection* of any sort between the belief and the true proposition. There is simply a correspondence. And that is enough.[17]

First it is important to remember that I am not asking what it is that "makes" strongly certain beliefs reliable. Suppose the naturalist claims that "Any causal explanation which is sufficient to explain the existence of our strongly certain beliefs is sufficient to explain their veridical nature (absolute reliability), luminosity, and immediacy." I agree. Any causal explanation which is sufficient to explain the existence of a Snickers Bar is sufficient to explain its having peanuts. In cases like "2+2=4" it is right to say that, "...whatever explains the undeniable fact that we have intuitions with specific contents, suffices as an explanation of the actual reliability of our intuitions as it surely excludes contradictory content."[18]

My question, however, is not what explains the *reliability* of the strongly certain belief, but what explains the strongly certain belief. Not just any explanation will do.

Suppose Anne expresses her puzzlement over the source of her strongly certain belief that 2+2=4 to her mother. And suppose her mother answers that the complete causal explanation for Anne's belief is that when sentences are inscribed on crystal tablets and then the tablets are ground up and fed to small children, the children will come to believe what was written on the tablets with strong certainty. Anne ingested the ground crystal bearing the sentence "2+2=4" with her strained peas, and that is why she believes 2+2=4 with strong certainty. Hearing this odd theory about its cause will not shake Anne's commitment to that belief that 2+2=4. *Whatever* caused the belief, the belief is true, luminous, and immediate. But is the strained pea theory adequate as a causal explanation for the belief?

The strained pea theory suggests several serious questions. Ordinarily in our thinking about belief acquisition the digestive system plays little if any role because it presumably is not the part of the person which receives the sort of data which can be processed as information. Anne's mother might respond that Anne has made a mistake in assuming that the causes of strongly certain belief must involve the reception of data like the causes of other sorts of beliefs. Anne might note that the actual scratchings on the crystal, in the form of the Arabic numerals we use, are merely symbols without inherent meaning and could not possibly convey any concept to an infant. Anne's mother might respond that Anne is still making the mistake of assuming that the content of the belief must figure somehow in the cause of the belief. Anne's mother admits that the scratchings on the crystal do not somehow "contain" the actual content, 2+2=4, but her contention is this: the fact that 2+2=4 has no causal role to play in the production of Anne's belief.

Anne might respond that divorcing the content of 2+2=4 from the causes which produce the strongly certain belief that 2+2=4 leads to impossible consequences. On the strained pea theory, "2+2=5" could have been inscribed on the crystal, and then, according to the theory; she, Anne, would have the strongly certain belief that 2+2=5. But that is impossible. Anne's mother might argue that the latter point is irrelevant, since in fact it was "2+2=4" that Anne ingested with her peas. But Anne's criticism is not refuted. The theory entails that "2+2=5" really could have been scratched on the crystal, and then that Anne would have had a strongly certain belief that 2+2=5. But a strongly certain belief that 2+2=5 is an impossibility. A theory which entails an impossibility is not a good theory.

The naturalist's proposed "correspondence" theory is subject to roughly the same problems as the strained pea theory. The correspondence theory proposes that the belief that 2+2=4 is correct because it corresponds to the truth, and it is inherently reliable, but the fact that 2+2=4 plays no role in the causal history of the strongly certain belief that 2+2=4. The belief itself can be completely causally explained by naturalistic factors. As in the strained pea theory, there is no causal connection between the knower and the known, but, according to the correspondence theory, that doesn't matter.

The first claim, echoing Anne to her mother, is that it is standard to suppose that knowledge requires some sort of causal connection between the knower and the known. This is certainly true of perceptual knowledge. Suppose we were to tell a correspondence story of the causes of perception. There is no causal connection at all between the object "seen" and the experience of seeing it. Rather natural processes happen to have produced the experiences of seeing certain objects, and they happen to have produced the actual existence of those objects, and there just happens to be a consistent correspondence between the presence of the object and the experience. (It is not that natural processes "happen to have produced a correspondence" as some sort of causal connection between the perceiver and the perceived. The correspondence itself must be a brute fact.)

This seems a very strange story to tell about perceptual knowledge. On this theory the experience that we would ordinarily describe as "seeing a tree" seems better put as "having a tree-seeing experience", since there is absolutely no connection between you, the perceiver, and the tree. And if this is the story you tell about perceptual knowledge, then you invite skepticism. The scenario entails the possibility that natural processes have thrown up perceptions without the corresponding objects. Your theory *says* that the objects are there, but it also claims that your knowledge and absolutely all the phenomena of your experience are explained without any appeal to the reality of the objects.

A theory of the causes of perceptual knowledge which denies any causal role to the objects of perception seems a non-starter. Could it be that strongly certain belief is so different from perceptual knowledge that, while theories about the latter need to establish a connection between the knower and the known, theories about the former do not? The paradigm case of the strongly certain belief is "I exist". Here there seems to be a clear and direct cause of the belief – the knower's immediate presence to himself. But perhaps the story is different when the content of the belief is necessary truth. It seems to me that the burden of proof here is on the one who would deny the standard requirement that knowledge depend in some way upon the facts known. But perhaps the correspondence theory has an argument to show that knowledge of necessary truth *must* be treated differently from other sorts of knowledge.

One might argue that the fact that 2+2=4 could not possibly figure in any causal explanation. Joel Pust, developing an argument by David Lewis, writes:

> ... we can make little sense of the truth-makers of necessary propositions being causally implicated in the explanation of any fact, including the fact that we have reliable intuitions regarding necessity... This is because the counterfactuals upon which such an explanation would presumably rest, counterfactuals such as "If 2+2 were not equal to 4, then I would not find 2+2=4 intuitive," are deviant and, on standard semantics, uniformly and vacuously true.... Hence, a natural strategy often employed in the realm of contingent truth to show that our opinions depend upon the truth — that of showing that if the facts were different, so too would be our opinions — simply has no application to the necessary.[19]

Does this argument show that our knowledge of necessary truth must be causally independent of that truth? An alternative conclusion would be that there are difficulties with the analysis of causation which reduces it to nothing but counterfactual dependence, and these problems become glaring when the question is how we know necessary truth. A general discussion of the nature of causation would take us too far afield. Here I will simply suggest that what Pust's argument actually proves is that some claims figuring in causal explanations resist counterfactual analysis.

In saying that necessary truth can play a constitutive role in a causal explanation, I do not mean to say that necessary truth per se or platonic abstracta can act as causal agents. But the claim that they can play no role at all is false. Suppose I ask my son how it is that I owe him $11. He responds that on Friday I borrowed $8 and then last Tuesday I borrowed $3, and 8+3=11. He has given me a causal explanation involving not only the historical facts of our financial transactions, but an additional piece of mathematical information without which the explanation would be incomplete. I might jokingly respond, "So if it's not the case that 8+3=11, then I don't owe you $11!" Of course, if it is not the case that 8+3=11 anything and everything follows. But that does not mean that my son's explanation is either non-causal or incoherent. And it doesn't show that "8+3=11" was not part of the explanation.

And there are deep problems with saying that the content of the necessary truth does not play a role in the causal explanation of our strongly certain beliefs – that there need be no causal connection between the knower and the known. The correspondence theorist grants that "2+2=4" is not a phenomenon of the spatio-temporal universe. He goes on to hold that my strongly certain belief that 2+2=4 is wholly the product of natural processes, perhaps beginning with Quine's "triggering of our nerve endings by light rays and molecules from our environment,..." Nerve endings get triggered, a long chain of events occurs in the spatio-temporal universe, and I come to have the strongly certain belief that 2+2=4. I have no doubt that my belief is veridical and utterly reliable, but is this "triggered nerve" theory plausible? (Let the "triggered nerve" stand for the natural processes invoked to explain belief.)

It seems in principle to be in the same family with the strained pea theory. It gives a causal explanation for how the belief comes to be, and it holds that the content of the belief, 2+2=4, plays no role at all in the causal history. That being the case, the theory ought to hold that, had the natural processes followed a slightly different path, as of course they could have done being contingent, a belief with all of the properties of a strongly certain belief but with a different content, say "2+2=5", could have resulted. This is impossible.

It will not do to say that there is no problem because the natural processes in fact threw up a belief that "2+2=4".[20] Analogous to the strained pea theory, the correspondence theory entails that the light rays *really could have* triggered the nerves in a "2+2=5" kind of way. There would then have been no correspondence to the truth, but the claim of the theory is that every aspect of the belief is explicable through the natural causes which simply have no connection to the content of the platonic abstracta. The theory entails that the strongly certain belief, with its content and phenomenology, would exist as the contingent phenomenon caused by the natural processes even if its content were "2+2=5". And that is impossible. The triggered nerve theory, like the strained pea theory, entails an impossible consequence, and thus is not a good theory to explain the existence of the strongly certain belief.

Naturalism seems unable to provide a causal connection between belief and platonic abstracta, and denying the need for some connection, as does the correspondence theory, leads to impossible consequences. But does the God hypothesis do any better?

The claim is that God (or a god-like being) provides what naturalism is lacking. He is a powerful causal agent who can produce human beliefs, and He knows necessary truths necessarily so there is no issue of explaining how He came to possess them. No contingent being – even a powerful angelic spirit, or a lesser god like Zeus – supplies what is required here, since for any contingent being, its beliefs must be contingent phenomena and hence in need of further causal explanation. It is true that a necessarily existent knower with great power might fall short of the God of classical theism. Still the argument points to a being who is at least very god-*like*. With the possible exception of Anselm's *Proslogion* argument, this is the case for all of the attempted proofs and adduced evidence for God.

There are different possible analyses of the relationship of God to necessary truth. The fact that He knows necessary truths necessarily means that there is no question of how He came to know them, and that may be enough for my purposes here. A full discussion lies beyond the scope of this paper, but a brief mention of some of the possibilities should assure the reader that the job of providing a coherent analysis can be done.[21] I should note that Descartes' suggestion that God somehow "creates" necessary truth is *not* among the viable options, in my opinion. It is subject to the insurmountable problem that it places God "above" the laws of logic. But if the laws of logic do not apply to God then nothing coherent can be said about Him.[22]

Many contemporary philosophers of religion go to the opposite extreme and embrace what is in essence the other horn of the logician's version of the Euthyphro problem. If God does not create the laws of logic and mathematics, then, it is assumed, such laws must exist independently of God. This view might be adequate for my argument here. On the thesis that the necessary truths exist independently of God, perhaps the claim that God is necessarily omniscient is enough to explain His knowledge of necessary truth, and so it may be sufficient for my present purposes.

From the perspective of (*very*) traditional theism, though, this position demeans God. It reduces Him to the role of a sort of Platonic demiurge, a being whose knowledge and power must depend upon and conform to a "World of the Forms" outside itself. This is not the God of the classical theism of philosophers like Augustine and Anselm and Aquinas. The classical theist God is the absolute source of all. All that exists is God or what He makes. On this view, God's knowledge of necessary truth does not depend on anything outside Himself. Rather, He is Perfect Being, and necessary truth – the laws of logic and mathematics – are the way all being has to be. They reflect the nature of God. Classical theism holds that God is simple – His nature is identified with His omnipotence, His omniscience, and His perfect goodness. On this view, not only can there be no demand for how God "comes to know" necessary truths, but there is no explanation at all for God's knowledge of necessary truths beyond the simple fact of His necessary existence.[23]

This "anti-platonic" analysis of the relationship of God to necessary truth has the further advantage that it does not hypothesize a world of ontologically dubious platonic abstracta just "there" in the universe. Absent God, the platonist understanding of numbers seems preferable to the alternative, the claim that numbers are an aspect of the physical universe. But nevertheless, the universe of the naturalist who allows this platonic realm seems a strange, unparsimonious, and indeed schizophrenic place. All of the causal action is set among the objects of perceptual experience, but in addition to spatio-temporal things there are these other…what? Besides the problem of how the abstracta could play a role in the beliefs of corporeal creatures such as ourselves, there is an intrinsic puzzle about their ontological status. The theist who sees necessary truth as existing independently of God seems to face this question as well. What sort of "things" are these platonic abstracta? As Robert Adams notes, they *seem* like ideas.[26] Classical theism solves the problem by placing necessary truth in the mind of God and identifying it with the nature of God. This seems to me by far the best move.

There may be various ways to tell the story of how God causes our strongly certain beliefs. Perhaps, as Augustine thought, He implants them directly in our minds. This may accord best with the phenomenological quality of immediacy that I have taken to be characteristic of strongly certain belief. Perhaps other stories might do the job as well. The most important claim is that God is involved as an agent who establishes the required *causal connection* between the believer and the propositions believed.

But if God is omnipotent couldn't he produce a strongly certain belief in a false proposition, "2+2=5", for example? That is, doesn't the theist hypothesis face the same problem as the correspondence theory and the strained pea theory? No. First note that God is good and would not Himself deliberately deceive. But more fundamentally, a strongly certain belief with the content "2+2=5" is an impossibility. A belief in "2+2=5" is not veridical or luminous, and does not have the sort of immediacy which consists in a "grasping" of a fact. The problem with the strained pea theory and the correspondence theory as causal explanations of strongly certain belief is that both divorce the content of the belief from the causal processes that produced it and so could not avoid the impossible entailment that a strongly certain belief could have a falsehood as its content. The theist theory, on the other hand, insists that only a cause which could "implant" the content of necessary truth in our minds could possibly be the source of strongly certain belief. God is omnipotent, but omnipotence does not include the ability to do the impossible. God is in a position to cause strongly certain belief, but this does not entail the impossible consequence that God could cause a strongly certain belief in a false proposition.

But doesn't invoking God as the cause of our strongly certain beliefs generate a problem of what might be termed epistemic theodicy? That is, the vast majority of our beliefs are held with less than strong certainty. We are, in fact, woefully ignorant. Surely if there were a good God who loves us and produces our strongly certain beliefs, He would *want* us to know as much of the truth with as much certainty as possible. Undoubtedly many beliefs are not of the sort that could be held with strong certainty, but couldn't we have more strongly certain knowledge than we do? Isn't our ignorance evidence that there is no belief-producing God? No. The premises of the argument from epistemic evil are weak. For all we know, our ignorance may be a necessary part of the divine plan. Perhaps the struggle to overcome it is valuable for the development of human virtues. And perhaps our ignorance ultimately stems from human free choices so God cannot eradicate it without doing damage to the freedom which is a terribly important human property. This question in epistemic theodicy is amenable to the same sorts of responses that any version of the theist problem of evil raises.

Only a god-like being can provide a sufficient explanation for our strongly certain beliefs concerning platonic abstracta (and necessary truth in general), and so the existence of such beliefs provides some evidence for the existence of God. There are responses open to the committed atheist. He can simply deny that there are strongly certain beliefs regarding mathematical propositions and hold that no belief involving platonic abstracta can be held with the proposed unique phenomenology such that the belief entails the truth of the proposition believed, is luminous and immediate. Possibly it is not the case that 2+2=4. And then he can provide a causal history of his belief that 2+2=4 through any of the naturalist theories proposed above. These theories fail as explanations of strongly certain belief, but they might succeed as explanations for beliefs of a different sort.

An alternative move would be to grant the strongly certain beliefs about mathematical entities, allow the necessity of some connection between the believer and the abstracta, but radically revise one's platonism. One might propose that the platonic entities themselves do have some sort of causal powers.[25] But it is difficult to see how "3" might be an agent or interact causally with the citizens of the spatio-temporal universe. And a theory depending on a possibly infinite number of agent abstracta at work in the world seems to depart from the empiricist and parsimonious motivations behind naturalism at least as much as, and perhaps more than, the religious thesis.

Another alternative for the atheist is to stick with standard platonism, embrace strongly certain beliefs regarding platonic abstracta, and admit that they defy explanation. A more optimistic move would be to grant that there is not a satisfactory causal story *yet*. Although now the inherent difficulties of explaining how the contingent phenomena of our physical universe could produce strongly certain beliefs about mathematical propositions seem insurmountable, we may trust that the Science of the Future will find a way. These responses are problematic, but one or another seems unavoidable for the atheist. Someone who is not powerfully committed to the non-existence of God, though, granting that we sometimes do have strongly certain beliefs about necessary propositions, ought to conclude that this provides some evidence for God.[26]

Notes

1 Timothy Williamson, *Knowledge and its Limits* (Oxford: Oxford University Press, 2000) p.107.
2 William Alston, 'Does God Have Beliefs?' in *Divine Nature and Human Language* (Ithaca, NY: Cornell University Press, 1989) pp.178–193, see p.187. Reprinted from *Religious Studies* 22 (1987): 287–306. Alston goes on to say that this sort of knowledge may be reserved to God.
3 Williamson, *Knowledge and its Limits*, 107–108.
4 From Quine's 'Philosophical Self-portrait' in the *Penguin Dictionary of Philosophy*, ed. Thomas Mautner (Penquin Books, 1997), 466.
5 Ibid.
6 Mark Heller, 'Painted Mules and the Cartesian Circle', *Canadian Journal of Philosophy* 26: (1996) 29–56.

7   It does not seem to me that the problem of mathematical knowledge can be solved by reducing it to logical knowledge. The problem only gets pushed back a step. Bob Hale ('Is Platonism Epistemologically Bankrupt?' in *The Reason's Proper Study*, eds. Bob Hale and Crispin Wright (Oxford: Clarendon Press, 2001) 169–188)) notes the analogous nature of knowledge about mathematical statements and knowledge about logical statements.

8   There are a variety of theories suggesting that the necessity of mathematical statements can be preserved while locating mathematical "objects" within the confines of the physical universe. See for example, D.M Armstrong, *A Combinatorial Theory of Possibility* (Cambridge: Cambridge University Press, 1989) Chapter 10; P. Maddy, *Naturalism in Mathematics* (Oxford: Oxford University Press, 1997).

9   The apparent impossibility of describing the causal interaction between the World of the Forms and the physical world was one of Aristotle's chief criticisms of Plato in the first book of the *Metaphysics*. The contemporary *locus classicus* for the epistemic problem with mathematical platonism is Paul Benacerraf, 'Mathematical Truth', *Journal of Philosophy* 70 (1973): 661–679. See also Colin Cheyne, 'Existence Claims and Causality', *Australasian Journal of Philosophy* 76 (1998): 34–47.

10 Saul A. Kripke, *Naming and Necessity* (Cambridge, MA: Harvard University Press, 1980): 91–93.

11 Richard Swinburne, *Is There a God?* (Oxford, Oxford University Press: 1996): 87–88.

12 Steven Stich calls into question the very existence of "rationality" as a cognitive faculty aimed at discovering the truth (*The Fragmentation of Reason* (Cambridge, Massachusetts: MIT Press, 1993), Chapter 3). Alvin Plantinga defends the reliability of our reasoning, but argues that it is unlikely that evolution alone would produce reliable cognitive faculties (*Warrant and Proper Function* (Oxford: Oxford University Press, 1993), Chapter 12). Thus he holds that the theist is in a better position than the naturalist with regard to trusting his cognitive faculties.

13 Roger Penrose, *The Large, the Small, and the Human Mind* (Cambridge: Cambridge University Press, 1997): 114.

14 Michael Rea, *World Without Design* (Oxford: Clarendon Press, 2002): 193–195.

15 Thomas Nagel, *The Last Word* (Oxford, Oxford University Press; 1997): 132–133.

16 George Bealer, 'Intuition and the Autonomy of Philosophy' in *Rethinking Intuition* eds. Michael DePaul and William Ramsey (Lanham, MD: Rowman & Littlefield, 1998): 201–240, see p.208.

17 Joel Pust, 'On Explaining Knowledge of Necessity', *Dialectica* 58 (2004): 71–87. Jerrold Katz, if I am understanding him correctly, advances this thesis in *Realistic Rationalism* (Cambridge, MA: MIT Press, 1998).

18 Pust, 'On Explaining Knowledge of Necessity', 78–79.

19 Ibid. p.74. See David Lewis *On the Plurality of Worlds* (Oxford: Basil Blackwell, 1986): 111.

20 Pust, 'On Explaining Knowledge of Necessity', 80.

21 For other suggestions regarding the relationship of God to necessary truth see: C. Menzel, 'Theism, Platonism and the Metaphysics of Mathematics', *Faith and Philosophy* 4 (1987): 365–382; C. Menzel and T. Morris, 'Absolute Creation', *American Philosophical Quarterly* 23 (1986): 353–362. See also Plantinga's Presidential Address, 'How to be an Anti-Realist' in *Proceedings and Addresses of the American Philosophical Association*, 56 (1982): 47–70.

22 Katherin A. Rogers, *Perfect Being Theology* (Edinburgh: Edinburgh University Press, 2000): 94–96. Brian Leftow discusses a more moderate analysis of God's causing

necessary truth in 'A Leibnizian Cosmological Argument', *Philosophical Studies* 57 (1989): 135–155.
23 The question of whether or not humans have libertarian freedom, and how God knows human choices is a difficult one which would take us far, *far* afield.
24 Robert Adams, 'Divine Necessity', *Journal of Philosophy* 80 (1983): 741–751, see p.751.
25 There does seem to be some sort of connection between the physical world and the world of platonic abstracta. The physical world does behave in a mathematically describable way. Plato invoked the mysterious relationship of "participation", but a more plausible proposal might find "the hand of God" in this connection between the physical world and mathematical truth.
26 I would like to thank William Hasker and anonymous readers for this journal for lengthy and constructive criticism on earlier versions of this paper, and my colleague Joel Pust for his more than generous help over several years of revisions.

11

The Argument from the Applicability of Mathematics[1]

William Lane Craig

1. Introduction

One of the perennial and burning questions in the philosophy of mathematics concerns mathematics' indispensability and applicability. Though often conflated in the literature, these are actually distinct questions. Indispensability has to do with our inability to get along in science or in even ordinary life without quantifying over or using singular terms having as their referents mathematical objects. Applicability concerns mathematics' reliability or utility in helping us to navigate successfully the physical world.

Indispensability is thus first and foremost linguistic in character and only secondarily ontological. Most philosophers of mathematics acknowledge that our best scientific theories cannot be purged of quantification over, and singular terms for, mathematical objects; but many, if not most, will deny that we are thereby ontologically committed to the mind-independent reality of mathematical objects. Most of the philosophers who reject indispensability arguments for the reality of mathematical objects will be anti-realists about such objects, since these arguments are today the main motivation for the affirmation of mathematical realism, though even some realists may themselves eschew indispensability arguments in favor of other justifications of their realism. The indispensability of mathematics is, then, not widely contested, but the ontological implications of such indispensability is strongly contested across a wide variety of anti-realist perspectives.[2]

Applicability has to do with what mathematician and physicist Eugene Wigner famously called "the unreasonable effectiveness of mathematics in the natural sciences."[3] Mathematics is the language of nature. That is to say, the laws of nature may be expressed as mathematical equations which describe the phenomena to an astonishing degree of accuracy. In his important study *The Applicability of Mathematics as a Philosophical Problem* Mark Steiner has characterized the question raised by Wigner as a problem of *description*, to be differentiated from Steiner's own problem of *discovery*.[4] While the distinction is a helpful one, we must be careful not to attribute to Wigner a sort of literalism or naïve realism about the descriptive character of nature's laws. Wigner speaks rather of "an unexpectedly close and accurate description of the *phenomena*" and "the enormous *usefulness* of mathematics in the natural sciences."[5] As we shall see, he insists that nature's laws are useful and thus applicable even though they often cannot be taken as literal descriptions of the physical world. They accurately describe physical phenomena, and a multiplicity of such descriptions may be possible. Steiner, on the other hand, is concerned with the applicability of mathematics in the way in which mathematics serves as a means of scientific discovery. In this essay I shall be concerned only with Wigner's problem of the describability of the universe via mathematics rather than with its discoverability.

The applicability of mathematics is only indirectly related to the indispensability of mathematics. A Platonic realist like Peter van Inwagen does try to draw a connection between mathematics' applicability and indispensability by casting Platonic realism as at least a partial explanation of mathematics' applicability. He claims that, given the indispensability of mathematical terms and quantificational statements, arguments for even conclusions which are nominalistically acceptable, like "We shall need two gallons of paint for this room," are undermined by anti-realism, leaving us with no reason to think that truth should be ascribed to such conclusions. He writes:

> Anyone who denies the existence of numbers ... must therefore regard the empirically verifiable fact that applying these principles to the physical world always yields the right result as a *mystery*....
>
> Nominalism is therefore to be rejected because it renders the applicability of mathematics to the physical world a mystery.[6]

Realism presumably renders the applicability of mathematics non-mysterious.

In fact, however, van Inwagen's real target here is not anti-realism but fictionalism, the view that statements involving quantification over or reference to mathematical objects are, strictly speaking, false.[7] Fictionalism is but one of a cornucopia of anti-Platonic perspectives on mathematics, most of which affirm mathematical truth. Van Inwagen thus misleads in playing off Platonism solely against fictionalism, as though fictionalism were the only alternative to Platonic realism. The fundamental issue raised by fictionalism is mathematical truth, not the ontology of mathematical objects. The salient point made by van Inwagen is that we have good reason to think that many statements involving quantification over or reference to mathematical objects are true, in contradiction to fictionalism. It is only the conjunction of this conclusion with van Inwagen's neo-Quinean criterion of ontological commitment, which takes singular terms and the first-order existential quantifier to be devices of ontological commitment, that yields Platonism or, at least, realism.[8] Anti-realists who reject the neo-Quinean criterion may actually themselves press indispensability/applicability arguments for the truth of mathematical statements against their fictionalist colleagues without fear of ontological commitment to mathematical objects.

Our interest, then, is not in the indispensability of mathematics, nor in the ontological implications of such indispensability, but rather in the applicability of mathematics to the physical world, as evident from its utility in science.

2. The "unreasonable effectiveness of mathematics"

In his seminal paper Wigner makes two main points:

(i) Mathematical concepts turn up in "entirely unexpected connections" in physics and often permit "an unexpectedly close and accurate description" of the phenomena in these connections.[9]

(ii) Because we do not understand the reasons for the usefulness of mathematical concepts, we cannot know whether a scientific theory formulated in terms of such concepts is uniquely appropriate.

Wigner declines to develop (ii), which is not, in any case, germane to our interest.

3. The nature of mathematical inquiry

Turning to (i), Wigner first makes some preliminary remarks on the question, "What is mathematics?" which will prove to be relevant later. Here he stresses the *a priori* nature of mathematical inquiry, especially of the mathematics that is so valuable in physics:

> whereas it is unquestionably true that the concepts of elementary mathematics and particularly elementary geometry were formulated to describe entities which are directly suggested by the actual world, the same does not seem to be true of the more advanced concepts, in particular the concepts which play such an important role in physics ... Most more advanced mathematical concepts, such as complex numbers, algebras, linear operators, Borel sets—and this list could be continued almost indefinitely—were so devised that they are apt subjects on which the mathematician can demonstrate his ingenuity and sense of formal beauty.[10]

Wigner's point is well-taken. As philosopher of mathematics Penelope Maddy emphasizes, what justifies the use of various set-theoretical axioms by the mathematician is fruitfulness: axioms are properly adopted which are rich in mathematical consequences, or what Maddy calls "mathematical depth."[11] This fact is important because set theory is typically regarded as foundational for the rest of mathematics, since the whole of mathematics can be reductively analyzed in terms of pure sets.[12] Whereas Wigner represents the mathematician as inventing new concepts outside his axioms, Maddy represents him as inventing new axioms. Mathematicians are at liberty to craft and explore different axiomatic systems at will.

So set theorists have felt free to formulate quite a variety of set theories, some featuring even different mathematical objects. Maddy observes that mathematicians employ "maximizing principles of a sort quite unlike anything that turns up in the practice of natural science: crudely, the scientist posits only those entities without which she cannot account for our observations, while the set theorist posits as many entities as she can, short of inconsistency."[13] Maddy identifies quite a few of these "rules of thumb" followed by set theorists in choosing their axioms and constructing their theories, such as *maximize, richness, diversity, one step back from disaster, etc.*[14] Similarly Wigner observes, "The great mathematician fully, almost ruthlessly, exploits the domain of permissible reasoning and skirts the impermissible."[15]

The "principal point" which will be relevant to the uncanny effectiveness of mathematics is that mathematicians are not bound by customary axiomatic concepts but are free to define new concepts with a view, not of applicability or scientific utility, but of "permitting ingenious logical operations which appeal to our aesthetic sense both as operations and also in their results of great generality and simplicity."[16] That historically there has been a cross-pollination between physics and mathematics, physics sometimes spurring developments in mathematics,[17] does not nullify Wigner's point. Wigner finds a particularly striking example in complex numbers:

> Certainly, nothing in our experience suggests the introduction of these quantities. Indeed, if a mathematician is asked to justify his interest in complex numbers, he will point, with some indignation, to the many beautiful theorems in the theory of equations, of power series, and of analytic functions in general, which owe their origin to the introduction of complex numbers. The mathematician is not willing to give up his interest in these most beautiful accomplishments of his genius.[18]

Who, then, would have anticipated the centrality and utility of complex numbers in physical theory?[19]

4. Mathematics' role in physics

Wigner now inquires as to the role of mathematics in physics and why mathematics' success in that role appears "so baffling." With respect to mathematics' role in physics, Wigner notes that while mathematics is useful in physics for evaluating the consequences of the laws of nature, a role which he associates with applied mathematics, it also plays a more "important" and "sovereign" role in physics, namely, to enable the formulation of the laws of nature themselves in the language of mathematics in order to be an apt object for the use of applied mathematics. By laws of nature Wigner understands statements of various regularities of the inanimate world which are conditional and limited in scope.[20]

To illustrate the importance of mathematical concepts in the formulation of the laws of physics, Wigner turns to Paul Dirac's formulation of the axioms of quantum mechanics. Wigner identifies two basic concepts in Dirac's formulation: vectors in Hilbert space, a peculiar, infinite-dimensional, mathematical space, and mathematical operators which act on these vectors to give the real (that is, neither complex nor imaginary) value of various observables or measurable quantities like position, momentum, spin, and so forth.[21] So we have two foundational mathematical concepts at play in Dirac's formulation of the laws of quantum mechanics: vectors in Hilbert space and special operators on those vectors. Wigner pulls up at this point "lest we engage in a listing of the mathematical concepts developed in the theory of linear operators."[22]

Wigner rejects the suggestion that the physicist had to choose this particular formulation of quantum mechanics because of its simplicity. He reminds us that the Hilbert space of quantum mechanics is a complex space and that complex numbers are far from simple and cannot be suggested by physical observations. Moreover, the use of complex numbers in this case is not a calculational trick of applied mathematics but comes close to being a necessity in the formulation of the laws of quantum mechanics.

It now appears, Wigner comments, that not only complex numbers but so-called analytic functions are destined to play a decisive role in the formulation of quantum theory.[23] Thus, mathematical concepts are of decisive importance in the formulation of the laws of quantum theory and cannot be regarded as forced upon us by simplicity.

At this point Wigner muses, "It is difficult to avoid the impression that a miracle confronts us here."[24] The closest thing to an explanation of mathematical concepts' cropping up in physics, Wigner reflects, is Einstein's assertion that the only physical theories which we are willing to accept are the beautiful ones and, hence, the mathematically formulated ones, since mathematical concepts have the quality of beauty. Wigner rightly rejects this suggestion, since it explains at best why the theories we are willing to believe are mathematically formulated, not why the accurate, that is, empirically applicable, theories are mathematically formulated.

Thus far, Wigner has argued merely that mathematics plays a central role in the formulation of successful laws of physics, a conclusion which no one, I think, would contest. This conclusion is reinforced by the indispensability of mathematics for physical theories. The key question comes in the next section of Wigner's paper, "Is the Success of Physical Theories Truly Surprising?"

5. Is the success of physical theories truly surprising?

In this section Wigner argues that "the mathematical formulation of the physicist's often crude experience leads in an uncanny number of cases to an amazingly accurate description of a large class of phenomena."[25] He provides three examples in support.

The first example is Newton's second law of motion, $F = ma$ (where F is the force on an object, m is the mass of that object, and a is the acceleration of the object). Newton's law proved applicable, not merely to mundane objects, but to planetary motion. According to Wigner, the law though simple to the mathematician, is not simple for the untrained because a second derivative, namely, acceleration (change in change-in-displacement over time) appears in it. "Newton's law, quoted over and over again, must be mentioned first as a monumental example of a law, formulated in terms which appear simple to the mathematician, which has proved accurate beyond all reasonable expectations".[26] Wigner alludes as well to Newton's gravitational law $F = G(m_1 m_2 / r^2)$,[27] which is algebraically related to the second law and has also been confirmed to a fantastic degree of accuracy. Newton's gravitational equation was eventually superseded by Einstein's ten equations for the gravitational field, which may be expressed as $R_{\mu\nu} - \frac{1}{2} R g_{\mu\nu} + \Lambda g_{\mu\nu} = 8\pi G/c^4 \, T_{\mu\nu}$.[28] The General Theory of Relativity based on the Einstein equations affords even more accurate predictions than Newton's theory, solving, for example, the mystery of Mercury's orbit, which Newton's theory had failed precisely to predict.

Wigner's second example is ordinary, elementary quantum mechanics. At the instigation of Max Born, who had noted specific similarities between the behavior of matrices and some of Werner Heisenberg's earlier quantum work,[29] Heisenberg replaced the position and momentum variables in his equations with matrices and applied the rules of matrix mechanics to a few highly idealized problems, with satisfactory results. "The miracle occurred only when matrix mechanics, or a mathematically equivalent theory, was applied to problems for which Heisenberg's calculating rules were meaningless."[30] Heisenberg's original rules presupposed that the equations of classical mechanics had solutions with certain periodicity properties, that is to say, solutions which exhibit a regular, repetitive, wavelike pattern. But the equations of motion for the electrons of the helium atom, not to mention the electrons of heavier atoms, did not have these same properties. Therefore, Heisenberg's rules could not be applied to them. Nevertheless, alternative theories that utilized the ideas of matrix mechanics yielded calculations for the helium atom which Wigner says had an accuracy of "one part in ten million." A disagreement would have provoked a crisis in atomic physics. Wigner reflects, "physics as we know it today would not be possible without a constant recurrence of miracles similar to the one of the helium atom, which is perhaps the most striking miracle that has occurred in the course of the development of elementary quantum mechanics, but by far not the only one."[31]

Wigner's third example is quantum electrodynamics, a theory which unites quantum mechanics and relativity to describe electromagnetism, and in particular the Lamb Shift, which described a small difference of about 0.00003% in the energy levels of the hydrogen atom not predicted by Dirac's equations. The theory is one of the most accurate ever devised, predicting the value of the fine structure constant α to an accuracy of 10^{-8}.

Wigner notes that his three examples represent an increasing independence of empirical experience in favor of reliance on mathematics: "Whereas Newton's theory of gravitation still had obvious connections with experience, experience entered the formulation of matrix mechanics only in the refined or sublimated form of Heisenberg's prescriptions. The quantum theory of the Lamb shift ... is a purely mathematical theory and the only direct contribution of experiment was to show the existence of a measurable effect."[32]

Wigner takes his examples—"which could be multiplied almost indefinitely"—to illustrate the "appropriateness" and "almost fantastic accuracy" of the mathematical formulation of the laws of nature in terms of mathematical concepts chosen for their "manipulability," that is to say, their "amenability to clever manipulations and to striking, brilliant arguments."[33]

6. Reconstruction of Wigner's argument

Steiner, without disputing the legitimacy of Wigner's mystery of nature's mathematical describability, does fault him for his "flawed presentation," which has hindered philosophers from giving him his due. Steiner reconstructs Wigner's argument as follows:[34]

(1) Mathematical concepts arise from the aesthetic impulse in humans.
(2) It is unreasonable to expect that what arises from the aesthetic impulse in humans should be significantly effective in physics.

(3) Nevertheless, a significant number of these concepts are significantly effective in physics.
(4) Hence, mathematical concepts are unreasonably effective in physics.

Steiner thinks that this formulation is problematic for two reasons: (i) It ignores the failures, that is, the instances in which scientists fail to find appropriate mathematical descriptions of natural phenomena, which outnumber the successes by far, as well as the mathematical concepts that have never found an application. (ii) Each individual success of applying a mathematical statement might have nothing to do with its being a *mathematical* concept.

I must confess that I fail, despite my best effort, to see the force of these alleged shortcomings. With respect to (i), the fact that scientists often fail to find mathematical laws to describe physical phenomena (in biology, for example) does nothing to nullify the fact that many such phenomena, especially in physics, are so describable, as Wigner illustrates, and so cry out for explanation. Moreover, it is to be expected that many of the infinitude of mathematical concepts will not be physically applicable, nor does Wigner's argument suggest otherwise.

As for (ii), Steiner later expands on the perceived flaw. Wigner, he says,

> gives persuasive examples of successes that cry out for explanation—but he doesn't prove that they add up to one phenomenon that cries out for explanation. Each success is a story in itself, which may or may not have an explanation. Wigner does not make a case that what is unreasonably effective is *mathematics*, even though the individual examples he gives are of concepts that happen to be mathematical. In other words Wigner may give examples of a number of applications which are "unreasonably effective"—applications of concepts which happen to be mathematical. But he doesn't show that these successes have anything to do with the fact that the concepts are mathematical.[35]

This is an odd complaint. Steiner grants that each of the examples of applicability that Wigner gives is mathematical and that each "is so extraordinary that it requires explanation."[36] To complain that Wigner's argument focuses on isolated examples is to suggest that his examples may not be representative. But of what? Of physics? Wigner justifiably maintains that examples such as he gives pervade physics. Of mathematics? Wigner has no interest in showing that physical applicability pervades mathematics, nor should he. *Pace* Steiner, Wigner does *not* want to show that "these successes have [some]thing to do with the fact that the concepts are mathematical." The examples of successful application are not to be explained by the concepts' being mathematical; indeed, in Wigner's view mathematical concepts successfully apply *despite* their being mathematical. The concepts' being mathematical contributes, not to their successful application, but to the inexplicability of their successful application. For Wigner there is no explanation for their successful application, and so we are left with mystery. To refute Wigner one would need to show either that the relevant concepts, despite their mathematical nature, do have some explanation of their applicability, or else that the examples of inexplicable applicability are truly exceptions and that most of the successful applications of mathematics in physics are explicable.[37]

In any case Steiner seems to regard his alleged shortcomings of Wigner's argument as merely a flaw of presentation. Appealing to physicists who maintain that mathematical concepts as a whole require explanation for their applicability, Steiner says that this is "a separate question" and "I believe the most profound. It concerns the applicability of mathematics as such, not as this or that concept ... It is the question raised by Eugene Wigner."[38] Since the focus on isolated examples is merely a flaw of presentation, "Wigner's thesis is not in fact vulnerable to the objection that one is ignoring the evidence of failure."[39]

Furthermore, Steiner's reconstruction of Wigner's argument, which is nowhere explicitly formulated by Wigner, seems somewhat maladroit. For it follows from (1) and (2) that:

(4*) It is unreasonable to expect that mathematical concepts should be significantly effective in physics.

which is practically synonymous with (4). Yet this makes (3) superfluous to Wigner's argument, even though it represents the heart of his paper! Worse, (3) gives one the premiss for a *modus tollens* argument from (2) against (1).

We can avoid denying (1) if we take (2) to be an implicit conditional. (2) is plausibly true only on the assumption of metaphysical naturalism, the view that the physical world is all there is.[40] Accordingly, we could revise (2) to:

(2*) If naturalism is true, then it is unreasonable to expect that what arises from the aesthetic impulse in humans should be significantly effective in physics.

Then (3) would lead to a rejection of naturalism. Wigner, however, does not argue for theism but rests with mystery. Accordingly, we should take (2) to mean something like:

(2**) It would be surprising to find that what arises from the aesthetic impulse in humans should be significantly effective in physics.

Recall that this section of the paper asks "Is the Success of Physical Theories Truly Surprising?", not "Is the Success of Physical Theories Truly Unreasonable?" When, therefore, we learn that mathematical concepts are significantly effective, it occasions a mystery, something meriting explanation.[41]

Steiner's reconstruction also misses out completely on Wigner's strong emphasis on the laws of nature as mathematical descriptions of the phenomena.[42] Wigner is not concerned with how many mathematical concepts, for example, arithmetic concepts, are significantly effective in physics. He is concerned with nature's laws. Accordingly, (3) ought to be reformulated as something along the lines of:

(3*) The laws of nature can be formulated as mathematical descriptions (concepts) which are often significantly effective in physics.

Wigner rightly emphasizes that this is a pervasive feature of the laws of physics. That scientists often fail in their fumbling attempts to discover or formulate nature's laws does nothing to undercut (3*). (Such botched efforts would again seem more relevant to Steiner's discoverability argument.) That an indefinite number of mathematical concepts fail to find application in the universe is to be expected, given the infinitude of the one and the finitude of the other, and does nothing to undercut the truth of (3*). To refute Wigner one would need to show that scarcely any physical phenomena are covered by laws of nature or that the relevant natural law is not mathematically formulable. While that may be the case in some fields of science, it does not seem to be the case in physics.

Steiner's formulation of (1) is unobjectionable, so long as we keep in mind that Wigner is not talking about aesthetics in the artistic sense, but in the sense of mathematical beauty, what Maddy calls *mathematical depth*. Mathematics is an a priori discipline which is independent of the physical world. Moreover, when we reflect that mathematical objects, even if they exist, are causally effete, it is surprising that such objects should be significantly effective in physics.[43] Indeed, the abstractness of mathematical objects would serve to explain in general terms, not just in isolated examples, why their applicability is so surprising.

Accordingly, the following seems to be a more suitable formulation of Wigner's argument:

(1**) Mathematical concepts arise from the aesthetic impulse in humans and have no causal connection to the physical world.
(2**) It would be surprising to find that what arises from the aesthetic impulse in humans and has no causal connection to the physical world should be significantly effective in physics.
[Therefore, it would be surprising to find that mathematical concepts should be significantly effective in physics.]
(3**) The laws of nature can be formulated as mathematical descriptions (concepts) which are often significantly effective in physics.
(4**) Therefore, it is surprising that the laws of nature can be formulated as mathematical descriptions that are often significantly effective in physics.

Given that something surprising merits *prima facie* an explanation, we wonder as to the explanation of the fact that the laws of nature can be formulated as mathematical descriptions that are often significantly effective in physics.

7. Accounting for mathematics' applicability

Wigner, despite his characterization of the applicability of mathematics to the physical world as a miracle, in the end regarded it as a mystery. He concluded, "The miracle of the appropriateness of the language of mathematics for the formulation of the laws of physics is a wonderful gift which we neither understand nor deserve."[44] Wigner, however, never actually considered in his essay whether theism might not furnish a good explanation of mathematics' applicability. He considered at most naturalistic explanations of it and, finding none to be satisfactory, therefore concluded "that the enormous usefulness of mathematics in the natural sciences is something bordering on the mysterious and that there is no rational explanation for it."[45] But suppose we take the theistic hypothesis seriously. Since the question of mathematics' applicability to the physical world is already a metaphysical, not a physical, question, there can be no objection stemming from the corner of methodological naturalism to considering a metaphysical answer to a metaphysical question.

Theists will have a considerably easier time, I think, explaining the applicability of mathematics than will naturalists. Theists hold that there is a personal, transcendent being (a.k.a. God) who is the Creator and Designer of the universe. Naturalists hold that all that exists concretely is space-time and its physical contents. Now whether one is a realist or an anti-realist about mathematical objects, it appears that the theist enjoys a considerable advantage over the naturalist in explaining the uncanny success of mathematics.

8. Realism: non-theistic and theistic

Consider first realism's take on the applicability of mathematics to the world. For the *non-theistic* realist, the fact that physical reality behaves in accord with the dictates of acausal mathematical entities existing beyond space and time is, in the words of philosopher of mathematics Mary Leng, "a happy coincidence."[46] For consider: If, *per impossibile*, all the abstract objects in the mathematical realm were to disappear overnight, there would be no effect on the physical world. This is simply to underscore the fact that abstract objects are causally inert. The idea that realism somehow accounts for the applicability of mathematics "is actually very counterintuitive," muses Mark Balaguer. "The idea here is that in order to believe that the physical world has the nature that empirical science assigns to it, I have to believe that there are causally inert mathematical objects, existing outside of spacetime," an idea which is inherently implausible.[47]

It might be said that the applicability of mathematics is not puzzling because there are unlimited realms of mathematics which have no applicability whatsoever to the physical world. So it is hardly surprising that out of this infinite range of options, the physicist will find some mathematics to describe the laws of nature. Wigner seemed to anticipate this sort of response when he acknowledged:

> It is true, of course, that physics chooses certain mathematical concepts for the formulation of the laws of nature, and surely only a fraction of all mathematical concepts is used in physics. It is true also that the concepts which were chosen were not selected arbitrarily from a listing of mathematical terms but were developed, in many if not most cases, independently by the physicist and recognized then as having been conceived before by the mathematician. It is not true, however, as is so often stated, that this had to happen because mathematics uses the simplest possible concepts and these were bound to occur in any formalism.[48]

As Wigner sees, the question is not, why are there mathematical concepts and structures which are applicable to physical reality, for the question is not about the fecundity of the mathematical realm. Quite the reverse, the question is why the physical world exhibits a structure that is so amenable to mathematical description of its natural laws. As Wigner states, there is nothing about the mathematical formalism discerned in the laws of nature that renders its instantiation inevitable.[49]

By contrast, the *theistic* realist can argue that God has fashioned the world on the structure of the mathematical objects He has chosen. This is essentially the view that Plato defended in his dialogue *Timaeus*. Plato draws a fundamental distinction between the realm of static being (that which ever is) and the realm of temporal becoming (that which is ever becoming). The former realm is to be grasped by the intellect, whereas the latter is perceived by the senses. The realm of becoming is comprised primarily of physical objects, while the static realm of being is comprised of logical and mathematical objects. God looks to the realm of mathematical objects and models the world on it. The world has its mathematical structure as a result. Plato writes:

> We must in my opinion begin by distinguishing between that which always is and never becomes from that which is always becoming but never is. The one is apprehensible by intelligence with the aid of reasoning, being eternally the same, the other is the object of opinion and irrational sensation, coming to be and ceasing to be, but never fully real ... Whenever, therefore, the maker of anything keeps his eye on the eternally unchanging and uses it as his pattern for the form and function of his product the result must be good; whenever he looks to something that has come to be and uses a model that has come to be, the result is not good.
>
> ... If the world is beautiful and its maker good, clearly he had his eye on the eternal; if the alternative (which it is blasphemy even to mention) is true, on that which is subject to change. Clearly, of course, he had his eye on the eternal; for the world is the fairest of all things that have come into being and he is the best of causes. That being so, it must have been constructed on the pattern of what is apprehensible by reason and understanding and eternally unchanging; from which again it follows that the world is a likeness of something else ...
>
> ... For god's purpose was to use as his model the highest and most completely perfect of intelligible things, and so he created a single visible living being, containing within itself all living beings of the same natural order.[50]

Thus, the realist who is a theist has a considerable advantage over the naturalistic realist in explaining why mathematics is so effective is describing the physical world.

The main objection confronting this view is theological: the realm of mathematical objects is thought to exist independently of God, so that God is not the sole ultimate reality. There are on the contemporary scene Christian realists who limit God's creation to Plato's realm of temporal becoming and exempt the intelligible realm from creation.[51] But other Christian realists construe mathematical and other putative abstract objects to be in fact concrete objects, namely, thoughts of various sorts in the mind of God and so dependent upon God for their being.[52] Still others advocate absolute creation, the view that the realm of abstract objects, including mathematical objects, though necessary in its existence, is nonetheless causally dependent upon God.[53]

9. Anti-realism: non-theistic and theistic

Now consider anti-realism of a *non-theistic* sort. It might be said by certain thinkers of post-modernist bent that mathematics is merely a projection of the human mind, and so it is hardly surprising that physicists should concoct the mathematical concepts and structures they need for their theories. Again Wigner seemed to anticipate such a response:

> A possible explanation of the physicist's use of mathematics to formulate his laws of nature is that he is a somewhat irresponsible person. As a result, when he finds a connection between two quantities which resembles a connection well-known from mathematics, he will jump at the conclusion that the connection is that discussed in mathematics simply because he does not know of any other similar connection. It is not the intention of the present discussion to refute the charge that the physicist is a somewhat irresponsible person. Perhaps he is. However, it is important to point out that the mathematical formulation of the physicist's often crude experience leads in an uncanny number of cases to an amazingly accurate description of a large class of phenomena.[54]

Whatever other failings a postmodern view of mathematical truth might have, the salient point here is that the amazing accuracy of physics in a vast range of cases is most plausibly explained by there being an objectively existing physical world which one discovers to be amenable to mathematical description. It is irrelevant whether the mathematical realm is a mere pretense. The world really operates in accord with mathematically formulated laws; this is not plausibly an illusion of human consciousness.

Leng, on the other hand, says that on anti-realism relations which are said to obtain among pretended mathematical objects just mirror the relations obtaining among things in the world, so that there is no happy coincidence. Philosopher of physics Tim Maudlin muses, "The deep question of why a given mathematical object should be an effective tool for representing physical structure admits of at least one clear answer: because the physical world literally has the mathematical structure; the physical world is, in a certain sense, a mathematical object."[55]

Well and good, but what remains wanting on naturalistic anti-realism is an explanation *why* the physical world should exhibit so elegant and stunning a mathematical structure in the first place. After all, there is no necessity that a physical world exist at all, in which case mathematical truths would not have been descriptive of the physical world. Perhaps the universe, in order to exist, had to have *some* mathematical structure—though couldn't the world have been a structureless chaos?[56]—but that structure might have been describable by elementary arithmetic. For example, one thing and another thing make two things. But, as Wigner is at pains to emphasize, modern physics shows the physical world to be breathtakingly mathematically elegant. When Einstein was struggling to craft his General Theory of Relativity, for example, he had first to go to a mathematician to be tutored in tensor calculus before he could advance further to formulate his equations of the gravitational field. The laws of nature are contingent, at least in the sense that the states of affairs described by them did not have to obtain. By using as his examples laws of nature which are fearsomely complicated mathematically, Wigner already forced the question to a higher plane.

Not only so, but by choosing examples like the infinite-dimensional Hilbert space and complex numbers, Wigner implicitly precluded the explanation that physical reality is isomorphous to such mathematical structures, since these cannot be physically realized in the universe. According to Steiner, physicists see no difficulty in the applicability of arithmetic to the world, since this is just a matter of logic, not physics; rather they concentrate upon the seemingly miraculous appropriateness of physically meaningless concepts like matrix algebra or Hilbert spaces for quantum mechanics.[57] It is the burden of Steiner's book to provide numerous examples of the applicability of mathematical concepts that cannot be physically instantiated.[58] Some of his examples are the same ones to which Wigner already appealed, such as the descriptive applicability of analytic functions of complex variables, Heisenberg's utilization of matrix mechanics in his classical equations, a procedure for which, Steiner says, "there is no physical rationale" and which replaces all the variables by matrices "which have no physical meaning," and the descriptive applicability of the Hilbert space formalism to quantum mechanics, which Steiner calls "physically unintelligible." So even if the physical universe had to have some mathematical structure, that fails to address the question raised by Wigner. In the end Balaguer admits that he has no explanation why, on anti-realism, mathematics is applicable to the physical world or why it is indispensable in empirical science. He just observes that neither can the realist answer such "why" questions.

By contrast, the *theistic* anti-realist has a ready explanation of the applicability of mathematics to the physical world: God has created it according to a certain blueprint which He had in mind. There are any number of blueprints He might have chosen. Maddy observes:

> contemporary pure mathematics works in application by providing the empirical scientist with a wide range of abstract tools; the scientist uses these as models—of a cannon ball's path or the electromagnetic field or curved spacetime—which he takes to resemble the physical phenomena in some rough ways, to depart from it in others ... The applied mathematician labors to understand the idealizations, simplifications and approximations involved in these deployments of his abstract structures; he strives as best he can to show how and why a given model resembles the world closely enough for the particular purposes at hand. In all this, the scientist never asserts the existence of the abstract model; he simply holds that the world is like the model is some respects, not in others. For this, the model need only be well-described, just as one might illuminate a given social situation by comparing it to an imaginary or mythological one, marking the similarities and dissimilarities.[59]

On theistic anti-realism the laws of nature have the mathematical form they do because God has chosen to create the world according to the abstract model He had in mind. This was the view of the first century Jewish philosopher Philo of Alexandria, who maintained in his treatise *On the Creation of the World* that God created the physical world on the mental model in His mind. For a Jewish monotheist like Philo, the realm of Ideas does not exist, as Plato thought, independently of God but as the contents of His mind. Philo referred to the mind of God as God's Logos (Word). The sensible world (*kosmos oratos*) is made on the model of the conceptual or intelligible world (*kosmos noētos*) that preexists in the Logos. Philo explains:

> God, because He is God, understood in advance that a fair copy would not come into existence apart from a fair model, and that none of the objects of sense-perception would be without fault, unless it was modeled on the archetypal and intelligible idea. When he had decided to construct this visible cosmos, he first marked out the intelligible cosmos, so that he could use it as a incorporeal and most god-like paradigm and so produce the corporeal cosmos, a younger likeness of an older model, which would contain as many sense-perceptible kinds as there were intelligible kinds in that other one.
>
> To declare or suppose that the cosmos composed of the ideas exists in some place is not permissible. How it has been constituted we will understand if we pay careful attention to an image drawn from our own world. When a city is founded, in accordance with the high ambition of a king or a ruler who has laid claim to supreme power and, because he is at the same time magnificent in his conception, adds further adornment to his good fortune, it can happen that a trained architect comes forward. Having observed both the favourable climate and location of the site, he first designs in his mind a plan of virtually all the parts of the city that is to be completed—temples, gymnasia, public offices, market-places, harbours, shipyards, streets, construction of walls, the establishment of other buildings both private and public. Then, taking up the imprints of each object in his own soul like in wax, he carries around the intelligible city as an image in his head. Summoning up the images by means of his innate power of memory and engraving their features even more distinctly in his mind, he begins, like a good builder, to construct the city out of stones and timber, looking at the model and ensuring that the corporeal objects correspond to each of the incorporeal ideas.
>
> The conception we have concerning God must be similar to this, namely that when he had decided to found the great cosmic city, he first conceived its outlines. Out of these he composed the intelligible cosmos, which served him as a model when he also completed the sense-perceptible cosmos. Just as the city that was marked out beforehand in the architect had no location outside, but had been engraved in the soul of the craftsman, in the same way the cosmos composed of the ideas would have no other place than the divine Logos who gives these (ideas) their ordered disposition. After all, what other place would there be for his powers sufficient to receive and contain, I do not speak about all of them, but just a single one of them in its unmixed state? If you would wish to use a formulation that has been stripped down to essentials, you might say that the intelligible cosmos is nothing else than the Logos of God as He is actually engaged in making the cosmos. For the intelligible city too is nothing else than the reasoning of the architect as he is actually engaged in the planning the foundation of the city.[60]

Especially noteworthy is Philo's insistence that the world of ideas cannot exist anywhere but in the divine Logos. Just as the ideal architectural plan of a city exists only in the mind of the architect, so the world of ideas exists solely in the mind of God. Philo's view can be interpreted as either a conceptualist realism or as an anti-realism, for he says that the intelligible world may be thought of as either formed by the divine Logos or, more reductively, as the Logos itself as God is engaged in creating. Since Philo believed that time had a beginning at creation, the formation of the intelligible realm in the divine mind should probably be thought of as timeless and as explanatorily prior to God's creation of the sensible realm.

10. Conclusion

Thus, the theist—whether he be a realist or an anti-realist about mathematical objects—has the explanatory resources to account for the otherwise unreasonable effectiveness of mathematics in physical science—resources which the naturalist lacks.

We may thus extend Wigner's argument:

(1*) Mathematical concepts arise from the aesthetic impulse in humans and have no causal connection to the physical world.
(2**) It would be surprising to find that what arises from the aesthetic impulse in humans and has no causal connection to the physical world should be significantly effective in physics.
   [Therefore, it would be surprising to find that mathematical concepts should be significantly effective in physics.]
(3*) The laws of nature can be formulated as mathematical descriptions (concepts) which are often significantly effective in physics.
(4**) Therefore, it is surprising that the laws of nature can be formulated as mathematical descriptions that are often significantly effective in physics.
5. Therefore, the fact that the laws of nature can be formulated as mathematical descriptions that are often significantly effective in physics merits explanation.
6. Theism provides a better explanation of the fact that the laws of nature can be formulated as mathematical descriptions that are often significantly effective in physics than does atheism.
7. Therefore, the fact that the laws of nature can be formulated as mathematical descriptions that are often significantly effective in physics provides evidence for theism.

Notes

1   I am grateful to David Hutchings, David Sherrill, and Matthew Probert for their valuable input to this essay.
2   For a survey of anti-realist and realist perspectives as well as non-Platonic realisms, see my *God and Abstract Objects: The Coherence of Theism III: Aseity* (Berlin: Springer Verlag, 2017).

3   Eugene Wigner, "The Unreasonable Effectiveness of Mathematics in the Natural Sciences," in *Communications in Pure and Applied Mathematics* 13 (New York: John Wiley & Sons, 1960), 1–14.
4   Mark Steiner, *The Applicability of Mathematics as a Philosophical Problem* (Cambridge, MA: Harvard University Press, 1998), 9. Steiner's project is to show that physicists' use of mathematical analogies to guess at the laws of nature is anthropocentric, that is, it presupposes that human beings have a special importance in the scheme of things. The stunning success of such a procedure, attested by numerous examples, calls into question naturalism, which holds that the universe is indifferent to the goals and values of humanity (ibid., 3–8; cf. 55, 176). Steiner contends that "If we examine the analogies actually used to discover the major laws of physics in our century, we find that the analogies used are anthropocentric. On naturalist grounds, then, they should have failed, just as a dowser should fail to find oil. And this is a difficulty for naturalism, because what the evidence suggests is, on the contrary, that nature looks 'user-friendly' to human inquiry" (ibid., 72). Not only is Steiner's project compatible with Wigner's, but Steiner recognizes that his conclusion is consistent with natural theology as well (ibid., 10).
5   Wigner, "Unreasonable Effectiveness of Mathematics," my emphasis, 2.
6   Peter van Inwagen, "'Fictionalist Nominalism and Applied Mathematics," *The Monist* 97, no. 4 (2014): 486; cf. 495–496. The "principles" to which he here alludes are correspondence principles correlating adjectival use of numerals with nominal use of numerals, which are employed as premises to obtain a true, nominalistically acceptable conclusion. Since the truth of the conclusion is not guaranteed by the truth of the premises, he wants to know, why does mathematics work?
7   For an account of fictionalism, see Mark Balaguer, "Fictionalism in the Philosophy of Mathematics," in *The Stanford Encyclopedia of Philosophy*, ed. Edward N. Zalta (Stanford University, 1997–). Article published September 21, 2013. Retrieved from http://plato.stanford.edu/archives/fall2013/entries/fictionalism-mathematics/; Mark Balaguer, *Platonism and Anti-Platonism in Mathematics* (New York: Oxford University Press, 1998).
8   On the neo-Quinean criterion of ontological commitment, see Mark Balaguer, "Platonism in Metaphysics," in *The Stanford Encyclopedia of Philosophy*, ed. Edward N. Zalta (Stanford University, 1997–). Article published April 7, 2009. Retrieved from <http://plato.stanford.edu/archives/sum2009/entries/platonism/>
9   Wigner, "Unreasonable Effectiveness of Mathematics," 2. Wigner rephrases this first point as "mathematics plays an unreasonably important role in physics."
10 Ibid., 2–3.
11 Penelope Maddy, *Defending the Axioms: On the Philosophical Foundations of Set Theory* (Oxford: Oxford University Press, 2011), 82.
12 See Penelope Maddy, "Set Theory as a Foundation," in *Naturalism in Mathematics* (Oxford: Clarendon Press, 1997). Maddy comments:

> The astounding achievement of the foundational studies of the late nineteenth and early twentieth centuries was the discovery that these fundamental assumptions could themselves be proved from a standpoint more fundamental still, that of the theory of sets. The idea is simple: the objects of any branch of classical mathematics— numbers, functions, spaces, algebraic structures—can be modeled as sets, and resulting versions of the standard theorems can be proved in set theory. So the most fundamental of the fundamental assumptions of mathematics, the only such assumptions that truly cannot be proved, are the axioms of the theory of sets itself.

In this sense, then, our much-valued mathematical knowledge rests on two supports: inexorable deductive logic, the stuff of proof, and the set theoretic axioms. (Ibid., 1)

13 Ibid., 131.
14 Penelope Maddy, "Believing the Axioms I," *Journal of Symbolic Logic* 53, no. 2 (1988): 481–511.
15 Wigner, "Unreasonable Effectiveness of Mathematics," 3.
16 Ibid.
17 Ivor Grattan-Guiness, "Solving Wigner's Mystery: The Reasonable (Though Perhaps Limited) Effectiveness of Mathematics in the Natural Sciences," in *Mathematical Intelligencer* 30, no. 3 (2008): 7–17.
18 Ibid.
19 See now the possible relevance of so-called octonions, two steps beyond complex numbers, Natalie Wolchovern, "The Peculiar Math that Could Underlie the Laws of Nature," *Quanta Magazine* (July 28, 2018) Retrieved from <https://www.wired.com/story/the-peculiar-math-that-could-underlie-the-laws-of-nature/>
20 He summarizes: "All the laws of nature are conditional statements which permit a prediction of some future events on the basis of the knowledge of the present, except that some aspects of the present state of the world, in practice the overwhelming majority of the determinants of the present state of the world, are irrelevant from the point of view of the prediction" (Wigner, "Unreasonable Effectiveness of Mathematics," 5). For a good discussion of the nature of nature's laws see Jeffrey Koperski, *Divine Action, Determinism, and the Laws of Nature* (London: Routledge, 2020), chap. 5.
21 Wigner refers to these as self-adjoint operators. They are also known as Hermitian operators. Self-adjoint operators are those which guarantee real values as an outcome. The presence of such an operator tells us that its corresponding quantity can indeed be measured—hence Wigner's calling the operators themselves "observables" in his paper.
22 Wigner, "'Unreasonable Effectiveness of Mathematics," 7.
23 Analytic functions are those which are highly amenable to the calculus of Newton and Leibniz. They are smooth, meaning that their derivatives will yield meaningful results. This is vital in quantum mechanics because many of the observables, such as momentum, are indeed derivatives.
24 Wigner, "Unreasonable Effectiveness of Mathematics," 7.
25 Ibid., 8.
26 Ibid., 8–9.
27 In this equation G is the gravitational constant, which has a precise, contingent value, and r is the distance between the objects whose masses are m_1 and m_2 respectively.
28 The terms of this equation are as follows: $R_{\mu\nu}$ is the Ricci curvature tensor, R is the scalar curvature, $g_{\mu\nu}$ is the metric tensor, Λ is the cosmological constant, G is the gravitational constant from Newton's equation, c is the velocity of light, and $T_{\mu\nu}$ is the stress-energy tensor. The left-hand side of the equation describes the curvature of spacetime and the right-hand side the mass-energy density.
29 Viz., certain pairs of variables in Heisenberg's theory did not commute, that is to say, the calculations gave a different answer when done in reverse. It is this behavior which gave rise to his famous uncertainty principle because the first measurement "interferes" with the second. On the sole grounds of the fact that matrix manipulation is likewise non-commutative, Born and Heisenberg proposed to use matrices in Heisenberg's equations, with surprising success!

30 Wigner, "'Unreasonable Effectiveness of Mathematics," 9.
31 Ibid., 10.
32 Ibid.
33 Ibid.
34 Steiner, *Applicability of Mathematics*, 46.
35 Mark Steiner, "Mathematics—Application and Applicability," in *Oxford Handbook of Philosophy of Mathematics and Logic*, ed. Stewart Shapiro, Oxford Handbooks in Philosophy (Oxford: Oxford University Press, 2005), 631.
36 Ibid.
37 For example, Steiner thinks that the applicability of a mathematical concept can be explicable by a physical structure in the world. So, he writes, "To eliminate the mystery of a *particular* mathematical concept describing a *particular* phenomenon, we match the concept to a nonmathematical property, as before with linearity" (Steiner, *Applicability of Mathematics*, 44). Concerning the property of linearity, Steiner had written, "Whatever we are to say about this question, we can at least conclude this: there is no mystery concerning the applicability of linearity; the mathematical property of linearity can be reduced to physical properties which nature may either exhibit or not exhibit" (ibid., 32). For Steiner. linearity, which applies whenever multiple solutions can combine by simple addition to provide further solutions, is simply a consequence of some natural behaviors' being the sum of many small parts. We shall take up below whether such isomorphism really resolves the mystery of applicability rather than merely shifts it; in any case Steiner provides abundant examples where such isomorphism does not hold.
38 Steiner, *Applicability of Mathematics*, 45.
39 Ibid., 73; cf. Steiner, "Mathematics—Application and Applicability," 631. So Steiner in fact takes Wigner's mystery to be a profound one. Unfortunately, Steiner imagines Wigner countering the above flaws by contending that his thesis applies to the set of mathematical concepts, not to the set of attempts to apply mathematical concepts, that is to say, it can be said of the mathematical concepts that a significant number of them prove significantly effective. This friendly advice strikes me as altogether wrong-headed. Wigner nowhere tries to assess what proportion of scientific attempts to apply mathematical concepts have proved successful (such a concern would be more relevant to Steiner's discoverability argument). And it would be inept to try to determine that a significant number of the untold infinity of infinities of mathematical concepts find application to the physical world. Rather Wigner may be understood, not to be focusing on isolated examples, but to be using a few examples merely to illustrate for his reader the general truth that mathematical concepts permeate physical science and have been singularly successful in describing the phenomena.
40 As Peter Simons remarks, "the natural *Weltanschauung* for [the anthropocentric] view is theistic, with *Homo sapiens* as the chosen species." See Peter Simons, "MARK STEINER The Applicability of Mathematics as a Philosophical Problem," *British Journal for the Philosophy of Science* 52, no. 1 (2001): 182.
41 *Pace* critics (e.g., Grattan-Guiness, "Solving Wigner's Mystery: The Reasonable (Though Perhaps Limited) Effectiveness of Mathematics in the Natural Sciences," *Mathematical Intelligencer* 30, no. 3 (2008): 7–17) who interpret "unreasonable" to mean "irrational" and would refute Wigner by arguing that it is not irrational to think that mathematics should be effective in science. I think it is clear that for Wigner belief in the effectiveness of mathematics in physics is not irrational, since he himself believed in it, but rather surprising or unexpected.

42 Contrast Steiner's later rendition in Steiner, 'Mathematics—Application and Applicability', 631. There he says more accurately that Wigner argues that (i) mathematical concepts are subject primarily to criteria internal to the mathematical community and (ii) in physics the reliance on mathematical concepts in formulating the laws of nature has led to laws of unbelievable accuracy.

43 Even those who maintain that mathematics plays an explanatory role in science (e.g., Manfred R. Schroeder, "The Unreasonable Effectiveness of Number Theory in Physics, Communication and Music," *Proceedings of Symposia in Applied Mathematics* 46, (1992): 1–19, retrieved from <http://dx.dol.org/10.1090/psapm/046/1 195839>; Alan Baker, "Are there Genuine Mathematical Explanations of Physical Phenomena?" *Mind* 114, no. 454 (2005): 223–238; Marc Lange, "What Makes a Scientific Explanation Distinctively Mathematical?," *British Journal for the Philosophy of Science* 64, no. 3 (2013): 485–511) recognize that such is a case of acausal explanation. It amounts to nothing more than the broadly logical necessity of mathematical truths, e.g., Mother cannot divide 23 strawberries among her 3 children evenly because 23 is not divisible by 3 without remainder. Lange writes, "these explanations explain not by describing the world's causal structure, but roughly by revealing that the explanandum is more necessary than ordinary causal laws are . . . These necessities are stronger than causal necessity, setting distinctively mathematical explanations apart from ordinary scientific explanations" (Lange, "What Makes a Scientific Explanation Distinctively Mathematical?" 491).

44 Wigner, "Unreasonable Effectiveness of Mathematics," 14.

45 Ibid., 2.

46 Mary Leng, *Mathematics and Reality* (Oxford: Oxford University Press, 2010), 239.

47 Balaguer, *Platonism and Anti-Platonism in Mathematics*, 136.

48 Wigner, "Unreasonable Effectiveness of Mathematics," 7.

49 One must be wary in this connection of committing the fallacy of the Anthropic Principle, reasoning that the applicability of mathematics is the result of a self-selection effect, since we could not observe worlds that are not mathematically describable. As J. L. Mackie explains in another context, "this is not a good reply. There is only one actual universe, and it *is* therefore surprising that the elements of this unique set-up are just right for life when they might easily have been wrong. This is not made less surprising by the fact that it had not been so, no one would have been here to be surprised" (J. L. Mackie, *The Miracle of Theism* (Oxford: Oxford University Press, 1974), 141). The Anthropic Principle requires for its legitimate employment the postulation of world ensemble, in this case featuring worlds varying in their mathematical describability, in which our universe appears.

50 Plato, *Timaeus*, 3–4.

51 Peter van Inwagen, Richard Swinburne, and Keith Yandell come to mind. For a discussion of competing views on this issue see ed. Paul Gould, *Beyond the Control of God? Six Views on the Problem of God and Abstract Objects* (Bloomsbury Academic, 2014) with articles, responses, and counter-responses by K. Yandell, S. Shalkowski, R. Davis, P. Gould, G. Oppy, and G. Welty.

52 This is the option advocated by Alvin Plantinga and defended most extensively by Greg Welty. See Alvin Plantinga, "Theism and Mathematics," *Theology and Science* 9, no. 1 (2011): 27–33; Alvin Plantinga, *Where the Conflict Really Lies: Science, Religion, and Naturalism* (Oxford: Oxford University Press, 2011), 284–86; Greg Welty, "Theistic Conceptual Realism," in *Beyond the Control of God? Six Views on the Problem of God and Abstract Objects*, ed. Paul Gould (Bloomsbury Academic, 2014), 81–96.

53 Thomas V. Morris and Christopher Menzel, "Absolute Creation," *American Philosophical Quarterly* 23, no. 4 (1986): 353–362.
54 Wigner, "Unreasonable Effectiveness of Mathematics," 8.
55 Tim Maudlin, "On the Foundations of Physics," (July 5, 2013). Retrieved from <http://www.3ammagazine.com/3am/philosophy-of-physics/3>
56 Albert Einstein thought so: "One should expect a chaotic world which cannot be grasped by the mind in any way. One could (yes *one should*) expect the world to be subjected to law only to the extent that we order it through our intelligence … By contrast, the order created by Newton's theory of gravitation, for instance, is wholly different. Even if the axioms of the theory are proposed by man, the success of such a project presupposes a high degree of ordering of the objective world, and this could not be expected *a priori*. That is the 'miracle' which is being constantly reinforced as our knowledge expands" (Albert Einstein, *Letters to Solovine*, translated by Wade Baskin, with an introduction by Maurice Solovine (New York: Philosophical Library, 1987), 132–133. I am indebted to Melissa Cain Travis for this reference.
57 Steiner, *Applicability of Mathematics*, 15, 27. See also Nancy Cartwright, *How the Laws of Physics Lie* (Oxford: Clarendon Press, 1983), 5, who argues that mathematical physics cannot be regarded as directly describing the true structure of the physical world.
58 The turning point from examples of descriptive applicability which Steiner deems not mysterious because they can be explained in terms of physical properties of nature to examples of descriptive applicability which do seem mysterious because they have no physical basis, occurs at pp. 35–36 of Steiner's book. For discussion of the following examples, see Steiner, *Applicability of Mathematics*, 36–40, 95–97, 102.
59 Penelope Maddy, *Defending the Axioms: On the Philosophical Foundations of Set Theory* (Oxford: Oxford University Press, 2011), 89–90.
60 Philo, *On the Creation of the World*, 16–20; 24.

Bibliography

Baker, Alan, "Are there Genuine Mathematical Explanations of Physical Phenomena?" *Mind* 114, no. 454 (2005): 223–238.

Balaguer, Mark, "Fictionalism in the Philosophy of Mathematics," in *The Stanford Encyclopedia of Philosophy*, edited by Edward N. Zalta, Stanford University, 1997–, September 21, 2013, http://plato.stanford.edu/archives/fall2013/entries/fictionalism-mathematics/.

Balaguer, Mark, *Platonism and Anti-Platonism in Mathematics*, New York: Oxford University Press, 1998.

Balaguer, Mark, "Platonism in Metaphysics," in *The Stanford Encyclopedia of Philosophy*, edited by Edward N. Zalta, Stanford University, 1997–, April 7, 2009, http://plato.stanford.edu/archives/sum2009/entries/platonism/.

Cartwright, Nancy, *How the Laws of Physics Lie*, Oxford: Clarendon Press, 1983.

Craig, William Lane, *God and Abstract Objects: The Coherence of Theism III: Aseity*, Berlin: Springer Verlag, 2017.

Einstein, Albert, *Letters to Solovine*, translated by Wade Baskin, with an introduction by Maurice Solovine, New York: Philosophical Library, 1987.

Grattan-Guinness, Ivor, "Solving Wigner's Mystery: The Reasonable (Though Perhaps Limited) Effectiveness of Mathematics in the Natural Sciences," *Mathematical Intelligencer* 30, no. 3 (2008): 7–17.

Koperski, Jeffrey, *Divine Action, Determinism, and the Laws of Nature*, London: Routledge, 2020.
Lange, Marc, "What Makes a Scientific Explanation Distinctively Mathematical?" *British Journal for the Philosophy of Science* 64, no. 3 (2013): 485–511.
Leng, Mary, *Mathematics and Reality*, Oxford: Oxford University Press, 2010.
Mackie, J. L., *The Miracle of Theism*, Oxford: Oxford University Press, 1974.
Maddy, Penelope, "Believing the Axioms. I," *Journal of Symbolic Logic* 53, no. 2 (1988): 481–511.
Maddy, Penelope, *Defending the Axioms: On the Philosophical Foundations of Set Theory*, Oxford: Oxford University Press, 2011.
Maddy, Penelope, *Naturalism in Mathematics*, Oxford: Clarendon Press, 1997.
Morris, Thomas V., and Christopher Menzel, "Absolute Creation," *American Philosophical Quarterly* 23, no. 4 (1986): 353–362.
Maudlin, Tim, "On the Foundations of Physics," *3:am Magazine*, July 5, 2013, http://www.3ammagazine.com/3am/philosophy-of-physics/.
Plantinga, Alvin, "Theism and Mathematics," *Theology and Science* 9, no. 1 (2011): 27–33.
Plantinga, Alvin, *Where the Conflict Really Lies: Science, Religion, and Naturalism*, Oxford: Oxford University Press, 2011.
Schroeder, Manfred R., "The Unreasonable Effectiveness of Number Theory in Physics, Communication and Music," *Proceedings of Symposia in Applied Mathematics* 46, (1992): 1–19, http://dx.dol.org/10.1090/psapm/046/1 195839.
Steiner, Mark, "Mathematics—Application and Applicability," in *The Oxford Handbook of Philosophy of Mathematics and Logic*, edited by Stewart Shapiro, Oxford Handbooks in Philosophy, Oxford: Oxford University Press, 2005.
Steiner, Mark, *The Applicability of Mathematics as a Philosophical Problem*, Cambridge, MA: Harvard University Press, 1998.
Simons, Peter, "MARK STEINER The Applicability of Mathematics as a Philosophical Problem," *British Journal for the Philosophy of Science* 52, no. 1 (2001): 181–184.
van Inwagen, Peter, "Fictionalist Nominalism and Applied Mathematics," *The Monist* 97, no. 4 (2014): 479–502.
Welty, Greg, "Theistic Conceptual Realism," in *Beyond the Control of God? Six Views on the Problem of God and Abstract Objects*, edited by Paul Gould, 81–96, Bloomsbury Academic, 2014.
Wigner, Eugene, "The Unreasonable Effectiveness of Mathematics in the Natural Sciences," *Communications in Pure and Applied Mathematics* 13, no. 1 (1960): 1–14.
Wolchovern, Natalie, "The Peculiar Math that Could Underlie the Laws of Nature," *Quanta Magazine*, July 28, 2018, https://www.wired.com/story/the-peculiar-math-that-could-underlie-the-laws-of-nature/.

12

The Conceptualist Argument

Greg Welty

According to conceptualist reductions [of propositions to thoughts], the entities designated by 'that'-clauses are identified with mental entities (mind-dependent conceptual entities) ... [These reductions fail, but] if you knew that, necessarily, God exists and has all the requisite concepts, you might be able to avoid this conclusion.[1]

This chapter clarifies, augments, and further defends material I have written elsewhere in support of a conceptualist argument for God's existence.[2] The argument is a piece of *noncausal broad natural theology*. It is *natural* theology, rather than revealed theology, because it seeks to argue for God's existence from publicly available premises not derived from putative special verbal revelation (such as the Hebrew Bible, the Christian Bible, or the Qur'an). It is *broad* natural theology, rather than strict natural theology, because the theistic theory that accounts for the facts is not *deduced* from the facts but is an inference to the best explanation of the facts, where "best" is relative to the chief alternative theories. And it is *noncausal* broad natural theology, rather than causal natural theology, because rather than God *causing* a range of empirical facts, God is claimed to be the best explanation for a range of metaphysical facts about the world, for his very existence *constitutes* this range of facts.

1. Precis of the argument

Realism (argument for entity-existence): Five intuitions and four arguments drawing upon these intuitions give us good reason to believe in the existence of propositions.

Functionalism (argument for entity-role): The previous realist arguments—supplemented with a "meta-argument" about the conditions of good argument—indicate that whatever propositions turn out to be (metaphysically speaking), they must satisfy the six conditions of objectivity, necessity, alethicity, doxasticity, plenitude, and simplicity.

Metaphysics (argument for entity-identification): Identifying propositions with the mental particulars of "conceptualism"—rather than with the non-mental particulars of "nominalism" or with the abstract universals of "Platonism"—is the only metaphysical account of propositions which satisfies all six conditions on any such account, at least if the mental particulars are *divine* thoughts.

Conclusion: Therefore, if we have good reason to be realists about propositions (and we do), then we have good reason to be theistic conceptual realists about propositions, and therefore good reason to be theists.[3]

2. Step 1 – Realism (argument for entity-existence): "Propositions exist"

2.a. Five intuitions

Consider one of our fundamental mathematical beliefs: $1 + 1 = 2$. Since every reader believes this, we'll focus our attention and start there. Imagine four of us take a pop quiz in our philosophy class, and the first question is: "Write down one of your simple mathematical beliefs." The following four answers are written down and turned in:

"$1 + 1 = 2$"

"$I + I = II$"

"One plus one equals two"

"Uno más uno es igual a dos"

Reflecting on these answers reveals some pretty strong intuitions in support of the following five claims. First, we all believe *the same thing*—namely, that $1 + 1 = 2$—regardless of the language used to express that claim. We are each of us committed to the same mathematical claim, for we distinguish between the claim believed and the differing bits of language that can be used to express that claim. We certainly don't believe *different* things here; rather, there is just one thing each of us believes, even if we have chosen to express our belief in different ways. It seems to follow that this single thing (which we all believe) isn't even linguistic, since otherwise we wouldn't all be believing the same mathematical claim. But we are.

Second, we all believe this claim *is* true, and therefore has a property which distinguishes it from false claims. We register this commonsense distinction between true and false, and categorize claims in this way, regardless of what we might think the property "true" ultimately amounts to. Perhaps we think that truth is correspondence between claims and a mind-independent reality. Or maybe we think that truth is coherence among the claims we believe. Or maybe we haven't given the topic much thought at all. Nevertheless, even without a consensus on what "truth" amounts to, we will definitely put $1 + 1 = 2$ into a special category: it is one of the *true* claims. Many other claims, such as $1 - 1 = 2$, $1 \times 1 = 2$, and $1/1 = 2$, go into a different category: the *false* claims. These different claims have different properties, and we believe this too.

Third, we all believe that this claim *is true no matter what*. No matter how many world wars get fought, or which people are born or die, or which mountain ranges there are, or what the fundamental constants of the laws of nature are, it would still be true that 1 + 1 = 2. Across the whole diverse range of ways things could be, whether in our actual universe or in a world which consists of a single atom or no atoms at all, the claim would still be true.

Fourth, we all believe that this claim (and many claims like it) *is true quite independently of our thinking or expressing it*. This seems to follow from the third point, but it's helpful to state this explicitly. This claim would be true in the absence of humans and the thoughts, sound waves, and inscriptions they produce.

Fifth, we believe *there are innumerable claims like this*. Perhaps there's a complicated mathematical claim that neither we nor anyone else has actually thought of, for instance that 5820820109860594 + 3489104812728453 = 9309924922589047. But when we work this out, and—verifying it for ourselves—come to believe this claim, our intuition isn't that we invented the claim or its truth. Rather, we discovered both the claim and its truth. These were awaiting our discovery, and there are likely an infinite number of claims just like this one in these two respects. We could even put our conviction this way: "There are true claims which no one has ever expressed in language." Such claims *are* true, and even if we discover them, they *were* true independent of our expressing them in language or thinking about them. That is, they are the kinds of things which have the property of being true while lacking the property of being expressed in a language.

Now take "alethicity" to refer to the capacity to be true or false, and "doxasticity" to refer to the capacity to be believed or disbelieved. It follows from the five intuitions above that we have good reason to believe in *a plenitude of necessarily existing objects possessing alethicity and doxasticity*. We'll call these objects "propositions." The pop quiz in the philosophy class was designed to lead us to this conclusion.

2.b. Four arguments for propositional existence

It's quite understandable to think this case for realism has proceeded a bit too fast. For one thing, what do we mean by "objects"? For another, why must we think these propositions *exist*, indeed *necessarily* exist? These are good questions, and some answers will be given in the next section. For now, let's consider four reasons why it's quite reasonable to be committed to the *existence* of these propositions, given the preceding intuitions.[4]

First, an argument from ordinary language seems to imply propositional existence. We could easily summarize our quiz answers by saying, "Isn't it interesting that there is something we all believe?" The use of "there is" typically indicates existential commitment in an extraordinarily wide range of cases (e.g., "There are some bears," "There is Los Angeles."). In fact, we seem to subscribe to a very general but defeasible principle: *normally* (that is, unless we have a good reason to think otherwise), we are committed to the existence of the entities we say there are. Imagine trying to understand ordinary language, and the ontological commitments we express through it, in the *absence* of this principle![5]

Second, an appeal to our basic ontological intuitions seems to imply propositional existence. Only *existing* things can make a difference to our lives, and the fact that these claims are true does make a difference. For instances, bridges will fall and cars won't start if 1 + 1 = 2 isn't a true claim. Adding parts together needs to *preserve* the parts in their integrity, rather than making them disappear, but this won't happen if 1 + 1 = 2 isn't a truth.

Third, propositional verbs like "intend," "think," "believe," and "judge" have existential presuppositions. Once we study how we use verbs that take propositions as their objects, we discover two things. We seem to take their objects as *distinct from the attitudes* we take up toward them (for we all believe the same claim rather than each believing different claims). And we seem to take their objects as *intersubjectively available* (for if one of us *failed* to believe the claim, it would still be available to be believed by the others—otherwise, what are the others doing?). Since the objects are available to all subjects and yet distinct from these subjects, they are perfect candidates for being objects which *exist* quite independently of our subjective mental states. Indeed, in all these respects the objects of propositional verbs seem perfectly parallel to the objects of *cognitive* verbs, which uncontroversially exist. In "I see the house," "I smell the rose," "I taste the steak," "I feel the blanket," and "I hear the gong," the objects of these cognitive verbs are both intersubjectively available and distinct from the cognitive attitudes we take up toward them. In the end, both cognitive *and* propositional verbs denote the attitudes we take up toward the objects denoted by the grammatical accusatives of these verbs, and these objects exist independently of the attitudes themselves.

Fourth, the ontological preconditions of property attribution seem to imply propositional existence. How could objects bear properties if they don't exist? Could my next-door neighbor have the property of being friendly if he doesn't even exist? Likewise, could 1 + 1 = 2 have the property of being true if it doesn't even exist? It seems very hard to make sense of the idea that non-existing objects can have properties.

3. Step 2 – Functionalism (argument for entity-role): "Propositions must be the kind of things which play six specific roles"

3.a. The connection between Step 1 (entity-existence) and Step 2 (entity-role)

So far, we have some arguments for the existence of propositions, for a plenitude of necessarily existing objects possessing alethicity and doxasticity. But these arguments do not by themselves indicate what *kind* of thing propositions are, metaphysically speaking. Are they bits of ink on paper, acoustic waves in the air, or magnetized regions on hard drives? Are they thoughts in our head, or in all our heads put together? Are they built out of abstract "stuff" which is neither material nor mental? On these points the realist arguments themselves say next to nothing, but that is not to say they are entirely mute. Further reflection on the realist arguments reveals that propositions can't be just *anything*. For example, a prime minister might propose propositions for our consideration, perhaps at a party conference, hoping to persuade us of her point of view. But she couldn't *be* a proposition. That wouldn't make sense. Nor, apart from some pretty convincing argument, can propositions be a coat of paint. As we'll see in step 3, about entity-identification, some promising accounts might involve propositions as sentences, or as thoughts, or as abstractions of some sort. *These* candidates aren't immediately ruled out, as are prime ministers and coats of paint.[6]

There is a connection, then, between entity-existence and entity-role. Typically, arguments for the former will imply something about the latter, imposing constraints on the kind of things these entities can be, that is, upon entity-identification. If "we need X's because X's do *that*" (step 1's entity-existence arguments), then X's must be able to *do* that (step 2's entity-role prescription). If they can't, then we haven't gotten the right X's into our ontology and need to continue the search for how best to characterize metaphysically the X's we've argued to exist. This connection between entity-existence and entity-role, and its implication for step 3's entity-identification, is familiar to us from the philosophy of mind. For example, our being committed to the existence of *persons* involves our being committed to entities who are subject to ascriptions of moral praise and blame, who possess the capacity to deliberate and realize intentions, who are causal agents in the world, and who experience qualia, self-awareness, and the unity of consciousness. What *kind* of thing could possibly satisfy all those roles? Perhaps the materialists are right, and persons are brains. Perhaps the dualists are right, and persons are immaterial souls with bodies. But though these candidates are worth debating about, there are limits here: no person could be a number, or a grain of sand, or the taste of roast beef, or a credit card.

Recognizing the relevance of the functional role of concepts in settling metaphysical disputes tends to greatly lessen (although it does not eliminate) the phenomenon of question-begging which often arises in these disputes. It would be quite easy for dualists about persons to contend that materialists about persons don't "really" believe in the existence of persons (on the grounds that materialists don't believe in immaterial souls). But of course, this criticism simply presupposes that dualism *is* the best account of personhood, and that is exactly what should be argued for in this debate, not assumed. Likewise, materialists about persons might be tempted to say that dualists don't "really" believe that genuine persons exist either (on the grounds that dualists don't recognize the bodily side of personhood as they ought). But this seems to assume, rather than argue, that being embodied is of the essence of personhood. Foisting your preferred metaphysical account on your detractors is not the best way to convince them of your account. Rather, we proceed stepwise: from a consensus about the *existence* of persons, to reflection on the common-sense kinds of things persons are said *to be or do*, to a metaphysical account that best satisfies those conditions. Perhaps only immaterial souls can be or do all of the things earlier mentioned. Or perhaps not, since this approach doesn't preclude at the outset materialism offering a better account than dualism.

Ditto for the debate over propositions. We proceed from realism to functionalism to metaphysics, from arguments for propositional existence, to reflection on the functional roles of "proposition" which emerge from these realist arguments, to identifying the best metaphysical account of the entities which play these roles. John Divers' discussion of "ontological applications" of "possible-worlds talk" illustrates this promising strategy for adjudicating among rival ontological conceptions of propositions:

... the conception of an equivalence thesis as grounding an ontological identification is inevitably informed by some conception of the analysis of the concept. For example, we should expect the analysis of the concept of a proposition (e.g. a specification of the proposition-role) to exert some constraints on the kind of thing that a proposition can be. Such constraints are conditional. They are of the form: if there are things that play the proposition-role then they must be thus and so.[7]

3.b. Six conditions on a successful account of propositions

Thus, what emerges from the preceding realist arguments (granting their *prima facie* plausibility), and from the intuitions which back such arguments, are several conditions on a successful ontological identification of propositions, and that metaphysical theory of propositions which best satisfies these conditions is to be preferred to its rivals. These conditions are objectivity, necessity, alethicity, doxasticity, plenitude, and simplicity. Whatever propositions are, metaphysically speaking, they must play these roles. Entity-identification (step 3) must answer to the constraints of entity-role (step 2), and these emerge naturally from the arguments for entity-existence (step 1).

First there is *objectivity*—propositions are *objects*. That is, they are entities which are intersubjectively available and mind-independent, existing independently of the subjects who take up various attitudes towards them. Our first, fourth, and fifth intuitions seem to support this condition. Multiple subjects believe the same thing, this thing has the property of truth independently of the thoughts and expressions of these subjects, and these things are discoverable rather than constituted by our thoughts and attitudes.

Second there is necessity—propositions *necessarily* exist. That is, they exist no matter how the universe turns out to be—for instance, whether there are many atoms, or just one, or none. Propositions exist in all possible worlds and couldn't have failed to exist. Our third intuition, combined with our fourth reason to assert propositional existence, seems to support this condition. If these mathematical claims are *true* no matter what (third intuition), then since nothing can have a property without existing (fourth reason), then they *exist* no matter what.

Third there is *alethicity*—propositions are the kinds of things which can be *true or false*. Our second, third, and fourth intuitions seem to support this condition, since for just about any claim (not just the mathematical ones) we register the commonsense distinction between the true and the false and categorize them accordingly. (Note that this is more modest than the controversial claim that every proposition *has* a determinate truth-value. Alethicity simply refers to the capacity to be truth-valued.)

Fourth there is *doxasticity*—propositions are the kinds of things which can be *believed or disbelieved*. All five of our intuitions and all four subsequent arguments seem to support this, since the entire discussion has been about *the things we believe*, or (as the fifth intuition has it) about *the things we could come to believe*. In particular, the various propositional verbs which featured in the third argument denote the attitude of belief (or disbelief) in the entity which is its grammatical accusative.

Fifth, there is *plenitude*—there is an *infinity* of propositions. That is, whatever propositions are, there must be enough of them to do the job they are supposed to do. Our fifth intuition seems to support this. Here we don't have to restrict ourselves to claims like 1 + 1 = 2, for intuitively there are an infinite number of other kinds of propositions. As Plantinga puts it, "For each real number r, for example, there is the proposition that r is distinct from the Taj Mahal."[8] Or, somewhat less whimsically: "Platonists never tire of pointing out, for example, that there is a nondenumerable infinity of propositions specifying, in turn, that each irrational less than the number one is less than the number two."[9]

In addition, there need to be enough propositions to cover all the *possibilities* there are, since there are truths about these as well, and therefore need for truth-bearers. So, for instance, for each real number r there is the proposition which asserts there could be two atoms r millimeters apart. (Or, restricting ourselves to the natural numbers, we could say that for each natural number r there is the proposition which asserts there are r atoms.) In the end, while no single argument can generate reference to *all* of the propositions which exist, intuitively there do seem to be an infinite number of propositions, such that any theory of the ontological status of propositions which cannot supply enough propositions to meet this intuition is thereby a defective theory.

Sixth and finally, there is *simplicity*—explanations should not multiply beyond explanatory necessity the number of entities or kinds of entity they posit. This is the only condition on a successful account of propositions which doesn't emerge from the realist intuitions and arguments in step 1. Rather, simplicity is a constraint on metaphysical theories in general, insofar as metaphysical theories are explanations or accounts of what there is. If we are committed not only to realism about propositions but also to a principle of ontological kind-economy, then we are committed to not multiplying ontological kinds beyond necessity. Even as our explanatory accounts should not multiply *entities* beyond necessity (say, by positing two planets when one will do), so they should not multiply *kinds* of entity beyond necessity (say, by positing mental and physical events as fundamental categories of being when physical events will do). Therefore, if propositions can be satisfactorily understood as belonging to an ontological kind we already accept, this in itself is an argument that we should so understand them. As we will see in step 3, all sides appeal to this principle in debates over the nature of propositions.

To summarize, the realist arguments, supplemented with a general constraint on metaphysical theories, indicate that whatever propositions turn out to be (metaphysically speaking), they must satisfy conditions of objectivity, necessity, alethicity, doxasticity, plenitude, and simplicity (subsequently summarized as ONADPS). It is time to turn from entity-existence and entity-role to entity-identification.

4. Step 3 – Metaphysics (argument for entity-identification): "Only propositions as divine thoughts can play all six roles"

4.a. Distinguishing the chief alternatives

Broadly speaking, there are three main theories of propositions on offer: conceptualism, nominalism, and Platonism. Each theory is a "realism" about propositions, accepting the *existence* of propositions based on the kinds of arguments offered in step 1, but disagreeing about the *nature* of the propositions said to exist. Conceptualist theories identify propositions with mental particulars (such as thoughts), and so propositions end up being mental entities. Nominalist theories identify propositions with material particulars and subdivide into linguistic nominalism (propositions are written or spoken sentences) and set-theoretic nominalism (propositions are sets of familiar objects). On these views, propositions end up being material entities. Platonist theories identify propositions with abstract entities that are neither mental nor material.

There is no need to contend that this threefold division is exhaustive. Perhaps there is a fourth type of entity-identification that involves a very different kind of metaphysical entity, distinct from the three just mentioned. Who are we to think we have exhausted the alternatives? Possibilities like these are perfectly acceptable. As in science so in metaphysics—there's always another theory just around the corner. That is no bar to coming to well-justified conclusions in both science and metaphysics. In science, perhaps cold fusion can explain what hot fusion cannot explain. It depends—what does the theory say, and how well does it account for the facts we need to explain? In the absence of further information on both these points, we're certainly not warranted in *disbelieving* (or even suspending judgment about) the hot fusion theories we currently believe to be the best explanations of the data. Likewise in philosophy (here, the philosophy of mind), perhaps pan-psychism can explain what a more traditional materialism or dualism cannot explain. But unless the explanation is both given and defended, current philosophical arguments remain untouched. You can't beat something with nothing.

So, of the main theories of propositions on offer (conceptualism, nominalism, Platonism), the best theory will satisfy all six of the conditions on a successful theory, or (failing that) more conditions than any of its competitors. Because nominalism subdivides into linguistic and set-theoretic, and these each have relevantly different features for the purposes of assessment, the following analysis interacts with four alternatives: propositions as thoughts, sentences, sets, and abstracta.

4.b. Initial comparative assessments

4.b.1. *Propositions as thoughts?* +ADS –ONP

On conceptualism, propositions are mental particulars of some sort, such as the tokening of sentences in Mentalese (cf. Sellars 1975), or some other kind of thought. If so, then conceptualism passes the alethicity, doxasticity, and simplicity conditions *par excellence*. It is obvious that our thoughts can be true or false, and can be beliefs (or disbeliefs), and that in positing thoughts we do not multiply ontological kinds beyond necessity. Rather, we remain committed to a kind of thing we already accept. So, +ADS.

Indeed, thoughts have an *intentional* character; they variously claim, assert, attribute, predicate, and represent. Thus they are natural candidates for doing the philosophical work of propositions. In addition, it is not merely that thoughts (like propositions) have "aboutness," being about objects and their properties. It is also that thoughts (like propositions) pick out these objects and properties in a fine-grained way. The thought "Lois Lane loves Superman" is *distinct* from the thought "Lois Lane loves Clark Kent," even though both thoughts are "about" the same things, attributing the same properties to the same objects. This fine-grained "aspectual shape" of beliefs exactly matches that of propositional intentionality. So there is a one-to-one correspondence between thoughts and propositions with respect to directedness and aspectual shape.[10]

But these advantages are limited, for the obvious problem with conceptualism is its failure to satisfy the objectivity, necessity, and plenitude conditions. If propositions are thoughts, then *whose* thoughts are they? If I have the thought that the sky is blue, and so do you, whose thought is the "real" proposition, and whose is the imposter? Any answer here looks arbitrary.[11] The *one* thing we all believe can't also be *many* things, the thoughts *we* come up with can't also be entities existing *independently* of us, and if we are each trafficking in *our own* thoughts then propositions aren't the *intersubjectively available* entities we thought they were. Beyond this, surely our thoughts only contingently exist, and there are not nearly enough of them to serve as all the propositions there are, not even if we add in all the conceptual activity of all the existing people in the world.[12] So, –ONP.

4.b.2. *Propositions as sentences?* +ADS –ONP

On linguistic nominalism, propositions are linguistic-tokens of some sort.[13] Perhaps they are simply the sentences we speak or write down. As with conceptualism, linguistic nominalism surely satisfies the alethicity, doxasticity, and simplicity conditions, at least if sentences can be true or false, believed or disbelieved, and don't multiply ontological kinds. But we already accept "audio waves" and "ink inscriptions" into our ontology. In addition, sentences seem just as fine-grained in their directedness and aspectual shape as thoughts. So, +ADS.

But sentences fail here for the same reason as thoughts: they fail the objectivity, necessity, and plenitude conditions. *Whose* sentences are the propositions? Can't our sentences *fail* to exist? And don't we generate only a small fraction of the required linguistic activity? There is even a kind of reverse plenitude problem here—in some respect there are *too many* propositions. Not only are there a multiplicity of human persons, but in addition there are a multiplicity of languages. Which is the real proposition that it is raining, the English sentence "It is raining," or the French sentence "Il pleut"? So, –ONP.

4.b.3. *Propositions as sets?* +ONS –ADP

On set-theoretic nominalism, "a proposition is a set of possible worlds"; indeed, "any set of worlds is by definition a proposition."[14] Possible worlds themselves are just spatiotemporal wholes (like our universe), and each of these wholes is spatiotemporally isolated from the others in logical space. So, for instance, the proposition "There are talking donkeys" is just the set of all spatiotemporal wholes (read: possible worlds) in which there are talking donkeys.[15]

This theory seems to satisfy the objectivity and necessity conditions. If propositions are sets of this sort, then propositions just exist "out there" in logical space, as objects existing independently of our beliefs and activities. And the existence of these sets is necessary in some significant sense, since their existence isn't contingent on anything and doesn't vary across possible worlds. One might say: since the same possible worlds exist no matter *which* world we find ourselves in, then any *set* of possible worlds (read: proposition) exists no matter what. So, +ON.

It has seemed to many that this theory grossly violates the simplicity condition, by multiplying spatiotemporal entities beyond what we normally accept, and to an infinite degree. Nevertheless, realists about propositions must posit *something* as the propositions, and a realist theory needs an infinity of them. So it's not clear that an infinity of sets is really *worse* than an infinity of sentences, thoughts, or abstracta on this score. Indeed, set-theoretic nominalism doesn't posit any new *kind* of entity, since the other worlds are just more of the kinds of things which constitute us and our surroundings. There is certainly no need for abstract, Platonistic entities, and this may at least be an advantage over Platonism. So, +S.

Unfortunately, set-theoretic nominalism doesn't fare so well when it comes to the alethicity, doxasticity, and plenitude conditions. Sets just don't seem to be the kind of things that can be true or false, and believed or disbelieved.[16] Nor are there enough of them, since on this theory all necessarily true propositions turn out to be the *same* proposition: the set of all possible worlds. Likewise for all necessarily false propositions, which also turn out to be the *same* proposition: the null set. So, -ADP.

4.b.4. *Propositions as abstracta?* +ONADP –S

On Platonism, propositions are abstract entities that are neither material nor mental. They have no spatiotemporal location or extension, and they are causally inert. Imagine Platonism as an induction over past failure: for reasons we've just seen, propositions can't be our thoughts or sentences, or sets of material objects. So just *stipulate* entities that satisfy +ONADP, since these are precisely the entities needed. Therefore, they can't be spatiotemporal, lest they inherit the contingency and finitude of the material universe. They can't be thoughts or sentences, because this way lies subjectivity. But they are *like* thoughts and sentences in *representing* the world as it is or could be, and so can be true or false, believed or disbelieved. So, +ONADP.

The challenge to Platonism is simplicity. Platonism multiplies ontological kinds by identifying propositions with "abstract objects" that have a distinct kind of being, inhabiting a "third realm" which is neither material nor mental, "distinct both from the sensible external world and from the internal world of consciousness."[17] It was partly the failure of both conceptualist and nominalist theories of propositions that led Gottlob Frege to posit abstract "senses" of declarative sentences.[18] Of course, theorists of propositions as thoughts, as sentences, or as sets claim to satisfy simplicity. But if all *those* theories fail, then another theory *is* needed, and so while Platonists multiply ontological kinds, they claim not to do so beyond *explanatory necessity*. Since the latter is a crucial (but often overlooked) qualification to the principle of parsimony, Platonists will say they have not violated it. Perhaps it's best to say: Platonists do multiply kinds, and so violate simplicity (so, –S), but if they *are* correct that no material or mental theories are adequate, then their multiplication isn't beyond explanatory necessity after all (so, +S).

4.b.5. *Propositions as divine thoughts?* +ONADPS

But are no mental theories adequate? Is Platonistic appeal to a "third realm" necessary for explanation? Although *human* conceptualism obviously suffers from –ONP, construing propositions as *divine* thoughts seems to mitigate these three deficiencies. First, a divine mind (being omniscient) can certainly have enough thoughts for all the truths and possibilities we intuitively think there are. Second, if necessarily existent thoughts are required, they must be the thoughts of a necessarily existent mind, and the most plausible candidate here is God. Third and finally, objectivity is secured by there being just *one* omniscient and necessarily existent person whose thoughts are uniquely identified as propositions. These thoughts would have extramental existence, at least *relative to finite minds*. Propositions would exist independently of any human cognition, although they would not exist independently of divine cognition. Does this crucial qualification pose an insuperable barrier to the claim of objectivity? It doesn't appear to. In the realist arguments of step 1, propositions were deemed to exist as the objects of *human* propositional attitudes, and to be the referents of that-clauses associated with the propositional verbs *humans* employ. There is no reason why divine thoughts cannot supply the requisite objectivity by being the objects and referents of these human attitudes and verbs. We humans would be taking up attitudes to propositions which exist independently of our cognitive activities. Surely this is sufficient to secure the requisite objectivity demanded by the relevant realist arguments for the existence of propositions.

So theistic conceptualist theories satisfy all six conditions, something managed by no other theory. A kind of "inference to the best explanation," characteristic of noncausal broad natural theology, leads us to theism as the best account of propositional existence, once the functional roles of the latter are given prominence in our reflections (+ADS follows from the conceptualist component, while +ONP follows from the theistic component). Ontologically disambiguating the conclusion of the realist arguments in a conceptualist direction, and then specifying that conceptualism in terms of theism, provides the best way to satisfy the relevant conditions on a successful theory of propositions. To the extent, then, that we have reason to be realists and conceptualists about propositions, to that extent we have reason to be theists.

4.c. The assessment so far[19]

Thoughts	+ADS –ONP
Sentences	+ADS –ONP
Sets	+ONS –ADP
Abstracta	+ONADP –S
Divine thoughts	+ONADPS

5. Updating these assessments—all theories require conceptualism!

5.a. Thoughts simpler than sentences and sets after all

A further and very significant opportunity to reassess these alternatives arises once we consider the *intentionality* of propositions, that is, their "aboutness." Propositions *make claims*, representing reality to be such-and-such, and so are "about" the reality they represent. "1 + 1 = 2" is about mathematical reality (regardless of what numbers are), rather than about the color of my house, or about the praiseworthiness of courage. "The cat is on the mat" is about an object (the cat) and about the property it possesses (being on the mat). Three points can be made about this intentionality.

First, the intentionality of propositions explains why they have alethicity and doxasticity. If propositions represent reality, then this representation is either accurate or inaccurate. This explains their capacity to be either true or false. We also agree or disagree with whether a proposition accurately represents reality. So, they can be believed or disbelieved. This intentionality of propositions seems to be one of their "deepest" features, because it explains these other aspects of them, and so differences among the theories in accounting for this feature may further help us decide between such theories.

Second, there is a distinction between intrinsic and derived intentionality. Sentences and sets seem to have *derived* intentionality, since their status as representations is derived from the thinkers or speakers who confer intentionality on them. Rocks randomly arranged on a seashore by waves, even if they happen to spell out "MOM," make no claim at all. But I can *use* such rocks to express my answer to a question, and therefore impose an intentional status upon them by way of my own thoughts and intentions. I can use the same rocks, unchanged in relative position, to give a different answer to a different question ("WOW"). Or I can (somewhat whimsically) tell my students that if they see a set of rocks on my lectern at the beginning of tomorrow's class, they can safely infer the class will be let out early. Tomorrow, that set of rocks will be *making a claim* (and therefore have intentionality), but only because that intentionality was derived from my thoughts and intentions. Ink marks on a page, audio waves in the air, and rocks on a lectern are not *intrinsically* intentional. Instead, their intentionality presupposes the intentionality that inheres in the mind or minds which interpret and use them. As Tim Crane puts it:

> Words and pictures gain the interpretations they do, and therefore represent what they do, because of the states of mind of those who use them. The intentionality of the book's sentences is derived from the original intentionality of the states of mind of the author and reader who interpret those sentences.[20]

By way of contrast, intentionality seems *intrinsic* to the thoughts or minds in question. But if no non-mental states have intrinsic intentionality, but at least some mental states can have it, then mental states can alone supply the intentionality from which all other forms of intentionality are derived.[21]

Third, from the perspective of *simplicity*, the intrinsic intentionality of thoughts would therefore further favor thoughts over sentences or sets as the most appropriate identification of propositions. Propositional intentionality can ultimately be accounted for most simply in terms of mental states, not material objects like sentences or sets, since the intentionality of the latter *presupposes* mental states. (Failing the simplicity condition is the price they pay for satisfying the intentionality condition.) So, both propositions-as-sentences and propositions-as-sets are at best +AD −ONPS.[22] The intentionality of the mental is *doubly* primitive: it not only explains other aspects of thoughts (their alethicity and doxasticity), but also the intentionality of other entities besides thoughts.

So an updated assessment, sorted by degree of success, would now be:

Divine thoughts	+ONADPS
Abstracta	+ONADP –S
Thoughts	+ADS –ONP
Sentences	+AD –ONPS
Sets	+AD –ONPS

5.b. The fate of *abstracta*

Clearly, the only two theories "in the running" here are theistic conceptualism and Platonism. The others have faded away as serious contenders. Is there anything further a defender of theism could say to break this impasse? Four points are worth considering.

First, theists can continue to hinge their whole case on simplicity. This just is the criterion which breaks the impasse. If we already accept persons with thoughts as items in our ontology, theistic conceptualism doesn't ask us to go beyond the categories of being we already accept. By way of contrast, Platonists must posit an infinite realm that is neither material nor mental. Since theists are continually accused of violating simplicity by invoking God in their explanations of empirical phenomena, it is understandable for them to emphasize cases where the shoe seems to be on the other foot!

Second, the way that Platonism violates simplicity is different from how propositions-as-sentences or -sets violates simplicity. It is one thing to multiply entities beyond explanatory necessity by positing the material when just the mental will do, or positing the mental when just the material will do. The problem there is just the gratuitous *addition*. But it is quite another thing to posit abstract "stuff" which is neither material nor mental. The problem here is gratuitous addition *of mystery*. We know quite a bit about material entities: they have spatiotemporal location and extension, and enter into causal relations. We know quite a bit about mental entities: thoughts possess qualia, privacy, and inherence in a thinker. But what do we know about abstract entities as a category of being? They lack the six things just noted. Platonism isn't like positing waves when atoms will do, or positing blueness when redness will do. We seem to lack *any* familiarity with what this being is like. Not all violations of simplicity are created equal.

Third, why think abstracta have intentionality at all apart from thinkers? This question doesn't arise for thoughts, obviously, since we are intimately familiar with these intrinsically intentional entities. Nor does it arise for sentences or even for sets, for we can clearly see *how* these latter entities can derive their intentionality from the thinkers who use them. Of course, abstracta can just have *stipulated* intrinsic intentionality. But doesn't that just add to the mystery noted under point two? Our access to intrinsic intentionality is via access to our own thoughts. To have a thought is to "see" its aboutness. Reflecting on just about any thought shows this. (There could be exceptions here—a sense of "undirected anxiety" might be a mental state without aboutness. But this doesn't affect the main point of familiarity.) By way of contrast, what *is* an intrinsically representational entity that neither is a thought nor presupposes thought? Again, this seems utterly mysterious to us.

Fourth, thinkers are causal agents who are themselves both subject to causation and able to bring about causal effects in others. I perceive the tree and know it's there because the tree brings about my perception of it via its causal relation to me. No such story can be told for "perception" of abstracta. So how do they bring about our awareness of them? Again, this seems to be an utter mystery. We aren't in causal contact with abstracta as we are with materiality and mentality, so how do we know of them?

So the negative verdict against Platonism does not just depend on its being a less simple theory, although that is significant. Rather, the abstract status, intentionality, and knowability of its entities all seem puzzling and unnatural, and this triple mystery doesn't arise on theistic conceptualism (or on any other view, for that matter). Theists will say: better to have a theory that satisfies simplicity *and* avoids the triple mystery.[23]

Notes

1 George Bealer, "Universals and Properties," in *Contemporary Readings in the Foundations of Metaphysics*, ed. Stephen Laurence and Cynthia Macdonald (Blackwell, 1998), 136, 145 fn21.

2 Greg Welty, "Truth as Divine Ideas: A Theistic Theory of the Property 'Truth,'" *Southwestern Journal of Theology* 47 (2004): 57–70; Greg Welty, *Theistic Conceptual Realism: The Case for Interpreting Abstract Objects as Divine Ideas* (DPhil diss., Oxford: University of Oxford, 2006); Greg Welty, "Theistic Conceptual Realism" in *Beyond the Control of God? Six Views on the Problem of God and Abstract Objects*, ed. Paul Gould (Bloomsbury Academic, 2014); Greg Welty, "Do Divine Conceptualist Accounts Fail?," *Philosophia Christi* vol. 21, no. 2 (2019): 255–266; James Anderson and Greg Welty, "The Lord of Noncontradiction: An Argument for God from Logic," *Philosophia Christi* vol. 13, no. 2 (2011): 321–338; James Anderson and Greg Welty, "In Defense of the Argument for God from Logic," *Evangelical Philosophical Society*, 2013, <http://www.epsociety.org/userfiles/art-Anderson-Welty%20(In%20Defense%20of%20the%20Argument%20for%20God%20from%20Logic).pdf>

3 Note that there are at least *four* arguments for God in the vicinity: (i) an argument for God from propositions (this chapter), (ii) an argument for God from the laws of logic (James Anderson and Greg Welty, "The Lord of Noncontradiction: An Argument for God from Logic"; James Anderson and Greg Welty, "In Defense of the Argument for God from Logic," Evangelical Philosophical Society), (iii) an argument for God from propositions and possible worlds (Greg Welty, *Theistic Conceptual Realism: The Case for Interpreting Abstract Objects as Divine Ideas*, and Greg Welty, "Theistic Conceptual Realism"), and (iv) an argument for God from properties (Greg Welty, "Truth as Divine Ideas: A Theistic Theory of the Property 'Truth.'" This chapter freely draws upon these earlier presentations.

4 See Welty, *Theistic Conceptual Realism: The Case for Interpreting Abstract Objects as Divine Ideas*, 28–61; Anderson and Welty "The Lord of Noncontradiction: An Argument for God from Logic," 327–329; and Welty, "Theistic Conceptual Realism," 82–83 for elaborations of these arguments.

5 Notice that this qualified principle of ontological commitment is different from the *unqualified* principle which William Lane Craig critiques and rejects as "obviously false and wholly implausible." See William Lane Craig, *God Over All: Divine Aseity and the Challenge of Platonism* (Oxford: Oxford University Press, 2016), 143.
6 In step 1 above I suggested that we already know propositions can't be our linguistic expressions or mental attitudes. But some philosophers demur, so these accounts will be given a fair hearing in step 3.
7 See John Divers, *Possible Worlds* (Routledge, 2002). See also Peter van Inwagen, "Two Concepts of Possible Worlds," in *Midwest Studies in Philosophy*, eds. P. French, T. Uehling and H. Wettstein, vol. 11: Studies in Essentialism (University of Minnesota Press, 1986), 192–193 for this functionalist insight as applied to arguments in both philosophy of mind and ontology more generally.
8 Alvin Plantinga, "God, Arguments for the Existence of," in *The Routledge Encyclopedia of Philosophy*, ed. Edward Craig, vol. 4 (London: Routledge, 1998), 91.
9 Michael Loux, "Toward An Aristotelian Theory of Abstract Objects," in *Midwest Studies in Philosophy*, eds. P. French, T. Uehling, and H. Wettstein, vol. 11: Studies in Essentialism (University of Minnesota Press, 1986), 499.
10 On propositional intentionality, see Alvin Plantinga, "Two Concepts of Modality: Modal Realism and Modal Reductionism," in *Philosophical Perspectives, I, Metaphysics*, ed. James Tomberlin (Ridgeview, 1987), 190. On directedness and aspectual shape as the "two main elements of the concept of intentionality as discussed by recent philosophers," see Tim Crane, "Intentionality as the Mark of the Mental," in *Current Issues in Philosophy of Mind*, ed. A. O'Hear (Cambridge: Cambridge University Press, 1998), 243; Tim Crane, "Intentionality," in *The Routledge Encyclopedia of Philosophy*, ed. Edward Craig (Routledge, 1998); Tim Crane, *Elements of Mind* (Oxford: Oxford University Press, 2001), 13–21.
11 Richard Gale, "Propositions, Judgments, Sentences, and Statements," in *The Encyclopedia of Philosophy*, ed. Paul Edwards (New York: Macmillan, 1967), 500.
12 Loux, "Toward An Aristotelian Theory of Abstract Objects," 499.
13 Sellars, Wilfrid, "Abstract Entities," *Review of Metaphysics*. vol. 16, no. 4 (1963): 627–671.
14 David Lewis, *On the Plurality of Worlds* (Blackwell, 1986), 53, 105.
15 See David Lewis, *On the Plurality of Worlds*, 5–69 for the exposition of this theory.
16 Plantinga, "Actualism and Possible Worlds," in *The Possible and the Actual: Readings in the Metaphysics of Modality*, ed. Loux, 267; Plantinga, "Two Concepts of Modality: Modal Realism and Modal Reductionism," 206–207.
17 Gideon Rosen, "Abstract Objects," *Stanford Encyclopedia of Philosophy* (2018): <http://plato.stanford.edu/entries/abstract-objects>, §2.
18 Gottlob Frege, "Der Gedanke: Eine Logische Untersuchung" in *Beiträge zur Philosophie des Deutschen Idealismus*, ed. Peter Geach and R. H. Stoothoff (1919), Part I: 351–72.
19 Notice that different theories satisfy different conditions. Their satisfying at least *some* of these conditions helps to partly explain the attraction of each theory. No theory flouts *all* the conditions, and many satisfy several. The "role-filler" strategy illuminates why each of these theories have an attraction of their own. Intuitively, each theory gets *something* right.
20 Crane, "Intentionality," §3.
21 For the distinction between intrinsic and derived intentionality, and argument for the point made in the text, see John Searle, *Intentionality* (Cambridge: Cambridge University Press, 1983), 27–29.

22 In particular, propositions-as-sets now acquires –ONPS because—presupposing conceptualism—it is less simple than conceptualism (–S) *and* inherits its weaknesses (–ONP).
23 In addition, we have many other arguments for God's existence, as evidenced by the rest of this volume. But do we have other arguments for abstractly-conceived propositions? If not, then divine thoughts are less *ad hoc* than abstracta in the context of a cumulative case.

Bibliography

Anderson, James, and Greg Welty, " 'The Lord of Noncontradiction: An Argument for God from Logic," *Philosophia Christi* vol. 13, no. 2 (2011): 321–38.

Anderson, James, and Greg Welty, "In Defense of the Argument for God from Logic," *Evangelical Philosophical Society* (September 1, 2013): 1–16, http://www.epsociety.org/userfiles/art-Anderson-Welty%20(In%20Defense%20of%20the%20Argument%20for%20God%20from%20Logic).pdf

Bealer, George, "Universals and Properties," in *Contemporary Readings in the Foundations of Metaphysics*, edited by Stephen Laurence and Cynthia Macdonald, 131–147, Blackwell, 1998.

Craig, William Lane, *God Over All: Divine Aseity and the Challenge of Platonism*, Oxford University Press, 2016.

Crane, Tim, "Intentionality as the Mark of the Mental," in *Current Issues in Philosophy of Mind*, edited by A. O'Hear, 229–251, Cambridge: Cambridge University Press, 1998.

Crane, Tim, "Intentionality," in *The Routledge Encyclopedia of Philosophy*, edited by Edward Craig, Routledge, 1998.

Crane, Tim, *Elements of Mind*, Oxford: Oxford University Press, 2001.

Divers, John, *Possible Worlds*, Routledge, 2002.

Frege, Gottlob, "Der Gedanke: Eine Logische Untersuchung," in *Beiträge zur Philosophie des deutschen Idealismus* 1, 1919, translated by Peter Geach and R. H. Stoothoff in *Logical Investigations*, Part I: 351–372.

Gale, Richard M., "Propositions, Judgments, Sentences, and Statements," in *The Encyclopedia of Philosophy*, edited by Paul Edwards, 494–505, New York: Macmillan, 1967.

Lewis, David, *On the Plurality of Worlds*, Blackwell, 1986.

Loux, Michael J., *The Possible and the Actual: Readings in the Metaphysics of Modality*, Ithaca: Cornell University Press, 1979.

Loux, Michael J., "Toward An Aristotelian Theory of Abstract Objects," in *Midwest Studies in Philosophy, vol. 11: Studies in Essentialism*, edited by P. French, T. Uehling, and H. Wettstein, 495–512, Minneapolis: University of Minnesota Press, 1986.

Plantinga, Alvin, "Two Concepts of Modality: Modal Realism and Modal Reductionism," in *Philosophical Perspectives, I, Metaphysics*, 1987, edited by James Tomberlin, 189–231, Ridgeview, 1987.

Plantinga, Alvin, "God, Arguments for the Existence of," in *The Routledge Encyclopedia of Philosophy*, edited by Edward Craig, 85–93, London: Routledge, 1998.

Rosen, Gideon, "Abstract Objects," in *Stanford Encyclopedia of Philosophy*, edited by Edward N. Zalta, Winter 2018 edition, http://plato.stanford.edu/entries/abstract-objects.

Searle, John, *Intentionality*, Cambridge: Cambridge University Press, 1983.
Sellars, Wilfrid, "Abstract Entities," *Review of Metaphysics* vol. 16, no. 4 (1963): 627–671.
van Inwagen, Peter. "Two Concepts of Possible Worlds," in *Midwest Studies in Philosophy, vol. 11: Studies in Essentialism*, edited by P. French, T. Uehling and H. Wettstein, 185–213, Minneapolis: University of Minnesota Press, 1986.
Welty, Greg, "Truth as Divine Ideas: A Theistic Theory of the Property 'Truth,'" *Southwestern Journal of Theology* 47 (2004): 57–70.
Welty, Greg, "Theistic Conceptual Realism: The Case for Interpreting Abstract Objects as Divine Ideas," DPhil diss. Oxford: University of Oxford, 2006.
Welty, Greg, "Theistic Conceptual Realism," in *Beyond the Control of God? Six Views on the Problem of God and Abstract Objects*, edited by Paul Gould, 81–96, Bloomsbury Academic, 2014.
Welty, Greg, "Do Divine Conceptualist Accounts Fail?" *Philosophia Christi* vol. 21, no. 2 (2019): 255–266.

13

The Argument from Desire

William A. Lauinger

Most of us live primarily in the everyday mode, where we have ordinary thoughts and feelings that accompany our engagement in ordinary activities such as working, eating, paying bills, driving, sleeping, exercising, and shopping. Even when we are with friends and family members, most of our thoughts, feelings, and actions are of the everyday variety. However, there are certain moments, rare and ephemeral though they may be, where the everyday mode of life is unexpectedly pierced and where some kind of difficult-to-explain experience of lifting or transcendence occurs. Often these moments of lifting or transcendence are triggered by the awareness of beauty— for instance, the beauty of a song, a story, a beach, or a green field. And often these moments have a wistful quality.[1] Though they are deeply fulfilling and, indeed, are more fulfilling than any of the moments that we experience in the everyday mode of life, they are nevertheless tinged with disappointment in that (a) they do not last and (b) they seem to point beyond themselves to something even better, but which seems just out of reach. C. S. Lewis took these moments to be intimations of heavenly existence, and he thought that they revealed to us that we have an inborn desire for heaven—and, with it, God. Lewis referred to this inborn desire as Joy (always with a capital "J"), and in different writings he advanced the argument from desire; that is, he argued that our inborn desire for heaven and God provides us with evidence that heaven and God exist.[2] Though Lewis is probably more closely associated with the argument from desire than anyone else, there are others who are closely associated with this argument, notably, Aquinas.[3] In this chapter I will examine the argument from desire, and while doing so I will often focus on points that Aquinas and Lewis have made.

It will help here at the start if I lay out a working formulation of the argument from desire:

(1) *Assumption*: Humans have an inborn desire for a kind of fulfillment that is attainable only in a wonderful afterlife outside the natural world and only with the help of God or something very much like God.
(2) *Assumption*: For any inborn desire that humans have, it is far more reasonable to think that it can be fulfilled than that it cannot be fulfilled, that is, unless we are able, through observation, to determine that it cannot be fulfilled.

(3) *Assumption:* Observation does not tell us that the desire referenced in (1) is incapable of being fulfilled (i.e., we cannot observe that there is no wonderful afterlife available to us).
(4) *Conclusion:* It is far more reasonable to think that the inborn human desire referenced in (1) can be fulfilled than that it cannot be fulfilled, and in turn it is far more reasonable to think that God or something very much like God exists than that this is not the case.

The third assumption from above is uncontroversial, and the conclusion clearly follows if all three assumptions are granted. However, each of the first two assumptions is controversial and should be examined. In what follows I will discuss the first assumption from above (section 1) and then the second assumption from above (section 2). After that, I will discuss a different formulation of the argument from desire than the one from above, namely, the inference-to-the-best-explanation formulation (section 3). Finally, I will conclude this chapter (section 4).

1. Do humans have an inborn desire for a state of fulfillment beyond the natural world?

Plato is well known for depicting the human soul as longing to rise out of the physical-sensible realm and into the realm of the Forms, where the Forms are entities that are immaterial, eternal, indestructible, changeless, and the most real of all things.[4] If this sounds like a religious longing, perhaps that is because it is. Indeed, as W. K. C. Guthrie says:

> Plato reaffirmed the truth of the Pythagorean religious doctrine that the soul belongs in essence to the eternal world and not the transitory. It has had many earthly lives, and before and between them, when out of the body, has had glimpses of the reality beyond. Bodily death is not an evil for it, but rather a renewal of true life.[5]

Augustine was deeply influenced by Platonic thought, and so it is perhaps unsurprising that, like Plato, he viewed each human being as longing to leave the natural world behind and, in turn, to unify closely with something immaterial—though, of course, for Augustine, the ultimate target of each human's longing was not union with any impersonal Form, but rather union with God. As Augustine famously says at the beginning of his *Confessions,* "[Y]ou have made us for yourself, and our heart is restless until it rests in you."[6] To be clear about the meaning of this quote: Though Augustine thought that we could find a good degree of rest in God during our lives in the natural world, he also thought that, in order to attain the eternal rest in God for which we yearn, we must be in heaven.

Aristotle is generally thought to be more level-headed (i.e., less prone to flights of fancy) than both Plato and Augustine, and so it might help to ask whether he thought that humans long for a state of fulfillment beyond the natural world. It seems that

Aristotle did not believe in any personal form of immortality for human beings.[7] That said, he did maintain (a) that humans by nature desire to attain *eudaimonia* (roughly: true happiness) and (b) that one characteristic of *eudaimonia* is that it is self-sufficient, in that it "makes life desirable and lacking in nothing."[8] This self-sufficiency criterion for *eudaimonia* is, admittedly, open to interpretation.[9] Yet we might plausibly say this: Aristotle held that humans by nature desire *eudaimonia*, where this is a state of fulfillment that is so complete that it ensures that one is lacking in nothing; and, since the natural world does not offer humans any state of fulfillment that is *that* complete, it follows that Aristotle was, if only implicitly, committed to the view that humans by nature desire a state of fulfillment beyond the natural world.

Aquinas placed a large emphasis on Aristotle's self-sufficiency criterion for *eudaimonia*, as, indeed, Aquinas held that humans by nature desire perfect happiness or complete fulfillment, where this is understood as something that must "so fulfill the whole of man's desire that there is nothing further left to desire outside it."[10] But what could fulfill a human being's appetites in this totalizing way? Aquinas's answer is the same as Augustine's: Only the attainment of union with God in heaven, the beatific vision, can give us all that we want; unless we reach this state of fulfillment, there will inevitably be some degree of restlessness inside us. Aquinas thought of this inborn desire for complete fulfillment, and so implicitly for union with God in heaven, as underpinning all other human desires, such that they somehow flow out of it.[11] And Aquinas also thought of this inborn desire for complete fulfillment as providing humans with a natural but confused knowledge of God. As Aquinas says:

> To know that God exists in a general and confused way is implanted in us by nature, inasmuch as God is man's beatitude. For man naturally desires happiness, and what is naturally desired by man must be naturally known to him. This, however, is not to know absolutely that God exists; just as to know that someone is approaching is not the same as to know that Peter is approaching, even though it is Peter who is approaching; for many there are who imagine that man's perfect good which is happiness, consists in riches, and others in pleasures, and others in something else.[12]

Here Aquinas seems to be thinking as follows. Every human has an inborn desire for complete fulfillment, and since this consists in union with God, it follows that, in desiring complete fulfillment, each of us is at least implicitly desiring union with God. Further, this inborn desire for union with God impacts our intellects so as to provide us with some kind of intellectual awareness of God's existence. However, taken just as it stands, this intellectual awareness of God's existence is inchoate, and it is highly susceptible to becoming confused. This is evidenced by the fact that a great many people, if asked, would deny that God exists and, moreover, would say that, in wanting to be fulfilled (or "happy"), they are not wanting union with God, but rather are wanting something else, such as wealth and material comfort, or certain pleasures, or the experience of earthly beauty.

According to Aquinas, confusion easily arises here partly because this is a case where desire is outstripping what one can positively cognize or positively intellectually see. One by nature wants union with God, but, on Aquinas's view, it is impossible for a human being, during his or her present life, to have a positive insight into God's nature, as God's nature exceeds what the human intellect can positively grasp during this present life. As Aquinas puts this point:

> [T]he human intellect is not able to reach a comprehension of the divine substance through its natural power. For, according to its manner of knowing in the present life, the intellect depends on the senses for the origin of knowledge; and so those things that do not fall under the senses cannot be grasped by the human intellect except in so far as the knowledge of them is gathered from sensible things. Now, sensible things cannot lead the human intellect to the point of seeing in them the nature of the divine substance; for sensible things are effects that fall short of the power of their cause.[13]

Given that humans are unable to have a positive insight into God's nature during this present life, and given also that humans naturally desire union with God (or, for short, God), it follows that humans naturally desire something (i.e., God) that they cannot positively cognize. And, in any case where a human wants an object that he or she cannot positively cognize, there is presumably a good chance that he or she will make a mistake about just what it is that he or she wants.

Like Aquinas, Lewis believed that humans have an inborn desire for a kind of fulfillment that is unattainable in the natural world. As Lewis says in the last chapter of *The Problem of Pain*:

> There have been times when I think we do not desire heaven; but more often I find myself wondering whether, in our heart of hearts, we have ever desired anything else ... Are not all lifelong friendships born at the moment when at last you meet another human being who has some inkling (but faint and uncertain even in the best) of that something which you were born desiring, and which, beneath the flux of other desires and in all the momentary silences between the louder passions, night and day, year by year, from childhood to old age, you are looking for, watching for, listening for? You have never *had* it. All the things that have ever deeply possessed your soul have been but hints of it—tantalizing glimpses, promises never quite fulfilled, echoes that died away just as they caught your ear.[14]

The above quotation—and especially the phrase "beneath the flux of other desires"—makes it clear that, like Aquinas, Lewis thinks of the inborn desire for complete fulfillment in heaven as underpinning all other human desires, such that they somehow flow out of it. Indeed, for both Aquinas and Lewis, this desire is the deepest of human desires, and the fountain of all of them.

So far I have focused primarily on thinkers who were religious. However, it is worth emphasizing that there are some non-religious thinkers who have affirmed, either for themselves or for humans more generally, the existence of a seemingly inborn desire for a kind of fulfillment that is unavailable in the natural world. Camus and Lacan provide us with two examples here.[15] Moreover, while discussing Lewis's argument from desire, Alister McGrath quotes from a letter that the atheistic philosopher Bertrand Russell wrote in 1916:

> The center of me is always and eternally a terrible pain . . . a searching for something beyond what the world contains, something transfigured and infinite—the beatific vision, God—I do not find it, I do not think it is to be found—but the love of it is my life . . . it is the actual spring of life within me.[16]

Russell is among the most strident of atheists ever to live, and yet there he is, affirming that above all else he wants the beatific vision.

How might one object to the claim that humans have an inborn desire for a kind of fulfillment that is unavailable in the natural world? One might say: "I have searched inside myself for the desire in question, but I cannot find it. All that I find are desires for things such as good relationships with others, the experience of earthly beauty, achievement, and pleasure. And surely these things can be had here in the natural world. While I admit that I sometimes have moments of lifting or transcendence, where such moments are often triggered by the awareness of beauty, I see no reason to interpret these moments as pointing to the possibility of heavenly existence, for they seem to be rather easy to explain in naturalistic terms. Indeed, these moments do not seem to reveal the presence within me of a desire for a kind of fulfillment that can only be had outside the natural world; rather, these moments seem to reveal the presence within me of a desire for something great but merely earthly—say, the desire for earthly aesthetic experience."

In responding here, proponents of the argument from desire will admit that it is easy to interpret these moments as revealing the presence of a desire for something great but merely earthly—say, for earthly aesthetic experience. In *Surprised by Joy*, Lewis details how he spent much of his life wrongly taking his desire for heaven and God to be a desire for other objects; and, obviously enough, Lewis is assuming that *all* of us are prone to making this same mistake. There is a nebulousness to what one wants here—one wants, to use Peter Kreeft's way of putting it, "an unknown x"[17]—and it is this nebulousness that so easily allows for differing interpretations. But, of course, if proponents of the argument from desire are right, a thorough examination will reveal that this unknown x is heaven, understood as entailing God. The claim here is that, for whatever earthly thing or combination of things you might think can stand in for this unknown x, this earthly thing or combination of things will not quite quell the desire within you. Aquinas argues for this claim at length in Questions 1 to 5 (and especially in Question 2) of the First Part of the Second Part of the *Summa Theologica*.[18] And Lewis's most famous argument for this claim comes in *Mere Christianity* when he says:

> Most people, if they had really learned to look into their own hearts, would know that they do want, and want acutely, something that cannot be had in this world. There are all sorts of things in this world that offer to give it to you, but they never quite keep their promise. The longings which arise in us when we first fall in love, or first think of some foreign country, or first take up some subject that excites us, are longings which no marriage, no travel, no learning, can really satisfy. I am not

now speaking of what would be ordinarily called unsuccessful marriages, or holidays, or learned careers. I am speaking of the best possible ones. There was something we grasped at, in that first moment of longing, which just fades away in the reality. I think everyone knows what I mean. The wife may be a good wife, and the hotels and scenery may have been excellent, and chemistry may be a very interesting job: but something has evaded us.[19]

Even if Lewis goes too far when he says that everyone knows what he means, I do think that most of us know what he means. We often think to ourselves, "I'll be happy when . . ." and then fill this out in different ways, such as "when I finish college," "when I am financially stable," "when I am in a healthy romantic relationship," "when I finally move to California," and so on. Often we are significantly happier when we attain these desired objects. But, even so, we also often find that attaining these objects did not give us all that we thought it would. Something has, as Lewis says, "evaded us." The something in question is complete fulfillment. We want this more deeply than anything else, and at times we find ourselves believing, if only implicitly, that we can attain it here in the natural world. Yet nothing here in the natural world actually gives it to us. That, in sum, is Lewis's claim, and, in my view, this claim is convincing.

Before proceeding to section 2, let me note two more objections that might be raised in this context. (1) One might say: "Humans generally do want God and a wonderful afterlife, but, with Freud, we should hold that the desire for God and for fulfillment connected to God is not an inborn desire, but rather is a displaced, unconscious desire that goes back to one's infancy. We can partially fill this out by saying (a) that, when we are infants, we want to be safe and in turn want our earthly father's protection, and (b) that, as we age, we unconsciously displace this infantile desire onto the idea of God the Father, such that we end up desiring God the Father's protection from bad things that might happen to us."[20] (2) One might say: "Bernard Williams has argued that living forever, whether in the natural world or beyond it, is undesirable.[21] And many people who have thought about living forever in an afterlife have explicitly said that they do not want this. Thus it seems that the argument from desire is wrong to assume that humans by nature desire a wonderful afterlife."

Due to space constraints, I will be very brief—indeed, overly brief—in addressing each of the above two objections. With regard to the first objection: If we assume a naturalistic framework, as Freud does, then, in my view, a Freudian explanation of the origin of the desire for God and for fulfillment connected to God is highly plausible. But we should not approach the matter in this way. Rather, we should approach the matter from a neutral perspective, where this entails our being just as open to a theistic explanation as we are to a naturalistic explanation. If we do that, then, in my view, a Freudian explanation is no more convincing, and probably less convincing, than the explanation given by Aquinas and Lewis—that is, the explanation that says that the desire for God and for fulfillment connected to God is instilled in humans by God, such that humans have this desire by nature. Turning now to the claim that many people explicitly deny wanting to live forever in an afterlife, we can ask these people the following question: Do you want *a wonderful afterlife*, that is, *a totally fulfilling eternal afterlife*? When the question is put this way, these people are apt to answer, "If I thought that it were possible to have a totally fulfilling eternal afterlife, I suppose I would want to have this. But it is not possible to have this. Indeed, living forever in an afterlife would inevitably grow intolerably boring at some point. In view of this, I have given up all desires related to living forever." I think the following: These people really do want a totally fulfilling eternal afterlife, but, because they do not believe that it is possible to have this, they convince themselves that they do not want this. A certain man might in fact want to date a certain woman, but, because he believes that she will never agree to date him, he might convince himself that he does not want to date her. I think that it is the same, *mutatis mutandis*, with those who deny that they want a totally fulfilling eternal afterlife.

2. Are inborn desires always, or at least usually, capable of being fulfilled?

We can now turn to the second assumption from the working formulation of the argument from desire that I put forth near the start of this chapter. That assumption says that, for any inborn desire that humans have, it is far more reasonable to think that it can be fulfilled than that it cannot be fulfilled, that is, unless we are able, through observation, to determine that it cannot be fulfilled.

I have formulated this assumption more weakly than Aquinas formulates it. He holds that it is impossible for any given inborn or natural desire to be in vain.[22] His point here is not that every natural desire will be fulfilled. Rather, his point is that, for every natural desire, it must at least be possible for it to be fulfilled. Aquinas is here applying the Aristotelian dictum that nature does nothing in vain to the desires that humans have by nature. Or, put more fully, Aquinas is here doing two things. First, he is following Aristotle in assuming that all living beings have internal organizing principles or natures that direct them toward their fulfillment or completion, where their fulfillment or completion is truly possible, even if it is not inevitable (e.g., a flower that is directed by its nature to grow and bloom might actually wither and die if a drought blocks it from receiving needed water). Second, Aquinas is claiming that, in the case of humans, there are certain desires that are aspects of each human's own human nature, where these desires join in the directing-toward-fulfillment-or-completion work that each human's own human nature does.

In presenting Lewis's version of the argument from desire, Kreeft takes Lewis to assume, as Aquinas does, that every natural desire is capable of being fulfilled. Kreeft says, "The major premise of the argument is that every natural or innate desire in us bespeaks a corresponding real object that can satisfy the desire".[23] In *Mere Christianity* Lewis states,

> The Christian says, "Creatures are not born with desires unless satisfaction for those desires exists. A baby feels hunger: well, there is such a thing as food. A duckling wants to swim: well, there is such a thing as water. Men feel sexual desire: well, there is such a thing as sex."[24]

So far, then, it seems as though Kreeft has the correct interpretation of Lewis. However, Lewis's next few sentences say:

> If I find in myself a desire which no experience in this world can satisfy, the *most probable* explanation is that I was made for another world. If none of my earthly pleasures satisfy it, that does not prove that the universe is a fraud. *Probably* earthly pleasures were never meant to satisfy it, but only to arouse it, to suggest the real thing.[25]

I have added the italics to the above quote to stress that Lewis here puts the conclusion of the argument in probabilistic terms. Given this, it might be best to interpret Lewis's assumption that creatures "are not born with desires unless satisfaction for those desires exists" as not asserting what it seems on its face to assert (i.e., that every natural desire is capable of being fulfilled), but rather as asserting something weaker, such as that, for any given natural or inborn desire, we should hold that it is highly likely that it can be fulfilled (i.e., unless we have observational evidence to the contrary).

Why might a weaker formulation of this assumption be better than the strong one that says that every natural desire can be fulfilled? The answer here concerns the possibility of counterexamples. Kreeft doubts that there are any counterexamples available. He says, "No case has ever been found of an innate desire for a nonexistent object."[26] And Joe Puckett Jr., in his book on Lewis's argument from desire, says, "Clearly Lewis believed that *all* innate desires just so happen to have objects that satisfy them. Even if this truth is not a *logically necessary* truth, it is a truth that happens to exist within the world of human nature nonetheless."[27] I do not know whether there are any counterexamples available here. In short, I am agnostic on the matter. Consider the desire *never to be in any significant pain*. This is a widespread human desire. Furthermore, for any human being, it does not seem possible, in the relevant sense of "possible," for this desire to be satisfied, as there does not seem to be any way for a human to live in the natural world without experiencing significant pain. Here consider (a) that, if a birth is healthy, the baby comes out screaming, which indicates an experience of significant pain, and (b) that, if a birth is unhealthy, the pain for the baby is presumably even worse. Thus, right from birth, life for humans in the natural world involves significant pain. We should admit, then, that *if* the desire *never to be in any significant pain* is in fact an inborn or natural desire for humans, it is a successful counterexample to the claim that every natural desire can be fulfilled. I myself do not know whether the desire *never to be in any significant pain* is in fact an inborn or natural desire for humans. It is the word "never" that makes me hesitate here. I am sure that the desire *to be free from significant pain* is an inborn or natural desire for humans, for I am sure that we are born desiring to be free from significant pain. I am not sure, though, that we are born with sophisticated enough mental capacities to have the temporal term "never" included within the content of the desire in question, that is, right from birth.[28] Note that it does matter whether the word "never" is included in the desire in question right from birth or, instead, is added later in life. After all, the desire without "never" included—that is, the desire *to be free from significant pain*—is one that *is* capable of being fulfilled, as, indeed, most humans live some of their lives free from significant pain.

As I have said, I do not know whether there are successful counterexamples to the claim that every natural desire can be fulfilled. But, because I think that there might be, I find it best to formulate the argument from desire such that it assumes not that every natural desire can be fulfilled, but rather something weaker, such as that, for any given natural or inborn desire, we should hold that it is highly likely that it can be fulfilled (i.e., unless we have observational evidence to the contrary). Yet, even when the assumption in question is put in this weaker way, one might object to it. In particular, one might say (a) that inborn or natural desires fall into two different types, the type that is clearly biological and the type that is not, and (b) that, although it is clearly true that inborn or natural desires of the clearly biological type are always, or at least usually, capable of being fulfilled, it is by no means clearly true that inborn or natural desires of the not-clearly-biological type are always, or at least usually, capable of being fulfilled. John Beversluis seems to have this objection in mind when he says:

> [Lewis's argument] is based on a judicious selection of examples—human hunger and sexual drives and ducklings' desire to swim—and it is on this selectivity that its apparent persuasiveness depends. No one is likely to deny that his (almost amusingly uncontroversial) examples are natural desires. But their relevance to Joy [i.e., the desire for heaven and God] is not apparent. Surely he is not suggesting that the highly elusive (and almost exotic) phenomenon he calls Joy is a natural desire *in the same sense* as garden variety desires like the desire to eat, to splash about in ponds, and to engage in sexual intercourse.[29]

One response to this objection from Beversluis is to note that humans seem to have inborn desires for knowledge and aesthetic experience, where these inborn desires are neither clearly biological nor "almost exotic" in the same way that Joy is.[30] These inborn desires form a bridge in humans' desire-sets between (a) inborn desires that are clearly biological and that fit cleanly with naturalistic, evolutionary thinking about humans (e.g., inborn desires to eat, drink, survive, be healthy, and have and care for children) and (b) the inborn desire for a state of fulfillment beyond the natural world. To see the "bridge" point that I have in mind, consider knowledge in particular. On the one hand, humans gain in naturalistic, evolutionary terms by knowing about their physical environment—for instance, by knowing truths about dangerous animals and about what is required to build shelters. But, on the other hand, humans seem to have an inborn desire for much more knowledge than is helpful in naturalistic, evolutionary terms. Thus, while it is true that Lewis's discussion in *Mere Christianity* jumps abruptly from inborn desires that are clearly biological to Joy, there are "bridging" inborn desires that Lewis *could have* invoked. Imagine that, after reading Lewis's comment that humans feel sexual desire and that there is such a thing as sex, we ourselves mentally add that humans want knowledge and aesthetic experience and can get knowledge and aesthetic experience. If we incorporate this mental addition while reading Lewis's passage, then Lewis's transition from discussing clearly biological desires to the desire for heaven will no longer seem nearly as abrupt and, in turn, Beversluis's objection will no longer seem nearly as strong as we might initially have thought it to be.

3. The inference-to-the-best explanation formulation of the argument from desire

I will now turn to the inference-to-the-best explanation formulation of the argument from desire. This formulation can be put in different ways.[31] I will put it as follows:

(1) *Assumption:* Humans have an inborn desire for a kind of fulfillment that is attainable only in a wonderful afterlife outside the natural world and only with the help of God or something very much like God.
(2) *Assumption:* Out of all of the explanations for the existence of the desire referenced in (1), the best explanation is the theistic one, which says that God instilled this desire in humans, such that humans have this desire by nature. (Also, the theistic explanation is a good explanation. Thus we should not think of it as being a bad explanation that happens to be the best of a bad lot of explanations.)
(3) *Conclusion:* We have good reason to think that God exists and that he instilled in humans the desire referenced in (1), such that humans have this desire by nature.

To reject the argument from above, one must reject either the first or the second assumption. I discussed objections to the first assumption in Section 1. Let me now discuss an objection to the second assumption.

The objection that I have in mind here comes from Erik Wielenberg. He thinks that a naturalistic, evolutionary explanation for the existence of the desire referenced in (1) from above is available, where this naturalistic, evolutionary explanation is at least as plausible as the theistic explanation (Wielenberg 2008: 119). Wielenberg follows Lewis in referring to the inborn desire in question as Joy, and Wielenberg says:

> [O]ne of the main effects of Joy is that it prevents a person from deriving lasting contentment from earthly things. This fact is important because deriving lasting contentment from earthly things can be quite disadvantageous, evolutionarily speaking... To see the evolutionary drawbacks of lasting contentment, consider a male human who is perfectly content as long as his basic needs (food, shelter, and sex) are satisfied. Once such needs are satisfied, he will have no motivation whatsoever to acquire additional wealth, power, status, or success; indeed, he will have no motivation to do anything at all, other than perhaps ensure that his basic needs continue to be satisfied. Contrast this male with a second male who has the same basic drives but who *never* achieves lasting contentment, regardless of his earthly accomplishments. Everything else being equal, the second male will likely do better than the first in the competition for limited resources and access to the most desirable females.[32]

Wielenberg fills the foregoing out with further remarks, all of which supplement his view that, because Joy "causes us to strive for the infinite, it prevents us from being entirely satisfied by the finite, and in this way causes us to survive and reproduce better than we otherwise would."³³ The upshot of this, then, is that Wielenberg finds it reasonable to think that Joy was ingrained in humans by naturalistic, evolutionary processes.

What Wielenberg says here is somewhat plausible, but I nevertheless find it problematic. The restless desire for a state of fulfillment outside the natural world that Aquinas and Lewis have in mind does not seem to be quite the same as the restless desire that Wielenberg discusses here. Wielenberg purports to be discussing Joy, understood as a natural desire for a state of fulfillment beyond the natural world. But his discussion does not really focus on a desire for anything beyond the natural world. Rather, it focuses on wanting more and more and more earthly items—for instance, more and more and more wealth, power, status, and success, all of which might help with survival and attracting mates. But wanting earthly items *ad infinitum* is not quite the same as wanting a state of fulfillment beyond the natural world. Furthermore, Wielenberg's discussion makes no mention of beauty and no mention of wistfulness, and this is further evidence that Wielenberg's discussion is not quite on target. Indeed, the restlessness of which Wielenberg speaks seems somewhat ugly and harsh, as its function is to propel one to be acquisitive and ambitious in attaining more and more and more earthly items that would help one with survival and reproduction. This is not the same as the restlessness of which Aquinas and Lewis speak. The function of *that* restlessness is to make one yearn for a beautiful and peaceful state of fulfillment outside the natural world, where this state of fulfillment is characterized by harmony with God and others, not by a competitive advantage over others (e.g., for limited resources and desirable mating partners). In sum, then, although Wielenberg has given us a good naturalistic, evolutionary explanation for the existence of a natural desire for an infinite number of earthly items, what we really need here is an explanation for the existence of Joy, that is, of the natural desire for a state of fulfillment beyond the natural world.³⁴

The foregoing remarks do not compel us to conclude that the theistic explanation is the best explanation of Joy. After all, it is possible, for all I know, that Wielenberg's explanation could be modified so as to end up being at least as plausible as the theistic explanation. Or perhaps some entirely different naturalistic explanation could be provided here, one that is at least as plausible as the theistic explanation. Or maybe there is even some good explanation available that is neither theistic nor naturalistic. That said, I cannot help but think (a) that the real internal battle, for most people, is between theism and naturalism and (b) that there is a deep problem with any naturalistic explanation of Joy. This deep problem is as follows. If naturalism is true, then (a) reality is, at its most fundamental level, constituted by matter and energy that swirl around in accordance with laws of nature and (b) there is presumably nothing that exists outside this nexus of matter and energy that swirl around in accordance with laws of nature—that is, it is presumably true that this nexus is exhaustive of all that has ever been, now is, and ever will be.³⁵ The whole idea that this nexus would give rise to beings who deeply yearn for something outside this nexus is very strange. Indeed, it is, going into the issue, not at all what we would expect. Obviously enough, this deep problem does not plague the theistic explanation of Joy.

4. Conclusion

I will now end this chapter by returning to the moments of lifting or transcendence that I mentioned at the start. In *Surprised by Joy* Lewis describes some "transcendence" moments from his own life. For Lewis, these moments were very intense. When I myself have these moments, they are definitely not as intense as the ones Lewis had. But I do occasionally have them, and this has been so since my childhood. For me, these moments are usually triggered by the experience of a beautiful song or something beautiful in nature. Sometimes they involve other people; sometimes they do not. Sometimes life is generally going well for me when I have them; sometimes it is not. The last one that I had was in late April in Connecticut, near my sister's home in the countryside, watching my six-year-old and ten-year-old daughters and their cousins run through a graveyard at dusk, with the green grass beneath their feet.[36] The moon in the endless sky, the very old gravestones, the green grass, and the smiling children all combined, and the lifting happened. When I have these moments, they are fleeting, so fleeting that by the time I am fully conscious of them, they are gone. Though this will sound like a kind of theistic romanticism, these moments do make me think of, hope for, and believe in another, much better place, one filled with beauty and peacefulness, where serious worries and suffering dissipate to nothing, and where finitude and contingency do not bring with them any lasting death. Freud would say that, in reacting to these moments as I do, I am surely engaging in wishful thinking. And I take it that anyone with strong naturalistic leanings will be inclined to say: "True, many of us have these 'transcendence' moments from time to time. But they very quickly go away, and everyday life comes right back. And, for the sake of honesty, it is important not to make these moments into something more than they are."

Thus it is difficult to determine the significance of these moments. For people like me, who are convinced theists, these moments are apt to be construed as pointing beyond themselves, that is, toward God and heaven. For convinced naturalists, by contrast, these moments are apt to be interpreted as wonderful, but also as fairly easy to explain in naturalistic terms. To make progress in settling this matter, we should listen to people who are truly neutral between theism and naturalism as they go into these moments. Listening to these people's reactions to these moments will help us not only in determining the significance of these moments, but also, more generally, in determining how strong the argument from desire really is.

Notes

1 The literature on the argument from desire sometimes references the German word *Sehnsucht* to capture this wistful quality: Robert Holyer, "The Argument From Desire," *Faith and Philosophy* 5, no.1 (1988): 61–71.
2 Lewis's best known version of the argument from desire is in *Mere Christianity* (New York: HarperCollins Publishers, 1952), 134–137. In *Surprised by Joy* (New York: HarperCollins Publishers, 1955), which is an autobiography, Lewis details his own experiences of Joy. And there are other places where Lewis advances the argument

from desire—on this point, see Alister McGrath, *The Intellectual World of C. S. Lewis* (Malden, MA: Wiley-Blackwell, 2014), 108–109.

3   Aquinas has an explicit argument from desire for the immortality of the soul in Question 75, article 6 of the First Part of the *Summa Theologica* in Thomas Aquinas, *Introduction to St. Thomas Aquinas*, ed. Anton Pegis (New York: The Modern Library, 1948), 289.
And, in his writings on happiness (i.e., fulfillment) in Questions 1 to 5 of the First Part of the Second Part of the *Summa Theologica* in Thomas Aquinas, *Thomas Aquinas, Selected Writings*, ed. and trans. Ralph McInerny (New York: Penguin Books, 1998), 482–550, Aquinas implicitly advances the following argument from desire.
(1) Humans naturally desire perfect fulfillment, which entails unmediated union with God in heaven. (2) Nature does nothing in vain, which entails that all natural desires are capable of being fulfilled. From (1) and (2), it follows that the natural human desire for perfect fulfillment, which entails unmediated union with God in heaven, is capable of being fulfilled; hence, God and heaven exist. Thomas Aquinas, *Introduction to St. Thomas Aquinas*, ed. Anton Pegis, (New York: The Modern Library, 1948).

4   For instance, see Plato's *Symposium* in Plato, *The Collected Dialogues of Plato*, ed. E. Hamilton and H. Cairns (Princeton: Princeton University Press, 1961), 554–563.

5   William Guthrie, *The Greek Philosophers* (New York: Harper and Row, 1975), 95.

6   Augustine, *Confessions*, trans. H. Chadwick (New York: Oxford University Press, 1991), 3.

7   On this point, see W. K. C. Guthrie, *The Greek Philosophers* (New York: Harper and Row, 1975), 145–146.

8   Aristotle, Chapter 7 of *The Nicomachean Ethics*, trans. David Ross (New York: Oxford University Press, 1925), 12.

9   For discussion, see Julia Annas, *The Morality of Happiness* (New York: Oxford University Press, 1993), 40–42.

10 Thomas Aquinas, *Thomas Aquinas, Selected Writings*, Question 1, article 5 of the First Part of the Second Part of the *Summa Theologica*, 491.

11 On this point, see ibid., Question 1, article 6 of the First Part of the Second Part of the Summa Theologica, 493.

12 Thomas Aquinas, *Introduction to St. Thomas Aquinas*, Question 2, article 1 of the First Part of the *Summa Theologica*, 22.

13 Thomas Aquinas, *Summa Contra Gentiles*, trans. Anton Pegis (Notre Dame, IN: University of Notre Dame Press, 1975), Chapter 3, 64.

14 C. S. Lewis, *The Problem of Pain* (New York: HarperCollins Publishers, 1940), 149–151.

15 For a discussion of this point, see William Lauinger, *Well-Being and Theism: Linking Ethics to God* (New York: Continuum, 2012), 166–169.

16 In Alister McGrath, *The Intellectual World of C. S. Lewis* (Malden, MA: Wiley-Blackwell, 2014), 107.

17 Peter Kreeft, *Heaven* (San Francisco: Ignatius Press, 1989), 205.

18 Thomas Aquinas, *Thomas Aquinas, Selected Writings*, 482–550.

19 C. S. Lewis, *Mere Christianity* (New York: HarperCollins Publishers, 1952), 135.

20 For more on this Freudian line of objection, see Lauinger, *Well-Being and Theism: Linking Ethics to God*, 171–178.

21 Bernard Williams, *Problems of the Self* (Cambridge: Cambridge University Press, 1973), 82–100).

22 Thomas Aquinas, *Introduction to St. Thomas Aquinas*, Question 75, article 6 of the First Part of the *Summa Theologica*, 289.

23 Kreeft, *Heaven*, 201.
24 Lewis, *Mere Christianity*, 136.
25 Ibid.
26 Kreeft, *Heaven*, 203.
27 Joe Puckett Jr., *The Apologetics of Joy* (Wipf and Stock, 2012). Italics in original.
28 In thinking about temporal terms in this context, I have been influenced by a blog post by Edward Feser. See Edward Feser, "Arguments from Desire," 2017. Retrieved from http://edwardfeser.blogspot.com/2017/06/arguments-from-desire.html.
29 John Beversluis, *Lewis and the Search for Rational Religion* (Amherst, New York: Prometheus Books, 2007), 45.
30 For a defense of the claim that almost all humans have inborn desires for items such as knowledge and aesthetic experience, see William Lauinger, *Well-Being and Theism: Linking Ethics to God* (New York: Continuum, 2012), 84–120.
31 McGrath, *The Intellectual World of C. S. Lewis*, 121; Erik Wielenberg, *God and the Reach of Reason* (New York: Cambridge University Press, 2008), 115.
32 Wielenberg, *God and the Reach of Reason*, 116.
33 Ibid., 117.
34 For a response to Wielenberg that differs from the one that I have provided here, see Stewart Goetz, *C. S. Lewis* (Hoboken, NJ: Wiley Blackwell, 2018), 174–177.
35 One caveat here: Some naturalists accept that there are certain non-causally efficacious entities (e.g., non-natural values) that exist outside this nexus of matter and energy that swirl around in accordance with laws of nature. Perhaps, if one is a naturalist of this sort, it would not be that strange to think that the natural world would give rise to beings who deeply yearn for something outside the natural world. Then again, there is a reason why most naturalists deny that there are non-natural entities: They deny this because non-natural entities do not fit well with a naturalistic view of reality.
36 It is now late June of 2019. The moment I am referencing took place about two months ago.

Bibliography

Aquinas, Thomas, *Introduction to St. Thomas Aquinas*, edited by Anton Pegis, New York: The Modern Library, 1948.

Aquinas, Thomas, *Summa Contra Gentiles*, translated by Anton Pegis, Notre Dame, IN: University of Notre Dame Press, 1975.

Aquinas, Thomas, *Thomas Aquinas: Selected Writings*, edited and translated by Ralph McInerny, New York: Penguin Books, 1998.

Aristotle, *The Nicomachean Ethics*, translated by David Ross, New York: Oxford University Press, 1925.

Augustine, *Confessions*, translated by H. Chadwick, New York: Oxford University Press, 1991.

Beversluis, John, *C. S. Lewis and the Search for Rational Religion*, revised and updated, Amherst, NY: Prometheus Books, 2007.

Feser, Edward, "Arguments from desire," 2017, http://edwardfeser.blogspot.com/2017/06/arguments-from-desire.html.

Goetz, Stewart, *C. S. Lewis*, Hoboken, NJ: Wiley-Blackwell, 2018.

Guthrie, W. K. C., *The Greek Philosophers*, New York: Harper and Row, 1975.

Holyer, Robert, "The Argument From Desire," *Faith and Philosophy*, 5, no. 1 (1988): 61–71.

Kreeft, Peter, *Heaven*, San Francisco: Ignatius Press, 1989.
Lauinger, William, *Well-Being and Theism: Linking Ethics to God*, New York: Continuum, 2012.
Lewis, C. S., *The Problem of Pain*, New York: HarperCollins Publishers, 1940.
Lewis, C. S., *Mere Christianity*, New York: HarperCollins Publishers, 1952.
Lewis, C. S., *Surprised by Joy: The Shape of My Early Life*, New York: HarperCollins Publishers, 1955.
McGrath, Alister. *The Intellectual World of C. S. Lewis*. Malden, MA: Wiley-Blackwell, 2014.
Plato, *The Collected Dialogues of Plato*, edited by E. Hamilton and H. Cairns, Princeton: Princeton University Press, 1961.
Puckett Joe Jr., *The Apologetics of Joy*, Wipf and Stock, 2012.
Wielenberg, Erik, *God and the Reach of Reason*, New York: Cambridge University Press, 2008.
Williams, Bernard, *Problems of the Self*, Cambridge: Cambridge University Press, 1973.

14

The Argument from Religious Experience

Kai-man Kwan

1. The Experiential Roots of Religion

Religion is characterized by the passion that it can arouse. Why is religion capable of such enormous effects on human life? Apart from the fact that religion is about the ultimate concern of human beings, we also need to bear in mind that religion often has an *experiential* basis. God is not just a hypothesis for the religiously devoted. He is a Living Reality who permeates all their lives. Those people who experience God will echo with Job: "I have heard of thee by the hearing of the ear, but now mine eye seeth thee" (Job, 42.5). Religious experiences sometimes convey such a heightened sense of reality that the conviction they instill transforms the lives of the experients. Furthermore, religious experiences are often world-transforming as well; just contemplate the immense impact of people like Moses, St. Paul, Augustine, etc. on Western civilization.

Some clarification of related terms and concepts is needed here. By a *religious experience* I mean an experience which the subject takes to be an experience of God or some supernatural being. Such an experience is *veridical* if what the subject took to be the object of his experience actually existed, was present, and caused him to have that experience in an appropriate way. The claim that "S has an experience of God" does not entail "God exists". So the fact that religious experiences have happened does not automatically assume that God exists. The argument from religious experience (hereafter ARE) claims that the occurrence of religious experience provides grounds for the belief in God. Before discussing the epistemological issues surrounding the ARE, let me introduce its development in the twentieth century.

2. The Argument from Religious Experience: From the Twentieth to the Twentieth-first century

Earlier defenders of religious experience included both theologians and philosophers, e.g., Farmer and Knudson.[1] Some of them claimed that religious experiences provide immediate knowledge of God, and that they were *self-authenticating* because within the experience the subject directly encountered God and received God's revelation. For example, according to the British theologian H. H. Farmer:

> the Christian experience of God ... in the nature of the case must be self-authenticating and able to shine in its own light independently of the abstract reflections of philosophy.[2]

However, philosophers tended to be critical of claims to self-authentication (the major reasons will be examined below). They pointed out that religious experiences were heavily shaped by the conceptual framework of the experient and that no knowledge could be inferred from mere emotional states or conviction, no matter how intense they were. They also suggested that it was hard to make sense of the notion of self-authenticating experience. Keith Yandell, himself a defender of religious experience, raised many criticisms to this notion.[3] No matter whether these criticisms were cogent or not, they were influential and accounted for the rise of a form of argument from religious experience which did not rely on claims to self-authentication.[4]

C. D. Broad anticipated an early version of the ARE that is hotly debated nowadays:

> The practical postulate which we go upon everywhere else is to treat cognitive claims as veridical unless there be some positive reason to think them delusive. This, after all, is our only guarantee for believing that ordinary sense-perception is veridical. We cannot *prove* that what people agree in perceiving really exists independently of them; but we do always assume that ordinary waking sense-perception is veridical unless we can produce some positive ground for thinking that it is delusive in any given case. I think it would be inconsistent to treat the experiences of religious mystics on different principles. So far as they agree they should be provisionally accepted as veridical unless there be some positive ground for thinking that they are not.[5]

From the fifties to the seventies, defenders of religious experience included John Hick, Elton Trueblood, and Rem Edwards.[6] However, they had not drawn much attention from professional philosophers because at that time, verificationism, roughly the doctrine that only in principle verifiable sentences were cognitively meaningful, was still influential and hence even the meaningfulness of religious language was in doubt. The situation by now is very different. As Taliaferro has noted:

> Since then many philosophers have conceded that concepts of God and other components of different religions cannot be ruled out as obvious nonsense or clear cases of superstition. Important work has gone into building a case for the intelligibility of the concept of God ... the debate on these matters is now more open-ended without being less rigorous.[7]

Starting from the end of 1970's, a number of analytic philosophers had produced increasingly sophisticated defenses of religious experience. Richard Swinburne defended religious experience via his Principle of Credulity in *The Existence of God*.[8]

The Principle of Credulity says that it is rational to treat our experiences (including religious experience) as innocent until proven guilty. In other words, religious experiences are to be treated as *prima facie* evidence for the existence of God unless there are reasons for doubting them. This attracted quite a lot of attention in the circle of philosophy of religion. There were of course many critics of Swinburne, e.g., William Rowe, Michael Martin, but he had also inspired the support of quite a few professional philosophers, e.g., the philosopher of science Gary Gutting.[9] Many books were written on religious experience which essentially followed Swinburne's line of reasoning, expanding it, modifying it, and replying to objections. These books included Caroline Davis's *The Evidential Force of Religious Experience*, George Wall's *Religious Experience and Religious Belief*, and Jerome Gellman's *Experience of God and the Rationality of Theistic Belief* and *Mystical Experience of God: A Philosophical Inquiry* (2001).[10] Other philosophers also worked independently towards a similar conclusion, e.g., William Wainwright and Keith Yandell.[11]

One landmark of this debate is William Alston's *Perceiving God*.[12] In this book, Alston brought his analytical skills to the issue of religious experience and defended a doxastic practice approach to epistemology. This approach said that it was practically rational to trust our socially established doxastic practices, including the Christian Mystical Practice. His arguments were discussed in major analytic philosophy journals, e.g. *Nous*, *The Journal of Philosophy*. Both *Philosophy and Phenomenological Research* and *Religious Studies* have organized symposia to discuss his book in 1994.

The resurgence of the ARE has continued into the twenty-first century (for a survey, see Kwan 2011, chapter 1). I have extensively defended Swinburne's ARE.[13] I have also renamed his Principle of Credulity as the Principle of Critical Trust to highlight the importance of integrating trust and criticism in a coherent epistemology that I call the Critical Trust Approach. I have further developed this epistemological approach in my book *The Rainbow of Experiences, Critical Trust, and God*.[14] Moreover, a parallel development in epistemology has strengthened the ARE. Epistemic principles similar to the Principle of Credulity are now defended by analytic philosophers. One notable example is Michael Huemer's Phenomenal Conservatism,[15] which "has become quite a significant player among internalist positions in epistemology".[16] Such principles have also been defended by epistemologists such as James Pryor,[17] Chris Tucker,[18] and William Lycan.[19] The ARE, then, appears to be alive and well, having both able defenders and detractors. It is also exciting and fascinating because it helps us rethink deep issues in epistemology. Let us examine this debate in some details.

3. The Demise of Foundationalism and Traditional Objections to the Argument from Religious Experience

Foundationalists believe that our knowledge has to be built upon the foundation of sense experiences because only they are the indubitably given free from interpretations, and are open to public confirmation. Religious experiences, if they are to be trusted, have to be vindicated on the basis of this foundation: sense experience. However, the

ARE has strong intuitive force for many. For example, Hick thinks that we are "in the last resort thrown back upon the criterion of coherence with our mass of experience and belief as a whole; there is no further criterion by which the criteriological adequacy of this mass can itself be tested. This is surely our actual situation as cognizing subjects."[20] Is it not plausible to say that "it is proper for the man who reports a compelling awareness of God to *claim* to know that God exists"? At least it seems to Hick that the "onus lies upon anyone who denies that this fulfills the conditions of a proper knowledge claim to show reasons for disqualifying it".[21] The allegation that religious experience as a type is unveridical amounts to the claim that *not a single instance* of the myriad religious experiences of humankind is veridical, i.e., all these experiences are totally delusory. Is it reasonable to believe that all "God-experients" are either deceiving themselves or others? Gutting, for one, does not think so:

> [R]eligion, throughout human history, has been an integral part of human life, attracting at all times the enthusiastic adherence of large numbers of good and intelligent people. To say that something that has such deep roots and that has been sustained for so long in such diverse contexts is nothing but credulity and hypocrisy is . . . extraordinary.[22]

Suppose we come to know the life story of a person who has dramatic experiences of God *throughout his life*. We find that person honest, sane, and intelligent. We also find his story corroborated by many others' stories throughout history in many cultures. Is it not rash to say that *all of them are entirely and chronically deluded*? Nevertheless, for empiricist-minded philosophers, the trustworthiness of religious experiences is hard to swallow. In many introductory books on philosophy, the ARE is usually dismissed on the basis of stock objections like the following:

1) *The Logical Gap Objection*: We have to distinguish the experience and the subjective conviction it produces from the objectivity (or veridicality) of the experience, for example, a very "real" hallucination or dream is a live possibility. Critics such as Antony Flew admit that religious experiences often produce subjective certitude in subjects. However, it does not follow that the experience is objectively certain. In other words, there is a logical gap between the psychological data and the ontological claim of the religious experiences. To bridge the gap, we need independent certification of the religious belief. For example, Flew challenges the defenders of religious experiences to answer this basic question when he says:

   > How and when would we be justified in making inferences from the facts of the occurrence of religious experience, considered as a purely psychological phenomenon, to conclusions about the supposed objective religious truths?[23]

2) *The Theory-Ladenness Objection*: The religious experiences are heavily (or even entirely) shaped by the conceptual framework of the experients. Hence they are not useful as evidence for ontological claims.[24]

3) *The Privacy Objection*: According to Edwards, "the foremost accusation leveled at the mystics is that mystical experiences are private, like hallucinations, illusions, and dreams, and that like these "nonveridical' experiences", religious experience is really of no noetic significance at all".[25]

However, theists have provided reasonable responses to these objections. First, we should note that the logical gap objection to religious experiences basically conforms to the structure of the general skeptical argument.[26] This can be seen from Gutting's parody of Flew's question:

> How and when would we be justified in making inferences from the facts of the occurrence of experiences of material objects, considered as a purely psychological phenomenon, to conclusions about the supposed objective truths about material objects?[27]

The certitude/certainty distinction applies to almost all kinds of experience, *including* sense experience. A hallucination is exactly an unveridical sense experience which nevertheless produces subjective conviction. If the certitude/certainty distinction *in itself* threatens religious experiences, it will also threaten sense experience. So anyone who pushes this objection needs to show why the logical gap is not damaging in other cases. If the critics only apply the objection to religious experiences but not to other experiences, it would be arbitrary. This would also confirm Alston's charge that critics of religious experiences often adopt a double standard with regard to sense experiences:

> I have identified certain recurrent fallacies that underlie many of these objections-epistemic imperialism and the double standard ... They involve unfavorable epistemic comparisons between mystical perception and sense perception; it is not difficult to show that they either condemn the former for features it shares with the latter (double standard) or unwarrantedly require the former to exhibit features of the latter [imperialism].[28]

The Theory-ladenness Objection again raises a general problem in epistemology. Even ordinary perception is theory-laden.[29] The empiricists and positivists have searched hard for the rock-bottom "given" which is interpretation-free, so that it can be the neutral arbiter of different theories or interpretations. However, the developments of contemporary philosophy of science bespeak the downfall of this project. All major philosophers of science, for example, Popper, Hanson, Kuhn, Lakatos, Feyerabend, agree that all observations are to some extent theory-laden. For example, Nancy Cartwright writes:

> We can be mistaken about even the most mundane claims about sensible properties, and once these are called into question, their defense will rest on a complicated and sophisticated network of general claims about how sensations are caused, what kinds of things can go wrong in the process, and what kinds of things can and cannot be legitimately adduced as interferences.[30]

Modern psychology also confirms the idea that interpretation "is absolutely essential to there occurring a perceptual experience at all.... We are not passive recipients of ready-made representations of our environment; rather, stimuli from that environment must be processed by various interpretive mechanisms before they can have any significance for us."[31] Now the critic requires that the interpretive elements of religious experience be independently supported before we deem the experiences reliable. However, because sense experiences also have interpretive elements, "if we were always required to provide independent evidence that the beliefs in terms of which we had unconsciously "interpreted" a perceptual experience were probably true before we could take the perceptual experience to be probably veridical, we would be trapped in [scepticism]."[32] If the critic is to avoid the charge of double standard, he needs to explain in what way this is a special problem for religious experiences. So again, the Theory-Ladenness Objection in itself is not decisive. Perhaps to avoid scepticism, the wiser policy is to treat the incorporated interpretations in our experiences as *prima facie* justified.[33] Furthermore, prior religious frameworks need not be corrupting; they may instead help to "tune" people to perceive a reality that they would otherwise miss.[34]

The Privacy Objection claims that, unlike sense experience, religious experience is private and subjective. In what sense is a sense experience public? My *experience* of a chair occurs essentially in my mind – it is every bit as private as other experiences in this aspect. I cannot directly experience how you experience the chair and vice versa. There is a danger that the critics are "confusing the claim that the experience is private with the quite different claim that the object of the experience is private".[35] What makes a sense experience public is that verbal reports of different persons can be compared. However, reports of people having religious experiences can also be compared. For example, experiences of God are present in almost all ages and all cultures. The reports to a considerable extent match. So in these aspects religious experience is also public. As Edwards emphasizes:

> the experience of the Holy seems to be very much *unlike* dreams and hallucinations. Extremely large numbers of people from extremely diverse cultural backgrounds claim to experience the Holy One, and there is a significant amount of transcultural agreement about what the experienced object is like. This is not the case with the objects of hallucinations – most hallucinators do not see pink elephants ... *Pink elephant* is simply a convenient symbolic abbreviation for the immense variety of weird entities encountered by people having hallucinations."[36]

It seems that the force of many stock objections to religious experience depends upon the traditional foundationalist framework, which "is rarely found now outside discussions of religious experience,"[37] and in fact widely regarded as untenable. The demise of foundationalism does not mean an automatic victory for the ARE. However, both defenders and critics of religious experience need to take seriously this development. They need to spell out and defend the epistemological framework they use to evaluate religious experience. Let us examine Richard Swinburne's attempt in this direction.

4. Swinburne's Defense of Religious Experience via the Principle of Credulity

Swinburne proposes a defense of religious experiences by espousing an epistemological principle that accords religious experiences with *prima facie evidential force* (hereafter PFEF). An experience has PFEF if the claims of the experience are probably true unless there are positive reasons to the contrary. The idea is that all experiences should be treated as innocent until proven guilty. Religious experiences should also be accorded PFEF then – that is, the claims of religious experiences should be trusted unless counter-evidence can be brought forward.[38] This epistemological principle is called the Principle of Credulity (hereafter PC) defined as follows:

> (PC) If it seems (epistemically) to me that x is present on the basis of experience, then probably x is present unless there are special considerations to the contrary.

Swinburne argues that PC is a fundamental principle of rationality apart from which we cannot provide any noncircular justification of either ordinary perception or memory. Then, using this principle, Swinburne formulates the following argument for the existence of God:

A) It seems (epistemically) to me that God is present.
B) There is no good reason to think either God is non-existent or not present; nor any good reason to think the experience unveridical.
C) Hence, probably God is present.

The PC does not stand alone in Swinburne's epistemological approach. It has to be used together with other epistemological principles like the following:

(a) The Principle of Testimony: other things being equal, others' experiences are likely to be as they report them to be.
(b) The Principle of Simplicity: "[I]n a given field, we take as most likely to be true the simplest theory which fits best with other theories of neighbouring fields to produce the simplest set of theories of the world".[39]
(c) The Principle of Charity: other things being equal, we suppose that other men are like ourselves.

These principles are important. If we just take the PC alone, the principle may look unduly egocentric. However, the Principle of Testimony shows that Swinburne is equally emphatic on trusting others' experiences and the social dimension of knowing. Second, Swinburne's approach has to be distinguished from an "anything goes" approach. It is recognized that man's ability to know is far from perfect: his initial epistemic seemings are fallible. The hope lies in the ability of man to sift and correct these initial data. For example, an erroneous epistemic seeming can be corrected by other epistemic seemings. However, to do this we need some rational principles to organize our data. For Swinburne the supreme principle is the Principle of Simplicity. This principle explains what can be counter-evidence to a prima facie justified claim:

> We should not believe that things are as they seem to be in cases when such a belief is in conflict with the simplest theory compatible with a vast number of data obtained by supposing in a vast number of other cases that things are as they seem to be.

So Swinburne's approach includes a way to sift the data and establish an orderly noetic structure. Swinburne's argument has engendered a lot of controversy. Some critics challenge the validity of the PC, and others argue that (B) above is false in that Swinburne has neglected some defeaters of religious experiences. Since space is limited, I can only discuss three major objections below.

4.a. The No Criteria/Uncheckability Objection

Critics allege that there is no criterion to distinguish the veridical religious experiences from the nonveridical ones. If so, it is not rational to believe that a certain religious experience is veridical. Hence it cannot be used as evidence for religious claims. Even if there are criteria from within the religious framework, we still lack objective, noncircular criteria. In contrast, when we doubt a sense experience, it can be subjected to further tests, for example, others' reports and photographs. C. B. Martin put it this way:

> the presence of a piece of blue paper is not to be read off from my experience as a piece of blue paper. Other things are relevant: What would a photograph reveal? Can I touch it? What do others see?[40]

Since religious experiences cannot be tested in similar ways, they are unreliable.

The defenders of ARE point out that religious experiences can be checked in principle, for example, by other experiences (religious or non-religious) or by the Bible. The critics will surely say, "These checks already assume some religious beliefs, and hence are circular. We need some non-circular checks." This requirement, however, is not even satisfied by sense experience. Checking by others' reports depends on our hearing experiences and capacity for understanding, and so on. All checks are ultimately circular. This point is made trenchantly by Mavrodes:

> Suppose that I do try to photograph the paper. What then? Martin asks, "What would a photograph reveal?" To discover what the photograph reveals I would ordinarily look at it. But if the presence of blue paper is not to be "read off" from my experience then the presence of a photograph, and *a fortiori* what the photograph reveals, is not to be read off from my experience either. It begins to look as though I must take a photograph of the photograph, and so on ... I send for my friend to look at the paper ... But his presence is not to be read off from my experience either. Perhaps I must have a third man to tell me whether the second has come and the infinite regress appears again ... Martin's thesis fails because it

converts into a general requirement something that makes sense only as an occasional procedure. At most we can substitute one unchecked experience for another.[41]

Ultimately, the veridicality of a sense experience can only be checked with respect to other sense experiences. So to hold this as a debilitating factor for religious experience *alone* is again to commit the double standard fallacy.

Despite the above responses, Michael Martin still insists that the PC should not be applied "unless one has a right to assume that perceptual conditions hold under which the entity at issue is likely to appear to an observer if the entity is present. This right may be justified on inductive grounds, by one's background theory or in other ways".[42] He concludes that we have the right to use a principle like PC in the case of sense experience but not in the case of religious experience.

However, is it really the case that our belief in the general reliability of sense experience can be justified by inductive evidence? The story goes like this. Usually our perceptual claims can be checked to see whether they are correct or not. In this way we can keep a track-record of our perceptual process and see that it is generally reliable. If we accumulate enough inductive evidence for the validity of our perceptual claims in the past, we can be justified in believing that they will continue to be reliable.

However, we can still ask, "How is the checking of a belief-forming process possible?"

> The most direct approach would be to compare its output beliefs with the facts that make them true or false, and determine the track record of the practice in a suitable spread of cases. Sometimes this is possible. It is possible, e.g., when we are dealing with what we might call "partial" or "restricted" practices, like determining temperature on the basis of mercury thermometers ... In these cases we have other modes of access to the facts in question, modes which we can use to check the accuracy of the practice under examination. But we fairly quickly arrive at more inclusive practices where this technique is no longer available. If we are assessing SP (i.e., sensory practice) in general, e.g., we have no independent access to the facts in question ..., i.e., no access that neither consists in nor is based on reliance on sense perception; and so we have no non-circular check on the accuracy of the deliverances of SP.[43]

If, in the end, we still insist that our checks, for example, asking for others' corroboration, provide justification for the perceptual claims, it can only be because we already accord PFEF to others' perceptual experiences. If others' perceptual claims are to corroborate ours, we have to assume that they possess sense organs which are in good order and a brain which is functioning properly. But how can one justify all these assumptions apart from a basic prima facie trust in our perceptual experiences? A commitment to PC seems to be inescapable.

The second problem concerning this argument is pointed out sharply by Swinburne:

> an induction from past experiences to future experiences is only reliable if we correctly recall our past experiences. And what grounds have we got for supposing

that we do? Clearly not inductive grounds – an inductive justification of the reliability of memory-claims would obviously be circular. Here we must rely on the principle that things are the way they seem, as a basic principle not further justifiable ... The principle that the rational man supposes that in the absence of special considerations in particular cases things are the way they seem to be cannot always be given inductive justification. And if it is justifiable to use it when other justifications fail in memory cases, what good argument can be given against using it in other kinds of case when other justifications fail?[44]

So in the end to "justify" ordinary perception inductively, we have to rely on the prima facie reliability of memory. The attempt to provide non-circular justification for our memory claims is notoriously difficult. Again we seem to need the PC as a fundamental principle.

4.b. The Naturalistic Explanation Objection

Many critics think that religious beliefs formed by having religious experiences are susceptible to naturalistic explanations, psychological, sociological and the like. The religious experiences are hence discredited. At least their evidential force, if there is any in the beginning, is then cancelled.[45]

However, many suspect that there are as yet no general naturalistic explanations of religious experiences which are empirically well-established and theoretically plausible. For example, the Freudian explanation of religion is a prominent example of naturalistic explanation: it regards religious belief as wishful thinking generated by the mechanism of projection. But nowadays Freudianism itself is in doubt.[46] Its explanation of religious belief has been carefully examined and found wanting, even by atheists.[47] A researcher in cognitive science of religion even says:

> It might be an overstatement to say that among working sociologists, psychologists and anthropologists of religion ... the theories of Freud and Marx are considered relics rather than serious scientific hypotheses, but it would probably not be far off the mark.[48]

Indeed, Alston comments:

> the most prominent theories in the field invoke causal mechanisms that themselves pose thus far insoluble problems of identification and measurement: unconscious psychological processes like repression, identification, regression, and mechanisms of defense; social influences on ideology and attitude formation. It is not surprising that theories like those of Freud, Marx, and Durkheim rest on a slender thread of evidential support and generalize irresponsibly from such evidence as they can muster. Nor do the prospects seem rosy for significant improvement.[49]

Of course, this general assertion needs to be supported by more detailed discussions.[50] Let us further examine some recent proposals.

One popular type of naturalistic explanation is the neurophysiological one. Some argue that the fact that mysticism can be induced by drugs provides a reductive explanation of mysticism. However, some scholars contend that drugs are not sufficient to produce genuine mystical experiences. The experimental evidence only suggests that it can raise the likelihood and enhance the intensity of the experiences.[51] Even if drugs are causally sufficient to produce mystical experiences, it does not follow that they are unveridical. God may have laid down some psychophysical laws to the effect that whenever certain brain states are produced, a certain perception of the divine would be produced. There is no reason why those brain states cannot be caused by taking drugs. As long as the whole process is set up and upheld by God, such perception of God should be counted as veridical. In any case, even if drug-induced mystical experiences are unveridical, it does not follow that those numerous non-drug-induced religious experiences are unveridical. What is shown is that on the experiential level, mystical experience can be faked. This is neither surprising nor uniquely true of mystical experience as sense experiences can also be faked and caused by drugs like LSD.

Neuroscientist, Michael Persinger, has suggested that the stimulation of the brain can generate religious experiences. Persinger is famous for his "God Helmet" which, when placed on the head of an experimental subject, stimulates the brain's temporal lobes with fluctuating magnetic fields. Upon wearing the God Helmet, some subjects have reported experiences using the same words used to describe spiritual and mystical experiences. Persinger claims that these religious experiences are correlated with transient electrical instabilities within the temporal lobe of the human brain, and have emerged within the human species as a means of "dealing with the expanded capacity to anticipate aversive events".[52]

Persinger's claims, however, have been forcefully challenged by a team of Swedish researchers at Uppsala Universtiy who attempted to replicate Persinger's findings using equipment from Persinger's own lab. This team, led by Pehr Granqvist, used a double-blind protocol, so that neither experimenters nor subjects knew what was being tested and who, while wearing the helmet, had the magnetic fields turned on. What Granqvist found was that under these tightly-controlled conditions, the magnetic fields had no effect whatsoever in that the subjects reported the very same sorts of experiences irrespective of whether the helmet was turned on or off. According to Granqvist, the most reasonable explanation for the reports of a sensed presence of God was *suggestibility*: according to Granqvist, the more suggestible subjects were more likely to report a sensed presence of God and other mystical experiences.[53]

Eugene d'Aquili and Andrew Newberg's neurophysiological theory of mysticism has also caught much attention.[54] According to d'Aquili and Newberg, mystical practices, such as meditation and ritual, can lead to the hyperactivation of the prefrontal cortex of the brain, which can in turn activate the hippocampus, causing it to inhibit neural signals into parts of the parietal lobes – specifically, the posterior superior parietal lobules. It is this inhibition or "deafferentation" of neural signals into the posterior superior parietal lobules that causes the experience of an "absolute unitary being" along with other kinds of mystical experiences.

The theory of d'Aquili and Newberg is highly controversial and by no means proven at this stage. Moreover, d'Aquili and Newberg admit that "tracing spiritual experience to neurological behavior does not disprove its realness ... both spiritual experiences and experiences of a more ordinary material nature are made real to the mind in the very same way – through the processing powers of the brain and the cognitive functions of the mind."[55] The neurophysiological theory by itself does not disprove the mystical experiences just as psychophysical laws governing sense experiences would not disprove those experiences.[56]

They also ask, "Why should the human brain, which evolved for the very pragmatic purpose of helping us survive, possess such an apparently impractical talent?"[57] They in fact tend to think their biology of transcendence is congenial to religion. The neurophysiological theory by itself does not disprove the mystical experiences just as psychophysical laws governing sense experiences would not disprove those experiences.[58]

The above discussions already show that regardless of the merits of the naturalistic explanations, one prior philosophical question needs to be asked: in what ways is the availability of naturalistic explanation relevant? If we infer from the availability of naturalistic explanation of a religious experience to its unveridicality, we seem to commit the genetic fallacy. Even the fact that an experience of God has proximal natural causes seems to be compatible with its ultimate origin in God. As Wainwright says:

> Suppose we are presented with a causal account of religious experience which is believed by the scientific community to be fully adequate. Are we entitled to infer that the experiences are not genuine perceptions of God, etc? We are entitled to draw this conclusion ... only if we have good reason to believe that the causes which are specified in that account can, when taken alone, i.e. in the absence of (among other things) any divine activity, produce the experiences in question. Without a disproof of the existence of God and other supra-empirical agents, it is totally unclear how we could know that this was the case.[59]

In fact, sense experiences can likewise be adequately causally explained in terms of brain processes without mentioning the perceived objects. Since this does not in itself render sense experiences unreliable or cancel their evidential force, it is not clear why the corresponding fact will do harm to religious experiences.

4.c. The Conflicting Claims Objection

Many critics argue that since the claims of religious experiences are so various and mutually contradictory, we should regard all these claims with suspicion. In other words, these conflicts show that the alleged process to form religious beliefs is not reliable. Even if we grant some force to the religious experiences, different religious experiences cancel one another's force in the end.[60]

The first question we should settle is whether the existing contradictions between religious experiences make the PC inapplicable to them. It is a totally different one from the question: "*if we grant some evidential force to religious experiences*, will such conflicts cancel this force?" To apply the PC to some experiences is to have *initial* trust in them and, if they are defeated, to salvage as much as possible from them. It does not entail that they are all or mostly reliable. There is no contradiction in saying that we should have initial trust in conflicting experiences. Let me illustrate this by the Parable of the Remnants.

Suppose a nuclear holocaust occurs and the remnants are badly hurt by radiations. Mutations occur such that during their seeing the proximal stimuli produced by external objects are *always* blended with internally generated noise. The result is that the apparent size, shape and color of a nearby object can vary for different individuals and can also vary from time to time for the same individual. The saving grace is that the noise level does not exceed the threshold which would destroy altogether the capability of object recognition. So the people can still, with difficulty, know that a *certain* object is around. The result is a kind of "vision" which can roughly locate a medium-sized object nearby but all others are blurred and unstable. Notice that the erroneous perceptions are always integrated with the roughly correct identifications. Phenomenologically speaking, we can't separate these two kinds of perceptions: the bare recognition of object versus the more detailed perception of color, shape and size.

In this case should those people accord some evidential force to their perceptions? Suppose they don't and instead they adopt initial scepticism towards their "perceptions". Namely, they insist that their perceptions have to be treated as "guilty until proven innocent". Can they demonstrate the reliability of their "perceptions" by another means? Hardly! What about the availability of tests? There may not be effective tests which have consistent results. Scepticism surely results and it would rob the people of the little information they still possess! This consequence seems to be counter-intuitive. Instead it is plausible to say the PC is applicable here. By applying it, the remnants will come to trust their ability to locate medium-sized objects while not giving undue confidence to their color and shape perceptions. The PC is "charitable" enough here without being unduly uncritical. The idea here is that although the "perceptions", described at the highest level of epistemic seeming, are grossly inconsistent, they do convey information about the reality at a lower level of description. Indeed the parable is suggestive. It shows that it is quite conceivable that even though religious experiences as a whole are not entirely accurate, they can be reasonably informative at a lower level of description. There is no a priori reason for believing that contradictions of experiences would entail their total unreliability.

Furthermore, almost all sorts of experience or cognitive practices produce conflicting beliefs. (Just think of the empiricists' "argument from illusion".) So why do we think that the presence of contradictions in religious experience should debar us from having initial trust in religious experience?

The above argument, however, does not license the irrationality of swallowing a grossly inconsistent set of beliefs. To have initial trust in contradictory experiences does not mean to accept them all. This, contrarily, is only the first step to ensure a proper initial base on which then, and only then, we can exercise our critical faculty rigorously. First, consider the alternative, the Skeptical Rule (SR), which can be defined as follows:

SR: When experiences or claims conflict with one another, we should reject all of them.

Should we adopt the SR? I don't think so. Consider the conflict of witnesses in the courts. It would be indeed stupid to reject all their accounts just because they conflict! It seems to be a rational strategy to try to reconcile their reports as much as possible. For example, a common core[61] can be identified. Take another example: suppose a phenomenon occurred very briefly which led to conflicting reports – A reported seeing an aeroplane, B a spaceship, and C an air-balloon. It is absurd to suggest that we should reject all their statements and think that nothing has ever happened! It is possible that one of them may actually be correct. At the very least we should accept the common content of their experiences. *Unidentified flying object*, vague though it is, is not a completely uninformative term. Moreover if the SR is adopted, history would also be imperiled. It is well known that historical documents are liable to massive contradictions. However we do not deduce from this phenomenon that historical enquiry is entirely pointless. The job of the historian is to utilize all these materials to reconstruct the past by harmonizing them without producing too much strain in the overall interpretation. Many historical accounts of a momentous historical event, for example, China's Cultural Revolution, are contradictory. It is difficult to determine the exact course or nature of this event but it would be preposterous to deny that the Cultural Revolution has happened. All the above examples count against the sceptical policy and show that conflict of presumptive data is not irremediable.

Consider now Martin's conflicting claims objection to religious experience, Martin states:

> Swinburne advises us when considering a new sense to assume first that by and large things are what they seem.... This initial assumption must be quickly abandoned in the case of religious experiences. religious experiences are often conflicting, and thus things *cannot* be what they seem.[62]

Suppose Martin is correct about the degree of conflicts of the religious experiences. Does it follow that the whole lot of religious experiences has no evidential force at all and we can just dismiss them? If my arguments are so far correct, this conclusion is unwarranted. The conflicts of religious experience may indeed show the type-unreliability of religious experience at the highest level of description. However, a certain common core can still be extracted from the diverse religious experiences at a lower level of description. Let's elaborate the Parable of the Remnants. Consider their "perceptions" of the sun. When they look at the sun, they see some object *up there* but one sees it as round while another as square and so on. Even worse, for an individual he sees it as square on Monday but round on Tuesday and hexagonal on Wednesday and so on. Obviously an object can't be both round and square at the same time. So the object *cannot* be identical to what it seems at most of the times. However, by the application of the PC, the people at least can arrive at the conclusion that there is a bright object of *some* shape up there. There is no need to adopt a reductionist account of the "sun" as nothing but productions of their minds, that is, to discount their experiences of the sun as absolutely unreliable. Similarly, despite the conflicts of the religious experiences, they still point to the fact that there is another realm *up there* or *beyond*. In other words, although the religious experiences taken as a whole hardly point to a determinate supernatural reality, they still cohere in that they all point to *something beyond* the naturalistic world, that is, the Transcendent realm.

The most important contradiction remains has to do with the *nature of the ultimate reality*. Is it personal or impersonal? I believe the "contradiction" is not as stark as it is commonly made out to be. For example, Davis carefully sifts through the data of diverse religious experiences and suggests a common core.[63] If this attempt can be backed up by detailed and substantial arguments, then it can plausibly be maintained that we can extract a common core from the diverse religious experiences which at least points to the fact that this spatio-temporal world is not the Ultimate. There is more to reality than what we can see. Religious experience as a loose type at least supports this modest conclusion. It is a tricky question whether the argument from religious experience can be used to support some particularistic religious traditions. I have a fuller treatment elsewhere,[64] and argue that theistic experience is still largely warranted despite the diversity of religious experiences.

5. Conclusion

The ARE is still hotly contended. I just hope to highlight the crucial issues surrounding this debate, and show that there are weighty considerations for both sides. Swinburne's route of taking religious experience as prima facie evidence for the transcendent realm is a promising one but his approach depends crucially on the PC, the further defence of which will inevitably raise many deep epistemological issues. In the end, the epistemic assessment of religious experience will probably depend on the ability of this radically new epistemology to withstand objections.

It is difficult to have a quick solution here because problems of circularity always loom in the background. How one judges the epistemic status of religious experience depends crucially on one's fundamental epistemic principles. Since there is no consensus about fundamental epistemic principles, each side of this debate needs to defend his epistemology. But epistemic principles like PC or Phenomenal Conservatism need to be taken seriously and cannot be simply dismissed. So even if the ARE may not be able to gain consensus, it is not as easy as some critics think to show that religious experiences are entirely unreliable, and some forms of ARE may well be defensible, especially for those who have vivid religious experiences themselves.

Notes

1   H. H. Farmer, *The World and God* (London: Nisbet and Co. Ltd, 1935); Albert C. Knudson, *The Validity of Religious Experience* (New York: Abingdon, 1937).
2   Farmer, *The World and God*, 158.
3   See Keith E Yandell, *The Epistemology of Religious Experience* (Cambridge University Press, 1993), ch.8. I also eschew the claim that religious experience has to be ineffable. I take the core of truth in this claim is that God is intrinsically beyond the capacity of human language to describe *fully*. This does not entail that human concept as such is not applicable to God.

4 Robert Oakes continues to defend some form of self-authentication. See Robert Oakes, "Transparent Veridicality and Phenomenological Imposters: The Telling Issue," *Faith And Philosophy* 22 no.4 (2005): 413–425.
5 C. D. Broad, *Religion, Philosophy and Psychical Research* (London: Routledge and Kegan Paul, 1953), 197.
6 John Hick, *Faith and Knowledge*. 2nd edition (London: Macmillan, 1967); Elton Trueblood, *Philosophy of Religion* (Grand Rapids, Michigan: Baker, 1957), ch.11; Rem Edwards, *Reason and Religion: An Introduction to the Philosophy of Religion* (New York: Harcourt Brace Jovanovich, 1972), chs.13–14.
7 Charles Taliaferro, *Contemporary Philosophy of Religion* (Oxford: Blackwell, 1998), 3.
8 Richard Swinburne, *The Existence of God* (Oxford: Clarendon Press, 1979), ch.13.
9 William Rowe, "'Religious Experience and the Principle of Credulity," *International Journal for Philosophy of Religion* 13 (1982): 85–92; Michael Martin, "The Principle of Credulity and Religious Experience," *Religious Studies* 22 (1986): 79–93; Gary Gutting, *Religious Belief and Religious Skepticism* (Notre dame: University of Notre Dame Press, 1982).
10 Caroline Davis, *The Evidential Force of Religious Experience* (Oxford: Clarendon Press, 1989); George Wall, *Religious Experience and Religious Belief* (Lanham, MD: University Press of America, 1995); Jerome Gellman, *Experience of God and the Rationality of Theistic Belief* (Ithaca: Cornell University Press, 1997); Jerome Gellman, *Mystical Experience of God: A Philosophical Inquiry* (Aldershot: Ashgate, 2001).
11 William Wainwright, *Mysticism* (Brighton: The Harvester Press, 1981); Yandell, *The Epistemology of Religious Experience*.
12 William Alston, *Perceiving God: The Epistemology of Religious Experience* (Ithaca and London: Cornell University Press, 1991).
13 Kai-man Kwan, "The Argument from Religious Experience," in *The Blackwell Companion to Natural Theology*, eds. William Craig and J. P. Moreland (Oxford: Blackwell, 2009), 498-552.
14 Kai-man Kwan. *The Rainbow of Experiences, Critical Trust, and God: A Defense of Holistic Empiricism* (New York: Continuum, 2011).
15 Michael Huemer, *Skepticism & the Veil of Perception* (Lanham, Maryland: Rowan & Littlefield, 2001), 99.
16 Michael Bergmann, "Externalist Justification and the Role of Seemings," *Philosophical Studies* 166 (2013): 165.
17 James Pryor, "The Skeptic and the Dogmatist," *Nous* 34 (2000): 517–549.
18 Chris Tucker, "Why Open-minded People Should Embrace Dogmatism," *Philosophical Perspectives* 24 (2010): 529–45.
19 William Lycan, "'Phenomenal Conservatism and the Principle of Credulity," in *Seemings and Justifications: New Essays on Dogmatism & Phenomenal Conservatism*, ed. Chris Tucker (Oxford: Oxford University Press, 2013), 293–305.
20 John Hick, *Faith and Knowledge*, 205.
21 Ibid., 210.
22 Gutting, *Religious Belief and Religious Skepticism*, 2–3.
23 Antony Flew, *God and Philosophy* (London: Hutchinson and Co. Ltd., 1966), 129.
24 Peter Donovan, *Interpreting Religious Experience* (London: Sheldon Press, 1979), ch.5.
25 Edwards, *Reason and Religion*, 318.
26 A. J. Ayer, *The Problem of Knowledge* (London: Macmikllan, 1956), ch.2; Michael Williams, *Groundless Belief: An Essay on the Possibility of Epistemology* (Oxford: Basil Blackwell, 1977), 14ff.

27 Gutting, *Religious Belief and Religious Skepticism*, 147.
28 Alston, *Perceiving God*, 255.
29 David Papineau, *Theory and Meaning* (Oxford: Clarendon Press, 1979).
30 Nancy Cartwright, "How We Relate Theory to Observation," in *World Changes: Thomas Kuhn and the Nature of Science*, ed. Paul Horwich (Cambridge, Massachusetts: The MIT Press, 1993), 259.
31 Davis, *The Evidential Force of Religious Experience*, 149.
32 Ibid., 144.
33 Ibid., 153.
34 Ibid., 163ff. I have also provided a critique of the constructivist view of religious experience in Kai-man Kwan, *The Rainbow of Experiences, Critical Trust, and God: A Defense of Holistic*, chapter 16.
35 Edwards, *Reason and Religion*, 318.
36 Ibid., 320–21.
37 Davis, *The Evidential Force of Religious Experience*, 143.
38 Swinburne, *The Existence of God*, chapter 13.
39 Richard Swinburne, *The Evolution of the Soul* (Oxford: Clarendon Press, 1986), 13–15.
40 C. B. Martin, *Religious Belief* (Ithaca: Cornell University Press, 1959), 87–88.
41 George Mavrodes, *Belief in God: A Study in the Epistemology of Religion* (Washington, DC: University Press of America, 1970), 75–76.
42 Michael Martin, "The Principle of Credulity," 85–86.
43 William Alston, "Religious Diversity and Perceptual Knowledge of God," *Faith and Philosophy* 5 (1988): 436.
44 Swinburne, *The Existence of God*, 256.
45 John Mackie, *The Miracle of Theism* (Oxford: Clarendon Press, 1982), 183.
46 See Hans Eysenck, *Decline and Fall of the Freudian Empire* (London: Penguin Books, 1985); Richard Webster, *Why Freud Was Wrong: Sin, Science and Psychoanalysis* (Fontana, 1995).
47 See Robert Banks, "Religion as Projection: Re-appraisal of Freud's Theory," *Religious Studies* 9 (1973): 401–26.; Adolf Grunbaum, "Psychoanalysis and Theism," *Monist* 70 (1987): 152–192.
48 Aku Visala, *Naturalism, Theism and the Cognitive Study of Religion: Religion Explained?* (Farnham, Surrey: Ashgate, 2011), 1.
49 William Alston, *Perceiving God*, 230.
50 See my detailed examination of projectionism in Kai-man Kwan, "Are Religious Beliefs Human Projections?" in *A Religious Atheist? Critical Essays on the Work of Lloyd Geering*, eds. Raymond Pelly and Peter Stuart (Dunedin, New Zealand: Otago University Press, 2006), 41–66.
51 Davis, *The Evidential Force of Religious Experience*, 220; Antoine Vergote, *Religion, Belief and Unbelief: A Psychological Study* (Amsterdam: Rodopi, 1997), 197ff.
52 Michael Persinger, *Neuropsychological Bases of God Beliefs* (New York: Praeger, 1987), x.
53 Pehr Grandqvist, et al. "Sacred Presence & Mystical Experiences Are Predicted by Suggestibility, Not by the Application of Transcranial Weak Complex Magnetic Fields" ed. Justin Barrett, *Psychology of Religion: Critical Concepts in Religious Studies, Volume 1: Explaining Religion & Spirituality* (London & New York: Routledge, 2010): 367.
54 Andrew Newberg, Eugene D'Aquili and Vince Rause, *Why God Won't Go Away: Brain Science and the Biology of Belief*.
55 Andrew Newberg, Eugene D'Aquili and Vince Rause, *Why God Won't Go Away: Brain Science and the Biology of Belief*, 37.

56 Gellman, *Mystical Experience of God*, 99.
57 Newberg et al, *Why God Won't Go Away: Brain Science and the Biology of Belief*, 123.
58 Gellman, *Mystical Experience of God*, 99.
59 William Wainwright, "Natural Explanations and Religious Experience," *Ratio* 15 (1973): 100–101.
60 Flew, *God and Philosophy*, 126–127; Michael Martin, "The Principle of Credulity," 87–88.
61 Indeed, it is not the case that a "common core" has to be shared by *all* the eye-witness accounts. *Sometimes* it is sufficient that it is shared by the large majority of the accounts, provided that either the error of the deviant witness in that aspect can be explained or overwhelming explanatory power is attained by adopting the common core.
62 Michael Martin, *Atheism: A Philosophical Justification* (Philadelphia: Temple University Press, 1990), 183–184.
63 Davis, *The Evidential Force of Religious Experience*, 191.
64 Kai-man Kwan, "Is the Critical Trust Approach to Religious Experience Incompatible with Religious Particularism? A Reply to Michael Martin and John Hick," *Faith and Philosophy* 20, no. 2 (2003): 152–169.

Bibliography

Alston, William. "Religious Diversity and Perceptual Knowledge of God." *Faith and Philosophy* 5 (1988): 433–448.
Alston, William. *Perceiving God: The Epistemology of Religious Experience*. Ithaca and London: Cornell University Press, 1991.
Ayer, A. J. *The Problem of Knowledge*. London: Macmillan, 1956.
Banks, Robert. "Religion as Projection: Re-appraisal of Freud's Theory." *Religious Studies* 9, (1973): 401–426.
Bergmann, Michael. "Externalist Justification & the Role of Seemings." *Philosophical Studies* 166 (2013): 163–184.
Broad, C. D. *Religion, Philosophy and Psychical Research*. London: Routledge and Kegan Paul, 1953.
Cartwright, Nancy. "How We Relate Theory to Observation," in *World Changes: Thomas Kuhn and the Nature of Science*, edited by Paul Horwich. Cambridge, Massachusetts: The MIT Press, 1993, 259–273.
Davis, Caroline. *The Evidential Force of Religious Experience*. Oxford: Clarendon Press, 1989.
Donovan, Peter. *Interpreting Religious Experience*. London: Sheldon Press, 1979.
Edwards, Rem. *Reason and Religion: An Introduction to the Philosophy of Religion*. New York: Harcourt Brace Jovanovich, 1972.
Eysenck, Hans. *Decline and Fall of the Freudian Empire*. London: Penguin Books, 1985.
Farmer, H. H. *The World and God*. London: Nisbet and Co. Ltd., 1935.
Flew, Antony. *God and Philosophy*. London: Hutchinson and Co. Ltd., 1966.
Gellman, Jerome. *Experience of God and the Rationality of Theistic Belief*. Ithaca: Cornell University Press, 1997.
Gellman, Jerome. *Mystical Experience of God: A Philosophical Inquiry*. Aldershot: Ashgate, 2001.
Grandqvist, Pehr, et al. "Sacred Presence and Mystical Experiences Are Predicted by Suggestibility, Not by the Application of Transcranial Weak Complex Magnetic Fields."

In *Psychology of Religion: Critical Concepts in Religious Studies, Volume 1: Explaining Religion & Spirituality*, edited by Justin Barrett (London & New York: Routledge), (2010): 365–376.

Grunbaüm, Adolf. "Psychoanalysis and Theism." *Monist* 70 (1987): 152–192.

Gutting, Gary. *Religious Belief and Religious Skepticism.* Notre Dame: University of Notre Dame Press, 1982.

Hick, John. *Faith and Knowledge.* 2nd edition. London: Macmillan, 1967.

Huemer, Michael. *Skepticism & the Veil of Perception.* Lanham, Maryland: Rowan & Littlefield, 2001.

Kwan, Kai-man. "Is the Critical Trust Approach to Religious Experience Incompatible with Religious Particularism? A Reply to Michael Martin and John Hick." *Faith and Philosophy* 20, no. 2 (2003): 152–169.

Knudson, Albert C. *The Validity of Religious Experience.* New York: Abingdon, 1937.

Kwan, Kai-man. "Are Religious Beliefs Human Projections?" In *A Religious Atheist? Critical Essays on the Work of Lloyd Geering*, edited by Raymond Pelly and Peter Stuart. Dunedin, New Zealand: Otago University Press, 2006, 41–66.

Kwan, Kai-man. "The Argument from Religious Experience." In *the Blackwell Companion to Natural Theology*, edited by William Craig and J. P. Moreland. Oxford: Blackwell, 2009, 498–552.

Kwan, Kai-man. *The Rainbow of Experiences, Critical Trust, and God: A Defense of Holistic Empiricism.* New York: Continuum, 2011.

Lycan, William G. "Phenomenal Conservatism & the Principle of Credulity." In *Seemings & Justifications: New Essays on Dogmatism & Phenomenal Conservatism*, edited by Chris Tucker. Oxford: Oxford University Press, 2013, 293–305.

Mackie, John. *The Miracle of Theism.* Oxford: Clarendon Press, 1982.

Martin, C. B. *Religious Belief.* Ithaca: Cornell University Press, 1959.

Martin, Michael. "The Principle of Credulity and Religious Experience." *Religious Studies* 22 (1986): 79–93.

Martin, Michael. *Atheism: A Philosophical Justification.* Philadelphia: Temple University Press, 1990.

Mavrodes, George. *Belief in God: A Study in the Epistemology of Religion.* Washington, DC: University Press of America, 1970.

Newberg, Andrew, Eugene D'Aquili and Vince Rause. *Why God Won't Go Away: Brain Science and the Biology of Belief.* New York: Ballantine Books, 2001.

Oakes, Robert, "Transparent Veridicality and Phenomenological Imposters: The Telling Issue," *Faith And Philosophy* 22, no.4 (2005): 413–425.

Papineau, David. *Theory and Meaning.* Oxford: Clarendon Press, 1979.

Persinger, Michael A. *Neuropsychological Bases of God Beliefs.* New York: Praeger, 1987.

Pryor, James. "The Skeptic & the Dogmatist." *Nous* 34 (2000): 517–549.

Rowe, William. "Religious Experience and the Principle of Credulity." *International Journal for Philosophy of Religion* 13 (1982): 85–92.

Swinburne, Richard. *The Existence of God.* Oxford: Clarendon Press, 1979.

Swinburne, Richard. *The Evolution of the Soul.* Oxford: Clarendon Press, 1986.

Swinburne, Richard. "Does Theism Need a Theodicy?" *Canadian Journal of Philosophy* 18 (1988): 287–312.

Taliaferro, Charles. *Contemporary Philosophy of Religion.* Oxford: Blackwell, 1998.

Trueblood, Elton. *Philosophy of Religion.* Grand Rapids, Michigan: Baker, 1957.

Tucker, C. " 'Why Open-minded People Should Embrace Dogmatism." *Philosophical Perspectives* 24 (2010): 529–45.

Vergote, Antoine. *Religion, Belief and Unbelief: A Psychological Study.* Amsterdam: Rodopi, 1997.

Visala, Aku. *Naturalism, Theism & the Cognitive Study of Religion: Religion Explained?* Farnham, Surrey: Ashgate, 2011.

Wainwright, William. "Natural Explanations and Religious Experience." *Ratio* 15 (1973): 98–101.

Wainwright, William. *Mysticism.* Brighton: The Harvester Press, 1981.

Wall, George. *Religious Experience and Religious Belief.* Lanham, MD: University Press of America, 1995.

Webster, Richard. *Why Freud Was Wrong: Sin, Science and Psychoanalysis.* Fontana, 1995.

Williams, Michael. *Groundless Belief: An Essay on the Possibility of Epistemology.* Oxford: Basil Blackwell, 1977.

Yandell, Keith E. *The Epistemology of Religious Experience.* Cambridge: Cambridge University Press, 1993.

15

The Wager Argument

Joshua Golding

1. Summary

Traditional arguments for the rationality of religious belief such as the ontological, cosmological, and teleological arguments seek to demonstrate that God exists or to show that God's existence is probable on the basis of the evidence of the senses. These may be referred to as *cognitive* arguments since they aim to show that we can know with certainty or probability that God exists. In contrast, the argument known as "Pascal's Wager"[1] aims to show that it is rational to believe in God, based on consideration of the potential value of having this belief. Hence, the Wager may be referred to as a *pragmatic* argument for belief in God.

A summary of Pascal's Wager is as follows. We are faced with a decision about whether or not to believe in God. Since God is conceived as infinite and the human mind is finite, it is impossible for us to assess whether or not God exists. Using our cognitive capacities alone, we cannot make this decision rationally. But the decision is forced. We must somehow decide what to believe. Therefore, we should base our decision on consideration of what possible effect belief (or disbelief) in God will have on our welfare or happiness. At first glance, it seems we have everything to gain and nothing to lose if we choose to believe in God. For, if God exists and we believe in him, we shall attain great happiness in the afterlife. If God does not exist, and we believe in him, we haven't lost much. (Momentarily, Pascal will refine this last step.) On the other hand, if we choose not to believe in God, we shall not attain great happiness under any circumstance. The following diagram or "matrix" from Hacking[2] represents the features of this decision problem:

	Relevant possible states of affairs and outcomes:	
	God exists	*God does not exist*
Option 1: Believe in God	great gain	no great gain
Option 2: Do not believe in God	no great gain	no great gain

Under the assumptions set out in the diagram, Pascal claims the rational choice is to believe in God. Using modern terminology, the option of belief in God "dominates" over the option of disbelief, since it has a better result if God exists and no worse result if God does not exist. However, Pascal reconsiders the initial and perhaps hasty assumption that one has nothing to lose by being a believer. For, if it turns out God does not exist, the believer will have believed in vain and perhaps lost many goods he would have enjoyed otherwise. So, Pascal refines the argument by introducing the notion that if God exists, the gain in the next world for the believer is not merely great but *infinite*. Pascal holds fast to the assumption that one has no chance of attaining the infinite gain if God does not exist, nor if one opts for disbelief. (Interestingly, Pascal does *not* claim that the disbeliever will suffer great harm if God exists; he claims only that the disbeliever will *lose* the infinite gain.) The following matrix represents this refined version of the decision problem:

	Relevant possible states of affairs and outcomes:	
	God exists	God does not exist
Option 1: Believe in God	infinite gain	some finite loss
Option 2: Do not believe in God	some finite gain	some finite gain

Given these assumptions, Pascal argues again that it is more rational to choose belief rather than disbelief. For, an option which has even a small probability of gaining infinite value is a more rational choice than an option which has a high probability of gaining a very large finite value. Using modern terminology, the option of belief in God has a higher *expected value* than the option of disbelief. The expected value of an option is computed by (1) multiplying the probability of each possible state of affairs by the value of the outcome on that option, and (2) summing all the products obtained, for all possible states of affairs on that option. The rationale behind the expected value principle is that it provides a sensible procedure for taking into account both the probabilities and the potential values of available options. Thus, if (as Pascal assumes) the probability of God's existence is ½, the expected value of belief in God may be computed as follows:

½ × infinite gain + ½ × some finite loss = infinite gain.

Note that the same result would be attained even if the probability of God's existence is less than ½, so long as it is assumed to be a real probability greater than zero. Furthermore, given Pascal's assumptions, the expected value for not believing in God is computed as follows:

½ × finite gain + ½ × some finite gain = some finite gain.

The result is that the expected value of belief in God is infinite, and the expected value of disbelief is finite. Hence, belief in God is the rational choice. At this stage, Pascal considers one final objection. Having been shown that it is pragmatically rational to believe in God, the atheist may complain that he can't help himself; the fact is that he does not believe in God. What's an atheist to do? Pascal responds by recommending that if a person acts and speaks like a religious believer, sooner or later he will become one. While we may not be able to choose to believe in some proposition, we can choose to do certain things which are likely to induce that belief. In closing, Pascal intimates that a person who follows this route will ultimately arrive at a devout and sincere belief in God, in which the calculation of the Wager is somehow left behind.

2. Pascal's Wager: critique

So much for a summary of Pascal's Wager. Since its publication, the argument has been criticized on several grounds. While many philosophers regard the Wager as woefully unsuccessful, since the late twentieth century a number of philosophers have come to its defense. We may group the standard objections into four categories. We shall also discuss defenses and revisions of the Wager.

(1) One set of objections concerns Pascal's claims at the outset regarding the cognitive features of the decision problem. Pascal claims that our cognitive capacities are unable to make the decision about whether to believe in God. The only ground Pascal supplies for this claim is that the idea of God is infinite and the human mind is finite. It doesn't follow that one cannot cognitively assess whether or not God exists. After all, we are able to form some conception of an infinite being; otherwise we would not be having this discussion. Moreover, infinity is not the only feature of our concept of God. Pascal himself conceives of God as intelligent, powerful, benevolent, and yet also as a judge, since God rewards those who believe in him. These features of our concept of God may be (and indeed have been) used in cognitive arguments for, or against, God's existence. At the very least, Pascal needs to defend more substantively the claim that cognitive reason is unable to assess whether God exists.

A related objection concerns Pascal's apparent assumption that the probability of God's existence should be assigned ½. Pascal uses this assumption as a basis for saying that the decision to believe should be settled on pragmatic grounds. If God's existence (or nonexistence) had a probability of greater than ½, the move to pragmatic considerations would not be justified. (The notion that Pascal advocates throwing cognitive reason to the winds and making the decision solely on pragmatic grounds is a misreading of the Wager.) It may be argued that if our cognitive capacities cannot decide whether or not to believe in God, under such circumstances the cognitively rational choice is either to (a) leave the probability of God's existence unassigned, or (b) adopt the metaphysically more parsimonious hypothesis that God does not exist. A defense or reformulation of the Wager needs to show why these options are misguided, or why the argument succeeds in spite of these options.

Defenders of the Wager might respond that the argument is addressed to a specific audience, namely, those who find the cognitive arguments for and against God's existence inconclusive,[3] or those who find themselves in the predicament of believing that God's existence and nonexistence have roughly the same probability. However, even if the Wager can be salvaged in this manner, still another objection concerns Pascal's claim that the choice between belief in God and disbelief is "forced." If the decision is whether to *believe that God exists* or to believe *that God does not exist*, there seems to be a third option, namely, to *believe neither hypothesis*. Where *p* is any sentence, there is a genuine cognitive difference between *believing that not-p*, and *not believing p*. An analogy is helpful here. Some people believe that there exists life on other planets, and some people believe it is not the case that there exists life on other planets. But it seems quite possible to suspend belief, that is, to believe neither of these propositions. It is sometimes thought that Pascal can easily respond by saying that suspension of belief in God's existence is tantamount to believing that God does not exist, since God will not reward agnostics any more than he will reward atheists. But, aside from the problem of how Pascal can justify this theological claim, the objection remains that so long as suspension of belief is a genuine option, it is arguably the most cognitively rational choice, even if it does involve losing infinite bliss. By Pascal's own lights, if suspension of belief is a real possibility, the move to pragmatic considerations is blocked.

Still another possible revision is to recast the Wager as an argument in support of some religious commitment other than belief, such as the *assumption for practical purpose that God exists*.[4] It is a common occurrence that it may be pragmatically rational to assume some proposition is true, even if it is cognitively rational to suspend belief in that proposition. For example, a scientist might not know whether a cure for cancer is attainable. However, it may be pragmatically rational to assume for practical purpose that such a cure is attainable. A similar strategy might work in the case of religion. Even if there is insufficient cognitive proof for God's existence, it might very well be the case that there is pragmatic justification for assuming that God exists for practical purposes, if it can be shown that the only way or the best way of attaining some very valuable good is by making that assumption. This strategy escapes several criticisms of the Wager which focus on its attempt to provide a pragmatic justification of *belief*. We shall return later to this last suggestion.

(2) A second class of objections involves technical worries concerning the notion of an infinite value, and especially concerning the use of an infinite value in an expected value calculation. First, in what sense can a finite creature attain an infinite good? The notion of an infinite good needs to be explicated and defended. One natural way Pascal might begin to do this is by using the notion of God. God is conceived as the infinitely good being, and the infinite value is to be conceived as consisting in some kind of relationship with God in which a person participates or partakes of God's infinite goodness.[5] Whether this can be done successfully is beyond our scope here. But, as we shall see later, such a strategy would strengthen the Wager Argument in other ways as well.

Still, even on the assumption that an infinite value makes sense, it seems one should be wary of using an infinite value in an expected value calculation. In the course of his argument, Pascal claims that a tiny probability of attaining an infinite value always outstrips any large chance of gaining any large finite value. However, it also seems (absurdly) that an option that has a tiny probability of attaining an infinite value has the same expected value as an option with a large probability of resulting in an infinite value. For example, suppose that on one bet I have a ½ chance of winning an infinite value, and on a second bet I have a 1/20 chance of winning an infinite value. Common sense would say that it is rational to choose the first bet over the second bet. Yet if we employ the expected value calculus, the expected value of *both* bets turns out to be infinite! Perhaps the lesson to be derived is that one should not use infinite value in any expected value calculation at all.

One way in which proponents of the Wager might respond is to concede that in cases where an infinite value is at stake, one should not apply the expected value calculation directly, but rather one should treat that infinite value as *no worse than some astronomically high finite value*. Suppose that on bet (a) I have a ½ chance of attaining infinite value, and on bet (b) I have a 1/20 chance of attaining infinite value. If I apply the expected value in the standard way, I will indeed attain the counterintuitive result that both choices are equally rational. But if I treat the infinite value as no worse than some very high finite value, then the expected value of the first option will be higher than that of the second one. For, a ½ chance of attaining some very high finite value is obviously higher than a 1/20 chance of attaining that same value. On the other hand, suppose that on bet (c), I have a 1/20 chance of attaining an infinite value, whereas on bet (d) I have a ½ chance of winning a large finite value, call it z. I should indeed hesitate to apply the expected value directly to this case. However, I know that there is some finite value high enough—call it h—for a 1/20 chance of winning h to be preferable to a ½ chance of winning z. In particular, so long as h is more than 10 times z, the expected value of bet (c) would be higher than that of bet (d). But I know that an infinite value is no worse (indeed it is much better!) than h. Hence, I can safely conclude that (c) is the better bet.

Still another possible revision is to replace the notion of an infinite value with the notion of a supreme good that is *finite but qualitatively superior to any other competing good*.[6] One kind of good is qualitatively superior to another kind of good if any tiny bit of that first good is better than any large amount of the second kind of good, and any incremental increase in that first good is better than any large increase in that second kind of good. Using the expected value principle, even a tiny probability of attaining the first kind of good would be higher than a large probability of attaining any amount of a lesser kind of good. Yet, since that good is finite, a higher chance of attaining that superior good would be preferable to a lower chance of attaining that same kind of good. The strategy would then be to argue that the kind of good one might attain by having a certain kind of relationship with God is qualitatively superior to any other competing good. Since that good is conceived as finite, it would follow that any course of action which is deemed to have a higher chance of attaining that good would be more rational than any course of action which has a lesser chance of attaining that same good. We shall return to this strategy shortly.

(3) A third set of objections concerns Pascal's assumptions regarding the link between having certain specific religious beliefs and the attainment of an infinite gain (if it is attainable at all). Pascal assumes without argument that the only possibility of attaining an infinite gain is that a God (of a certain sort) exists and one believes in him. This raises what is probably the most widely discussed objection to the Wager, namely, the "problem of other gods." Pascal seems blithely to ignore several possible states of affairs. Just to list a few, perhaps God is all-forgiving, and he rewards everyone with infinite bliss in the afterlife, regardless of their beliefs. Alternatively, perhaps God rewards only those whose belief in him is *not* motivated by pragmatic considerations.

Still another possibility is that God rewards only certain theists, say for example, Muslims, but not Christians. Or perhaps he rewards only those who engage in some arbitrary or absurd action, such as jumping up and down three times every Tuesday. Alternatively, perhaps God will reward all and only atheists. Indeed, some critics of Pascal have attempted to use the Wager strategy as an argument for atheism as the safest choice under the circumstances.[7] Finally, although this is less commonly suggested, Pascal ignores the possibility that some infinite gain might be attainable even if there is no God at all. If any of these possibilities are considered, Pascal's Wager fails to establish its conclusion that it is pragmatically rational to believe in (a certain kind of) God.

Clearly, it would help Pascal's argument if there were some way of taking into account the relative probabilities of various hypotheses concerning what is the most plausible and/or probable way in which one might attain the ultimate gain. However, the present objection is exacerbated when taken together with the previous objection. As noted above, if Pascal relies on the strategy of trying to show that the expected value of belief in God is infinite, the problem arises that an option that has even a tiny chance of attaining infinite value is also infinite. Hence, it seems that so long as there is even some tiny probability that one can attain infinite value without believing in (a certain kind of) God, Pascal's argument fails.

By the same token, if the objection described previously can be met in either one of the two ways described above, then the present objection is mitigated, if not completely dissolved. Suppose we do not treat the ultimate gain of having a certain relationship with God as infinite but rather as *no worse than some very astronomically high finite value*. Or suppose we conceive of it as *finite but qualitatively superior to all other non-religious goods*. On either of these strategies, it turns out that an option which has a higher probability of resulting in that supreme (but finite) value has a higher expected value than any option which has a lower probability of resulting in that value. In this way, the relative probabilities of various hypotheses about how one might attain the supreme value become relevant.

With this in hand, defenders of the Wager could respond to the "problem of other gods" by arguing that it is more likely that the supreme gain will be attained if (a traditional sort of) God exists than if not. The strategy here is to establish a conceptual link between the traditional monotheistic conception of God and the conception of a supreme value. For example, it could be argued that only a supremely good and powerful being could supply a kind of good that is either astronomically high or qualitatively superior to any other competing good. Alternatively, it could be argued that the ultimate gain is best conceived as a relationship in which one partakes or participates in the goodness of a supremely good being, who is qualitatively superior to any other possible being. If this is correct, the kind of God who would reward all and only those who jump up and down three times every Tuesday is not the kind of God which can supply the best kind of good. In this way, it could be argued that it is more plausible that one will attain the supreme value if a certain traditional sort of God exists than if not. This in turn implies that it is more probable that one will succeed in attaining the supreme value if one casts one's lot with traditional theism rather than agnosticism or atheism.

Even if this strategy works, two problems still linger. First, how does one know which theistic religion to choose? Differently stated, why should one be a Christian rather than a Jew or a Muslim (or vice versa)? However, once the supreme value is no longer conceived as infinite, defenders of the Wager may respond that (1) one should choose the religion which seems most probably true on other grounds, or (2) one should at least choose some version of theism over non-theism. For, if there are equally plausible ways of attaining the supreme value, then they are all equally rational to choose. But one should choose at least *one* of those ways over none at all.

Still, a second lingering problem concerns the assumption that a *belief* in God is necessary or even conducive to the attainment of the supreme good. Suppose it is true that I will attain the supreme good only if a God of a certain sort exists. Why should I think that belief in God is necessary or conducive to the attainment of that supreme good? One possible response is that the doctrine that belief is necessary for attaining the ultimate value happens to be taught by the religion which seems overall to be the most probable of all available candidates. Of course, this response will only work if indeed it can be shown that the religion in question is more probably true than others. Another possible response is that if the good is conceived as a relationship with God, then I can only have that relationship if I believe in God. However, that does not in itself show that having the belief is itself conducive to attaining the relationship. Once again, a convenient strategy is to replace the attempt to justify a belief in God with the attempt to justify a *pragmatic assumption* that God exists, for the purpose of pursuing a good relationship with God.[8] If indeed one can attain the supreme value only if there is a God, then it is rational to guide one's actions on the assumption that there is a God, for the purpose of pursing that relationship. We shall return to this strategy shortly.

(4) The fourth set of objections claims that the Wager recommends that we do something immoral or religiously inappropriate. Suppose one could show that belief in God is our "best bet." Still, is it morally proper to believe in something on the basis of self-interest? Is it religiously pious to do so, even if God does exist? Moreover, Pascal's closing recommendation that one should get oneself to believe by acting as a believer seems to constitute a form of self-brainwashing.

Pascal might very well respond as follows. Surely there is nothing wrong with pursuing one's own self-interest, so long as one is not doing anything immoral in the process. The question is whether *believing* something on the basis of self-interest is somehow immoral or inappropriate. Now, Pascal has already argued that in this particular case, (a) cognitive reason cannot make the decision about whether or not to believe in God, and (b) we are forced to make a decision. If Pascal is right about these claims, then we have no choice but to make the decision on non-cognitive grounds. Since we are forced to make the decision on non-cognitive grounds, we might as well do what is in our best interest.

The same point applies in defense of his closing recommendation that one act as a believer. By Pascal's lights, the atheist's belief is just as cognitively unfounded as the theist's belief. Both are in the position of believing as a result of non-cognitive considerations. Perhaps the atheist's belief is a result of habit, or upbringing, or simply the desire to avoid the inconveniences of church. Arguably, the claim that it is immoral to "get oneself to believe" a proposition is valid only if one has the option of cognitively adjudicating whether or not to believe that proposition. Pascal has already argued that in this case, cognitive adjudication is not possible. To claim that he is wrong about that is to revert to other criticisms discussed above.

Moreover, with the regard to the worry about "self-interest," Pascal can easily reformulate the argument as an appeal to consideration of what is the best possible condition for a person to attain. The traditional conception of the afterlife is not merely one of *subjective* pleasure or bliss. It is also conceived as the *objectively* best possible state. Nothing could be better than having the best possible relationship with the best possible being (i.e., God). The only reason Pascal repeatedly uses the term "happiness" in the Wager is because he assumes his audience is (crassly?) self-interested. But for those who are interested in pursuing the best possible life, Pascal could also argue that taking a shot at beatitude is the best possible choice from a moral point of view. In fact, it has been argued that Pascal's strategy can be used to show that one has the obligation to help others become believers, since by doing so one furthers their chances of attaining what is best for *them*.[9] In short, the appeal to self-interest does not exclude an appeal to moral considerations as well.

The objection that a pragmatically based belief is *religiously* inappropriate can only be made from some religious standpoint. And, from a Christian point of view, there is arguably nothing wrong with believing in God as a means to personal gain. On the contrary, the Bible often exhorts us to believe and to worship because it is in our best interest to do so. The same is true for Judaism and Islam. Of course, this may not be the ideal or the only reason to believe in God, but it is certainly a common theme in many world religions. Pascal himself intimates toward the end of the argument that the Wager may be viewed as a stepping stone toward a more mature form of belief in God, to be developed later on in the believer's life or perhaps in some future state after death.

Alternatively, the Wager might be revised as a justification for some form of religious commitment other than belief, such as an assumption for practical purpose that God exists.[10] Suppose we grant that it is morally and intellectually problematic to *believe* some cognitively dubious proposition on pragmatic grounds. Surely, it need not be morally or intellectually problematic to assume that same proposition for practical purposes. It will be pragmatically rational to make that assumption, if the potential value of making that assumption is higher than that of not doing so. If that value is conceived as the best possible objective state for a person to be in, it may even be morally obligatory to make that assumption.

3. Concluding remarks

We have discussed several objections to the Wager and various ways in which defenders of the Wager might respond. Criticisms concern Pascal's claims that reason is unable to assess whether God exists and that the choice is forced; technical worries concerning the notion of infinite value; Pascal's assumptions linking a belief in (a certain sort of) God with the attainment of infinite value; and finally, moral and intellectual qualms about pragmatic justification of belief. We have discussed different strategies for defending and revising the Wager. For many philosophers, the Wager is hopelessly flawed.

In my opinion, the most promising strategy is to (1) replace the notion of an infinite value with a value that is finite but qualitatively superior to any other kind of good, and (2) replace the attempt to justify a *belief* in God with the attempt to pragmatically justify an *assumption for practical purpose* that God exists. The burden would then be to show why it is plausible to conceive of a certain relationship with God as qualitatively superior to any other kind of good, and why it is plausible to think that some theistic way of life is more probable than any non-theistic way of life to result in that good relationship with God. If these tasks can be carried out, the Wager strategy may be successfully used as a pragmatic justification for the assumption that there is a God.[11]

Notes

1 Pascal, Blaise, *Pensées* 1670. Translated by J. Warrington (London: J. M. Dent, 1973), 92–96.
2 Ian Hacking, "The Logic of Pascal's Wager," *American Philosophical Quarterly* Vol. 9 (1972): 186–92.
3 Nicholas Rescher, *Pascal's Wager: A Study of Practical Reasoning in Philosophical Theology* (Notre Dame, IN: University of Notre Dame Press, 1985), 25.
4 Golding, Joshua, "Toward a Pragmatic Conception of Faith," *Faith and Philosophy* Vol. 7 (1990): 486–503.
5 Joshua Golding, *Rationality and Religious Theism* (Aldershot: Ashgate, 2003), 55–66.
6 Golding, *Rationality and Religious Theism*, 79–81.
7 Michael Martin, "Pascal's Wager as an Argument for not Believing in God," *Religious Studies* Vol. 19 (1983).
8 See Joshua Golding, *Rationality and Religious Theism*.
9 Thomas Morris, "Pascalian Wagering," *Canadian Journal of Philosophy* Vol 16 (1986): 437–454.
10 Golding, "Toward a Pragmatic Conception of Faith."
11 For a detailed attempt to work out such a strategy, see Golding, *Rationality and Religious Theism*.

Bibliography

Golding, Joshua, "Toward a Pragmatic Conception of Faith," *Faith and Philosophy* Vol. 7 (1990): 486–503.
Golding, Joshua, *Rationality and Religious Theism,* Aldershot: Ashgate, 2003.
Hacking, Ian, "The Logic of Pascal's Wager," *American Philosophical Quarterly* Vol. 9 (1972): 186–192.
Martin, M., "Pascal's Wager as An argument for not Believing in God," *Religious Studies* Vol. 19 (1983): 57–64.
Morris, Thomas, "Pascalian Wagering," *Canadian Journal of Philosophy* Vol. 16 (1986): 437–454.
Pascal, Blaise, *Pensées*. 1670. Translated by J. Warrington. London: J. M. Dent, 1973.
Rescher, Nicholas, *Pascal's Wager: A Study of Practical Reasoning in Philosophical Theology,* Notre Dame, IN: University of Notre Dame Press, 1985.

16

The Argument from the Meaning of Life

Stewart Goetz

1. Introduction

The question "What is the meaning of life?" can plausibly be understood in many ways. If it is assumed the question is about the questioner's life as a human person, then three interpretations of it are reasonable.

First, the question can be interpreted as a question about purpose, so that when one asks "What is the meaning of life?" one is querying "What is the purpose of life?" Susan Wolf believes this understanding is first and foremost what a person has in mind when asking about life's purpose. She writes that "[t]hough there may be many things going on when people ask 'What is the meaning of life?' the most central among them seems to be a search to find a purpose or a point to human existence."[1]

Second, the question can be understood as a question about value. The historian of ideas Will Durant once wrote to the philosopher Bertrand Russell that "I am attempting to face, in my next book, a question that our generation ... seems always ready to ask ...—What is the meaning or worth of human life?"[2] By tweaking Durant's question, we arrive at "What, if anything, makes life worth living?" It will probably come as no surprise that the first two interpretations of the question are related. This is because purposes (ends) are things of value. Thus, the philosopher Iddo Landau has recently penned that "[i]t is not surprising that [people] relate meaningfulness to ends, since ... to understand why things are of value, we often search for their goal."[3] Landau believes that means pursued for ends derive their value (worth) from the value of the ends to which they are means.

Third, the question can be taken as a search for intelligibility in the form of things making sense or fitting together in the right way. Thus, to ask "What is the meaning of life?" is to ask "In what way, if any, do things ultimately make sense?"

In what follows, I will briefly set forth theistic answers to the first two questions and explain how they are interrelated. As an answer to the first question about the purpose of life, most Christian theists down through the ages have agreed that God creates each one of us for the purpose of experiencing perfect happiness (often referred to as beatitude or felicity). Because happiness is intrinsically good, it is what makes life worth living. So the answer to the second question concerning worth or value is that perfect happiness is what ultimately makes life worth living. I then spend a good bit of time considering the third question and the answer to it, which is that life ultimately makes sense only if there is an afterlife in which the experience of perfect happiness can be realized. While life in this world can be worth living to the extent that one experiences happiness, the happiness experienced here is imperfect. Thus, if there is no possibility of an afterlife, then there is no possibility of fulfilling the purpose/experiencing the happiness for which we were created, and life is ultimately absurd (meaningless). To explain the idea of things ultimately making sense, I will make use of what has become known as C. S. Lewis's argument from desire. After setting forth this argument, I will show how naturalists are committed to ultimately making sense of things, but to do so must embrace intuitively implausible positions concerning purposeful explanation and pleasure. Thus, while there is a way for the naturalist to ultimately make sense of things, that way of making sense of things is only as strong as the reasons for believing in naturalism. At this point, I provide a brief overview of Lewis's argument against naturalism, and conclude that theism ultimately provides a better account of the meaning of life.

2. Meaning as purpose

What is the purpose of life? David Benetar writes that "[t]he theist might plausibly respond that an omnibenevolent God, who ... loves us, would have only positive, ennobling purposes for us."[4] But, as Benetar goes on to point out, "'[s]erving God's purposes' is a placeholder for details that need to be provided."[5] Christian theists down through the ages have for the most part agreed that the purpose of life is that we be perfectly happy, where the word "perfect" is often either taken for granted, replaced with words like "blessed" or "eternal," or implied by such terms as "beatitude" or "felicity." Thus, in the early middle ages, Saint Augustine (354–430) wrote that "[w]e wish to be happy, do we not? ... Everyone who possesses what he wants is happy ... Therefore ... whoever possesses God is happy."[6] Not too long after Augustine, Boethius (480–524) wrote *The Consolation of Philosophy* in which his interlocutor Lady Philosophy reminded him that:

> [t]he whole concern of men, which the effort of a multitude of pursuits keeps busy, moves by different roads, yet strives to arrive at one and the same end, that of happiness ... In all of these things it is obviously happiness alone that is desired; for whatever a man seeks above all else, that he reckons the highest good. But we have defined the highest good as happiness; wherefore each man judges that state to be happy which he desires above all others ... And you also, earthly creatures that you are, have some image, though hazy, in your dreams of your beginning; you see, though with a far from clear imagination yet with some idea, that true end of your happiness. Your natural inclinations draw you towards that end, to the true good.[7]

And a few centuries later, Saint Anselm (1033–1109) affirmed the idea that God created us for the purpose that we be happy:

It ought not to be doubted that the nature of rational beings was created by God ... in order that, through rejoicing in him, it might be blessedly happy ... Man, being rational by nature, was created ... to the end that, through rejoicing in God, he might be blessedly happy ... God ... [made man] for the purpose of eternal happiness.[8]

Thomas Aquinas (1224/25-1274) agreed with Augustine, Boethius, and Anselm. According to Saint Thomas, "the ultimate end of man ... is called felicity or happiness, because this is what every intellectual substance desires as an ultimate end, and for its own sake alone."[9] Because "all creatures ... are ordered to God as to an ultimate end,"[10] and "the highest good for man ... is felicity,"[11] it follows that "man's ultimate felicity consists only in the contemplation of God."[12] John Calvin (1509-1564) also believed we were created for perfect happiness. According to him, in order that God "may encourage us in every way, he promises present blessings, as well as eternal felicity, to the obedience of those who shall have kept his commands."[13] Indeed, because the "holy patriarchs expected a happy life from the hand of God (and it is indubitable that they did), they viewed and contemplated a different happiness from that of a terrestrial life."[14] And, wrote Calvin, "[h]e who confesses that there is nothing solid or stable on the earth, and yet firmly retains his hope in God, undoubtedly contemplates a happiness reserved for him elsewhere."[15] According to Jonathan Edwards (1703-1758), "it is evident, by both Scripture and reason, that God is infinitely, eternally, unchangeably, and independently ... happy."[16] Moreover, God has "a real and proper pleasure or happiness in seeing the happy state of the creature,"[17] where the "happiness of the creature consists in rejoicing in God."[18] The Seventeenth of the Church of England's Thirty-Nine Articles of Religion assert that "Predestination to Life is the everlasting purpose of God" where those "chosen in Christ ... by God's mercy ... attain to everlasting felicity."[19] And the contemporary historian Keith Thomas explicitly links the ideas of happiness and meaning when he writes how "[i]n the late seventeenth and early eighteenth centuries, much was said by Anglican Divines about the 'pleasantness' of religion and the daily happiness it could bring to those who practised it. It ... gave meaning to their existence."[20]

More recently, C. S. Lewis (1898-1963) added his voice to the vast weight of the Christian tradition when he affirmed that the purpose for which God created human beings is that they be ultimately or finally perfectly happy. In his book *The Great Divorce*, which is about a fantastical bus trip from hell to heaven, Lewis had one of the ghostly heavenly visitors say "I wish I'd never been born ... What *are* we born for?" To which a Spirit answers, "For infinite happiness."[21] Lewis wrote elsewhere that infinite, complete, or ecstatic happiness is the life of the blessed and he stated that we must suppose "the life of the blessed to be an end in itself, indeed The End."[22] He thought a Christian "believes that men are going to live forever, [and] that they were created by God and so built that they can find their true and lasting happiness only by being united to God."[23]

Last, but certainly not least, there is *The Catechism of the Catholic Church*. According to it, "Man is made to live in communion with God in whom he finds happiness."[24] Moreover, "in [God] alone man can have the life and happiness for which he was created and for which he longs."[25] And finally, "[h]eaven is the ultimate end and fulfillment of the deepest human longings, the state of supreme, definitive happiness."[26]

3. Meaning as what makes life worth living

At this point, one might ask why so many luminaries in the Christian tradition have affirmed that the purpose of life is that we be perfectly happy. The most plausible answer is that happiness makes life worth living because it has the value of being intrinsically good and, as such, constitutes our well-being. While God has created us for perfect happiness, the fact that it is such a great good entails that it should not be had in just any way whatsoever. Sin is the immoral attempt to attain as much happiness as possible for oneself on one's own terms, which is the essence of pride. God, who is perfectly morally good, will not grant perfect happiness to anyone who does not die to self, where death to self is the renunciation of the demand to have perfect happiness on one's own terms. Perfect happiness, if it is to be had at all, must be received as a gift, and this gift can only be had ultimately in relationship with God. It is in this sense that God created us for Himself.

4. Meaning as things ultimately making sense

Because happiness is intrinsically good, we all desire it. Given this is the case, here are two statements by C. S. Lewis of what is known as his "Argument from Desire":

> [W]e remain conscious of a desire which no natural happiness will satisfy. But is there any reason to suppose that reality offers any satisfaction to it? "Nor does the being hungry prove that we have bread." But I think it may be urged that this misses the point. A man's physical hunger does not prove that man will get any bread; he may die of starvation on a raft in the Atlantic. But surely a man's hunger does prove that he comes of a race which repairs its body by eating and inhabits a world where eatable substances exist. In the same way, though I do not believe ... that my desire for Paradise proves that I shall enjoy it, I think it a pretty good indication that such a thing exists and that some men will. A man may love a woman and not win her; but it would be very odd if the phenomenon called "falling in love" occurred in a sexless world.[27]

And:

> Creatures are not born with desires unless satisfaction for those desires exists. A baby feels hunger: well, there is such a thing as food. A duckling wants to swim: well, there is such a thing as water. Men feel sexual desire: well, there is such a thing as sex. If I find in myself a desire which no experience in this world can satisfy, the most probable explanation is that I was made for another world. If none of my earthly pleasures satisfy it, that does not prove that the universe is a fraud. Probably

earthly pleasures were never meant to satisfy it, but only to arouse it, to suggest the real thing.[28]

Lewis's descriptions of an unsatisfied desire for Paradise as odd or fraudulent indicates he is concerned with the idea of things ultimately making sense. If there is no afterlife in which the desire for perfect happiness can be satisfied, things are ultimately absurd. In the words of the philosopher and historian of comparative religion, Edwyn Bevan, of whose work Lewis thought highly,[29] "*if* [the universe] is rational in the … sense [of the realization of value] … then it must provide a satisfaction of the exigence of spirit … [I]n a reasonable world exigencies would not arise which had not their proper satisfaction … If [the universe] … realizes no value … then [it] … would be absurd."[30] Stated otherwise, if the universe does not allow for the fulfillment of the desire for perfect happiness, then things ultimately do not fit together in the right way.

What might be said in response to Lewis? Thaddeus Metz has recently questioned whether everyone has a desire for perfect happiness: "In particular, many in the South and East Asian traditions simply do not hanker for … a [blissful] soul … Literally billions of adherents of Hinduism and Confucianism, for example, have desires radically different from believers in Judaism, Christianity, and Islam."[31] There is not sufficient space here to investigate in depth Hinduism and Confucianism, or any other suggested tradition about its position on the desire for perfect happiness. However, if one briefly considers Hinduism as represented in the *Bhagavad Gita*, one cannot help question Metz's implicit claim that adherents of Hinduism do not have the desire for perfect happiness. The *Gita* acknowledges that we desire to enjoy the fruits of our actions, where these fruits represent experiences of pleasure. At the same time, the *Gita* warns against the pursuit of those fruits because the quest for and failure to achieve the experience of them produces much pain and suffering. The *Gita* goes on (seemingly) to advocate a renunciation of the desire for the fruits of action and the supporting belief in the existence of a distinct, subsistent self as the subject of those desires. While people can debate the wisdom of a renunciation of this desire and belief, the fact that the *Gita* encourages it implies Hindus recognize that people at least initially desire the maximization of their happiness. However, even if there are human beings who do not initially desire to be as happy as they might be (it is difficult to understand how they could not initially desire this), many do so desire, and thus the issue of whether things ultimately make sense if that desire cannot be satisfied must still be addressed.

Contrary to Metz, one might concede that we all desire perfect happiness and attempt to make sense of it in non-theistic terms. The most popular non-theistic view in contemporary analytic philosophy is *naturalism*. As with so many other philosophical views, there are no necessary and sufficient conditions one can state for being a naturalist. Nevertheless, more than a few naturalists (from here on, naturalists) affirm that there is ultimately nothing irreducibly psychological in nature that enters into explanations of events in this world. This affirmation has two main components.

First, naturalists affirm that there is ultimately nothing irreducibly mental in nature that has any place in the explanations of events in this world, where something is mental in nature if it includes what philosophers refer to as *content*. For example, if one thinks about, desires, or chooses to attend university, the content of what one thinks about, desires or chooses is something like "that I attend university." Content is expressed in a "that" clause, which in this case is "that I attend university." If one chooses to attend university for the purpose that one acquire qualification for an occupation in which one is interested, then "that I acquire qualification for an occupation in which I am interested" is mental in nature. David Armstrong explains the implications of naturalism for what is mental in nature as follows:

> Naturalism I define as the doctrine that reality consists of nothing but a single all-embracing spatio-temporal system ... [I]f the principles involved [in the spatio-temporal system] were completely different from the current principles of physics, in particular if they involve appeal to mental entities, such as purposes, we might then count the analysis as a falsification of Naturalism. But the Naturalist need make no more concession than this.[32]

As Armstrong understands naturalism, because it ultimately excludes anything mental from the principles that describe what goes on in the spatial-temporal system that we think of as the physical world, it ultimately excludes purposeful explanations of what occurs in that world.

Richard Rorty is another naturalist who concurs with Armstrong about naturalism's ultimate disbarment of mental explanations. According to Rorty, "[e]very speech, thought, theory, poem, composition and philosophy will turn out to be completely predictable in purely naturalistic terms. Some atoms-and-the-void account of micro-processes within individual human beings will permit the prediction of every sound or inscription which will ever be uttered."[33] David Papineau agrees with Armstrong and Rorty about the exclusion of anything mental in nature from the final explanatory story:

> We may not know enough about physics to know exactly what a complete "physics" might include. But as long as we are confident that, whatever it includes, it will have no ineliminable need for any distinctively mental categorizations, we can be confident that mental properties must be identical with (or realized by) certain non-mentally identifiable properties.[34]
>
> When I say that a complete physics excludes psychology, and that psychological antecedents are therefore never needed to explain physical effects, the emphasis here is on "needed". I am quite happy to allow that psychological categories *can* be used to explain physical effects, as when I tell you that my arm rose because I wanted to lift it. My claim is only that in all such cases an alternative specification of a sufficient antecedent, which does not mention psychological categories, will also be available.[35]

A significant implication of naturalism is that while we might commonsensically explain our actions in terms of purposes, ultimately none of us acts for irreducible purposes. The explanatory story is ultimately irreducibly causal in nature. Thus, Alex Rosenberg writes about the nineteenth-century devious French diplomat Talleyrand standing in a palace and:

firings in his hippocampus ... sending sharp wave ripples out across his neocortex, where they stimulated one neural circuit after another, until combined with firings from the pre-frontal cortex and ventral striatum, and doubtless a half dozen or more other regions of Talleyrand's brain, causing his throat, tongue, and lips to move and him to speak. No [purposeful] narrative to report here—just one damn electrochemical process after another.[36]

Rosenberg recounts how Talleyrand spoke with others at the Congress of Vienna in 1815, which followed the defeat of Napoleon at Waterloo. Though the Congress was ostensibly convened for the purpose of achieving a stable European order, according to Rosenberg "[i]t had no purpose, and neither did the machinations of any of its participants. In fact, none of them—not Metternich, not Talleyrand, not Castlereagh, and not Tsar Alexander—came to the Congress with any purpose. There weren't and indeed aren't any purposes ... [though there] was and is the *appearance* of purpose."[37] In sum, "human behaviors aren't really driven by purposes, ends, or goals ... Every behavior that looks like it's driven by a purpose is just the result of physical processes, like those of blind variation and natural selection uncovered by Darwin."[38] However, because the belief that we act for purposes "is bred in the bone, we have even more trouble shaking it than we do belief in God."[39]

The second part of the claim that there is ultimately nothing irreducibly psychological that enters into explanations of events in this world concerns what is qualitative in nature. For present purposes, the form of the qualitative of most interest is the experience of pleasure, which, on any plausible understanding, is at least part of or completely constitutes happiness. Because we desire to be happy, we act for the purpose of experiencing pleasure. Jaegwon Kim makes clear how the naturalistic philosophical treatment of the explanatory relevance of the qualitative intrinsic goodness of an experience of pleasure starkly contrasts with that of ordinary people:

> For most of us, there is no need to belabor the centrality of consciousness to our conception of ourselves as creatures with minds. But I want to point to the ambivalent, almost paradoxical, attitude that philosophers [i.e., naturalists] have displayed toward consciousness ... [C]onsciousness had been virtually banished from the philosophical and scientific scene for much of the last century, and consciousness-bashing still goes on in some quarters, with some reputable philosophers arguing that phenomenal consciousness, or "qualia," is a fiction of bad philosophy. And there are philosophers ... who, while they recognize phenomenal consciousness as something real do not believe that a complete science of human behavior, including cognitive psychology and neuroscience, has a place for consciousness [as qualitative] in an explanatory/predictive theory of cognition and behavior ...
>
> Contrast this lowly status of consciousness in science and [naturalistic] metaphysics with its lofty standing in moral philosophy and value theory. When philosophers discuss the nature of the intrinsic good, or what is worthy of our desire and volition for its own sake, the most prominently mentioned candidates are things like pleasure, absence of pain, enjoyment, and happiness ... To most of us, a fulfilling life, a life worth living, is one that is rich and full in qualitative

consciousness. We would regard life as impoverished and not fully satisfying if it never included experiences of things like the smell of the sea in a cool morning breeze, the lambent play of sunlight on brilliant autumn foliage, the fragrance of a field of lavender in bloom, and the vibrant, layered soundscape projected by a string quartet ... It is an ironic fact that the felt qualities of conscious experience, perhaps the only things that ultimately matter to us, are often relegated in the rest of philosophy to the status of "secondary qualities," in the shadowy zone between the real and the unreal, or even jettisoned outright as artifacts of confused minds.[40]

How, then, do naturalists make sense of the desire for perfect happiness? This is not an easy question to answer, given that a desire is something mental in nature. For those naturalists who at least give the appearance of conceding the irreducible reality of the mental, the attempt to make sense of the desire for perfect happiness standardly invokes naturalistic evolution. The naturalist Erik Wielenberg reminds us that evolution selects for those characteristics in organisms that lead to their survival and reproduction. Thus, if a desire comes to exist that is advantageous for survival and reproduction, it will, all other things being equal, be preserved. In the following quote, Wielenberg explains how Joy, which is Lewis's term of art for the desire for perfect happiness, confers evolutionary advantage:

> The first important fact is that one of the main effects of Joy is that it prevents a person from deriving lasting contentment from earthly things. This fact is important because deriving lasting contentment from earthly things can be quite disadvantageous, evolutionarily speaking. Dissatisfaction can benefit us in the long run ... To see the evolutionary drawbacks of lasting contentment, consider a male human who is perfectly content as long as his basic needs (food, shelter, and sex) are satisfied. Once such needs are satisfied, he will have no motivation whatsoever to acquire additional wealth, power, status, or success; indeed, he will have no motivation to do anything at all, other than perhaps ensure that his basic needs continue to be satisfied. Contrast this male with a second male who has the same basic drives but who *never* achieves lasting contentment ... Everything else being equal, the second male will likely do better than the first in the competition for limited resources ... Evolutionarily speaking, a good strategy is never to be entirely satisfied with one's lot in life.[41]

Wielenberg concludes that "[b]y causing us to strive for the infinite, [the desire for perfect happiness] prevents us from being entirely satisfied by the finite, and in this way causes us to survive and reproduce more successfully than we otherwise would."[42]

What might Lewis have said in response to Wielenberg? He likely would have begun by pointing out that we should notice how Wielenberg, as a naturalist, turns the desire for perfect happiness into a cause of bodily behavior. While we ordinarily believe that a desire provides its subject with a purpose to pursue a course of action, Wielenberg assumes the desire for perfect happiness, given it ultimately enters the explanatory story as irreducibly mental in nature, does so as a cause. Irreducible purposes must ultimately not have any explanatory role to play.

What other points might Lewis have made in answer to Wielenberg? As someone who believed that perfect happiness is a qualitative state that is intrinsically good, he undoubtedly would have maintained that were this happiness experienced, it would not be disadvantageous in itself. Indeed, were one to be perfectly happy, one would not care in the least that one no longer had to compete to survive and reproduce. Lewis believed being perfectly happy is a far better state of existence than that in which there is competition and death in the struggle to survive. Moreover, in opposition to the naturalistic evolutionary explanatory story, he believed we are interested in surviving only if we believe we might or will be able to have a happy enough life in the future (where perfect happiness is the ultimate form of happiness). It is the goodness of happiness and the desire for it that explain our interest in survival; it is not the desire to survive that explains our desire to experience happiness. In short, Lewis would have maintained that Wielenberg (and naturalistic evolutionists generally) gets the explanatory story backwards.

However, for the sake of argument, Lewis might have conceded that the desire to experience perfect happiness is selected for and preserved because of the evolutionary advantage it bestows. Given this concession, he would have pointed out that on Wielenberg's naturalistic view it is impossible to satisfy this desire. Life would still be ultimately absurd, even given this concession to the naturalist. And as a matter of fact Wielenberg admits this point. "[T]here is," writes Wielenberg, "something 'out of kilter' about the universe in that it is part of human nature to desire something that does not exist ... That the universe fails to conform to our natural desires is an implication the atheist [naturalist] is unlikely to find surprising or implausible."[43] Lewis would likely have made clear that Wielenberg, with these comments, concedes his (Lewis') point, but would also have emphasized that Wielenberg, like the theist, is committed to making sense of things, and it is only because Wielenberg is so committed that he goes on to develop his naturalistic evolutionary explanation of how it is that we come to possess the desire for perfect happiness.

Here, Wielenberg might respond that while the desire for perfect happiness and the inability to satisfy it compose an absurdity on naturalism, nevertheless this absurdity ultimately makes sense within the naturalistic framework. In other words, that there are certain facts that do not make sense is something that itself ultimately makes sense, given the truth of naturalism. Wielenberg might go on to point out that the satisfaction of the desire for perfect happiness requires an afterlife, the existence of the soul, etc., and that these kinds of things are not possible, given the truth of naturalism.

Lewis devoted a good bit of space in his writings to refuting naturalism.[44] He believed the very fact that naturalists reason their way to a belief in naturalism falsifies naturalism, because reasoning involves a mental explanation of events in this world in the form of mental-to-mental causation. Briefly, he believed that it is the naturalist's apprehension of "If naturalism is true, then ultimately there are no irreducible mental explanations of events in this world" and "Naturalism is true" which causes apprehension of "Ultimately there are no irreducible mental explanations of events in this world." Moreover, Lewis made clear that when reasoning occurs it causes events to occur in the reasoner's brain, which is an instance of mental-to-physical causation and a falsification of naturalism. And Lewis would probably have made clear that a naturalist like

Wielenberg ultimately defends naturalism for an irreducible purpose (e.g., the purpose of showing the reasonableness of naturalism), which once again entails there is ultimate and irreducible mental explanation of events in this world. Finally, given all of these instances of ultimate and irreducible mental explanation, Lewis would have wondered why they could not originate in souls which can survive death and receive the perfect happiness which they desire. Things would ultimately make sense in a universe where God creates souls for the purpose that they be perfected by the experience of what makes life worth living. This purposeful creation by God would itself be an instance of ultimate and irreducible mental explanation which makes sense in light of our knowledge of our own reasoning and purposeful action, and life would be ultimately meaningful in the three senses described in this chapter.

Notes

1. Susan Wolf, "The Meaning of Lives," in *Exploring the Meaning of Life*, ed. Joshua Seachris (Oxford: Wiley-Blackwell, 2013), 304–305.
2. Bertrand Russell, *Bertrand Russell: Autobiography* (London: Routledge, 1967), 443.
3. Iddo Landau, *Finding Meaning in an Imperfect World* (Oxford: Oxford University Press, 2017), 135.
4. David Benatar, *The Human Predicament* (Oxford: Oxford University Press, 2017), 37.
5. Ibid., 38.
6. Saint Augustine, "The Happy Life," in *Happiness: Classic and Contemporary Readings in Philosophy*, ed. Steven M. Cahn and Christine Vitrano (Oxford: Oxford University Press, 2008), 52–53.
7. Boethius, *The Consolation of Philosophy*, transl. S. J. Tester (Cambridge, MA: Harvard University Press, 1973), 233, 235, 241.
8. Saint Anselm, *Anselm of Canterbury: The Major Works*, ed. Brian Davies and G. R. Evans (Oxford: Oxford University Press, 1998), 315–316.
9. Saint Thomas Aquinas, *Summa Contra Gentiles: Book Three*, transl. Vernon J. Bourke (Notre Dame, IN: University of Notre Dame Press, 1975), 102.
10. Ibid., 97.
11. Ibid., 113.
12. Ibid., 125.
13. John Calvin, *The Institutes of the Christian Religion*, transl. Henry Beveridge (Peabody, MA: Hendrickson, 2008), II. 8. 4.
14. Ibid., II. 10. 13.
15. Ibid., II. 10. 15.
16. Jonathan Edwards, *A Dissertation Concerning the End for Which God Created the World* (1765), I. 1. 1.
17. Ibid., I. 3.
18. Ibid.
19. *The Book of Common Prayer*, 1549, rev. edn. 1979, 871.
20. Keith Thomas, *The Ends of Life: Roads to Fulfillment in Early Modern England* (Oxford: Oxford University Press, 2010), 226.
21. C. S. Lewis, *The Great Divorce* (1954; New York: HarperSanFrancisco, 2001), 61.
22. C. S. Lewis, *Letters to Malcolm: Chiefly on Prayer* (1964; New York: Harcourt, 1992), 92.
23. C. S. Lewis, *God in the Dock* (Grand Rapids, MI: Eerdmans, 1970), 109.

24 *The Catechism of the Catholic Church* (1992; New York: Doubleday, 1995), #45.
25 Ibid., #1057.
26 Ibid., #1024.
27 C. S. Lewis, *The Weight of Glory and Other Essays* (1941; New York: HarperCollins, 2001), 32–33.
28 C. S. Lewis, *Mere Christianity* (1952; New York: HarperSanFrancisco, 2001), 136–137.
29 C. S. Lewis, *Miracles* (1947; New York: HarperCollins, 2001), 111.
30 Edwyn Bevan, *Symbolism and Belief* (London: George Allen & Unwin, n.d.), 367–369.
31 Thaddeus Metz, *God, Soul and the Meaning of Life* (Cambridge: Cambridge University Press, 2019), 33–34.
32 David Armstrong, "Naturalism, Materialism, and First Philosophy," *Philosophia* 8 (1978): 261–262.
33 Richard Rorty, *Philosophy and the Mirror of Nature* (Princeton, NJ: Princeton University Press, 1979), 387.
34 David Papineau, *Thinking about Consciousness* (Oxford: Oxford University Press, 2002), 41.
35 David Papineau, *Philosophical Naturalism* (Oxford: Blackwell, 1993), p. 31, n. 26.
36 Alex Rosenberg, *How History Gets Things Wrong* (Cambridge, MA: MIT Press, 2018), 160.
37 Ibid., 231. My emphasis.
38 Ibid., 206.
39 Ibid., 239.
40 Jaegwon Kim, *Physicalism, or Something Near Enough* (Princeton, NJ: Princeton University Press, 2005), 10–12.
41 Erik J. Wielenberg, *God and the Reach of Reason: C. S. Lewis, David Hume, and Bertrand Russell* (Cambridge: Cambridge University Press, 2008), 116–117.
42 Ibid., 117.
43 Ibid., 112.
44 Lewis, *Miracles*. See also Stewart Goetz, *C. S. Lewis* (Oxford: Wiley Blackwell, 2018), chap. 2.

Bibliography

Anselm, St., *Anselm of Canterbury: The Major Works*, edited by Brian Davies and G. R. Evans, Oxford: Oxford University Press, 1998, 315–316.

Aquinas, St. Thomas, *Summa Contra Gentiles: Book Three*, translated by Vernon J. Bourke, Notre Dame, IN: University of Notre Dame Press, 1975.

Armstrong, David, "Naturalism, Materialism, and First Philosophy," *Philosophia* 8 (1978): 261–262.

Augustine, St., "The Happy Life," in *Happiness: Classic and Contemporary Readings in Philosophy*, edited by Steven M. Cahn and Christine Vitrano, Oxford: Oxford University Press, 2008, 52–53.

Benatar, David, *The Human Predicament*, Oxford: Oxford University Press, 2017.

Bevan, Edwyn, *Symbolism and Belief*, London: George Allen & Unwin, n.d.

Boethius, *The Consolation of Philosophy*, 524, translated by S. J. Tester, Cambridge, MA: Harvard University Press, 1973.

The Book of Common Prayer, 1549.

The Catechism of the Catholic Church, 1992, New York: Doubleday, 1995.

Calvin, John, *The Institutes of the Christian Religion*, translated by Henry Beveridge, Peabody, MA: Hendrickson, 2008.
Edwards, Jonathan, *A Dissertation Concerning the End for Which God Created the World* I.1.1.
Goetz, Stewart, *C. S. Lewis,* Oxford: Wiley-Blackwell, 2018.
Kim, Jaegwon, *Physicalism, or Something Near Enough,* Princeton, NJ: Princeton University Press, 2005.
Landau, Iddo, *Finding Meaning in an Imperfect World,* Oxford: Oxford University Press, 2017.
Lewis, C. S., *God in the Dock,* Grand Rapids, MI: Eerdmans, 1970.
Lewis, C. S., *Letters to Malcolm: Chiefly on Prayer,* 1964, New York: Harcourt, 1992.
Lewis, C. S., *Mere Christianity,* 1952, New York: HarperSanFrancisco, 2001.
Lewis, C. S., *Miracles,* 1947, New York: HarperCollins, 2001.
Lewis, C. S., *The Great Divorce,* 1954, New York: HarperSanFrancisco, 2001.
Lewis, C. S., *The Weight of Glory and Other Essays,* 1941, New York: HarperCollins, 2001.
Metz, Thaddeus, *God, Soul and the Meaning of Life,* Cambridge: Cambridge University Press, 2019.
Papineau, David, *Philosophical Naturalism,* Oxford: Blackwell, 1993.
Papineau, David, *Thinking about Consciousness,* Oxford: Oxford University Press, 2002.
Rorty, Richard, *Philosophy and the Mirror of Nature,* Princeton, NJ: Princeton University Press, 1979.
Rosenberg, Alex, *How History Gets Things Wrong,* Cambridge, MA: MIT Press, 2018.
Russell, Bertrand, *Bertrand Russell: Autobiography,* London: Routledge, 1967.
Thomas, Keith, *The Ends of Life: Roads to Fulfillment in Early Modern England,* Oxford: Oxford University Press, 2010.
Wielenberg, Erik J., *God and the Reach of Reason: C. S. Lewis, David Hume, and Bertrand Russell,* Cambridge: Cambridge University Press, 2008.
Wolf, Susan, "The Meaning of Lives" in *Exploring the Meaning of Life,* edited by Joshua Seachris (Oxford: Wiley-Blackwell, 2013), 304–305.

17

The Argument from Common Consent

Jonathan Matheson

In this chapter, I will explain the common consent argument for theism, and its motivation. According to the common consent argument it is rational for you to believe that God exists because you know so many other people believe that God exists. Having motivated the argument, I will explain and motivate several pressing objections to the argument and evaluate their probative force. The paper will serve as both an accessible introduction to this argument as well as a resource for continued research on the topic.

1. Introduction

In its crudest form the common consent argument claims that God exists because most people believe that God exists. These days you are more likely to see the common consent argument referenced as an example of a logical fallacy (the bandwagon fallacy)[1] than you are to see it seriously considered as an argument for God's existence.[2] Things were not always this way.[3] J. S. Mill claimed of the common consent argument that "no argument for the truth of theism is more commonly invoked or confidently relied on than the general assent of mankind."[4] In what follows I will explain the common consent argument for God's existence and breathe new life into it through the emerging literature on higher-order evidence and recent findings in the social sciences. With this understanding of the argument in hand, we will turn to a brief examination of the most pressing problems with the common consent argument and a look at where the debates surrounding the argument may be headed.

2. The Argument

The common consent argument (hereafter CCA) is an *epistemic* argument, rather than a *metaphysical* one.[5] The argument is *not* that human opinions make it the case that God exists (i.e. that God's existence depends in any way on human attitudes toward God), but rather that human opinions *provide good evidence* to believe that God exists. In fact, the argument claims that the evidence provided by the pervasiveness of theistic belief is good enough to make it reasonable to believe that God exists.[6]

The CCA is best seen as a kind of inference to the best explanation, claiming that the prevalence of theistic belief is best explained by the existence of God. So, if we take the prevalence of theistic belief as our datum, the idea is that God's existence best explains the datum. We can formalize such an understanding of CCA as follows:

(1) The belief that God exists is very prevalent.
(2) God existing is a good explanation of the prevalence of the belief that God exists.
(3) God existing better explains the prevalence of the belief that God exists than any available rival explanation.
(4) Therefore, God exists.

Before turning to the particular premises of the CCA, we can pause to consider its form. It is not a valid argument—its premises do not entail its conclusion. It is possible for premises (1) to (3) all to be true, and yet nevertheless God does not exist. While not valid, proponents of the argument claim that its premises give good abductive support for its conclusion—enough to make it rational to believe the conclusion. We can see that arguments of this form can be good arguments by considering the following:

(1') The belief that the recycling is getting picked up today is prevalent in my neighborhood.[7]
(2') The recycling getting picked up today is a good explanation of the prevalence of the belief that it is.
(3') The recycling being picked up today better explains the prevalence of the belief that it is than any available rival explanation.
(4') Therefore, the recycling is getting picked up today.

Suppose that when sending the kids off to school I notice that most my neighbors have put out their full recycling containers. Knowing that the pesky HOA gets upset when people leave their recycling out for more than a day, and that my neighbors don't like getting in trouble with the HOA but do want their recycling picked up, I become justified in believing that most my neighbors believe the recycling truck is coming today. So, I am justified in believing (1'). Here, the datum is the prevalence (in my neighborhood) of the relevant recycling belief. What best explains this datum? Why might my neighbors believe this? Several explanations may come to mind:

A. The recycling is getting picked up today.
B. Most of my neighbors are mistaken about what day it is.
C. A mischievous individual, who sent most my neighbors fake recycling date change notifications, has deceived them.
D. Most my neighbors have excessive recycling and really want it to be picked up today, and this desire has caused them to believe that it will be picked up today.

While each of these explanations can account for the prevalence (in my neighborhood) of the belief that the recycling is coming today, they do not each explain this datum equally well. In fact, all besides (A) can be rejected quite quickly. Explanation (A) is a pretty good explanation of the datum. Given what I know about my neighbors, I would expect most of them to believe it was recycling day whenever it in fact was recycling day. Sure, one of them might occasionally get the recycling date wrong, but the odds that they're all wrong seems very low. This shows that I am justified in believing premise (2') as well. Given the how well the truth of my neighbors' beliefs explain their prevalence, there is a high bar for competitor explanation. Rival explanations (B) to (D) are all overly complicated or fail to explain the datum very well. So, it is reasonable to believe (3'). Finally, it seems clear that I am also justified in believing (4') on the basis of (1') to (3'). I am justified in believing (4'), and appealing to (1') to (3') is the best account of why. If my wife asks me why I think the recycling is being picked up today, referencing the beliefs of my neighbors looks like a legitimate response. So, the recycling argument looks perfectly good. Since the CCA shares this same logical structure, there are no issues with the general form of the CCA.

The recycling argument shows us that being aware of the prevalence of a belief in a community *can* make it reasonable for an individual to think likewise. Does it do so in CCA? Whether it does so will depend upon the plausibility of its premises. Let's consider each in turn. Premise (1) claims that the belief that God exists is very prevalent. A 2018 Pew Research Center survey found that 80% of Americans believe that God exists and over 90% believe in a higher power. According 2010 Pew Research Center data, close to 55% of the world's population belong to one of the big three monotheistic religions: Islam, Christianity, or Judaism.[8] The numbers are much higher for religious membership in general, with 84% of the world's population claiming some religious affiliation.[9] According to Zuckerman's analysis of the data to the converse question (how many people do not believe that God exists?), as of 2007, between 500 million and 750 million people in the world do not believe that God exists (a relatively small percentage of the 6.7 billion people at the time).[10] Further, the prevalence of theistic belief increases when we include the opinions of those no longer living.[11]

How popular must a belief be for it to be prevalent? There is no plausible and precise amount here. While not universal, belief that God exists is more prevalent than the belief that the recycling gets picked up today (at least in many instances of the recycling argument). For instance, the recycling argument does not require me to conclude that 75% or even 60% of my neighbors believe that the recycling is being picked up in my neighborhood today. The recycling belief is prevalent enough even when the numbers are comparable to the percentage of theistic believers. Given this, the numbers outlined above seem to suffice for making theistic belief prevalent enough for premise (1) to be accepted. In fact, premise (1) looks to be even better supported than (1'), at least on most recycling occasions.

Premise (2) also looks quite reasonable. In general, the truth of a belief is a pretty good explanation for the prevalence of that belief. Plausibly, what best explains the prevalence of the beliefs that being kind is good, that the Earth is roughly spherical, and that more than 100 people exist, is the truth of these beliefs. Similarly, God's existence is a very good explanation for the prevalence of the belief that God exists.[12] Of course, prevalently held beliefs can be false. It is not too difficult to think about beliefs that are both prevalent and false. Sometimes we have a better explanation for the prevalence of the belief than its truth. For instance, if I have framed the butler for a murder, I may know that the belief that the butler committed the crime is quite prevalent among the relevant parties, but such knowledge would not make it reasonable *for me* to believe that the butler did it![13] In such a case, I have a better explanation of the convergence of their opinions—my deceit. Other times, the best thing to think is that the prevalent belief was rationally held (and even rational due to its prevalence) at the time even though it turned out to be false. For example, it was rational for many in the early 1400s to believe that the Earth was flat, and for some, the rationality of this belief may have come solely from what they knew about what other people believed about the matter. While this belief was false, its falsity does not prevent it from being supported by the evidence (at the time).

Whether it is rational to believe premise (3) will depend upon the explanatory power of alternative explanations. Given (2), God's existence is a good explanation of the prevalence of theistic belief, so whether it is rational to accept (3) will depend upon whether any rival explanation does at least as good a job explaining the datum. For now, we will delay judgment on (3) as we will examine several rival explanations in the objections. Absent the discovery of a superior rival explanation, it will be rational to believe (3) as well.

So, there is reason to think the CCA is a successful argument. We have seen reason to accept (1) and (2), and we have seen that (1) through (3) provide good rational support for (4). If no superior rival explanation is found, it looks like the CCA is a success. Before turning to an examination of rival explanations, and other objections to the CCA, we will pause to note why interest in the CCA may be on the rise. Further reason to take the CCA seriously comes from current research in philosophy and the social sciences. Developments in these fields look to breathe new life into the CCA.

3. A new twist: higher-order evidence and the wisdom of groups

Interest in the CCA may be on the rise again given the recent interest in nature and value of higher-order evidence and social epistemology more generally. Social epistemology concerns the social dimensions of knowledge and rationality. Within the growing literature in social epistemology are emerging debates about higher-order evidence. Higher-order evidence is evidence that is about the evidence for some proposition. For instance, (your) evidence that someone else has evidence for a proposition is itself higher-order evidence (for you) regarding that proposition. That a generally reasonable person has a belief has been seen as one important kind of higher-order evidence. If I know that Jenna has been looking into the best landscaping companies and believes that Greener Grass is the way to go, then in knowing of her belief I get evidence that she has good evidence that Greener Grass is the company to go with. So, I have (higher-order) evidence that Greener Grass is the company to go with even without accessing the information on which Jenna is basing her belief. Given the kind of cognitive creatures that we are, knowing that someone believes a proposition is evidence that they have evidence in favor of that proposition—it is evidence that their belief is an appropriate response to the evidence that they possess.

The epistemic impact of the beliefs of others has been at the forefront of the burgeoning literature on the epistemic significance of disagreement. Here, much of the debate has been about whether discovering that someone else disagrees with you undermines the rationality of your belief by giving you higher-order evidence against what you believe.[14] Most in the debate agree that discovering a disagreement gives you at least *some* evidence against your belief,[15] but theorists still dispute how strong this evidence is as well as how it interacts with the pieces of first-order evidence you possess. While thinking about *disagreement* may have brought greater attention to the higher-order evidence provided by beliefs, such findings carry over to *agreement* as well.[16] Just as finding out that someone else *disagrees* with you can give you evidence *against* your belief, finding out that someone else *agrees* with you can give you evidence *in favor of* your belief. Finding out that many people agree about some issue, can provide strong evidence for what they believe. In fact, it is commonplace to rely on agreement within a community as our sole evidential basis for what we believe about it. For instance, because I have not directly studied the topics, the rationality of my beliefs about climate change, the effects of vaccines, and the health benefits of flossing entirely depends upon what I know about what people in a good epistemic position on the matters believe. In fact, Hilary Kornblith claims that "one would have to be a radical skeptic about mathematics, logic, probability, and decision theory to think that convergence of opinion is not, at this point in the history of those fields, evidence of truth."[17]

Further support for the evidential impact of agreement comes from the Condorcet Jury Theorem. According to the Condorcet Jury Theorem, so long as individuals are more likely than not to be correct on a dichotomous matter, the majority opinion becomes more and more likely to be correct as more individual opinions are added to the mix. For instance, in a group of 250 people who are each individually 0.51 likely to be correct on some matter, the majority opinion is 0.62 likely to be correct. In a group of 10,000 people with the same epistemic credentials, the majority opinion is 0.98 likely to be correct.[18] The Condorcet Jury Theorem thus shows the strong support that majority opinion can give, particularly as the numbers get large, and as we have seen, the agreeing parties in terms of theistic belief number in the *billions*!

Social scientists have also been appreciating the wisdom of crowds.[19] Here, research shows that relying on group opinions is a reliable way to go. The phenomenon of relying on a group average opinion is becoming commonplace. When deciding what movie to see, which restaurant to eat at, which plumber to call, or which car to buy, many of us rely on the average satisfaction report from a number of people who have utilized the service or product. Further, we take assurance when the average is backed by a large number of reviews. Such reliance on groups is backed up by social science as well. For instance, James Surowiecki[20] provides a number of real-world examples that show the benefits of relying on group wisdom. One example comes from the popular game show of the early 2000s, *Who Wants to be a Millionaire?* In this quiz show, players had three possible "lifelines": eliminating two of the four possible answers (the 50/50), calling a knowledgeable friend, and polling the studio audience. Analysis of the data has shown that polling the audience was a much better strategy than calling the expert friend. In particular, the expert friend had about a 65% chance of being correct, while the majority studio audience answer was correct 91% of the time.[21] So, while relying on an expert friend was a good strategy, there was more wisdom in the majority opinion of a somewhat random group of strangers. Cass Sunstein[22] notes than when a group of 56 individuals guessed the number of beans in a jar, their average guess (871) was closer to the correct answer (850) than all but one of the individual guesses. This data indicates that going with the prevalent opinion can be a pretty reliable way to navigate the world.

However, the CCA is not without its dissenters. And that's putting it mildly. In what follows, we will examine a series of objections to the argument. The objections will address the overall project, as well as each individual premise in the formalized argument above.

4. Objections to the project

One objection to the CCA has to do with the very idea of believing that God exists just because other people do. While the recycling argument shows that this is not always a problem, one might think that the recycling argument and the CCA are disanalogous in important ways. Recent debates about the appropriateness of moral deference have been concerned with the fact that something seems amiss about taking on a moral belief simply on someone else's say-so, even though in general there is nothing wrong with deferring to others (at least experts).[23] Religious deference might seem problematic in the same ways that moral deference does.[24] Some things, it might be thought, just simply shouldn't be believed on someone else's say-so. The idea here is that this secondhand evidence isn't always up to the task. For instance, while many items can happily be bought secondhand, swimsuits are a different matter. In the same way, secondhand evidence might not be the right kind of thing to base at least some beliefs upon. So, according to this objection, while the recycling argument might be perfectly fine, when the content of the argument shifts to something like belief in God, things break down. Mill maintains something along these lines, claiming that "to a thinker the argument from other people's opinions has little weight. It is but second-hand evidence; and merely admonishes us to look out for and weigh the reasons on which this conviction of mankind or of wise men was founded."[25] Further, as Kelly[26] notes, when it comes to investigating many important issues, we tend to look for arguments as opposed to surveys.

There is something preferable about having the very evidence that is the basis for those who believe, over merely knowing that they believe it, particularly concerning matters of morality and religion. While I might have little interest in the reasons why the meteorologist believes that it will rain this afternoon (her resulting belief sufficing for my interests), regarding whether an action is right or wrong, or whether God exists, things are importantly different than those more mundane matters. While no one has the time or resources to sort *everything* out for themselves, epistemic autonomy might be especially valuable regarding some matters. For instance, someone who believes an action is morally wrong simply on someone else's say-so will miss out on moral understanding even if they still get a true moral belief. If they only believe because of what someone else says, then they will fail to understand *why* it is that the belief in question is true. That's a significant loss. However, while it might be preferable, or epistemically better, to have the relevant (first-order) evidence for oneself, it does not follow that the secondhand evidence, or higher-order evidence, does not suffice in making the relevant belief rational. The defender of CCA will be happy if the argument shows that it is rational to believe that God exists, even while acknowledging that there are better epistemic positions to occupy on the matter. Just as we shouldn't let the perfect get in the way of the good, we should not let an epistemically better situation get in the way of a sufficiently good one. The defender of CCA may agree that it would be better for someone to understand why it is true that God exists, but if the argument succeeds in showing that it is rational to believe that God exists, this would still be a significant achievement.

5. Objections to (1)

Objections to (1) claim that theistic belief is either not prevalent, or not prevalent in the relevant way. The Condorcet Jury Theorem, and the appeal to the evidence of belief more generally, relied on two key factors: (i) the likelihood of individuals being correct, and (ii) the independence of their opinions. The evidential power in the numbers relied on both the individual opinions being more likely to be true than not, and the individual opinions being independently formed. Both factors can be seen to obtain in the recycling analogy. Most likely, my neighbors came to their recycling beliefs independently without consulting each other, and while they may miss a week here or there, they are more likely than not to be correct about the recycling day. However, things are not so straightforward regarding the CCA. In fact, there can be worries about each of the key factors pertaining to the prevalence of theistic belief.

The first worry concerns the likelihood of our being correct about God's existence. Are those appealed to in (1) more likely than not to be correct about whether God exists? If not, then the prevalence of theistic belief would actually count *against* God's existence. If the likelihood of a correct belief is less than 0.5, then adding individuals only makes the group opinion *less likely* to be correct! Unfortunately, it is difficult to assess the likelihood of our being correct on such matters without begging the question on the issue at hand. If God exists, then those who believe that are quite reliable in their theistic belief. If God does not exist, then they are quite unreliable. However, our likelihood to be right about a question is typically informed by our reliability regarding questions in the neighborhood. One way to push against the reliability of theistic belief/disbelief without begging the question regarding God's existence is to examine the diversity of religious beliefs outside of the belief that God exists. Even if we suppose that God does exist, there is *so much disagreement* in the details that it might be thought that on the whole we must be unreliable in forming religious beliefs in general.

Second, there are also issues surrounding belief independence. According to the Condorcet Jury Theorem, it is important for the result that the individual opinions are independently formed—that each individual in the group has come to their conclusion without influence from the other group members. Pinpointing exactly how to understand "independence" here is no easy matter,[27] but religious beliefs do not look like good candidates for independently formed beliefs. Individuals rarely form their theistic beliefs in isolation. The contingency of religious belief seems to indicate that where, and when, an individual exists plays a significant role in whether they believe God exists, as well as which other religious beliefs they have.[28] This is at least some indication that religious beliefs tend to not be independently formed. Further, the use of political and social power to promote religious belief has been all too common.[29] If the prevalence of an opinion was achieved without independence, it will have much less evidential value. If I find out that all my other neighbors just put out their recycling because Susan did (because they all just do what Susan does), then the prevalence of their recycling belief carries much less weight. Similarly, if the prevalence of theistic belief in some community is simply due to the fact that most people in the community are blindly believing whatever Pastor Steve says, their opinions will carry less evidential weight.[30]

While independence is of some epistemic value, we should be careful to not over-emphasize it.[31] Everyone conducting their own intellectual business in their own intellectual silos is hardly an intellectual ideal. There is great benefit from a shared epistemic division of labor. Recent epistemology has shifted from a more individualist model to one more appreciative of the social dimensions of knowledge and rationality. For instance, we want our scientist's views to be shaped by the work and insights of other scientists as well. So, while there is some evidential value in independently formed opinions, such opinions can also come with an epistemic cost.

A further response to the independence concern is to shift some of the evidential weight from the *independence* of theistic belief to the *persistence* of theistic belief. While religious belief may not often be independently formed, it very often persists through time. It persists through subsequent experiences and critical reflection. Such theistic belief is not entirely dependent upon its original source.[32] Along these lines, Kelly[33] gives the example of elementary mathematical claims. Few, if any, of us came to believe that 2 + 2 = 4 entirely on our own. The same goes for many of our basic historical, geographical, and scientific beliefs. Beliefs like these were instilled in us from a very young age; they were not independently formed. Nevertheless, such beliefs have stuck around. The fact that we *still* believe these claims with the addition of a lifetime of experiences, does something to make up for the lack of independence in the original formation of the belief.[34]

6. Objection to (2)

One reason to reject that God's existence is a good explanation of the prevalence of theistic belief is to appeal to divine hiddenness. Here the claim is that if God exists, we would expect that fact to be much more obvious than it is, and so the prevalence of theistic belief would be much higher than it is, if not universal. The problem of divine hiddenness is typically seen as an argument for atheism. In brief, it claims that if God existed there wouldn't be reasonable, non-culpable, non-belief, but since there is such non-belief in God's existence, God does not exist.[35] If God's existence is incompatible with reasonable, non-culpable, non-belief (or made implausible by such non-belief), then God's existence would not be a very good explanation of prevalence of theistic belief. According to this line of thought, if God existed we should expect *much more* (if not universal) theistic belief. So, even if theistic belief is much more prominent than non-belief, God's existence would not be a good explanation of the prevalence of theistic belief given that there is still far too much non-belief.

While the problem of divine hiddenness is worthy of more attention than we can give it here, we can briefly outline the debate.[36] Since it is clear that God could be less hidden than God is (and thus that there could be more theistic belief than there is), responses to the problem of divine hiddenness have either tried to identify a justifying reason for God to be hidden (at least to the extent that God is hidden),[37] or to deny that creatures like us are in a position to draw justified conclusions about what reasons God may or may not have.[38] The success of the CCA, and support for endorsing (2), will rely in part on how successful these responses to the problem of divine hiddenness are. If we should expect much more theistic belief given God's existence, then God's existence may not be a very good explanation of the theistic belief we do find.

The goodness of the theistic explanation of the prevalence of theistic belief will also depend upon how much theistic belief we should expect if God does *not* exist. Consider an analogy. Suppose that my yard is full of weeds, so I hire a gardener to take care of it while I am away for the weekend. When I return, I find my yard to have many fewer weeds than it did, but to also have many more weeds than I expected. Given that I had hired the gardener, I expect there to be next to no weeds in my yard, so if I find that only 60% of the weeds are gone, it would come as a shock and disappointment. Nevertheless, while I should expect to find even fewer weeds than I do, the fact that there has still been a significant reduction in weeds together with the fact that I hired the gardener makes it the case that the gardener explanation is the best explanation for the state of my yard.[39] Similarly, even if there is much less theistic belief that we should expect if God exists, if there is still significantly more theistic belief than we should expect if God does not exist, the theistic explanation of the prevalence of theistic belief will be a good explanation. Here too I might expect a 100% result and come to find only a 60% result, but if that 60% result would be quite surprising if God didn't exist, God's existence will be a good explanation of the result.

7. Objections to (3)

Objections to (3) put forward rival explanations of the prevalence of theistic belief that purport to better explain the datum (the prevalence of theistic belief). Put differently, they attempt to show why the prevalence of theistic belief should not be very surprising if God doesn't exist. Many such naturalistic rival explanations of the prevalence of theistic belief exist. Freud, Marx, and Nietzsche, among others, have each given a kind of debunking argument for theistic belief. For Freud, theistic belief is a kind of wish-fulfillment. For Marx, theistic belief is the result of a cognitive dysfunction resulting from the problematic social order. For Nietzsche, the origin of theistic belief is in the resentment of the oppressed and the adoption of their "slave morality."[40]

Perhaps the most pressing naturalistic challenge to theistic belief has come from the cognitive science of religion. The cognitive science of religion has been focused on explaining religious belief, and belief in God's existence in particular.[41] Utilizing resources in developmental psychology, anthropology, and evolutionary science, cognitive scientists of religion have argued that humans are naturally disposed to believe in God.[42] There are two broad ways to account for religious belief here. First, it could be that religious belief was selected for. For instance, Wilson[43] argues that religious beliefs are adaptive for groups, making the groups more cohesive, cooperative, with members who self-sacrifice for the greater good. Second, it could be that religious belief is an accidental by-product of other features that were selected for.[44] For instance, humans possess a hyperactive agency detective device (HADD), which strongly inclines them to interpret ambiguous information as having an agential cause. HADD was selected for because as Barrett[45] puts it, "if you bet that something is an agent and it isn't, not much is lost. But if you bet that something is not an agent and it turns out to be one, you could be lunch." While HADD was selected for other purposes, this cognitive mechanism, which leads us to conclude that agency is involved even when it isn't, also contributes to the formation of religious beliefs. On this picture, most people who believe that God exists arrive at their theistic beliefs not by way of argument, but non-inferentially in ways that are shaped by cognitive mechanisms like HADD. Further, it is argued that "unguided" explanations of theistic belief, explanations that do not rely on God playing some role in using these cognitive mechanisms, do better than "guided" explanations.[46] This is because it is unlikely that God would utilize such mechanisms to produce theistic belief. Marsh puts it this way:

> [T]here is no reason to expect that cognitive tools that were designed by natural selection for nonreligious purposes would, in turn, lead people to favor theism and disfavor alternatives to theism. In fact, since the outputs of our mental tools, like our agency detection devices, are likely to be highly nonspecific and highly sensitive to local factors in the environment, then the byproduct view gives us reason to expect serious religious diversity and early nonbelief in God ... Nothing about HADD or other capacities discussed in CSR requires that one will come to believe in God. If anything, it seems like theistic concepts would later evolve from nontheistic concepts that were initially triggered by mental tools like HADD.[47]

So, if God utilized these cognitive mechanisms to produce theistic belief, God would be doing so at the expense of bringing about substantial diversity in religious belief including a myriad of false beliefs.[48] If this is correct, then the best explanation of the prevalence of theistic belief is not its truth.

There are two lines of response to this threat from the cognitive science of religion.[49] First, it can be argued that while the cognitive mechanisms like HADD play some role in forming and sustaining religious belief, they are not the whole story. The greater the role played by other factors in forming and sustaining religious belief, the less good an explanation the evolutionary account is for the prevalence (and persistence) of theistic belief.[50] Other explanatory factors include religious experiences, theistic arguments, religious testimony from others, and so forth. A second response to the evolutionary explanation is to argue that the "guided" evolutionary explanation is superior to the "unguided" evolutionary explanation. If God utilized the cognitive mechanisms to bring about theistic belief, then theistic belief is still best explained by God's existence. Reformed epistemologists have argued along these lines that God designed humans to naturally believe that God exists.[51]

8. Other defeating evidence

Since, as formulated, the CCA is an inference to the best explanation, it is possible that the premises are all reasonable for you to accept, but that nevertheless other evidence in your total body of evidence prevents these premises from making it rational to believe the conclusion. Since abductive arguments are invalid, the truth of their premises is insufficient to guarantee the truth of the conclusion.[52] So, whether the CCA succeeds in making it reasonable to believe that God exists will depend upon what else it is reasonable for you to believe about God's existence. For instance, your appreciation of the problem of evil may provide defeating evidence that prevents the CCA from being a successful argument for you. So, a full evaluation of the CCA cannot occur in isolation from other considerations for and against God's existence. Whether it can succeed will depend up the success/failure of arguments and considerations against God's existence.

A final concern that confronts the CCA is how it may be turned on itself. Here, the worry is that common consent arguments are in some sense self-undermining. As noted at the outset, the CCA is not a very popular argument for God's existence these days. Most people who have considered the argument do not think that it is a good argument.[53] So, the belief that the CCA fails is quite prevalent among those who have considered it. One explanation of the prevalence of this belief is that the CCA is in fact not a good argument. So, unless a more compelling rival explanation exists, it might be thought that the very argumentative form utilized by the CCA in fact undermines a rational belief that the CCA is a good argument (even if it is)

9. Future directions

As mentioned above, there is not much contemporary discussion of the CCA. However, we have seen that a number of thriving philosophical debates all play an important role regarding what we should make of this argument. This shows that future directions in these neighboring debates will all have something to contribute in terms of how we assess the CCA. Hopefully, developments in these neighboring debates will also bring greater attention to common consent arguments in general and the CCA in particular.[54]

Notes

1 The common consent argument is often thought to illustrate an instance of the bandwagon fallacy or *argumentum ad populum*, a problematic kind of mental herd behavior where something is believed based on the majority believing it.

2. Thomas Kelly, "Consensus Gentium: Reflections on the 'Common Consent' Argument for the Existence of God," in *Evidence and Religious Belief*, eds. K. J. Clark and R. J. VanArragon (Oxford: Oxford University Press, 2011), 135–156 notes that the argument is not even mentioned in a number of central texts about arguments regarding God's existence: J. L. Mackie, *The Miracle of Theism* (New York: Oxford University, Press, 1983); John Howard Sobel, *The Miracle of Theism* (Cambridge University Press, 2003); Richard Swinburne, *The Existence of God* (Oxford University Press, 2004); William Wainwright, ed. *Oxford Handbook of Philosophy of Religion* (Oxford University Press, 2007). Of course, this list is far from exhaustive, but it does paint a picture.
3. For an overview of how the argument was seen historically, see Jasper Reid, "The Common Consent Argument from Herbert to Hume," *Journal of the History of Philosophy* 53, no. 3 (2015): 401–433.
4. J. S. Mill, *Three Essays on Religion: Nature, the Utility of Religion, and Theism* (London: Longman, Reader, Dyer, and Green, 1874 edition), 128.
5. See also Peter Kreeft and Ronald Tacelli, *Handbook of Christian Apologetics* (Downers Grove, IL: InterVarsity Press, 1994), 83–85.
6. Kelly, "Consensus Gentium: Reflections on the 'Common Consent' Argument for the Existence of God," has a more modest reading of CCA where the prevalence of theistic belief only gives some reason to believe that God exists.
7. This example follows Kelly, "Consensus Gentium: Reflections on the 'Common Consent' Argument for the Existence of God."
8. See "Pew-Templeton Global Religious Futures Project Worldwide Population Census," Pew Research Center's Religion & Public Life Project, The Pew Charitable Trusts, 2010, http://globalreligiousfutures.org/explorer#/?subtopic=15&chartType=pie&year=2010&data_type=number&religious_affiliation=all&destination=to&countries=Worldwide&age_group=all&gender=all&pdfMode=false. These numbers do not directly carry over to religious belief since individuals may identify with one of these religions without claiming to *believe* that God exists, seeing religious adherence as a form of non-doxastic faith or practice. A further complication arises regarding whether Christians, Jews, and Muslims who do believe that God exists, actually hold the same belief. On this issue, see Kelly, "Consensus Gentium: Reflections on the 'Common Consent' Argument for the Existence of God," and Tomas Bogardus and Mallorie Urban, "How to Tell Whether Christians and Muslims Worship the Same God," *Faith and Philosophy* 34, no. 2 (2017): 176–200.
9. "The Global Religious Landscape," Pew Research Center's Religion & Public Life Project, The Pew Charitable Trusts, 18 Dec. 2012, https://www.pewforum.org/2012/12/18/global-religious-landscape-exec/.
10. As Phil Zuckerman, "Atheism: Contemporary Numbers and Patterns," in *The Cambridge Companion to Atheism*, ed. M. Martin (New York: Cambridge University Press, 2007), 47 points out, data on this issue is fraught with methodological hurdles. Response rates are typically low, involve non-randomly selected samples, and involve surveying individuals in adverse political and cultural climates. Further, while the above numbers come from Zuckerman, he seems to include individuals who do not believe in a monotheistic or personal God in the category of theist believers.
11. For an argument as to why the beliefs of those no longer living are epistemically relevant, see Brandon Carey and Jonathan Matheson, "How Skeptical is the Equal Weight View?" in *Disagreement and Skepticism*, ed. D. Machuca (New York: Routledge, 2013), 131–149.

12 In fact, it might be thought that God's existing would come with near universal belief that God exists. We will examine this objection later in the paper.
13 This example is from Kelly, "Consensus Gentium: Reflections on the 'Common Consent' Argument for the Existence of God."
14 For a survey of the literature on the epistemology of disagreement and a more detailed discussion of the role of higher-order evidence in it, see Jonathan Matheson, *The Epistemic Significance of Disagreement* (New York: Palgrave, 2015).
15 For two notable exceptions, see Kelly, "The Epistemic Significance of Disagreement" in *Oxford Studies in Epistemology*, eds. Hawthorne and Gendler, Vol. 1 (Oxford: Oxford University Press, 2005), 167–196); and Michael Titelbaum, "Rationality's Fixed Point (or: In Defense of Right Reason)," in *Oxford Studies in Epistemology*, eds. Tamar Gendler and John Hawthorne, vol. 5, (Oxford: Oxford University Press, 2015), 253–294.
16 For more on the connection between disagreement and agreement, see Kenny Easwaran et al., "Updating on the Credences of Others: Disagreement, Agreement, and Synergy," *Philosopher's Imprint* 16, no. 11 (2016): 1–39; and Matheson, *The Epistemic Significance of Disagreement*.
17 Hilary Kornblith, "Belief in the Face of Controversy," in *Disagreement*, eds. Richard Feldman and Ted Warfield (Oxford University Press, Oxford, 2010), 40–41.
18 For more on the Condorcet Jury Theorem and this example, see David M. Estlund, "Opinion Leaders, Independence, and Condorcet's Jury Theorem," *Theory and Decision* 36 (1994): 131–162.
19 Miriam Solomon, "Groupthink vs. the Wisdom of Crowds: The Social Epistemology of Deliberation and Dissent," *The Southern Journal of Philosophy* 44 (2010): 28–42; James Surowiecki, *The Wisdom of Crowds* (New York: Doubleday, 2004); Cass Sunstein, *Why Societies Need Dissent* (Cambridge, MA: Harvard University Press, 2005); and Cass Sustein, *Infotopia: How Many Minds Produce Knowledge* (New York: Oxford University Press, 2008) are good examples.
20 James Surowiecki, *The Wisdom of Crowds*.
21 Surowiecki, *The Wisdom of Crowds*, 4.
22 Cass Sunstein, *Infotopia: How Many Minds Produce Knowledge*.
23 See Sarah McGrath, "The Puzzle of Pure Moral Deference," *Philosophical Perspectives* 23, no. 1 (2009): 321–344 for posing the problem of moral deference, and Alison Hills, "Moral Testimony," *Philosophy Compass* 8, no. 6 (2013): 552–559 for seeing the landscape of the debate.
24 See Scott McElreath, Jonathan Matheson, and Nathan Nobis, "Moral Experts, Deference and Disagreement," in *Moral Expertise: New Essays from Theoretical and Clinical Perspectives*, eds. J. Watson and L. Guidry-Grimes (Switzerland: Springer, 2018), 87–105 for more on this connection.
25 Mill (1885), 156.
26 Kelly, "Consensus Gentium: Reflections on the 'Common Consent' Argument for the Existence of God."
27 For in depth discussions on belief dependence and independence, see Zach Barnett, "Belief Dependence: How Do The Numbers Count?" *Philosophical Studies* 176, no. 2 (2019): 297–319; David Estlund, "'Opinion Leaders, Independence, and Condorcet's Jury Theorem"; and Jennifer Lackey, "Disagreement and Belief Dependence: Why the Numbers Matter," in *The Epistemology of Disagreement: New Essays*, eds. David Christensen and Jennifer Lackey (Oxford: Oxford University Press, 2013), 243–268.

28 See Tomas Bogardus, "The Problem of Contingency for Religious Belief," *Faith and Philosophy* 30, no. 4 (2013): 371–392 and Roger White, "You Just Believe That Because …," *Philosophical Perspectives* 24, no. 1 (2010): 573–615 for discussions of the problem of contingency.

29 Tiddy Smith, "The Common Consent Argument for the Existence of Nature Spirits," *Australasian Journal of Philosophy* (2019) notes that wars have been fought, taxes levied, marriages forbidden, and continents colonized, all of which led to a cultural diffusion of theistic belief.

30 Kelly, "Consensus Gentium: Reflections on the 'Common Consent' Argument for the Existence of God," notes the relevance of independence in claiming that no one would think that the intellectual case for Islam would be greater if only the majority of Muslim countries had a higher birth-rate over the past decade (nor would it be weaker had they had a lower birth-rate). Zuckerman, "Atheism: Contemporary Numbers and Patterns" points out that the distribution of theistic belief/disbelief *is* greatly affected by birthrates. Since religious nations tend to have higher birthrates than irreligious nations, people with religious views constitute a growing proportion of the world's population. See also Pippa Norris and Ronald Inglehart, *Sacred and Secular: Religion and Politics Worldwide* (New York: Cambridge University Press, 2004) on this point.

31 See Lackey, "Disagreement and Belief Dependence: Why the Numbers Matter," for a detailed discussion of varieties of belief independence and how non-independently formed beliefs can still have epistemic impact. Notice that even in the recycling case it is plausible that the neighbors came to their recycling beliefs from some shared source like an HOA mailing. In such cases, even their recycling beliefs lack an important kind of independence.

32 Lackey, "Disagreement and Belief Dependence: Why the Numbers Matter," calls this "autonomous belief dependence," 249.

33 Kelly, "'Consensus Gentium: Reflections on the 'Common Consent' Argument for the Existence of God."

34 A final worry is that even though theistic belief is more prevalent than not *right now*, once we appreciate how the numbers are changing across time, it looks like theistic belief is trending down. For instance, in the United States, belief in God has declined from 92% in 2007 to 89% in 2014, with sharper drops in categories that require being fairly certain that God exists from 88% in 2007 to 83% in 2014. If theistic belief is trending down, does that mean that the majority opinion is not to be trusted? It depends upon what the best explanation of the trend is. Is the decline of theistic belief merely a cultural trend, like intellectual bell bottoms, or does it indicate that we are making intellectual progress toward the truth? Further, one might question if theistic belief is indeed trending down. While there are decreases in theistic belief in the West, these changes appear to be compensated by much larger gains elsewhere (e.g. Africa, China).

35 This follows J. L. Schellenberg, *Divine Hiddenness and Human Reason* (Ithaca: Cornell University Press, 1993).

36 For a fuller treatment of the problem of divine hiddenness see eds. Daniel Howard-Snyder and Paul Moser, *Divine Hiddenness: New Essays* (New York: Cambridge University Press, 2002) and Schellenberg, *Divine Hiddenness and Human Reason*.

37 Andrew Cullison, "'Two Solutions to the Problem of Divine Hiddenness," *American Philosophical Quarterly* 47 (2010): 119–134, and Travis Dumsday, "'Divine Hiddenness, Free Will, and the Victims of Wrongdoing," *Faith and Philosophy* 27 (2010): 423–438.

38 See Justin McBrayer and Philip Swenson, "Skepticism About the Argument From Divine Hiddenness," *Religious Studies* 48 (2012): 129-150, and Daniel Howard-Snyder, "Divine Openness and Creaturely Nonresistant Nonbelief" in *Hidden Divinity and Religious Belief: New perspectives*, eds. Adam Green and Eleonore Stump (Cambridge: Cambridge University Press, 2015) for two examples.
39 Thanks to Tomas Bogardus for this helpful example.
40 For a discussion of these rival explanations, see Kelly, "Consensus Gentium: Reflections on the 'Common Consent' Argument for the Existence of God," and Alvin Plantinga, *Warranted Christian Belief* (New York: Oxford University Press, 2000) and *Where the Conflict Really Lies*, (New York: Oxford University Press, 2011).
41 In this literature, the focus of the debate has been on whether the cognitive science of religion lays the foundation for a kind of debunking argument against the rationality of religious belief. Our focus here is simply on how well it can explain the existence of religious belief (ignoring debates about the reliability of such mechanisms).
42 Matthew Braddock, "Debunking Arguments and the Cognitive Science of Religion," *Theologia and Science* 14, no. 3 (2016): 268-287.
43 D. S. Wilson, *Darwin's Cathedral* (Chicago: University of Chicago Press, 2002).
44 See J. L. Barrett, *Why Would Anyone Believe in God?* (Walnut Creek, CA: AltaMira Press, 2004) for a detailed defense of this view.
45 J. L. Barrett, *Why Would Anyone Believe in God?*, 31.
46 See Matthew Braddock, "Debunking Arguments and the Cognitive Science of Religion," 268-287.
47 Jason Marsh, "Darwin and the Problem of Natural Nonbelief," *The Monist* 96, no.3 (2013): 361-362.
48 This is due to the prevalence of pantheistic and finite god beliefs brought about by these cognitive mechanisms. For more on this point, see Braddock, 'Debunking Arguments and the Cognitive Science of Religion'.
49 Tiddy Smith, 'The Common Consent Argument for the Existence of Nature Spirits', *Australasian Journal of Philosophy* 98, no.2 (2019): 334-348 argues that such an evolutionary debunking argument has a stronger opponent in animism as opposed to theism.
50 See Joshua Thurow, 'Does Cognitive Science Show Belief in God to be Irrational? The Epistemic Consequences of the Cognitive Science of Religion', *International Journal for Philosophy of Religion* 74, no. 1 (2013): 77-98 for more on this point.
51 See Alvin Plantinga, *Warranted Christian Belief* (New York: Oxford University Press, 2000) and Alvin Plantinga, *Where the Conflict Really Lies* (New York: Oxford University Press, 2011) for a detailed defense of this claim.
52 It is important to remember that an argument being invalid is not itself a reason to reject it. Invalid arguments can still be very strong. The recycling argument is but one instance of a good (invalid) argument.
53 Since most people have never considered the CCA, most people do not have a belief about it. So, the version of a common consent argument that applies to itself must restrict the relevant population to those who have considered the argument. This parallels the way in which the relevant population was restricted to people in my neighborhood in the recycling argument.
54 Special thanks to Tomas Bogardus, Matt Frise, Nate King, and Ted Poston for helpful comments on this paper, and to Jamie Lang for her help as a research assistant.

Bibliography

Barnett, Zach, "Belief Dependence: How do the Numbers Count?" *Philosophical Studies* 176, no. 2 (2019): 297–319.

Barrett, J. L., *Why would Anyone Believe in God?* Walnut Creek, CA: AltaMira Press, 2004.

Bogardus, Tomas, "The Problem of Contingency for Religious Belief," *Faith and Philosophy* 30, no. 4 (2013): 371–392.

Bogardus, Tomas, and Mallorie Urban, "How to Tell Whether Christians and Muslims Worship the Same God," *Faith and Philosophy* 34, no. 2 (2017): 176–200.

Braddock, Matthew, "Debunking Arguments and the Cognitive Science of Religion," *Theologia and Science* 14, no. 3 (2016): 268–287.

Carey, Brandon, and Jonathan Matheson, "How Skeptical is the Equal Weight View?" in *Disagreement and Skepticism*, edited by D. Machuca, New York: Routledge, 2013, 131–149.

Cullison, Andrew, "Two Solutions to the Problem of Divine Hiddenness," *American Philosophical Quarterly* 47 (2010): 119–134.

Dumsday, Travis, "Divine Hiddenness, Free Will, and the Victims of Wrongdoing," *Faith and Philosophy* 27 (2010): 423–438.

Easwaran, Kenny, Luke Fenton-Glynn, Christopher Hitchcock, and Joel D. Velasco, "Updating on the Credences of Others: Disagreement, Agreement, and Synergy," *Philosopher's Imprint* 16, no. 11 (2016): 1–39.

Estlund, David M. "Opinion Leaders, Independence, and Condorcet's Jury Theorem," *Theory and Decision* 36 (1994): 131–162.

Hills, Alison, "Moral Testimony," *Philosophy Compass* 8, no. 6 (2013): 552–559.

Howard-Snyder, Daniel and Paul Moser (eds.), *Divine Hiddenness: New Essays*, New York: Cambridge University Press, 2002.

Howard-Snyder, Daniel, "Divine Openness and Creaturely Nonresistant Nonbelief," in *Hidden Divinity and Religious Belief: New Perspectives*, edited by Adam Green and Leonore Stump. Cambridge: Cambridge University Press, 2015, 126–138.

Kelly, Thomas, "The Epistemic Significance of Disagreement," in *Oxford Studies in Epistemology*, volume 1, edited by John Hawthorne and Tamar Gendler, Oxford: Oxford University Press, 2005, 167–196.

Kelly, Thomas, "Consensus Gentium: Reflections on the 'Common Consent' Argument for the Existence of God," in *Evidence and Religious Belief*, edited by K. J. Clark and R. J. VanArragon, Oxford: Oxford University Press, 2011, 135–156.

Kornblith, Hilary, "Belief in the Face of Controversy," in *Disagreement*, edited by Richard Feldman and Ted Warfield, Oxford: Oxford University Press, 2010, 29–52.

Kreeft, Peter, and Ronald Tacelli, *Handbook of Christian Apologetics*, Downers Grove, IL: InterVarsity Press, 1994.

Lackey, Jennifer, "Disagreement and Belief Dependence: Why the Numbers Matter," in *The Epistemology of Disagreement: New Essays*, edited by David Christensen and Jennifer Lackey, Oxford: Oxford University Press, 2013, 243–268.

McBrayer, Justin, and Philip Swenson, "Skepticism about the Argument from Divine Hiddenness," *Religious Studies* 48 (2012): 129–150.

McElreath, Scott, Jonathan Matheson, and Nathan Nobis, "Moral Experts, Deference and Disagreement," in *Moral Expertise: New Essays from Theoretical and Clinical Perspectives*, edited by J. Watson and L. Guidry-Grimes. Switzerland: Springer, 2018, 87–105.

McGrath, Sarah, "The Puzzle of Pure Moral Deference," *Philosophical Perspectives* 23, no. 1 (2009): 321–344.
Mackie, J. L., *The Miracle of Theism*, New York: Oxford University, Press, 1983.
Marsh, Jason, "Darwin and the Problem of Natural Nonbelief," *The Monist* 96, no.3 (2013): 349–376.
Matheson, Jonathan, *The Epistemic Significance of Disagreement*, New York: Palgrave, 2015.
Mill, J. S., *Three Essays on Religion: Nature, the Utility of Religion, and Theism*. London: Longman, Reader, Dyer, and Green, 1874 edition.
Norris, Pippa, and Ronald Inglehart, *Sacred and Secular: Religion and Politics Worldwide*, New York: Cambridge University Press, 2004.
Pew Research Center, "When Americans Say They Believe in God, What Do They Mean?" April 25, 2018, https://www.pewforum.org/2018/04/25/when-americans-say-they-believe-in-god-what-do-they-mean/
Plantinga, Alvin, *Warranted Christian Belief*, New York: Oxford University Press, 2000.
Plantinga, Alvin, *Where the Conflict Really Lies*, New York: Oxford University Press, 2011.
Reid, Jasper, "The Common Consent Argument from Herbert to Hume," *Journal of the History of Philosophy* 53, no. 3 (2015): 401–433.
Schellenberg, J. L., *Divine Hiddenness and Human Reason*, Ithaca: Cornell University Press, 1993.
Smith, Tiddy, "The Common Consent Argument for the Existence of Nature Spirits," *Australasian Journal of Philosophy* 98, no. 2 (2019): 334–348.
Sobel, John Howard, *The Miracle of Theism*, Cambridge University Press, 2003.
Solomon, Miriam, "Groupthink vs. the Wisdom of Crowds: The Social Epistemology of Deliberation and Dissent," *The Southern Journal of Philosophy* 44, (2010): 28–42.
Surowiecki, James, *The Wisdom of Crowds*, New York: Doubleday, 2004.
Sunstein, Cass, *Why Societies Need Dissent*, Cambridge: Harvard University Press, 2005.
Sunstein, Cass, *Infotopia: How Many Minds Produce Knowledge*, New York: Oxford University Press, 2008.
Swinburne, Richard, *The Existence of God*, Oxford University Press, 2004.
Thurow, Joshua, "Does Cognitive Science Show Belief in God to be Irrational? The Epistemic Consequences of the Cognitive Science of Religion," *International Journal for Philosophy of Religion* 74, no. 1 (2013): 77–98.
Titelbaum, Michael, "Rationality's Fixed Point (or: In Defense of Right Reason)," in *Oxford Studies in Epistemology*, Volume 5, edited by Tamar Gendler and John Hawthorne, Oxford: Oxford University Press, 2015, 253–294.
William Wainwright (ed.), *Oxford Handbook of Philosophy of Religion*, Oxford: Oxford University Press, 2007.
White, Roger, "You Just Believe That Because …," *Philosophical Perspectives* 24, no. 1 (2010): 573–615.
Wilson, D. S., *Darwin's Cathedral*, Chicago: University of Chicago Press, 2002.
Zuckerman, Phil, "Atheism: Contemporary Numbers and Patterns," in *The Cambridge Companion to Atheism* edited by Michael Martin, New York: Cambridge University Press 2007, 47–65.

18

The Argument from Ramified Natural Theology

Sandra Menssen and Thomas D. Sullivan

1. What is ramified natural theology, and why should anyone care?

Once upon a time, in the city of Seville, there lived a madman confined to an asylum, who came to think he had been cured.[1] The man was well-educated; in fact, he had been a canon lawyer, and his eloquent pleas for liberty persuaded the Archbishop that the lawyer had recovered his reason. A chaplain was sent to arrange a release. Before departing, the lawyer and the chaplain visited the area where the other inmates were incarcerated. One of them, learning of the lawyer's impending freedom, became enraged, saying: "I am the one who should be discharged, not you! I will take revenge: I am Jupiter the Thunderer, able to send the rains or withhold them; and for three years, I will not let a single drop of rain fall upon this ignorant town!" Upon which, the lawyer turned to the chaplain and said, with complete genuineness: "Do not worry; he is Jupiter, but *I am Neptune*, the father and god of waters; and *I will cause the rains to fall!*" After the bystanders' laughter died down, the chaplain decided the time had not yet come to free the insane lawyer.

Nobody takes seriously the claims of the likes of "Jupiter" and "Neptune" to be divinities. Yet across millennia and nations, men and women of every station in life have revered a first-century Nazarene Jew who purported to be a god. And more broadly, the venerable Abrahamic religions have been studied, respected, and believed by multitudes; indeed, they are thought to provide lenses through which we may view the world and our purposes within it.

Evidence supports our taking at least some bold claims of the great religious traditions seriously, all the while we reject lunatic pronouncements of a would-be Jupiter or Neptune. *Ramified natural theology excavates that evidence.*

Traditional or "bare" natural theology argues for the existence of God using evidence we access through our ordinary cognitive faculties, whereas ramified natural theology (RNT) uses that same sort of evidence to argue for more specific and robust claims of particular religions. An argument in RNT might conclude to a detailed claim *within* a religious tradition, such as that Jesus was resurrected or that Mohammad was a prophet of God; or, the argument might be more general, concluding to the claim that a particular religion (Christianity, for instance, or Lutheranism, or Islam) was divinely revealed.

The label "ramified natural theology" is relatively new. Richard Swinburne coined the phrase in 2004, focusing on the use of "generally agreed historical data" to support detailed doctrinal claims.[2] Commentators on RNT have expanded the allowable evidence to encompass *any* data that can be accessed through our ordinary cognitive faculties, or through sense and reason.[3] Paradigmatic examples of RNT include probabilistic arguments supporting miracle-claims, such as the contention that Jesus rose from the dead.[4] Since discussion of RNT has taken place largely within the Christian community of philosophers, that's where the paradigmatic examples are found.

The label for the enterprise is new, but the project itself is not, as Swinburne clearly noted when he introduced the terminology. John Locke, William Paley, and Blaise Pascal all argued that Christianity was more reasonable than other theistic religions, given our historical evidence. More specifically, John Henry Cardinal Newman argued that the historical development of Christian doctrine supports Roman Catholicism over Anglicanism; Martin Luther argued that the doctrine's development supported something other than the Roman Catholicism of his day.

Swinburne's own approach to RNT imagines an appropriate chronological order of investigation: first one undertakes "bare" natural theology (as he terms it), arguing for the existence of God, and next one examines detailed claims of a particular religious tradition.[5] It appears to be a widely shared, though tacit, presupposition of much twentieth and early twenty-first-century natural theology that one cannot obtain a convincing philosophical case for specific religious or revelatory claims without first obtaining a probable case for God's existence (a case that renders God's existence more probable than not).

Given this understanding of appropriate chronology, the imagery of ramification seems fitting. An inquirer into the truth of a religion, a revelatory claim, begins with a single trunk of arguments, the arguments of natural theology; at some point the trunk splits into several main branches (including Judaism, Christianity, and Islam), and these in turn present increasingly ramified options (some commentators speak of "doubly-ramified" natural theology, with arguments of particular denominations of Christianity in mind).

Still, even within the assumptions of this chronological approach, the imagery suggests too neat a division. What is packed into establishing God's existence? Typically, the effort involves showing the existence of some sort of originator or creator, and then arguing that the originator has the classic divine attributes. However, there is no consensus as to what these attributes are. And even if it's agreed, say, that *divine perfection* is among them, it might be argued that this attribute entails properties that some, but not all, specific religious traditions assign to God. For instance, Anselm argued that divine perfection entails a triune God; but not all monotheisms are trinitarian. So, do philosophical arguments that divine perfection entails the trinity belong to traditional natural theology (since they are arguments about what a classic divine attribute involves), or RNT (since they are arguments for specific religious doctrines)? The answer might well be that the arguments belong *both* to traditional and to ramified natural theology; but then the imagery of the branching tree is unhelpful.

And in fact, the underlying assumption Swinburne and others appear to make regarding the order of inquiry is mistaken. Why has it been supposed that the ordering protocol is appropriate? Perhaps due to logical considerations about complex questions: it may seem that to answer a complex question, one must first answer any embedded simpler question. More specifically, it may seem that if one is wondering whether there is a God who has revealed key doctrines of Christianity (for instance), one must first answer the embedded question: Is there a God? But counterexamples upend the ordering protocol. The statement "There is a planet beyond Uranus that is perturbing its orbit" embeds the sub-statement "There is a planet beyond Uranus," but investigators focused on proving the more complex, embedding statement, and thereby established the existence of Uranus.

Some arguments in RNT ignore the overly-rigid ordering protocol, embracing the possibility of establishing *at one and the same time* the existence of God and the truth of a particular religious or revelatory tradition.[6] Thus, the imagery of a tree trunk opening into branches that become increasingly ramified, insofar as it suggests a linear investigative protocol, can be misleading. If aspects of the image seem helpful, it might be good to particularize it by thinking of a banyan tree, whose branches grow down and become roots. In our view, *specific* religious doctrines and practices (the branches, in this image) nourish and sustain most *practical* inquiry into the existence of God (represented by the tree trunk), most inquiry aimed at deciding whether actually to believe, and live in accordance with, the claim that God exists.

Why should anyone care what RNT is? For multiple reasons. It may be used to help choose among competing revelatory claims, claims from different religious traditions and claims from different denominations of the same tradition. It may be used ecumenically, to explore commonalities that weave through traditions. It may be used to clarify theological doctrines and their implications (the line between RNT and "analytic theology" is not always sharp). Its applications are boundless, as the sweep of the literature signals. But perhaps the most important reason to care about RNT is the one suggested by the image of the banyan tree: RNT can be used to argue for the existence of God, *simultaneously* with arguing for detailed doctrinal claims. That approach provides an end-run around barriers to addressing the problem of evil, for it unlocks an array of resources unavailable at the level of "bare" natural theology. Critics of theism introduce evils as evidence against a good God; however, without listening to the voice of the accused, the evidence is incomplete. And the voice of the accused is heard in the scriptures and doctrines that anchor RNT.

2. The argument from revelatory content: argument frame

RNT ranges across multitudinous and disparate arguments, and we can't detail the entire span. Rather, in the remainder of this essay we'll develop an extended example of RNT which we'll call "the argument from revelatory content." It is, in our experience, powerful;[7] but it is little discussed. We speak of *the* argument from revelatory content, but along with classic arguments in natural theology (the cosmological argument, the ontological argument, etc.) this argument in RNT is actually a family of lines of reasoning.

In Section 2 we introduce an argument-frame that can generate a variety of specific arguments from revelatory content and we make a case that the frame is reasonable. In Section 3, we will illustrate how the frame might be used. The illustration will involve deploying a specific argument from the revelatory content of Christianity, which starts to point to the conclusion that the Christian revelatory claim is true. The illustration is intended to begin to make good on the promise of the general argument-frame. We hope all of this will invite longer and richer treatments of the argument from revelatory content: its ultimate effectiveness would reside in fuller discussions.

The entire business can be helped along by reflecting on an analogy.

Classical scholars interested in the *Iliad*'s authorship have long recognized that the text was transmitted orally across centuries, with improvisation along the way. But some twentieth-century classicists thought there was, nevertheless, a single individual (call him Homer) primarily responsible for the *Iliad*, and others denied there was a single major author. The dispute was resolved through analysis of the content of the epic poem. Its unity, the consistency of its language, particular vocabulary features such as use of Aeolic forms and patronymics, and similar considerations suggested that the best explanation of the content of the *Iliad* was that a Homer had existed and had authored the saga. Similarly, one might, through examination of the content of a specific revelatory claim, reach the compound conclusion that God exists, *and* that God authored or bestowed a revelation.

The so-called "unitary thesis" that a Homer existed (in the sense just mentioned) was out of favor for a time at least in part because it was thought a single individual couldn't, without the aid of writing, compose a poem the length of the *Iliad*. But the work of field linguists in southern Serbia in the 1930s dispelled this fiction: peoples without writing are better, not less, able to memorize long texts, and certainly capable of their composition. Once classicists recognized this, they were motivated to look for aspects of the content of the *Iliad* that could speak for or against the unitary thesis. Similarly, traditional arguments of natural theology might prepare the ground for the argument from revelatory content—without delivering the verdict that God's existence is more probable than not.

We take revelatory content to be content of a *revelatory claim*. A revelatory claim has the form: *G revealed that P*, where G is a supernatural being and P is a propositional content, perhaps a very complex content (which must be extracted from the language in which it's presented). Examples of the content of a revelatory claim include:

- God divided the Red Sea to allow the children of Israel to escape Pharaoh's army.
- The teachings of Islam are true.
- The lion-goddess wrote a mathematical theorem on my tongue last night.

The content of a revelatory claim may be specified variously, e.g. through reference to particular sacred scriptures or other authoritative pronouncements.

An argument from revelatory content employs the following argument-frame or template:

(1) The revelatory content R has the characteristic of being F [substitute for F: beautiful, sublime, resilient, fertile, original, unified, intelligent, wise, affecting, counter-cultural, uplifting to the hopeless and bedeviled – and the list goes on].

(2) If R has the characteristic of being F, then R can be recognized by an inquirer with an adequate cognitive and affective base to be F.
(3) If R can be recognized by an inquirer with an adequate cognitive and affective base to be F, then the plausibility of R and the plausibility that R was revealed can rightly be enhanced for the inquirer through recognition that R is F.
(4) [So,] The plausibility of R and the plausibility that R was revealed can rightly be enhanced for an inquirer with an adequate cognitive and affective base, through recognition that R is F.

A brief comment about each of the first three steps.

Some will say that the characteristics listed in (1) are merely subjective. It is, of course, the case that different people will perceive different characteristics more or less well. But there is a fact of the matter underlying what is perceived. The point is readily recognized by thinking about characteristics from the other end of the spectrum. There are ugly, vile doctrines in some religious texts, concerning genocide, for instance, and child sacrifice. These practices are *actually* horrible. Likewise, a reality that's actually beautiful and sublime may underlie religious teachings.

Moving to (2): What constitutes an inquirer's cognitive and affective base? It includes what's standardly, though vaguely, called "evidence." Further, though this is not widely recognized, it includes "quasi-facts," which the inquirer suspects are true but is not sure about. In plenty of cases one comes to accept as an actual fact something held tentatively, upon receiving an explanation of how it could be true. That's what we mean by a quasi-fact. You might, for instance, take it that *Humans have libertarian freedom* is a hypothesis conditional-upon-explanation: a quasi-fact. The base also includes non-propositional content. Suppose you have an experience of a pointillist painting, with its shimmering colors. How do you express, exactly, what that impression is? Here, and in an endless number of other cases, there is a mismatch between the sensuous experience and its verbalization. Further, the base includes various psychological states, some conscious and some unconscious; and memories, some deeply buried and others not; and dispositions to behavior; and *a priori* reasoning.

While much remains fixed in a person's psyche, a good deal of the cognitive and affective base changes, sometimes rapidly. One twist and things come into focus. In fact, our cognitive and affective bases *include* focal points. For Darwin, consciousness of the parasitoid wasp's activity served this role. Darwin said that given the way the wasp reproduces, he couldn't believe in a good God: the wasp injects caterpillars with eggs that eventually allow tiny larvae to eat the host, inside out. Another individual might have a centering experience pointing in a different direction. Imagine a man who has an encounter on a par with that of King David when the prophet Nathan unveiled him as a murderous adulterer. Suddenly, arguments leading to the cross and redemption are illuminated: somebody needs to pay the price. (That illumination might not yield the judgment that a revelatory claim is *true*. It might instead produce resolution to carry the inquiry forward and seek more evidence. But that would be no small thing.)

The cognitive and affective base must be *adequate*, (2) says. We don't mean that some individuals will luck into rightly formed bases; we don't take an "adequate" cognitive and affective base to be much akin to "properly basic" beliefs. But different background experiences will equip different individuals to recognize different features of a revelatory claim. Sometimes, for instance, the target characteristic F may be perceived only with knowledge of one's failures or limitations. We need sight to appreciate a spectacular sunset; we may need the experience of utter helplessness to understand the uplifting beauty of the Psalms.

Finally, a few words about (3): There's no doubt that people do come to find religious claims plausible based on perceptions such as those we've described. But why think this *rightly* happens? One may think it rightly happens if one believes (as we do) that the base is there in reality: the plausibility of the revelatory content referred to in the argument template is grounded on that ontological base.

The move made in (3) can be repeated: An argument involving revelatory content can build. You may begin by considering a particular doctrine R-1, perhaps concerning the incarnation, and the extent to which that doctrine has a specific characteristic, say the characteristic of *fittingness*. (That is the characteristic we will focus on in Section 3 of this paper.) If your reflection enhances the plausibility of R for you and the plausibility that R was revealed, then that conclusion will be part of a new, enlarged cognitive and affective base if and when you go on to consider a different doctrine, R-2, maybe a doctrine about resurrection.

And often there are linkages among the various specific doctrines making up the revelatory content (R-1, R-2, etc.), ties that strengthen the credibility of the overall revelatory claim. Sometimes so-called "cumulative case arguments" in natural theology are understood as additive: each new argument increases the probability of the conclusion that God exists, and over time the conjoined arguments build up into one strong argument. We certainly don't deny that happens. But a conjunction may give two reasons for the same conclusion, without any interconnections. The situation is different when there are linkages. Think of the way a friendship builds: over time, memories of earlier shared experiences stay with the new relationship, presuming it thickens. One reason the second day is nice is that the first one was: the memories are built into the developing relationship. Or, take an example from medicine. Clinicians making medical diagnoses recognize that it may be possible for a person who tests positive for a very rare disease to have only a small chance of actually having the disease, even if the test is highly accurate. A positive result in a second, independent test does not merely double the odds the first diagnosis was correct; it far more dramatically increases those odds.

2.a. Objections to the argument-frame, and replies

The argument from revelatory content, it may be said, is vulnerable to a logical objection. Our case implies that the whole interconnected body of content of a major revelatory claim—a long conjunctive proposition—might be more believable than a component conjunct or a consequence (such as "Jesus was resurrected from the dead"). However, an objector may aver, this is widely recognized as incorrect. As Richard Pettigrew says, "I ought not to believe a proposition more strongly than I believe a logical consequence of it."[8] (A conjunct of a proposition is, of course, a logical consequence of it.)

But the claim underlying this objection is false, as can be seen by counterexample. The Banach-Tarski theorem in set-theoretic geometry is so contrary to ordinary intuition that it is called a paradox: the theorem states that a solid ball can be decomposed into disjoint subsets that can be reassembled to yield two identical copies of the original ball. The theorem is a consequence of the axiom of choice in set theory, routinely regarded as non-controversial or even self-evident. Can we blame a person for attaching more credence to the axioms of set theory than to this bizarre (yet fascinating) logical consequence of the axioms? It may seem we are nit-picking: Wouldn't Pettigrew and others making the same point be presupposing that one sees how the conclusion is entailed by the premises? But in what manner "see" this? By a synoptic grasp of the mind? Or instead, step-by-step? There clearly are cases where no human can have a synoptic grasp: consider the four-color theorem. And if the manner is step-by-step, then there can be a reasonable worry that a mistake has been made at some prior step. Hence, it can be more reasonable to believe the starting point than the terminal point, even if the terminal point is entailed. Objective probability (if there is such a thing) and credence diverge.

A different protest has it that that our argument from revelatory content comes to little or nothing unless it's been snapped into proper, mathematized form—snapped into some standard schema.

But there is no agreed-upon form of non-demonstrative argument (often called "inductive" argument) that fits scientific and everyday reasoning. Three of the leading structures are frequentism, Bayesian reasoning, and likelihoodism. They have within them wide variations. And there are interesting competitors, such as Richard Jeffrey's probability kinematics. Every approach has serious limitations outside the realm of tightly controlled circumstances such as predicting whether the next card to be drawn from a fair deck will be the ace of spades. So, there's no such thing as snapping our argument in place: there's no place to snap it.

And since there isn't a system of probability that has a consensus behind it when it comes to scientific and everyday reasoning, when you choose to use one of those systems, you are making a risky commitment to a proposition regarding methodology. You have your substantive case, and then you add: the right way to package this case is through this particular (controversial) method. You may be far less sure of the applicability of the method than you are of the case itself.

We prefer to speak in terms of "plausibility" rather than "probability." Questions about the relationship between plausibility and probability are dark and deep. Karl Popper took the position that even theories that have been put to the most stringent falsification tests and have survived are not entitled to be deemed thereby more probable than they were before the tests. He spoke in terms of "corroboration" instead. He might just as well have spoken of "plausibility" and insisted that the concept of plausibility cannot be cashed out in terms of probability. The issue of the relationship between certain cognitive attitudes toward propositions, and probability, is an enormous and controversial field, about which we will say nothing more here.

Turning in yet another direction, we may find the complaint that we are running the characteristics that substitute for F through the concept of *explanation*. The beauty or fittingness of a doctrine, for example, is supposed to contribute to *explaining* it. That's a problem, it may be said, because though explanations are nice to have, they don't add to the probability or credibility of the thing explained.

Indeed, our argument-frame or template does involve explanation: a fittingness argument, for instance, is a kind of explanation.[9]

And it's true that some have thought explanations don't add to the probability or credibility of the thing explained. Distinguished theoreticians William Roche and Elliott Sober contended not long ago that "explanatoriness" is evidentially irrelevant. That is, they said, the probability of a hypothesis on a particular observation together with an explanation is equal to the probability of the hypothesis on the observation:[10]

Pr(H/O & EXPL) = Pr(H/O)

Happily, exchanges with critics led Roche and Sober to modify their original strong claim, and instead embrace one much weaker, that leaves the door wide open for the kind of argument we're giving here.[11]

We would note, too, that there are cases in the history of science in which explanation all but alone carried whatever credibility was given to a particular hypothesis. A distinguished example is Galileo's argument against the Aristotelian theory that a heavier body falls faster than a lighter body. While it's widely thought that Galileo took the trouble to actually experiment, whereas Aristotle didn't bother to look at evidence from the senses, the truth in this case is the exact opposite. A feather and a lead ball dropped at the same time will certainly not hit the ground at the same time: that's what we infer from the evidence of the senses. Galileo's elegant argument, on the other hand, is entirely *a priori*.

3. The argument from revelatory content: an illustration

How can one sort and arrange to good effect the massive data relevant to assessing putative revelatory content? Different organizing frameworks will appeal to different inquirers. One who's historically oriented might focus on *historical narratives*, which mark significant events and, through their teleology, point to new data. One with a literary bent might turn to *parables and stories*, and the commentaries, both verbal and imagistic, that help us fathom them. A philosophically inclined inquirer will look for a *logical framework*.

Here, we will work with Aquinas's logical framework for Christian revelation. His *Summa Theologiae* is not part of the Christian canon: while he treats of topics taken up within that canon, his own treatment of the topics does not have canonical status. However, his explicit aim in the *Summa* is to provide an account of sacred science, and sacred science is the science of revelation. We will focus on his discussion of the doctrine of the incarnation, the central mystery of Christianity. And, to narrow things even further (for this brief illustration), we will concentrate on what we'll call "fittingness arguments."

Aquinas, a sacred theologian, already accepted Christian doctrine, of course. He was intent on putting some systematic order into what he had received. Our aim is quite different: we are primarily interested in how fittingness arguments can contribute to the credibility of Christianity. So here and there, we will need to redirect what Aquinas asserts, to our purposes. Using an argument by a writer for one's own purposes, and not the author's, seems to trouble some individuals. But it shouldn't. Consider (to take just one example) that the first book about what we would today call *non*-Euclidean geometry, by the Jesuit Gerolamo Saccheri, was titled *Euclid Vindicated from Every Blemish*.

Fittingness arguments are fascinating, but under-explored. And they are seldom appreciated as a means of testing the credibility of a revelation. That is likely because the arguments typically are used in theological contexts in which the truth of the claims is assumed—so the arguments can easily be dismissed as having no philosophical value. But again, there is no need to refrain from using an argument for purposes that diverge from the author's.

It often will make sense for an inquirer into Christianity to begin with the mystery of the incarnation; but not always. It may be that when you call Christmas to mind, you recoil from the idea that a woman was supposed to have conceived without having had sex, and the notion of God becoming incarnate in a baby seems absurd. You're inclined to sweep it all away as myth. However, when you think of God as a reader of hearts and begin to wonder whether you might be in big trouble, you are drawn to the cross and the promise of salvation. In that case, the place to begin is not with the incarnation, but rather the crucifixion. Take what seem to be the strongest cases first; add the weaker ones later.[12] Imagine that somebody in your office composes strategic documents particularly well. She may make a puzzling decision, but all the other times she's handled things prudently speak to the reasonableness of the judgment at issue. If this had been the *first* decision of hers you'd observed, though, your reaction might be negative. Weaker arguments are enhanced by their inclusion in the unified whole. And so are the stronger ones—as the keystone essential to the stability of an arched bridge is itself suspended by the other stones.

So: At the beginning of Part III of the *Summa*, in the very first article, Aquinas poses the question of whether it was fitting that God should become incarnate. Aquinas is clearly thinking of Christ and puts the question in the past tense. But one might simply ask whether it would be fitting for a God to become incarnate. That would broaden the discussion, so an affirmative answer would be useful to a wide range of religions. And indeed, it's helpful to recognize that in India and elsewhere, there are stories about avatars and incarnations. As C. S. Lewis pointed out, the wealth of mythology and legend surrounding incarnations removes a stumbling block for those approaching Christianity.[13]

Often, the question about whether a thing is "fitting" will turn on *circumstances*. It's fitting for a 10-year-old to run around the playground, yelling, during recess; it's not fitting for her to run around the classroom, yelling, during quiet reading time. But some things are fitting at all times and places. In discussing the incarnation, Aquinas is talking about unconditional fittingness—even though he puts his question in the past tense and focuses on a particular individual, Christ.

Aquinas's account in this article of what it is for a thing to be *fitting* (conveniens) is very philosophical—and very terse. The expression, as he (and others) use it, is an analogical or "family resemblance" term, with a focal point, particularly in the theological context, of being *appropriate for a nature*.[14]

Aquinas raises two objections to the position he'll be defending in this article. In the first place, if God takes on flesh, it is objected, he will have changed from what he was from all eternity. What could be the point? He was perfect from all eternity. And in the second place, God is infinite, but, according to the doctrine of the incarnation, is to be squeezed into a baby. How can that make sense? Aquinas reserves answers to these objections until after his positive case is presented.

That positive case come in two stages. First, in the so-called *sed contra* (but on the other hand), Aquinas cites, with approval, authorities who itemize some relevant considerations. The upshot is that the incarnation was fitting because it does us so much good. The claims here are relatively easy to understand, and include points that would occur to most of us if we asked: "If there were a God, why might God take on human flesh?" God makes the invisible intelligible through the visible, and that's *helpful* to us.

In the body of the article, or *respondeo*, where Aquinas gives his own argument, we get something more profound. For Aquinas, the deepest reasons for the incarnation rest on two propositions: *God is the essence of goodness*, and *Goodness diffuses itself*. These claims regarding the essence of God and its natural overflow into the world involve difficult matters.[15] But the core idea can be seen on the human level, where goodness is also diffusive: there is such a thing as financial, and social, and emotional generosity. Those who've been lucky recipients of human kindness and munificence have a cognitive and affective base primed to appreciate Aquinas's account. The deprived and impoverished also have experiences that can fit into Aquinas's picture: the *absence* of human grace can point to the ontological need for divine beneficence. Newman contrasts Montaigne and his creature-comforts with the poor factory girl who says, "[I]f all I have been born for is just to work my heart and life away ... and if this life is the end, and ... there is no God to wipe away all tears from all eyes, I could go mad!"[16]

To help us understand why Aquinas deems the explanation in the *respondeo* to be deeper than the explanations in the *sed contra*, it's necessary to draw, as he did, on Aristotle, who sees ideal demonstration and explanation as rooted in understanding of the nature of things, from which properties flow. For a modern illustration, consider the question: Why does gold resist rust and corrosion? It's not because it's yellow, or because it's loved by the gods; rather, it's due to its atomic structure. An explanation in terms of atomic structure is rooted in the nature of the thing explained.

One of Aristotle's examples is particularly illuminating in the present context. It's possible to give three separate demonstrations showing that, and explaining why, all triangles have interior angles summing to 180 degrees (one demonstration for each kind of triangle – isosceles, scalene, and equilateral). These explanations aren't incorrect (just as Aquinas's arguments in the *sed contra* of the article aren't incorrect). But it's in virtue of the figures being triangles, not particular kinds of triangles, that they have the property at issue. A general demonstration of the point at issue knits things together and identifies what's per se; it's a deeper explanation. Aquinas's explanation that God's diffusiveness is fitting to God's nature is about as deep, and as unifying, an explanation as one can achieve.

Thus far, we've focused on the fittingness of the incarnation, given God's nature. But we also must ask about its fittingness given human nature. An important proposition in Aquinas' overall argument for fittingness, mostly implicit in the body of this article, is that *Human nature is a fit subject for bonding to a divinity*.[17] A great deal is said elsewhere in the *Summa* on this point. The underlying idea is that human rationality makes the union suitable. God's taking on human flesh is not like God's becoming a rock, or a crocodile, or even a gorilla. Aquinas, with Aristotle and the Greeks, held that reason is the best thing in us, and urged that it be turned toward the best object there is. To understand this, we may reflect on those who rave madly: "I am Jupiter"; "I am Neptune"; "My head is made of glass"; "I'm going to shoot everybody in the school." Reason is the glory of humankind. It makes language possible, as well as feelings of a higher order, including the best kind of love; it makes understanding possible, and insight into the infinite. And for these reasons, human nature is a fit subject of an incarnation.

Aquinas' answers to the objections at the head of the article—that if God becomes incarnate, he will change, and that God's infinity is a barrier to incarnation—follow the *respondeo*. Aquinas argues that the incarnation doesn't change God in any way: the change is on the side of creation, on the side of human beings. Aquinas has a theory, as did other medievals, that there are systematically misleading expressions that apply to God. The standard way of putting things makes it look like the changes are on God's end, but it's really a matter of creation, or particular parts of creation, being changed.[18] Aquinas accepts the conclusion of the second objection (about God's infinity), but in a restricted sense. To be united to God wasn't *naturally* fitting; however, it was fitting by reason of God's infinite goodness that he should unite a human nature to himself.

The fact that Aquinas knocks out one objection after another can by itself properly raise confidence in the doctrine. Some philosophers of science see as the supreme test of a hypothesis its ability to survive the most compelling attempts to disconfirm it. They are, of course, thinking primarily of experimental work. But there's also a long history of attempts of disconfirmation which take the form of tough objections, many of them *a priori*. The medievals' laboratory was an arena of dialectic.

Unless we're content to remain in that venerable but dated arena, however, we must move to a twenty-first-century counterpart. What are the best *contemporary* objections to Aquinas's case? Many would claim the title; but we have room to touch on only one.

The one we single out goes to a doubt about human nature. Aquinas thinks rationality confers immense and special dignity on humankind. But hasn't Darwin disabused us of this archaic notion? Aren't humans basically just higher apes? Some lines in Darwin's letters and in his *Origin of Species*, picked up by modern biologists, even suggest there are no species at all, no natural kinds—only individual organisms. But whether the Darwinian position is taken to involve a denial of human nature in favor of particulars, or acceptance of human nature as a mere variety of a larger class including advanced apes, or acceptance of humans as a distinctive species separated from chimps et al. only by degree, there is nothing so special about our nature that it can ground a divine incarnation.

The broad Darwinian understanding—radically naturalistic—is the received view, and it has stunning logical consequences. In the hands of a rigorous thinker, like Peter

Singer, willing to accept all the position's entailments, we wind up with the stance that "the life of a newborn baby is of less value than the life of a pig, a dog, or a chimpanzee"—because fully-grown non-human animals are more self-aware than human newborns.[19]

Is the naturalistic Darwinian understanding correct? It is often said that evolution is not a theory, but a fact. But what fact? The two co-discoverers of the theory of natural selection, and more broadly, evolution, Darwin and Wallace, eventually took fundamentally different views of evolution as it was applied to human beings. Darwin held that all human powers, including our cognitive capacities, spring from, and can be explained by, the history of "descent with modification." Wallace accepted this with respect to human bodies but over time became dissatisfied with the idea that this history of descent could explain human cognitive powers. He argued that our brains, our cognitive abilities, are more capacious than was necessary for the early humans to cope with their environment; so, there must be a cause extrinsic to nature to account for the oversupply of powers. Unlike Darwin, Wallace saw a clear gap between human mentation and the mentation of the other animals.

Thus, we ought to recognize two branches of evolution: Wallacian and Darwinian. We might well call the core they have in common, a fact (if we make some twenty-first-century revisions). It's supported by a mountain of evidence from a variety of fields. But we should resist the claim that evolution is a fact if evolution is identified with this common core *plus* the naturalistic Darwinian idea about our cognitive powers. Some will say Darwin and his followers refuted Wallace. But we should like to know when and where: we have seen no satisfactory refutation.

Extended inquiry into big questions raised by our single article on the fittingness of the incarnation (questions concerning differences between cognitive capacities of humans and other animals, questions concerning diffusiveness of goodness, and so forth) could draw in myriad additional considerations. For instance, an inquirer whose cognitive and affective base includes the quasi-facts that *Consciousness has a function*, or that *Humans have a special place in the* universe, or that *Humans have inalienable rights* might consider whether Aquinas's approach, supplemented by the Wallacian understanding of evolution, generates *explanations* of these quasi-facts—thereby transforming them into actual facts.

A skeptical but intrigued inquirer could eventually decide to seek additional evidence, personal evidence, through participating in practices the targeted revelatory claim encourages – practices open to a non-believer. Such an inquirer could sincerely pray the agnostic's prayer (O God, if there is a God, save my soul, if I have a soul), and try to live in accord with challenging religious teachings regarding forgiveness, say, or monogamous relationships. The practices may illuminate depths of the cognitive and affective base, may generate focal experiences. Reading about King David and Nathan, one may say: I should turn not to the parasitoid wasp, but toward the mirror, and my own wrongdoing. The particular organizing framework chosen to help explore a putative revelation can show where to look in mining one's cognitive and affective base or searching out new data. (The periodic table of elements permitted Dimitri Mendeleyev to predict discovery of new chemicals that would slot into the pattern of the table.)

At the same time that one seeks new evidence, one can study the way in which Aquinas's argument for the fittingness of an incarnation continues to build, beyond the article we've examined. He goes on to ask a sequence of questions connected with understanding the union between God and human beings. The specifics involve deep metaphysical issues, such as whether the union took place in the nature, in the person, or in the "hypostasis" (too technical a concept to expand on here). There are questions on the mode of union. And so forth. All the while we approach a more precise and nuanced definition of what the incarnation is, we move toward a more defensible doctrine. And along with the questions about the incarnation's fittingness, we find a host of related fittingness questions, including: Was the annunciation fitting? Was the virgin birth fitting? Was it fitting for Christ to pray for himself? Was it fitting that he never wrote anything? Linkages abound. We progress toward Aquinas's magnificent reflections on Christ's passion, where we find 36 references to fittingness (conveniens), and if we bring in synonyms and near-synonyms, quite a few more. And we are led back to the benefits the incarnation has for humankind: the greatest of these is salvation through the cross.

The *Summa Theologiae*'s organizing framework, which envelops fittingness arguments and a multitude of other gems of reasoning, is beautiful. But the real beauty is in what's framed. The rich resources of a revelatory claim—sublime, uplifting, fitting for the human condition, and much more—may themselves support a decision to accept, at one and the same time, the conclusion that God exists, *and* the conclusion that God vouchsafed this revelation to humankind.

Notes

1. So begins the barber's story in Miguel de Cervantes, *Don Quixote*, vol. 2, Ch. 1 (we've condensed and paraphrased).
2. See Richard Swinburne, "'Natural Theology, its 'Dwindling Probabilities' and 'Lack of Rapport'," *Faith and Philosophy* 21, no. 4 (2004): 533–546.
3. See Andrew Chignell and Derk Pereboom, "Natural Theology and Natural Religion," in *The Stanford Encyclopedia of Philosophy*, ed. Edward N. Zalta (Stanford University, 1997–), retrieved from https://plato.stanford.edu/archives/spr2017/entries/natural-theology/. See also: Angus Menuge and Charles Taliaferro, "Guest Editors' Introduction," *Philosophia Christi* 5, no. 2 (2013): 233.
4. Other examples of paradigmatic projects in the enterprise include Swinburne's "Natural Theology, its 'Dwindling Probabilities' and 'Lack of Rapport'," and the collection of essays on ramified natural theology in the special issue of *Philosophia Christi*, eds. Angus Menuge and Charles Taliaferro 5, no. 2 (2013).
5. As Swinburne puts it in "Natural Theology, its 'Dwindling Probabilities' and 'Lack of Rapport'," 'In order to pursue ramified natural theology, Plantinga claims correctly, we need first bare natural theology to argue for the existence of God" (538).
6. This may be becoming more widely recognized. See, for instance, Menuge and Taliaferro, "Guest Editors' Introduction"; Hugh G. Gauch, "Natural Theology's Case for Jesus's Resurrection," *Philosophia Christi* 13, no. 2 (2011); and Sandra Menssen and Thomas D. Sullivan, "The Existence of God and the Existence of Homer: Rethinking Theism and Revelatory Claims," *Faith and Philosophy* 19, no. 3 (2002).
7. Both of us are adult converts to theism and Christianity. The lines of reasoning we each (independently) traced many years ago as we moved toward Christian theism

were rough facsimiles of "the argument from revelatory content" articulated and illustrated in the remainder of this essay. Our earlier work along these lines includes Sandra Menssen and Thomas D. Sullivan, *The Agnostic Inquirer* (Grand Rapids, MI: Eerdmans, 2007). The present essay extends in several directions from our earlier work.

8   Richard Pettigrew, "Epistemic Utility Arguments for Probabilism," in *The Stanford Encyclopedia of Philosophy*, ed. Edward N. Zalta (Stanford University, 1997–), retrieved from https://plato.stanford.edu/archives/win2019/entries/epistemic-utility/.

9   See our discussion of inference to the best explanation and of ideal explanation in Menssen and Sullivan, *Agnostic Inquirer*, 171–196.

10 William Roche and Elliott Sober, "Explanatoriness is Evidentially Irrelevant, or Inference to the Best Explanation Meets Bayesian Confirmation Theory," *Analysis* 73 (2013): 659–668.

11 William Roche and Elliott Sober, "'Inference to the Best Explanation and the Screening-Off Challenge," *Teorema* XXXVIII, no. 3 (2019): 121–142.

12 Richard Jeffrey created probability kinematics (which violates the Kolmogorov axioms) in order to account for the reality that the order of consideration of evidence matters—though order does not matter in standard systems. Richard C. Jeffrey, *The Logic of Decision*, 2nd edn. (Chicago: University of Chicago Press, 1990).

13 See Lewis's discussion of differences between the Christian account of incarnation and the accounts found in other religions: C. S. Lewis, "Myth Became Fact," in *God in the Dock* (Grand Rapids, MI: Eerdmans, 1970).

14 "Conveniens" isn't the only term Aquinas used for the family of concepts. Among the other terms he employed are "congruens" (congruent) and various Latin expressions for what "ought to be the case."

15 We discuss some of them in Sandra Menssen and Thomas D. Sullivan, "Must God Create?" *Faith and Philosophy* 12, no. 3 (July 1995).

16 John Henry Newman, *An Essay in Aid of a Grammar of Assent* (Notre Dame, IN: University of Notre Dame Press, 1979), 247.

17 Homo sapiens alone, or other hominids? If the other hominids were rational, they are included in Aquinas's argument.

18 Aquinas's account of the ways in which human understanding and expression are limited provides the substance of a response to Alvin Plantinga's argument that God does not have a nature. If Plantinga's argument were correct, Aquinas's central argument in the body of the article we're focused on would fail. See Alvin Plantinga, *Does God Have a Nature?* (Marquette: Marquette University Press, 1980). And see Aquinas, *Summa Theologiae*, I.I., q.13., a.1.

19 Peter Singer, *Practical Ethics* (Cambridge: Cambridge University Press, 1979): 123. Singer reiterates the general point in the 1993 and 2011 editions of *Practical Ethics*, though in the 2011 edition he makes the abstract claim without reference to pigs, dogs, or chimpanzees.

Bibliography

Cervantes, Miguel de, *Don Quixote*, 1605, Vol. 2, ch.1.

Chignell, Andrew and Derk Pereboom, "'Natural Theology and Natural Religion," *The Stanford Encyclopedia of Philosophy*, edited by Edward N. Zalta, Spring 2017 edition, https://plato.stanford.edu/archives/spr2017/entries/natural-theology/.

Gauch, Hugh G., "Natural Theology's Case for Jesus's Resurrection," *Philosophia Christi* 13, no. 2 (2011): 339–355.
Jeffrey, Richard C., *The Logic of Decision*, 2nd edition, Chicago: University of Chicago Press, 1990.
Lewis, C. S., "Myth Became Fact," in *God in the Dock*, Grand Rapids, MI: Eerdmans, 1970.
Menuge, Angus, and Charles Taliaferro, "'Guest Editors' Introduction," *Philosophia Christi* 15, no. 2 (2013): 233.
Menssen, Sandra, and Thomas D. Sullivan, "Must God Create?"' *Faith and Philosophy* 12, no. 3 (July 1995): 321–341.
Menssen, Sandra, and Thomas D. Sullivan, *The Agnostic Inquirer*, Grand Rapids: Eerdmans, 2007.
Menssen, Sandra, and Thomas D. Sullivan, "The Existence of God and the Existence of Homer: Rethinking Theism and Revelatory Claims," *Faith and Philosophy* 19, no. 3 (2002): 331–347.
Newman, John Henry, *An Essay in Aid of a Grammar of Assent*, Notre Dame, IN: University of Notre Dame Press, 1979.
Pettigrew, Richard, "Epistemic Utility Arguments for Probabilism," *The Stanford Encyclopedia of Philosophy*, edited by Edward N. Zalta, Winter 2019 edition, https://plato.stanford.edu/archives/win2019/entries/epistemic-utility/.
Plantinga, Alvin. *Does God Have a Nature?* Marquette: Marquette University Press, 1980.
Roche, William, and Elliott Sober, "'Explanatoriness is Evidentially Irrelevant, or inference to the Best Explanation Meets Bayesian Confirmation Theory," *Analysis* 73 (2013): 659–668.
Roche, William, and Elliott Sober, "Inference to the Best Explanation and the Screening-Off Challenge," *teorema* XXXVIII, no. 3 (2019): 121–142.
Singer, Peter, *Practical Ethics*, Cambridge: Cambridge University Press, 1979.
Swinburne, Richard, "Natural Theology, its 'Dwindling Probabilities' and 'Lack of Rapport,'" *Faith and Philosophy* 21, no. 4 (2004): 533–546.

Index

Abbruzzese, John Edward 54
abductive inferences 118
abstracta 229–30
Achilles 39
Adams, Robert 151, 191
Aeolic forms 314
afterlife 9, 11–12, 236, 240–41, 244, 271, 278
agent causation 119
agnosticism 161, 274, 276
agnostic naturalism 160–61
Alberts, Bruce 99
alethicity 217, 219, 222–23, 225, 228–29
Alexander, Tsar 287
Alston, William P. 54, 180, 253, 255, 260
amino acid 102, 111–13
Anglicanism 312
Anscombe, Elizabeth 139
Anselm, St. 3, 13, 51–54, 57, 59, 61, 190, 278, 282–83
anthropic coincidences 121
Anthropic Objection 4
Anthropic Principle 205, 213n.49
anti-realism 8, 196, 206–9
The Applicability of Mathematics as a Philosophical Problem (Steiner) 195
Aquinas, St. Thomas,
    and Christian revelation 318–23, 324nn.14, 17–18
    and classical theism 190
    and desire 235, 237–38, 240–41, 245, 247n.3
    and the 'Fifth Way' 90
    and the KCA 35
    and meaning of life 283
    proving existence of God 53
ARE 252–54, 256, 258, 265
'Argument from Desire' (Lewis) 284–85
Aristotle 140, 150, 236–37, 241, 318, 320–21
Armstrong, D. M. 153, 286

Arnhart, Larry 134
assessment 227, 231n.19
atheism,
    and Bertrand Russell 239
    and certainty 192
    and divine hiddenness 300
    and existence of God 59, 272–74, 276
    and Freudianism 260
    and idea of God 52
    and mathematics 209
    and multiverse 84
    and origin of first life 120
Augustine, St. 167, 182, 190, 236, 282–83
Ayala, Francisco 109

bacterial flagellum 5, 99–102
Baker, Lynne Rudder 64
Balaguer, Mark 204, 207
Banach-Tarski theorem 317
Barcan formula 60
Barnes, Luke 73–74, 83
Barrett, J. L. 302
Bayesian reasoning 317
Bayes' Theorem 4, 75–77, 82
Bealer, George 186
beauty argument,
    conclusions 175–76
    explanatory regress 172–75
    introduction 167–68
    naturalistic 168–69
    subjective 169–70, 177n.16
    world with ugliness 171
Benetar, David 282
Bernstein, C'Zar 61
Bevan, Edwyn 285
Beversluis, John 243
Bhagavad Gita 285
Bible, the, 1, 217, 258, 278
Big Bang theory 36, 70, 73, 123, 149
Big Crunch 73

Biochemical Predestination (Kenyon/Steinman) 113
biological complexity,
  conclusion 104
  criticism and replies 101–4
  empirical argument 95–101
  philosophical argument 4, 89–95
Biology Direct (journal) 102
biophilia hypothesis 168–69
blob of everything 2, 19–20
Boethius 282–83
Bohm's pilot-wave model 43
Boltzmann brains 83
bootstrapping 25–26
Born, Max 199–200
Broad, C. D. 252
The Brothers Karamazov (Dostoevsky) 129

Calvin, John 283
Camus, Albert 238
Carroll, Sean 4, 72–73
Cartwright, Nancy 255
Castlereagh, Lord 287
The Catechism of the Catholic Church 283–84
Categorical Imperative 131, 139
causal adequacy 118–19
causal loops 42–43, 45
Causal Principle 35–36, 42–45
Cause of the Universe 35
cell autogeny 111
certainty argument 179–92, 193n.12, 255
Chamberlain, Thomas 118
Charity Principle 257
Chignell, Andrew 2
China 264
Christianity,
  choice of 277–78
  and common consent 295
  and key doctrines of 313
  and meaning of life 281–85
  monotheistic God of 130
  and moral belief 131
  Mystical Practice 253
  and realism 205
  reasonableness of 312–13
  revelatory claims of 13, 314, 318–19
  see also God; Jesus Christ
Church of England 283

Churchland, Paul 154
Collins, Robin 83
combination problem 160
common consent (CCA),
  argument 293–96
  future directions 303
  higher-order evidence 296–98
  introduction 293, 303n.1
  objections 298–303, 306nn.31, 34, 307nn.41, 48
  other defeating evidence 303, 307nn.52, 53
complicated mechanisms 167
composition fallacy 24–25
conceptualist argument,
  functionalism 220–23
  introduction 8–9, 217–18
  metaphysics 223–27
  realism 218–20, 231n.5
  and theory requirement 227–30
Condorcet Jury Theorem 297, 299
Confessions (St. Augustine) 167
conflicting claims objection 262–65
Confucianism 285
Congress of Vienna 287–88
consciousness,
  appearance of 160–61
  emergent 156–57
  phenomenal 287
  and theism 6
The Consolation of Philosophy (Boethius) 282
constructivism 140
contingency argument,
  existence question 17
  foundation theory 19–21, 31nn.6,8
  introduction 2
  more 26–30, 32n.21
  objections 23–26, 32nn.16,18
  possible explanations 21–23, 31–32nn.10–13
  results 30
  'why' principle 17–19
correspondence theory 187–89
cosmological constant 71–73, 80, 82, 84n.6
cosmos 152
Craig, William Lane 1, 35–36, 39–40, 45
Crane, Tim 228
Creator, the 36, 46, 204

credulity principle 10
Crick, F. H. 96, 110, 121
Critical Trust Principle 253, 257–65, 268n.61
crucifixion 319
Cultural Revolution (China) 264

Danielyan, E. 53
d'Aquili, Eugene 261–62
Darwin, Charles,
    and agnostic naturalism 160
    and Alfred Wallace 322
    and biological classification level of family 104
    and Charles Lyell 118, 120
    introduction 5
    life origin explanations 111
    and natural selection 89, 94–96, 154, 287
    and neo-Darwinism 109
    and *Origin of Species* 321
    and the parasitoid wasp 315
    and Richard Swinburne 184
Darwin Devolves (Behe) 103–4
Darwinian Natural Right (Arnhart) 134
Darwin's Black Box (Behe) 97, 102
David, King 315, 322
Davies, Paul 121
Davis, Caroline 253, 265
Dawkins, Richard 96, 109–10, 121, 123, 168, 176n.9
de Duve, Christian 112, 116–17
Descartes, René 3, 54, 56–57, 181–82, 190
designer, the 120–23
desire argument,
    best explanation 244–46
    conclusion 246
    in humans 236–41
    inborn 241–43, 248n.27
    introduction 235–36
    and meaning of life 282, 284–85
devolution 103–4
Dialogues Concerning Natural Religion (Hume) 93, 167, 172–73
Dirac, Paul 198, 200
disteleological features 171
disulfide bonds 102
Divers, John 221–22
divine beauty 173, 175

divine hiddenness 300–301
divine inscrutability 4, 80
divine perfection 312
divine revelation 2
DNA,
    digital code in 5, 109
    double helical structure of 89, 96
    enigma 110–11, 119
    mutations in molecules 103
    and protein synthesis 112–13
    and RNA 116
    and signature of intelligence 121
    structure of the molecule 114–15
    and X-ray diffraction 98–99
Dobzhansky, Theodosius 116
Dostoevsky, Fyodor 129
doxasticity 217, 219, 222–23, 225, 228–29
drugs 261
dualism 221, 224
Durant, Will 281
Durkheim, Émile 260

E. coli cells 104
Edwards, Jonathan 283
Edwards, Rem 252, 255–56
Einstein, Albert 83, 199, 206–7, 214n.56
Ellis, George 43
emergence 156, 158–59
entity-identification 222–23
epiphenomenalism 6, 153
epistemic probability 18, 75
error theory 131
Essay concerning Human Understanding (Locke) 172, 177n.24
eternalism 27, 32n.21
Euclid Vindicated from Every Blemish (Saccheri) 319
eudaimonia 237
Euthyphro problem 190
Everett's Many World's interpretation 43
evil 168, 171, 177n.20, 182, 191, 236, 303, 313
evolution,
    gradualness of 96
    inadequacy of explanations 153
    and satisfaction with life 288
    theory of 6
    and true belief 185
The Existence of God (Swinburne) 252

existentialism 140
Explanation Principle (PE) 17–21, 24, 27, 29–30
explanatoriness 318
explanatory regress objection 172–73

Farmer, H. H. 251–52
Farrer, Austin 129
fictionalism 196
Fifth Way (Aquinas) 90
fine-tuning (FTA),
  anthropic objection 74–75
  basic argument 72
  Bayes' theorem 77–79
  cosmological constant 70–72
  introduction 69
  and multiverse proposals 121–22
  objections 80–84
  probability theory 75–77, 85n.18
  Star Trek objection 72–74, 79–80, 84–85nn.8–9, 12
First Antinomy (Kant) 45
First Cause 35–36, 39, 42, 45–46
fittingness arguments 13, 316–19, 321–23
five intuitions 218–19
Flew, Antony 123, 254–55
Forgie, J. William 54
formalism 204–5, 207
Forrest, Peter 167–68, 175
Foundation Theory 2, 20, 30
four-color theorem 317
Frege, Gottlob 226
frequentism 317
Freud, Sigmund 240, 246, 260, 302
functionalism 217, 220–23

Galen 95
Galileo 318
gases 158
Gassendi, Pierre 57
Gates, Bill 110
Gaunilo 53, 59
Gauthier, David 136
Gellman, Jerome 253
Genealogy of Morals (Nietzsche) 130
General Theory of Relativity (Einstein) 199, 206–7
God,
  and afterlife 9
  and beauty 170, 172–75
  belief no longer credible 109
  and biochemical argument 90, 93–94
  and blueprint creation 207–8
  and certainty 179, 182–84, 189–91, 194n.23
  and Christianity 252, 254, 256–57, 261–62, 313
  and common consent 293–96, 298–303, 305n.12
  and conceptualism 217, 227
  and design of the world 154
  and desire 235–40, 243–44, 246
  direct activity of 159, 164n.23
  and empirical phenomena 229
  existence of 17, 149, 323
  and fine-tuning argument 4
  intelligent designer 120–21
  and libertarian freedom 153, 163n.11
  living reality 251
  and Logos (Word) 208–9
  and meaning of life 281–84, 287, 290
  and morality 5, 6, 129–30, 135, 138, 141–42
  and the multiverse 83
  nature and existence of 1–2, 10
  and objectively-binding moral obligations 132–33
  and ontological argument 3, 51–62, 62n.11
  rational to believe in 11
  and revelation 314, 316, 319, 321
  and theism 122
  and theistic realism 205
  and traditional natural theology 311–13
  and truths 8
  and the universe 78, 80–81
  and wager argument 271–79
The God Delusion (Dawkins) 5, 109
Gödel, Kurt 58, 61
God and Goodness (Wynn) 173
'God Helmet' (Persinger) 261
Gould, Stephen Jay 118
Grand Story 154–55, 157–58
Granqvist, Pehr 261
The Great Divorce (Lewis) 283
Greeks 321
Greene, Brian 70

Grim Reaper paradox 40, 42
Gruber, Howard E. 154
Guthrie, W. K. C. 236
Gutting, Gary 253, 255

HADD (hyperactive agency detective device) 302
Haeckel, Ernst 95, 111
happiness 11–12, 278, 281–85, 289
Harman, Gilbert 133, 136, 143n.29
Hawthorne, John 72, 82
Heisenberg, Werner 199–200, 207, 211n.29
Heller, Mark 182
heredity 95
Hick, John 252, 254
Higgs, Peter 8
Hilbert, David 38
Hilbert Hotel argument 38–39
Hilbert space 198, 207
Hinduism 285
Hobbes, Thomas 56, 135–36
Homer 314
Hood, Leroy 110
Horgan, Terence 153
Hoyle, Fred 121
Huemer, Michael 253
Hume, David 26, 56–57, 90, 93–94, 152, 167, 172, 177nn.24–5
Huxley, T. H. 111

Ideas 208
Iliad (Homer) 314
impartiality 134–35
incarnation 319, 321
infinite regress 3, 23, 36–37, 40–46, 172, 258
infinities 3, 37–40, 47n.6, 273
information argument,
    beyond chance 112–13
    chance and necessity 115–16
    the designer 120–23
    design hypothesis 117–19
    DNA enigma 110–11
    and intelligent design 119–20, 125n.38
    introduction 109
    life origin theories 111–12
    RNA world 116–17
    self-organizing scenarios 113–15
initial comparative assessments 224–25

intelligence 90–94
intelligent design,
    and bacterial flagellum 99–101
    the designer 120–23
    and fine-tuning 122
    and God 52
    hypothesis 117–19
    and information argument 119–20, 125n.38
    introduction 5
    and life-permitting universes 79, 84
    logical underpinnings of 95
    no evidence in nature 109
    and orderliness of world 167
    philosophical argument 89–90
    purposeful arrangement of parts 91–93
    and randomness 96
    and ribozyme engineering experiments 116
intentionality 150, 225, 227–30
intersubjectivity 170
irreducible complexity argument 4–5, 97
Isaacs, Yoaav 72, 82
Islam 277–78, 285, 295, 312
'Is the Success of Physical Theories Truly Surprising?' (Wigner) 199, 202
Is There a God? (Swinburne) 184

Jackson, Frank 155
Jeffrey, Richard 317, 319, 324n.12
Jesus Christ 1, 13, 311, 316, 323
    see also Christianity; God
Joy 235, 239, 243–45, 288
Judaism 130, 277–78, 285, 295, 312

Kalam Cosmological Argument (KCA) 35–46, 47n.2, 48n.36, 39
Kant, Immanuel 3, 45, 57, 131, 133, 138–40
Kelly, Thomas 298, 300, 306n.30
Kendrew, J. C. 96
Kenyon, Dean 113–14
Kierkegaard, Søren 138–39
Kim, Jaegwon 158, 287
kingdom of ends 138
knowledge 179–80, 183, 188
Knudson, Albert C 251
Koonin, Eugene 103
Koons, Robert 42
Koran 1

Kornblith, Hilary 297
Korsgaard, Christine 139–41
Kreeft, Peter 239, 241–42
Kripkean meaning 183
Küppers, Bernd-Olaf 110

Lacan, Jacques 238
Lamb Shift 200
Landau, Iddo 281
Laws (Plato) 1
Leftow, B. 60
Leibniz, Gottfried Wilhelm 3, 35, 54–56
Leng, Mary 204, 206
Lewis, C. S. 129, 131, 235, 238–46, 282–85, 289–90, 319
Lewis, David 188
Lewis, Geraint 73–74, 83
life-excluding universes 73
life-permitting universes 74, 78–81, 83–84
likelihoodism 317
Lipton, Peter 118
Lochhead, David M. 57
Locke, John 172, 312
Logical Gap Objection 254
'The Look-ahead Effect of Phenotypic Mutations' (Whitehead et al) 102
Lowe, E. 60
LSD 261
Luther, Martin 312
Lycan, William 253
Lyell, Charles 118–20
Lyons, William 149, 162n.3

McGinn, Colin 149, 160–61, 162n.2
McGrath, Alister 239
Mackie, J. L. 6, 131, 133, 141, 157
Maddy, Penelope 197, 203, 210–11n.12
Madell, Geoffrey 149, 160
Malcolm, N. 58
Mann, W. 61
Manson, Neil 80
Marsh, Jason 302
Martin, Michael 253, 258–59, 264
Marxism 131, 260, 301
materialism 221, 224
mathematics,
    and certainty argument 179–83, 187–89, 192, 193nn.7–8
    explanation 8

and realism 218–19
    truths 22
mathematics argument,
    and anti-realism 206–9
    applicability 203–4
    conclusions 209
    introduction 195–96
    nature of inquiry 197–98, 211n.19
    and physical theories 199–200, 211nn.27–8
    and physics 198–99
    and realism 204–5, 213n.49
    unreasonable effectiveness 196–97
    and Wigner reconstruction 200–203
matrix algebra 207
matrix mechanics 200, 207
Matthews, Gareth 60–61
Maudlin, Tim 206
Mavrodes, George 132–33, 258
Maydole, Robert 4, 60–61
Mayr, Ernst 96
meaning of life argument 11
    introduction 281–82
    life worth living 284
    making sense 284–90
    purpose 282–84
meditation 261
Meditations (Descartes) 54, 57
Mendeleyev, Dimitri 322
Mere Christianity (Lewis) 129, 239–41, 243
metaphysics 217–18, 221, 223
Metcalf, Thomas 61
Metternich, Klemens von 287
Metz, Thaddeus 285
Miller, Stanley 111
Millican, P. 61
Mill, J. S. 293, 298
Mivart, St. George 97
modal logics 57–58
modal ontological argument 4
modal perfection argument 4, 60
Modus Tollens argument 44
Mohammad 13, 311
Montaigne, Michel 320
Moore, G. E. 134
moral argument,
    and common consent 298
    conclusions 142
    introduction 129–30

naturalistic explanations 133–41
obeying God 141–42
objectively-binding 130–33
moral law 138–39
moral obligations/duties 5–6
Morriston, Wes 40–41
Muller, H. J. 97–98
multiverse 4, 82–84, 121
Muslims *see* Islam
myoglobin protein 89, 96
mysticism 261

Nagel, Thomas 159–60, 185
Napoleon Bonaparte 287
Nathan (prophet) 315, 322
naturalism,
  agnostic 160–61
  biological 155–61
  as a broad worldview 150–51
  and certainty 183, 186, 189–90, 192
  and consciousness 154–56, 161–62
  cumulative case arguments 316
  and Darwin 321–22
  and desire 245
  emergence 158–59
  and epiphenomenalism 153
  explanation 6, 8
  and Freudianism 260
  and mathematics 202–4, 206
  and meaning of life 11, 285–86, 288–90
naturalistic explanation objection 10, 260–62
naturalistic reductive accounts 6, 133–35
natural selection 4–5, 97, 104, 109, 115–16, 118–19
necessity 4, 82, 217, 222–23
neo-Darwinism 109
'New Atheist' movement 2, 5, 109, 123
Newberg, Andrew 261–62
Newman, Cardinal 129, 312, 320
Newton, Isaac 199
Nicolis, G. 113
Nietzsche, Friedrich 6, 130–31, 141, 301
no criteria/uncheckability objection 10, 258–60
Nolan, Lawrence 54
nominalism 9, 196, 218, 223–26
non-Euclidean geometry 319
non-limited 27–29

Oakes, Robert 252, 266n.4
objectivity 217, 222–23
Occam's Razor 172–73
O'Connor, Timothy 159
On the Creation of the World (Philo of Alexandria) 208
On Free Will (St. Augustine) 182
ontological argument,
  Anselm's version 51–54
  early modern period 54–57
  explanation 3, 51
  recent work 60–62
  Twentieth-century modal versions 57–60
Oparin, Alexander I. 111, 115–16
Oppy, G. 51, 53–54, 59, 60–61, 62n.7
organic models 167
organisms 153–54
The Origin of Species (Darwin) 96–97, 118, 321
Orr, H. Allen 97–98
other gods problem 276
Owen, H. P. 129

Padgett, Alan 45
pains 153–54
Paley, William 95, 312
panpsychism 158–60, 162, 164n.27, 224
panspermia 121
Papineau, David 286
Parable of the Remnants 263–64
Paradise 284–85
parallel universes *see* multiverse
parasitoid wasp 315, 322
Pascal, Blaise 13, 312
Pascal's Wager 11, 271–79
patronymics 314
Pauli-exclusion principle 83
PC (Principle of Credulity) 252–53, 257–60, 262–65
Peels, Rik 61
Penrose, Roger 184
Perceiving God (Alston) 253
Pereboom, Derk 2
Perlmutter, Saul 70–72
Persinger, Michael 261
Peter, St. 237
Pettigrew, Richard 316–17
Pew Research Center 295, 304n.8

PFEF (prima facie evidential force) 257, 259
phenomenal consciousness argument (AC),
   biological naturalism 156–58
   chief rivals 156–61
   conclusions 162
   and consciousness 151–54, 163n.9
   introduction 149
   naturalistic worldview 154–56
   preliminary points 149–50
   scientific theory acceptance 150–51
Phenomenal Conservatism 265
'Phenomenal Conservatism' (Huemer) 253
Philo of Alexandria 172–75, 207–9
physics 4, 38, 43, 71, 82, 198, 201–6, 209, 286
Planck units 71, 84n.4
Plantinga, Alvin 4, 58–59, 182, 223
Plato 133, 167, 205, 208, 236
Platonism,
   and conceptualism 223–24, 226, 229–30
   and entities with causal powers 192, 193n.9, 194n.25
   and entity-identification 218
   and God as a demiurge 190
   introduction 9
   mathematical 183
   and Peter van Inwagen 196
   and platonic abstracta 186
   a world of ultimate moral facts 133
plenitude 217, 222–23
Popper, Karl 317
possibility of nothing 26
Possible Explanations Argument (APE) 2, 22, 25
possible world notion 4, 58
presentism 27
Price, H. H. 180
Prigogine, Ilya 112–13
Principle of Charity 257
Principle of Credulity *see* Principle of Critical Trust
Principle of Critical Trust 253, 257–65, 268n.61
The Principles of Geology (Lyell) 118
Principle of Simplicity 257–58
Principle of Testimony 257

Privacy Objection 255–56
probability kinematics 317, 324n.12
The Problem of Pain (Lewis) 238
propositions,
   and conceptualism 226
   conditions 222–23, 225, 231n.6
   as divine thoughts 226–27
   existence arguments 219–20
   as sentences 225
   as sets 225–26
   and their 'aboutness' 227–28
   as thoughts 224–25
Proslogion (St. Anselm) 51, 190
protoplasm 111
Pruss, Alexander 42, 61
Pryor, James 253
Puckett, Joe Jr. 242
Pust, Joel 188–89
Pythagorean religious doctrine 236

quantum electrodynamics 200
quantum mechanics 198–99, 207, 211n.23
quantum theory 3
Quastler, Henry 117
Quine, Willard 181, 189, 196

The Rainbow of Experiences, Critical Trust, and God (Kai-Man Kwan) 253
ramified natural theology argument (RNT) 311–23, 323nn.6–7
random genetic variations 4–5
random mutation 109
randomness 96
Rashdall, Hastings 129
realism 196, 204–6, 209, 217–20, 223
recycling argument 294–95, 298–99
Reid, Thomas 90, 92
religious experience argument,
   conclusion 265
   experiential roots 251
   and foundationalism 253–56
   Principle of Credulity 257–65, 268n.61
   twentieth to twenty-first century 251–53
Return of the God Hypothesis (Meyer) 121–22
revelatory claims 314, 316–18
revelatory content argument 13
ribozymes 116

Riess, Adam 70–72
ritual 261
RNA 5, 111–17, 120
Roche, William 318
Roman Catholicism 312
    see also Christianity
Rorty, Richard 286
Rosenberg, Alex 286–87
Rosetta stone 120
Rowe, William 253
Russell, Bertrand 40, 132–33, 239, 281

S5 58
Saccheri, Gerolamo 319
Schmidt, Brian 70–72
scientism 154, 163n.16
Searle, John 160–61
secondhand evidence 298–99
second law of motion (Newton) 199
Second Law of Thermodynamics 36, 42
self-legislation 6, 138–41
self-organization theory 113, 115
self-replication 116
'sequence hypothesis' (Crick) 110
SETI (search for extraterrestrial intelligence) 120
Shannon, Claude 110
Signature in the Cell (Meyer) 113
simplicity 217, 222–23, 225, 257–58
sin 284
Sinclair, James 39–40
Singer, Peter 322–23, 324n.19
Skeptical Rule (SR) 263–64
Skrbina, David 159–60
slave morality 301
Sober, Elliott 4, 89, 318
social contract theories 6, 135–38
Socrates 181
Sorabji, R. 39
Sorley, W. R. 129
SP (sensory practice) 259
Standard Big Bang Model 36
Star Trek Objection 4
Steiner, Mark 195–96, 200–203, 207, 210n.4, 212nn.37–43, 214nn.57–8
Steinman, Gary 113
strained pea theory 187–88, 191
stringent vs. lax laws 4, 82
Sufficient Reason Principle (PSR) 18

Summa Theologica (Aquinas) 239, 318–21, 323
Sunstein, Cass 298
superstrings 83
Supreme Being 60
supreme good 277
supremity 29–30
Surowiecki, James 297
Surprised by Joy (Lewis) 239, 246
Swinburne, Richard 10, 167, 170, 184, 252–53, 256–65, 312–13, 323n.5
Symposium (Plato) 167

Taliaferro, Charles 252
Talleyrand 286–87
Talmud 1
Taylor, A. E. 129
TED talks 2
Tennant, F. R. 167–68, 170
Testimony Principle 257
theism,
    and anti-realism 206–9
    and beauty 167, 168, 171, 175, 176n.12
    as a broad worldview 150
    and certainty 190–91
    Christian 11–12
    and common consent 293–302, 306n.34
    and conceptualism 218, 227, 229–30, 230n.3
    and consciousness 161–62
    and desire 244–46
    and God 52, 122, 153
    and mathematics 202–4, 209
    and meaning of life 281–82
    and multiverse 84
    and naturalism 155, 158
    and panpsychism 160
    and Pascal's Wager 276–77, 279
    rationality of 59
    and realism 204–6
    and religious experience 255, 265
    and truths 8–9
    and the universe 132
theistic hypothesis 83
theology 13, 167
Theory-Ladenness Objection 254–56
Thomas, Keith 283
Thomistic Cosmological Argument 42

thoughts 227–29
Timaeus (Plato) 205
Tooley, Michael 59
Trueblood, Elton 252
Trump, Donald 58
truths,
    and certainty 182, 188, 190–91
    have an explanation 19
    and mathematics 22, 206
Tucker, Chris 253
2QS5 (modal logic) 60–61

uncertainty principle (Heisenberg) 43
unidentified flying objects 264
uniform inertial motion 150
uniform probabilities 4, 80
unitary thesis 314
universe-designer 72, 75, 78–79, 81–82
universes,
    life-excluding 73
    life-permitting 74, 78–81, 83–84
unsurpassable power 29
utilitarianism 134–35

van Inwagen, Peter 196, 210n.6
virtual particles 25

wager argument,
    conclusions 278–79
    introduction 11
    Pascal 273–78
    summary 271–73
Wainwright, William 253, 262
Wallace, Alfred Russel 322
Wall, George 253
Ward, Thomas M. 53
Warrant and Proper Function (Plantinga) 182
Watson, J. D. 96, 110
Weinberg, Steven 71
Weisberg, Jonathan 82
Whitcomb, Dennis 61
Who Wants to be a Millionaire? (game show) 297–98
Wielenberg, Erik 9–10, 132–33, 244–45, 288–90
Wigner, Eugene 8, 195–207, 209, 211n.20–21
Williams, Bernard 240
Williamson, Timothy 180
Wilson, E. O. 168, 302
Wolf, Susan 281
Wynn, Mark 167–69, 173–75

Yandell, Keith 252, 265n.3

Zeno's paradoxes of motion 39
Zeus 180
zombie worlds 157
Zuckerman, Phil 295, 304n.10

www.ingramcontent.com/pod-product-compliance
Lightning Source LLC
Chambersburg PA
CBHW052144300426
44115CB00011B/1511